Great American Bestsellers: The Books That Shaped America

Peter Conn, Ph.D.

THE
GREAT
COURSES®

PUBLISHED BY:

THE GREAT COURSES
Corporate Headquarters
4840 Westfields Boulevard, Suite 500
Chantilly, Virginia 20151-2299
Phone: 1-800-832-2412
Fax: 703-378-3819
www.thegreatcourses.com

Peter Conn, Ph.D.

Professor of English, University of Pennsylvania

Peter Conn is Professor of English at the University of Pennsylvania. He received his A.B. from Providence College in 1964 and his Ph.D. from Yale University in 1969.

Professor Conn's publications include *The Divided Mind: Ideology and Imagination in America, 1898–1917* and *Literature in America*, which was a main selection of Associated Book Clubs (UK). His Athenaeum Award–winning publication, *Pearl S. Buck: A Cultural Biography*, was named a *New York Times* Notable Book and was included among the five finalists for the National Book Critics Circle award in biography. Professor Conn's latest book is *The American 1930s: A Literary History*. His books and chapters have been translated into eight languages, including Chinese, Spanish, Japanese, and Korean.

Professor Conn has lectured at the Brooklyn Museum of Art, the Pennsylvania Academy of Fine Arts, the Whitney Museum, and other institutions on a number of American artists, including Edward Hopper, William Christenberry, Thomas Wilmer Dewing, Maxfield Parrish, Charles Sheeler, and The Eight.

Professor Conn is a John Simon Guggenheim Foundation Fellow and has directed National Endowment for the Humanities (NEH) seminars for college and high school teachers. He has received an NEH Humanities Focus Grant and several awards for distinguished teaching, including the University of Pennsylvania's senior teaching prize, the Lindback Award. His teaching projects have included College 005: The Great Books; English 401: Teaching American Studies, which places undergraduates as teaching assistants in a Philadelphia high school; and English 800, a graduate course that combines the study of literature and composition with teacher training.

Professor Conn has served as literary consultant on numerous television projects, including the Emmy-winning series *The American Short Story* and adaptations of novels by James Baldwin and Saul Bellow. In 2004, Professor Conn served as principal literary advisor to Oprah's Book Club for *The Good Earth*.

Since 1993, Professor Conn has served as visiting professor at the University of Nanjing in China. At the University of Pennsylvania, he is a member of the graduate groups in the history of art and American civilization, is an affiliated member of the East Asian Studies Center, and holds a secondary appointment in the Graduate School of Education. Professor Conn has served as dean of the college, chair of the graduate groups in American civilization and English, faculty master of Robert Hill College House and Community House, and deputy and interim provost. He was the founding faculty director of Civic House, the university's center for community service.

Professor Conn and his wife, Terry, have four children: Steven, David, Alison, and Jennifer.

Table of Contents
Great American Bestsellers:
The Books That Shaped America

Table of Contents

Great American Bestsellers:
The Books That Shaped America

Credits

Excerpts of no more than 4,000 words from the books listed below are used by permission of Cambridge University Press:

Conn, Peter. *The Divided Mind: Ideology and Imagination in America, 1898–1917*. London: Cambridge University Press, 1983.

Conn, Peter. *Literature in America: An Illustrated History*. Cambridge: Cambridge University Press, 1989.

Conn, Peter. *Pearl S. Buck: A Cultural Biography*. Cambridge: Cambridge University Press, 1996.

Conn, Peter. *The American 1930s*. Forthcoming from Cambridge University Press.

Permission to use excerpts from her e-mail correspondence to Peter Conn was granted by Maxine Hong Kingston.

Steiner, Wendy. "Hold Up the Mirror—Unlock the Door: The Symbol of the Model in Contemporary Culture." Manuscript in progress.

Great American Bestsellers:
The Books That Shaped America

Scope:

"Lincoln's doctor's dog." That was the response Bennett Cerf gave when he was asked what subject would produce a guaranteed bestseller. Cerf, a legendary editor at Random House, knew a lot about selling books. Despite his small joke, however, there is in fact no formula that will assure literary popularity. Nonetheless, the history of American book publishing does allow us to notice a few patterns. For example, certain types of fiction, sometimes referred to as genre novels, repeatedly turn up: Mystery stories, Westerns, historical romances, and harlequin romances have always been well-represented on lists of popular books along with political thrillers and tales of upward mobility. In the course of these lectures, I will have occasion to illustrate most of these genres with at least one text.

As we proceed in the course, I will discuss the distinctive qualities and particular accomplishments of each book, and I will also comment on the recurrence of certain themes, among them the meaning of America, the idea of success, the complex questions of race and gender, and the prominence of religion. And wherever I can do so, I will also try to answer the question, why was this book so popular?

In this course, I have chosen books by American authors. A steady focus on native writers provides a greater opportunity to examine some of the cultural and historical issues that link imaginative literature to the texture of its time. The lectures will follow a generally chronological sequence beginning with the first book published in the English-speaking New World, *The Bay Psalm Book* (1640), and concluding with contemporary popular literature. The chronological organization will also help us in tracing the permutations that mark certain themes and questions as they recur. Without pressing too hard on cause and effect, I will move back and forth from literary texts to their social and political context. I will also offer some comparisons between the texts themselves. Most of the lectures will take a single text as their principle focus. The exposition of those books will combine a close reading of literary techniques with an exploration of each book's major themes. The diversity of the readings will itself demonstrate how spacious the category of bestseller has proven to be. Furthermore, whether or not the featured books have earned a permanent place in the critical sortings of later decades—and several of them have—all of them will provide rich material for analysis and reflection.

Most of the works included are fiction. The exceptions, along with *The Bay Psalm Book* (1640), are Thomas Paine's *Common Sense* (1776), which helped to shape Colonial opinion in favor of independence; Dale Carnegie's *How to Win Friends and Influence People* (1936), a founding work in the ubiquitous self-help genre; and near the end of the course, examples of memoir and biography, two of the staples of popular nonfiction books.

The earliest novel on the list is James Fenimore Cooper's *The Last of the Mohicans* (1826), the most popular work by America's first bestselling novelist. *Uncle Tom's Cabin* (1852), by Harriet Beecher Stowe, put human faces on the struggle against slavery. It was almost certainly the bestselling American novel of the 19th century. Three more 19th-century bestsellers followed: *Ragged Dick* (1868), the first of more than a hundred novels by Horatio Alger Jr., popularized a version of the American dream. Louisa May Alcott's *Little Women* (1870) remains a much-loved and widely read account of the American family, and Mark Twain's *The Adventures of Huckleberry Finn* (1884), was the bestselling novel by the man who became the country's most popular writer and one of its most famous citizens.

The titles from the early 20th century include Owen Wister's *The Virginian* (1902), which more or less invented the Western as a major American genre; Edith Wharton's *The House of Mirth* (1905), a bestselling book about New York society that has also established itself securely in the canon of American literature; and Upton Sinclair's *The Jungle* (1906), a scarifying account of abuses in Chicago's meatpacking industry.

Some of the most popular American novels were published in the 1920s and 1930s. The first selection here is *Main Street* (1920), by Sinclair Lewis, which declared war on the small town. At the turn of the decade, Dashiell Hammett published his classic crime novel *The Maltese Falcon* (1930), which will be used to illustrate the centrality of the detective story, a major fictional genre in American literature. *The Good Earth* (1931), Pearl S. Buck's pioneering account of life in rural China, is still a widely read book. The same is true for two other popular novels of the 1930s: Margaret Mitchell's *Gone with the Wind* (1936), the bestselling novel of its time, and John Steinbeck's *The Grapes of Wrath* (1939), in which a family of displaced farmers poignantly embodied the sufferings of the Depression decade.

In the 1940s, Richard Wright's *Native Son* (1940) was the first novel by an African American to be a bestseller and to be selected by the Book-of-the-Month Club. The later half of the 20th century includes J. D. Salinger's *The Catcher in the Rye* (1951), Harper Lee's *To Kill a Mockingbird* (1960), and Joseph Heller's *Catch-22* (1961), which are all books of dissent in one form or another.

Maxine Hong Kingston's *The Woman Warrior* (1975) was the first book by an Asian American writer to make the bestseller lists, and it also deserves attention as an example of the memoir, which has become one of the mainstays of American popular writing in the past decade or so. Biographies have enjoyed a long history of success in American publishing, so to provide entry into this important genre, we will discuss David McCullough's phenomenally successful *John Adams* (2001). With 3 million copies sold, McCullough's *John Adams* is certainly the bestselling biography in American literary history.

The final lecture, "Recent Bestsellers," will provide a survey of the authors and books that have dominated the lists over the past couple of decades.

Lecture One
Why Do Bestsellers Matter?

Scope: A good place to start is probably with a definition: What is a bestseller? The phrase may seem self-evident, but in fact there is room for debate. To begin with, for books, the term "bestseller" dates back only to the 1890s. As several scholars of popular literature have pointed out, the word "bestseller" is misleading. A book termed a bestseller invariably appeared somewhere in a tabulation of 10 or 15 or more books. Recently, to add to the confusion, specialized categories of bestseller lists have proliferated. As we proceed in the course, I will discuss the distinctive qualities and particular accomplishments of each book we will examine, and I will also comment on the recurrence of certain themes, among them the meaning of America, the idea of success, the complex questions of race and gender, and the prominence of religion. And wherever I can do so, I will also try to answer the question, why was this book so popular?

Outline

I. How does one choose for this course two dozen or so bestselling titles from the vast library of possibilities? As I hope to demonstrate, the books on our list, whatever their academic ranking, deserve consideration for several reasons.

   A. To begin with, these books often provide access to the nation's social history.

   B. Many of the selections also shed light on our political history: the agitation over American independence, the debate over slavery, the place of women in society, the plight of the poor and working class, and so on.

   C. Finally, many and indeed most of these books are exceptionally entertaining.

II. Is there a formula that can identify or perhaps even predict a bestseller? Only one, addressed further in the final lecture: Certain contemporary writers have become what are called in the trade "brands" or even "franchises."

A. With the exception of superstar authors, there is simply no guaranteed path to literary popularity.

B. Nonetheless, the history of American book publishing reveals a few patterns. For example, certain types of fiction, or genre novels, have always been well represented on lists of popular books.

    1. Mystery stories, Westerns, historical romance, and chronicles of adventure are all popular genres, and in the course of these lectures, most of these genres are illustrated with at least one text.

    2. The persistence of these genres—and of their nonfiction counterparts, especially biography and memoir—tell us something about the making of bestsellers and about the book trade more generally.

III. Mainstream book selling was transformed in 1926, when a man named Harry Scherman founded the Book-of-the-Month Club. This spared readers the burden of choosing among the huge number of new titles on offer, and it provided entry into a virtual community of other readers.

A. For generations, authors and publishers knew that sales would multiply, sometimes many times, if a title were chosen as a main selection of the club. The Book-of-the-Month Club itself became a major brand in the industry.

B. Literary prizes can also propel sales. Though top prizes (such as the Pulitzer) are ostensibly intended to honor quality, not popularity, a good many bestsellers—including several on our list—were Pulitzer Prize winners.

C. Along with book clubs and book prizes, systematic marketing campaigns help propel sales with product tie-ins, celebrity endorsements, and even contests.

D. The past couple of decades have brought two of the most significant changes in the book-selling business: the big-box bookstore and the Internet.

    1. Hyperstores such as Borders and Barnes & Noble can stock thousands of titles, rather than hundreds, while providing amenities.

    2. The Internet has generated the other revolutionizing innovation: amazon.com and its many imitators. Internet publishing has also begun to have an impact on the book trade, though so far with marginal results.

IV. This course will review books by American authors. A steady focus on native writers provides a greater opportunity to examine some of the cultural and historical issues that link imaginative literature to the texture of its time.

   A. The lectures will follow a generally chronological sequence, beginning with the first book published in the English-speaking New World, *The Bay Psalm Book* (1640), and concluding with contemporary popular literature.

   B. The earliest novel on the list is James Fenimore Cooper's *The Last of the Mohicans* (1826), the most popular work by America's first bestselling novelist.

      1. Four more 19th-century bestsellers follow. *Uncle Tom's Cabin* (1852), by Harriet Beecher Stowe, was almost certainly the bestselling American novel of its time.

      2. Horatio Alger Jr.'s *Ragged Dick* (1868), Louisa May Alcott's *Little Women* (1870) and Mark Twain's *Huckleberry Finn* (1884) round out the 19th century selections.

   C. The titles from the early 20th century include Owen Wister's *The Virginian* (1902), which more or less invented the Western as a major American genre; Edith Wharton's *The House of Mirth* (1905); and Upton Sinclair's *The Jungle* (1906).

      1. Some of the most popular American novels were published in the 1920s and 1930s: *Main Street* (1920) by Sinclair Lewis, Dashiell Hammett's classic crime novel *The Maltese Falcon* (1930), and *The Good Earth* (1931) by Pearl S. Buck.

      2. Margaret Mitchell's *Gone with the Wind* (1936) was the bestselling novel of its time; it and Depression-era *The Grapes of Wrath* (1939) by John Steinbeck are still widely read today.

   D. Richard Wright's *Native Son* (1940) was the first bestselling novel (and Book-of-the-Month Club selection) by an African American writer.

   E. J. D. Salinger's *The Catcher in the Rye* (1951), Harper Lee's *To Kill a Mockingbird* (1960), and Joseph Heller's *Catch-22* (1961) are all books of dissent, in one form or another.

   F. Maxine Hong Kingston's *The Woman Warrior* (1975) was the first book by an Asian American writer to make the bestseller lists. It also deserves attention as an example of the memoir, which has become one of the mainstays of American popular writing in the past decade or so.

G. Biographies have long enjoyed a history of success in American publishing. Our selection is David McCulloughs's phenomenally successful *John Adams* (2001).

H. The final lecture, "Recent Bestsellers," will provide a survey of the authors and books that have dominated the lists over the past couple of decades.

Suggested Reading:

Hart, *The Popular Book.*

Sutherland, *Bestsellers.*

Questions to Consider:

1. In assessing literary value, what is your opinion about the relationship of popularity and quality? What do you think is the source of this distinction? Keeping in mind specific books you have read, both bestsellers and classics, develop a hypothesis that includes concrete reasons for both sides of the debate.

2. Why do you think popular books are popular? Using as reference points some bestsellers with which you are familiar, whether contemporary or earlier, construct an argument that might explain this phenomenon.

Lecture One—Transcript
Why Do Bestsellers Matter?

Let me open this course by telling you how much I have enjoyed preparing this series of lectures. To begin with, I have had a personal interest in this subject for quite a long time. In one of my books, a biography of the popular novelist and activist Pearl Buck, I had the chance to think about the phenomenon of the bestseller. Buck's novels have sold literally millions of copies, both in English and in translation into more than 70 languages. I found myself asking why she earned such conspicuous commercial success over several decades. I developed a few tentative answers, and I'll report those to you when we discuss Buck's most famous novel, *The Good Earth*. This course has given me the opportunity to consider the subject from all sorts of additional angles using a wide variety of fictional and nonfictional examples. I have had the chance to re-read, or—I confess it, in some cases—to read for the first time, a list of novels and nonfiction texts that have provided enjoyment for decades and in some cases even generations of American readers. Beyond that, the questions that bestselling books raise are interesting and important. By looking carefully at these texts, many of them still popular, we can gain valuable insights into our national history and culture. We will also have occasion to speculate on American values and the changing nature of American society.

A good place to start is probably with a definition. What is a bestseller? The phrase may seem self-evident, but in fact it contains more than a little room for debate. To begin with, as applied to books, the term "bestseller" dates back only to the 1890s. In 1895, a magazine called *The Bookman* published a list of books in what it called "the order of demand." The top-selling novel on that first list, by the way, was a Scottish romance by Ian Maclaren with the wonderful title, *Beside the Bonnie Brier Bush*. For every novel or work of nonfiction published earlier than the 1890s, we have to rely on reconstructed lists based on records that are usually incomplete. Indeed, through most of the 20th century, the sales figures on which newspapers relied for their bestseller lists remained sketchy and frequently erroneous. Counting is more reliable today, but that is a fairly recent development. Historically, the measurement of book sale transactions was primitive, subject to all sorts of human error. Furthermore, publishers realized early in the 20th century that success breeds success—that many people will often buy a book if many others have already done so, and it was commercially smart to have a bestseller. In response—I hope I do not shock you with this news—publishers sometimes manipulated book sales to promote more sales. Among other tricks, they would send hired help to visit bookstores and buy up every copy of a target title. If the scheme worked, the manufactured interest would provoke new orders, which would document a non-existent demand that might in turn become real.

Today, to avoid such self-promotion, the algorithm by which *The New York Times* establishes its counts is frequently adjusted and is treated as a state secret. Blocked in one direction, publishers will try to beat the system in others. A friend of mine, the book review editor of a major newspaper, became interested in the many paperback reprints that were festooned with the phrase "National Bestseller," always in large type. He started checking the original hardcover sales figures for some of these books and discovered that almost none of them had ever actually appeared on any bestseller list. His conclusion: Publishers simply make it up. Anyone who misused the name of *The New York Times* or *Publishers Weekly* in such fraudulent claims would probably face a lawsuit, but there is no law against simply asserting—regardless of the facts—that some book or other that in fact no one has ever heard of is a "bestseller." The same opportunistic logic applies: If a book is advertised as already popular, even if it isn't and wasn't, it is more likely to attract even more readers. So beware.

You should also be suspicious of the phrase "three—or four or five or more—hundred thousand copies in print." Who vouches for the numbers of copies in print? How many of the copies that were printed were actually sold? How many were returned to the publisher? How many wound up on that "dollar book" table on the sidewalk outside the bookstore? Whatever the method we use to identify bestsellers, a distinction must be made. As several scholars of popular literature have pointed out, the term "bestseller" is misleading. It is really a comparative phrase masquerading as a superlative. Here's what I mean. For any given period of time—weeks or years are the most familiar units—there is surely only one book that has actually sold more copies than any other, even if until recently we couldn't be absolutely sure which one it was. However, from that first reference in 1895 to the present, bestsellers have always appeared as lists, not as single titles. When we say that a book is a "bestseller," we invariably mean that it appeared somewhere in a tabulation of 10, or 15, or even more books. It is true that advertising copy will trumpet the phrase "Number One Bestseller" whenever possible, but the more general significance of the coveted label "bestseller" is, quite frankly, something like: "a book that has sold a lot of copies, along with a lot of other books that have also sold a lot of copies.

Recently, to add to the confusion, lists have proliferated in increasingly specialized categories. *The New York Times Book Review*, which is the most frequently cited authority, may include as many as a dozen lists of bestsellers. In addition to tabulations of fiction and nonfiction, each with 15 titles, readers can browse separate lists of paperback bestsellers in fiction further sub-divided into trade fiction and mass-market fiction, paperback nonfiction, and other groups of books called by such labels as "Advice, How-to, and Miscellaneous." Mysteries often get their own lists, as do children's books, science fiction, and cookbooks. The paper's business section adds two more lists, covering paperback and hardback sales in management and corporate strategy. In short, on any given Sunday, it would be possible to identify as many as 200 different titles, fiction and nonfiction, across multiple genres that had honestly earned the accolade: "*New York Times* Bestseller." Add all this up, and project backward into the earlier history of American publishing, and you will see that tens of thousands of books can legitimately claim the status of bestseller. Most of them have completely disappeared, leaving barely a trace. Even the number one bestselling books of most years have become nothing more than the answers to trivia questions: *To Have and To Hold* by Mary Johnston, *The Harvester* by Jean Stratton Porter, or *Soundings* by A. Hamilton Gibbs—to give just three examples from the early 20th century.

How to choose for this course two-dozen or so bestselling titles from the vast library of possibilities? The books I have chosen include many familiar titles, but only a few that have earned canonical status. This, in turn, leads to the next question in our exploration: the assumed distinction between serious and popular literature, which is often translated into a hierarchy of value. To put it bluntly, critics—and many readers—often sort literature into contrasting compartments: books that engage deeper questions and repay close study and re-reading, on the one hand, versus books that provide transient entertainment, on the other. That distinction is not relevant to these lectures. As I hope to demonstrate, the books on our list—whatever their academic ranking—deserve consideration for several reasons. To begin with, they often provide access to the nation's social history: the customs, behavior, and daily life of more or less ordinary men and women, past and present. In addition, since many of these books were written in response to particular events or movements, they can also shed light on our political history: the agitation over American independence, the debate over slavery, the place of women in society, the plight of the poor and the working class, and so on. In some cases, as we will see, these books went beyond recording hot-button issues and intervened on behalf of change. Quite a few of the titles on our list have been the center of literary or political controversy, a subject to which I will return in each case.

Finally, whether the word is considered praise or blame, many and indeed most of these books are exceptionally entertaining: "page turners," to use a favored phrase of reviewers. Indeed, to extend the crude distinction I mentioned a moment ago, it is taken for granted that popular books will be fun to read, while serious literature may not. What else do bestselling books share, beside their capacity for excitement? Is there a formula that can identify or perhaps even predict a bestseller? Only one, which I will sketch here and then come back to in the final lecture. Certain contemporary writers have become what are called in the trade "brands" or even "franchises.

These are the writers whose names appear in larger print than their titles. This has always been at least partly true: Pearl S. Buck and James Michener wrote dozens of bestsellers, and if Margaret Mitchell had ever published a sequel to *Gone With the Wind*, it would undoubtedly have dominated the list. (Indeed, when the sequel did appear, written after Mitchell's death by somebody else, it was the bestselling novel of 1991.) Over the past couple of decades, the franchise author has become an ever-larger presence on bestseller lists. Just about anything by John Grisham, or Stephan King, or Tom Clancy, or Danielle Steel will sell millions of copies—first in hardcover, then in paperback.

In yet another and related change, the numbers of copies a book must sell to qualify as a bestseller has grown exponentially over the years. Sir Walter Scott was almost certainly the bestselling novelist on either side of the English-speaking Atlantic in the first years of the 19th century. Scott probably sold 10,000 copies of each of his books.

A century later, *Gone With the Wind* sold an unprecedented million copies in its first six months. Today, initial print runs can exceed a million, and total sales can go much higher. Dan Brown's website claims that *The Da Vinci Code* has sold over 40 million copies, and I have no reason to doubt the number. The drawing power of superstar authors is one of the reasons that sales in seven figures have become almost commonplace. Beyond that, there is simply no formula that assures the popularity of any fiction or nonfiction book. Many years ago, Bennett Cerf, a legendary editor at Random House, was asked what subject would produce a guaranteed bestseller. His famous reply: "Lincoln's doctor's dog." Lincoln is always a magnet for readers, ditto medical yarns, ditto again tales of dogs. Why not put them together? Cerf knew a lot about selling books, and he also knew that he was making a joke. Despite the daydreams of agents, publishers, and writers themselves, there is simply no assured path to literary popularity. Indeed, several of the writers in this course had trouble finding a publisher, and the gossip of the book trade includes countless sad stories about the big one that got away from some editor.

Nonetheless, the history of American book publishing does allow us to notice a few patterns. For example, certain types of fiction—sometimes referred to as genre novels—repeatedly turn up. Mystery stories, Westerns, historical romances, and harlequin romances have always been well represented on lists of popular books, along with political thrillers and tales of upward mobility. In the course of these lectures, I will have occasion to illustrate most of these genres with at least one text. Over time, each genre tends to divide into specialized sub-categories. Mystery stories, for instance, come in both country house and police procedural flavors, and each of those large groupings has its local variants. The tough white guy sleuth has been joined by the tough white gal, and both now share a space on the shelf with detectives of both sexes who are African American, Native American, Asian American, gay and lesbian, and immigrant. Similar variety and mutations can be traced across most of the popular genres. Historical romances can be classed by period and region—the American Revolution and the Civil War have been extremely fruitful for this genre, and the South has long been home to a thriving industry in historical fiction. Subjects also change over time: Cold War thrillers went out of business with the end of the Cold War, to be replaced by thrillers about terrorism or global warming.

Persistence of genres—and of their nonfiction counterparts, especially self-help, biography, and memoir—tells us something about the making of bestsellers, and about the book trade more generally. Many books resemble comfort food, offering the security of familiar plots, character types, and even settings. Many of you might be willing to confess a weakness for one or another kind of genre fiction. Here is my own confession. I have an unquenchable appetite for mystery stories, preferably of the country house variety. I know how unfashionable this habit is. When we discuss Dashiell Hammett's *Maltese Falcon*, I will cheerfully quote from Raymond Chandler's contemptuous assessment of these artificial puzzle stories—but I won't stop reading them.

Genre is a species of marketing, and marketing matters. This is not a new phenomenon. Newspaper and magazine advertising has been a feature of book launches for a long time. In passing, I should also note that all books—whether they are considered works of art or pot-boilers—are embedded in commerce. James Joyce's *Ulysses*, a seldom-read masterpiece that is considered the epitome of high culture, continues to produce many thousands of dollars, pounds, and euros each year, and the copyright is fiercely protected by Joyce's heirs. Mainstream book selling was transformed in 1926 when a man named Harry Scherman founded the Book-of-the-Month Club. Sherman's scheme was a work of genius. A panel of high-profile judges selected a single title from the hundreds of new books published each month. That book was then offered to the Club members as the month's main selection and arrived by mail, accompanied by a brochure detailing the many virtues of the choice. The process spared readers the burden of choosing among the huge number of new titles on offer, and it also provided entry into a virtual community of other and perhaps like-minded readers.

The key was volume. Because the Club's executives bought in large quantities, they could demand deep discounts for specially printed editions. Part of the discount was passed along to members, thus making the books cheaper. The rest of the money was added to an accumulating profit that made the Club an exceptionally lucrative enterprise, with receipts that continued to grow even through the Great Depression. For generations, authors and publishers knew that sales would multiply—perhaps many times—if a title were chosen as a main selection of the Club. The Book-of-the-Month Club itself became a major brand in the industry. Over the subsequent decades, dozens of other clubs, often specialized by genre, joined Scherman's original organization: the History Club, the Mystery Club, the Cookbook Club, and so on. Commencing in the 1990s, Oprah's Book Club permanently altered the concept and reach of a business that had been limited to the United States Post Office and newspaper ads. Powered by the charisma and enthusiasm of its host, Oprah's Book Club promised to bring book talk into any household with a television. The consequences have been enormous. Whether classic or contemporary, the books chosen almost automatically enjoy sudden and stunning sales. In the course of her programming, Winfrey has single-handedly put Tolstoy's *Anna Karenina*, Faulkner's *Light in August*, Pearl Buck's *The Good Earth*, and Elie Wiesel's *Night* on the bestseller list (*The Good Earth* and *Night* for the second time). I'll return to Oprah Winfrey in the final lecture.

Literary prizes can also propel sales, although this presents a more complicated calculus. The Pulitzer Prizes were established in 1917 and have always enjoyed considerable prestige with the reading public. Ostensibly, the Pulitzer is intended to honor quality, not popularity. Nonetheless, a good many bestsellers—including several on our list—were Pulitzer winners: *The Good Earth, Gone With the Wind, The Grapes of Wrath, To Kill a Mockingbird,* and *John Adams.*

Along with book clubs and book prizes, systematic sales campaigns go back at least to the 1930s. Product tie-ins, celebrity endorsements, and even contests have been deployed in the tireless effort to bring novels and books of nonfiction to the public's attention. These exertions have increased in recent decades, when far more new books compete for space and attention each year than was true in the 19th century or even in the first half of the 20th. Keep this in mind: Over 100,000 new titles now appear each year in the United States alone, of an estimated 1 million worldwide.

The past couple of decades have brought two of the most significant changes the book-selling business has seen in its long history: the big-box bookstore and the Internet. Prior to the advent of Borders and Barnes & Noble, bookstores tended to be small, independent shops. They offered personal service, often provided by a staff of book lovers. But at their biggest, they were typically medium-sized spaces and could only offer a tiny sample of the new books published in any given month or season. The hyperstores, as they are sometimes called, moved books into huge palaces of print. Borders and Barnes & Noble can stock thousands of titles, rather than hundreds. They also provide a host of peripheral amenities: coffee shops, comfy chairs, wireless computer connections, music and film sections, and even bathrooms. Publishers now compete for placement: capturing space near the entrances or checkouts for their displays of favored new titles.

The Internet has generated the other innovation that has revolutionized the book business: Amazon.com and its many imitators. Literally millions of titles now change hands each year without the intervention of any traditional book dealer at all. It only takes a computer and a credit card. Internet publishing has also begun to have an impact on the book trade, although so far with marginal results—but stay tuned.

One final distinction, before I briefly introduce the specific titles in the course. American taste has reached out to books from other countries as well. In fact, some of the bestselling authors of the past 150 years or so have been foreign, usually English. Charles Dickens and William Thackeray in the 19th century, Arthur Conan Doyle across the turn of the century, and Agatha Christie and J. K. Rowling in the 20th century, to give just a few examples, have collectively sold tens of millions of copies to U.S. readers. Indeed, as I mentioned earlier, the first book ever identified as a bestseller in the United States, *Beside the Bonnie Brier Bush*, was a Scottish import. (I just wanted to say that title again.)

In this course, I have chosen books by American authors. A steady focus on native writers provides a greater opportunity to examine some of the cultural and historical issues that link imaginative literature to the texture of its time. The lectures will follow a generally chronological sequence, beginning with the first book published in the English-speaking New World, the *Bay Psalm Book*, and concluding with contemporary popular literature. The chronological organization will also help us in tracing the permutations that mark certain themes and questions as they recur. Without pressing too hard on cause and effect, I will move back and forth from literary texts to their social and political context. I will also offer some comparisons between the texts themselves. Most of the lectures will take a single text as their principal focus. The exposition of those books will combine a close reading of literary techniques with an exploration of each book's major themes. The diversity of the readings will itself demonstrate how spacious the category of bestseller has proven to be. Furthermore, whether or not the featured books have earned a permanent place in the critical sortings of later decades—and several of them have—all of them will provide rich material for analysis and reflection. Most of the works included are fiction. The exceptions (along with the *Bay Psalm Book*) are Thomas Paine's *Common Sense*, which helped to shape Colonial opinion in favor of independence; Dale Carnegie's *How to Win Friends and Influence People*, a founding work in the ubiquitous self-help genre; and, near the end of the course, examples of memoir and biography, two of the staples of popular nonfiction books. The earliest novel on the list is James Fenimore Cooper's *The Last of the Mohicans*, the most popular work by America's first bestselling novelist. *Uncle Tom's Cabin*, by Harriet Beecher Stowe, put human faces on the struggle against slavery. It was almost certainly the bestselling American novel of the 19th century. Three more 19th-century bestsellers followed. *Ragged Dick*—the first of over a hundred novels by Horatio Alger, Jr.—popularized a version of the American Dream. Louisa May Alcott's *Little Women* remains a much-loved and widely read account of the American family, and Mark Twain's *Huckleberry Finn* was the bestselling novel by the man who became the country's most popular writer and one of its most famous citizens.

The titles from the early 20th century include Owen Wister's *The Virginian*, which more or less invented "the Western" as a major American genre; Edith Wharton's *The House of Mirth*, a bestselling book about New York society that has also established itself securely in the canon of American literature; and Upton Sinclair's *The Jungle*, a scarifying account of abuses in Chicago's meat-packing industry.

Some of the most popular American novels were published in the 1920s and '30s. The first selection here is *Main Street* by Sinclair Lewis, which declared war on the small town. At the turn of the decade, Dashiell Hammett published his classic crime novel, *The Maltese Falcon*, which will be used to illustrate the centrality of the detective story, a major fictional genre in American literature. *The Good Earth* by Pearl Buck, the pioneering account of life in rural China, is still a widely read book. The same is true for two other popular novels of the 1930s: Margaret Mitchell's *Gone With the Wind*, the bestselling novel of its time; and John Steinbeck's *Grapes of Wrath*, in which a family of displaced farmers poignantly embodied the sufferings of the Depression decade. Richard Wright's *Native Son* was the first bestselling novel by an African American and the first that was selected by the Book-of-the-Month Club. J. D.

Salinger's *Catcher in the Rye* remains a byword for adolescent discontent, while Joseph Heller's *Catch-22* provides a different sort of dissent, in this case as one of the most popular anti-war novels in American literature.

Sales of Harper Lee's *To Kill a Mockingbird* remain strong. The book, which dramatized the national debate over civil rights at a moment of profound change, is often included on high school reading lists. Maxine Hong Kingston's *The Woman Warrior* was the first book by an Asian American writer to make the bestseller lists. It is still widely read: It was recently identified as the text most frequently assigned in college-level English courses. *The Woman Warrior* also deserves attention as an example of the memoir, which has become one of the mainstays of American popular writing in the past decade or so. Biographies have enjoyed a long history of success in American publishing. To provide entry to this important genre, we will discuss David McCullough's phenomenally successful *Life of John Adams*. With 3 million copies sold, and that prior to the HBO miniseries, McCullough's *John Adams* is certainly the bestselling biography in American literary history.

The final lecture, Recent Bestsellers, will provide a survey of the authors and books that have dominated the lists over the past couple of decades. In that lecture, I will elaborate on some of the topics I mentioned earlier: franchise writers and recent changes in the marketing of books. As we proceed in the course, I will discuss the distinctive qualities and particular accomplishments of each book, and I will also comment on the recurrence of certain themes, among them: the meaning of America, the idea of success, the complex questions of race and gender, and the prominence of religion, among others. Whenever I can do so, I will also try to answer the question: Why was this book so popular? I look forward to sharing ideas about these remarkable books with you.

Lecture Two
The Bay Psalm Book

Scope: *The Bay Psalm Book* was the first book printed in the English-speaking New World, and—as a proportion of the population—was also its first bestseller. Published in 1640, just 20 years after English settlers landed in Plymouth, the book was a new translation of the Psalms, the first written entirely in the English-speaking colonies. Early American Christians, also known as Puritans, thought of themselves as God's agents in a lonely wilderness, citizens of a Bible commonwealth that would embody their faith. Consequently, their literary achievement was mostly religious. *The Bay Psalm Book* was chosen as their first book following the customs of their Christian predecessors, who made the Psalms a focal point of their devotions. Rejecting all previous translations, including the graceful phrasing of the King James Version, they aspired to accuracy in plain translation. The motive was to provide the faithful with a literal account of the word of God, though ultimately the descendants of the Puritan settlers would eventually accommodate themselves to a rapidly expanding, heterogeneous society. The Puritan worldview, as seen in *The Bay Psalm Book*, however, continued to influence American ideas for generations.

Outline

I. Despite the primitive conditions, early American Christians, or Puritans, put a high value on education and literacy. They were people of the Book, and their educational philosophy had religious sources.

   A. Harvard was opened as a training ground for the ministry, and the college imported a printing press specifically to produce a new translation of the Psalms, a volume known as *The Bay Psalm Book*.

   B. Although the initial print run was under 2,000 copies, with less than 6,500 families in the colony, perhaps a third of households owned the book.

II. With their own version of the Psalms, the colonists claimed a distinctive religious identity and also added a chapter to the long history of biblical translation, a subject with profound political as well as religious and literary implications.

A. For 200 years, Christians fought over how and even whether to translate the Bible into local languages. The Church of Rome had insisted on Latin translations, as this was the language of the clergy and educated. This injunction against other translations precluded access of common people to the Word of God.

B. Reformists focused on the issue of biblical translation, and in the 16th century William Tyndale translated the Bible into early modern English. For this Tyndale was convicted of heresy and treason and burned at the stake.

C. Protestants rejected this control of biblical language—and the larger hierarchy it represented. They insisted that individuals could have direct access to divine wisdom, and the Bible was declared to be the sole source of religious certainty.

D. The Reformation came to England in the early 16th century when Henry VIII broke with the pope in an effort to divorce and remarry. Subsequently, he campaigned ruthlessly to disestablish the Roman Church and replace it with England's brand of Protestantism, which would be firmly established by the time of Elizabeth's reign.

III. By 1603, Elizabeth's cousin, King James VI of Scotland, a fervent Protestant, became King James I of England. He had a deep commitment to the idea of an English Bible and appointed a commission, mostly of clergy, to produce what would become the King James Bible.

A. Published in 1611, the King James Bible has proven to be one of the most widely read and influential texts in the English language, with extraordinary prose and poetry.

B. England's Puritans rejected the King James Bible, claiming that its poetic expressions led Christians away from the integrity of God's word. The king and his bishops punished the Puritans for their critiques of the Anglican Church and its leadership.

    1. While some Puritans stayed in England, many others left the country for safe havens in Europe or the farther shores of America.

    2. These refugee Puritans made up the earliest New England colonists. They sought refuge to practice religion without interference.

IV. Puritan literary achievements were primarily religious; these devout settlers believed their story was intimately linked with God's plan. Their efforts in transcribing their journeys and experiences in the New World were motivated by a desire to detail each pilgrim's progress toward the heavenly city.

    A. Puritan poetry also took religion as its central subject. The Bible provided a major source of ideas and imagery, as well as the justification for the poetry itself.

        1. Michael Wigglesworth, a minister and the most successful Puritan poet, wrote the most popular poem of the American 17th century, called "The Day of Doom."

        2. It illustrates the way in which religious orthodoxy shaped poetic expression.

    B. In the preface to *The Bay Psalm Book*, the author John Cotton insists that the criteria by which the translations should be judged are religious, not literary.

    C. The 150 Psalms were considered a universal mirror of human nature, a sacred refuge in troubled times, and a set of texts that brought closer the experience of divinity.

    D. Divided into five sections, the Psalms reach to every dimension of human life: prayer, repentance, history, anger, love, memory, and prophecy.

    E. The Puritans particularly identified their own journey and settlement with Biblical stories, especially the Psalms. They wanted to make the Psalms a centerpiece of their worship, leaving aesthetic criteria behind in their efforts to achieve the verbal equivalent of an "unpolished altar" rather than the glorious language of the King James Bible.

V. The consequences of approaching the Psalms as scripture rather than poetry are revealed in the lasting impact the King James Version has had on the English language.

    A. Despite *The Bay Psalm Book*'s literary weaknesses, it remained in use for over a century. The main motive was to provide the faithful with a literal account of the word of God.

    B. This single-minded commitment would evolve as the nation expanded into a vast, heterogeneous society. Though no longer read, *The Bay Psalm Book* remains a potent symbol of the long-term shaping spirit of America as "a city on the hill."

Suggested Reading:

Scheick, *Design in Puritan American Literature.*

Questions to Consider:

1. The publication of *The Bay Psalm Book* demonstrated the fervent desire of Colonial Protestant settlers to have their own version of the scriptures. Moving forward to our own time, consider the continuing importance of linguistic debates. For instance, the distinction between Standard English and dialect forms can provoke controversy, as can bilingual education and the spread of English as a "global language."

2. The lecture includes one extended comparison of the difference between the English of *The Bay Psalm Book* and that of the King James Bible. Aside from the aesthetic contrasts, does the meaning of the text change as a consequence of the word choices, metrical schemes, and rhymes?

Lecture Two—Transcript
The Bay Psalm Book

We begin this series with the first book printed in the English-speaking New World, which was also the New World's first bestseller. This was a volume called the *Bay Psalm Book*, published in 1640. Consider what a remarkable date that is—just 20 years after English settlers landed at Plymouth. At this time, only a few thousand men, women, and children lived in Massachusetts and Connecticut—some in a handful of towns and villages, most on small farms. Clinging mainly to the seacoast, these settlers were still threatened with famine and freezing winters. Pioneering English colonists had lost nearly half of their original company during their first winter in Plymouth in 1620. The settlers that followed, arriving in the area that would become Boston in the later 1630s, fared better, but conditions would continue to be formidably dangerous for decades, and death rates would remain high. The climate of New England was more punishing than that of the Old World, and the rocky soil was less hospitable to agriculture. They also faced the hostility of the native peoples. In some cases, this led to skirmishing and warfare. In other cases, the settlers tried to convert the Indians to Christianity. John Eliot, for example, became famous as "the Apostle to the Indians." He learned the Algonquian language and traveled from village to village preaching the Gospel in the local tongue. Along with physical challenges, New England's early white inhabitants suffered from the anxieties of homelessness. They knew that they were living in a tiny outpost of Great Britain, their villages no more than a collection of dots on the imperial map.

They still thought of themselves as English men and English women. They brought their language, tools, clothing styles, and furniture from the Old World, to which they remained attached by bonds of loyalty and affection. They had chosen exile, but they would feel the sting of that alienation from their homeland for generations. Although they were proud of their mission, they paid a heavy price for obedience to the demands of conscience. Dislocation and displacement would become major themes of their prose and poetry. They had chosen their exile in order that they might find a place to practice their version of Christianity without interference. They were called "Puritans," a word that their enemies had invented as a term of abuse. They were regarded as extremists in their beliefs and strict behavioral demands. These were the people, remember, who made dancing a punishable offense.

They have remained a byword for joyless piety for centuries. The journalist and critic H. L. Mencken memorably defined Puritanism as "the haunting fear that someone, somewhere, might be happy." The word "puritanical" is still used to ridicule morally squeamish attitudes.

The Puritans themselves were quite proud of their reputation for severity. They thought of themselves as God's agents in a lonely, howling wilderness—citizens of a Bible Commonwealth that would incorporate their faith. They had engaged in a covenant with God, and they firmly believed that God had personally designed their enterprise. John Winthrop, the first leader of the Massachusetts Puritans, insisted on the high destiny of his people. In a famous speech that he delivered on board the good ship *Arbella* before the settlers had even landed, Winthrop told his followers: "We must consider that we shall be as a city upon a hill. The eyes of all people are upon us.

Despite the primitive conditions they lived in, these early Christians put a high value on education and literacy. In 1636, they founded Harvard College—and in 1647, they made common schooling mandatory for their children. They were a people of the book, committed to more or less universal literacy, but they made it clear that their educational philosophy had religious sources. The laws that mandated common schools were intended to fight the devil. In a famous rationale the leaders of the colony declared that the people would learn to read because it was "one chief project of that old deluder, Satan, to keep men from the knowledge of the scriptures.

A couple of years after Harvard opened its doors to a handful of boys who would be trained for the ministry, the college imported a printing press for the specific purpose of producing a new translation of the Psalms, the first book written entirely in the English-speaking colonies. This is the volume that would become known as the *Bay Psalm Book*. By modern standards, the initial print run was rather modest: under 2,000 copies. However, since the entire population comprised fewer than 6,500 families, these figures suggest that perhaps a third of the households in the colony owned the book. As a ratio of population, the case could be made that this was, in fact, the bestselling book in American history.

Clearly, the production and ownership of this work was exceptionally important for the new Americans. By writing and publishing their own version of a central biblical book, the colonists laid claim to a distinctive religious identity. They also added a chapter to the long history of biblical translation, a subject that has had profound political as well as religious and literary implications.

In order to estimate the importance of the Massachusetts clergy, and their collaborators, and their printers, we need to look back at that earlier history. For over 200 years, Christians had debated, struggled, and sometimes killed each other over questions of how and even whether to translate the Bible into local languages. For centuries, the Church of Rome had prohibited the manufacture of any Bible except those that had been handed down in Latin. Since Latin was the language of the clergy and other educated people, these injunctions against translations meant that the common people had no access to the Word of God in a language they could understand. The men who set out to reform the Roman Church frequently put biblical translation near the top of their list of demands. Despite papal injunctions, John Wycliffe produced a complete translation of the Bible into Middle English in the late 14th century. Although Church authorities attempted to destroy them, these Wycliffe Bibles proved to be extremely popular, and hundreds of copies survive to this day. Wycliffe was condemned, but the pioneering work that he produced was the prelude to a whole library of English translations.

In the 16th century, William Tyndale translated the Bible into early modern English. The new technology of printing ensured a huge circulation for Tyndale's version of Scripture. In the view of Church leadership, Tyndale's Bible was a deliberate challenge to received authority. For example, he translated the Greek word *presbuteros* as "elder" rather than "priest" and *ecclesia* as "congregation" rather than "church." In both cases, he proved how an apparently simple choice of words could be incendiary—no priest, no church, no pope, and no infallible Roman authority. In 1535, Tyndale was arrested, convicted of heresy and treason, tied to a post, strangled, and then burned. As this history demonstrates, the stakes were very high. Those on both sides of the controversy realized that control of biblical language was a major weapon in the war over Christian souls.

Roman Catholicism had reserved ultimate religious authority to the Church and its leaders, headed by the pope. Protestants rejected that hierarchy, insisting that each individual could have direct access to divine wisdom. The Bible was declared to be the sole source of religious certitude; the mediation of priests and bishops was, therefore, irrelevant and even heretical.

The Reformation came to England in the early 16th century when Henry VIII, who had gained a great reputation as the defender of Rome, broke with the pope. The issue, Henry's desire to divorce and re-marry, is less important than the consequences. Henry embarked on a ruthless campaign to disestablish the Roman Church and replace it with an independent English system of beliefs and practices.

Monasteries and convents were taken over by the Crown. Monks and nuns were turned out, and the king named himself head of the English Church. Many English citizens retained a secret loyalty to the "old religion," as they called Roman Catholicism, but public compliance gradually became universal. England's brand of Protestantism was firmly established by the time of the first Elizabeth's reign. Several new translations of the Bible appeared in the 16th century; the most important of which were the Great Bible, the Geneva Bible, and the Bishop's Bible. These were remarkable feats of scholarship, but they are forgotten today because of the supreme English Bible that would appear in the first years of the 17th century.

When the childless Elizabeth died in 1603, she was succeeded by her cousin, King James VI of Scotland, who then became in addition King James I of England. James was a fervent Protestant and had a deep commitment to the idea of an English Bible. Like many of his subjects, he found the existing translations unsatisfactory. One of his first acts was the appointment of a commission of about 50 scholars, most of them clergymen. He charged these men to undertake a complete, new translation of the Bible. The work they produced, published in 1611, has proven to be one of the most widely read and influential texts in the English language. Although it was written by a committee, the new Bible set exceptionally high standards for the quality of its prose and poetry. In the 400 years that have passed since the publication, the King James Bible, as it is usually called, has had an enormous impact on literary style. Only the plays of Shakespeare, which were contemporary with the King James Bible, have had a more lasting influence. The Puritans, on both sides of the Atlantic, wanted no part of the King James Bible. For them, its verbal felicity was a potential trap leading Christians away from the integrity of God's Word into the dangerous beauties of human aesthetics. Their initial choice was a translation called the Geneva Bible, a name that denotes its strong Calvinist identification.

Their preference followed from their commitments. Insisting on their rigorous view of theology and religious practice, the Puritans spent much of the early 17th century criticizing the established Anglican Church and its leadership. For their part, the king and his bishops despised the Puritans and their theological allies and resorted to fines, imprisonment, and torture in the effort to eliminate dissent.

This conflict would shape the history of both the Old and New Worlds. In England, religious disputes were among the causes of the bloody civil war that would lead to the execution of a king, Charles I in 1649, followed by a dozen years of Puritan rule under Oliver Cromwell and his son, Richard.

While some Puritans stayed in England and fought, others left the country. Thousands emigrated to safe havens in Europe, while many took their chances in America. These are the people who made up the earliest New England colonists. Historians have demonstrated that they had political and economic motives, but the bond that united them, and gave them their identity, and strengthened their courage was their shared commitment to a certain kind of Protestant Christianity. As a consequence, most of their literary achievement was religious. The great majority of their writing had God and salvation at its center. The first Puritan historian was William Bradford, who worked for 20 years on the manuscript that was eventually published as *Of Plymouth Plantation*. This book is less a history than a sacred melodrama in which the piety and courage of the Christian saints are repeatedly tested by Satan's temptations.

Several decades later, Edward Johnson published a history of the colony whose title could serve as a summary of the Puritan worldview: *The Wonder-Working Providence of Sion's Savior in New England*. In other words, these devout settlers believed that their story was intimately linked with God's plan. A similar preoccupation with divinity invaded all Puritan writing. Their journals and diaries, which were never intended for publication, are filled with tortured questions about sanctity and sinfulness. The Puritans were not the first men and women to write down the stories of their interior and exterior lives, but the sheer scale of their effort in which so many of them participated makes them the great autobiographers of the early modern world. They spent a portion of each day engaged in searching inquiries into the state of their souls, hoping to find evidence of God's favor—terrified that they might find signs of God's disapproval.

The strenuous inward explorations recorded in Puritan diaries have a single motive. Puritan men and women wanted to transcribe the details of each pilgrim's progress toward the heavenly city. All of these men and women expressed a fervent belief in their personal relation with God, but all quite regularly expressed doubts about the condition of their own souls. They did not believe they could earn salvation. Theirs was a religion that believed in faith alone. However, they did believe that their deeds could provide evidence of their spiritual condition. Good deeds were not tallied up in the divine accounting, but good and bad deeds still loomed large as signs and signals of one's heavenly fate. A good person is one who does good things.

On this logic, note that even small, bad deeds could cause deep distress to the believer. After all, as Reverend John Hale says in Arthur Miller's *The Crucible*, his unsparing play about the Salem witch trials: "Theology is a fortress. No crack in a fortress may be accounted small." That is to say, one could not be "a little saved" or "a little damned." This was a demanding faith. Not surprisingly, Puritan poetry also takes religion as its central subject. Faith, and especially the dogmas of reformed Christianity, provided Puritan versifiers with their main material. The Bible claimed their attention, providing a major source of ideas and imagery as well as the justification for poetry itself.

The Puritans produced just two talented poets. The first was Ann Bradstreet, whose book *The Tenth Muse* was the first volume of verse published by an inhabitant of the New World. Theologically correct, Bradstreet's poems also revealed a passionate and intelligent woman. The second poet of importance was Edward Taylor, a clergyman whose complex religious meditations were not discovered and published until the 20th century. The most successful Puritan poet, as opposed to good, was a minister named Michael Wigglesworth, the author of a poem called *The Day of Doom*. This was probably the most popular poem of the American 17th century, outselling everything except the Bible and the many editions of the *Bay Psalm Book*. In *The Day of Doom*, Wigglesworth tells of Christ's second coming and the judgments he will make on an evil and complacent world. Dramatizing the terrifying majesty of Christ's return, Wigglesworth writes:

> Mean men lament, great men do rent their robes and tear their hair. They do not spare their flesh to tear through horrible despair. All kindreds wail. All hearts do fail. Horror the word doth fill with weeping eyes and loud outcries.

The poem lingers over Christ's judgments of the guilty, titillating its readers with the reminder that all sins will be dragged into the light no matter how deeply they have been concealed, or as Wigglesworth writes: "All filthy facts and secret acts however closely done and long concealed are there revealed before the midday sun." *The Day of Doom* is made up of 224 stanzas of this sort of verse. Most of the poem is given over to theological debate as Christ explains to each class of sinners the particular grounds for its damnation. One of the more bizarre of these conversations takes place when Christ is approached by those who died in infancy and, therefore, never sinned. Lecturing them that they bear the guilty legacy of Adam's original sin, Christ nevertheless concedes that those babies are less evil than those who live longer. He assigns them to what Wigglesworth calls "the easiest room in Hell. All of this may sound absurd to us, or at least I hope it does, but Wigglesworth's apocalyptic epic was continuously in print for nearly two centuries. Generations of New England school children actually committed it to memory. If the *Bay Psalm Book* was the first bestseller in the English colonies, *The Day of Doom* was the second. Although it is extreme even by Puritan standards, *The Day of Doom* accurately illustrates the way in which religious orthodoxy shaped poetic expression.

The New England colonists never produced a systematic exposition of their literary theory, but they did have strong views about the sort of imaginative writing that was acceptable. Poetry served its most productive purpose when it was directed toward religious edification. The Puritans treated sensuous images and complex metaphors with contempt. The best text in which to locate Puritan attitudes toward literary expression is the famous preface to the *Bay Psalm Book*. Almost certainly written by John Cotton, a major figure in the Massachusetts colony's early decades, this essay justifies poetry only insofar as it assists religious practice.

Repeatedly, Cotton insists that the criteria by which the translations in the *Bay Psalm Book* should be judged are religious, not literary. Several clergymen collaborated on the translation. They gave their work the title: *The Whole Book of Psalms Faithfully Translated into English Meter*. In his preface, John Cotton writes that the precise meaning of David's words has guided every verbal choice. The translators did not concern themselves with the demands of sound or rhythm. Confessing that such a criterion would lead to artistic failure, Cotton offered a robust defense.

> If therefore [he writes] the verses are not always so smooth and elegant as some may desire or expect, let them consider that God's altar needs not our polishings (Exodus 20) for we have respected rather a plain translation than to smooth our verses with the sweetness of any paraphrase and so have attended conscience rather than elegance, fidelity rather than poetry in translating the Hebrew words into the English language and David's poetry into English meter so that we may sing in Sion the Lord's song of praise according to His own will.

Why did these early English settlers choose the Psalms for their first book? They followed the customs of their Christian predecessors, both Protestant and Catholic, who had made the Psalms a focal point of their devotion. Psalms were featured in medieval prayer books, and each of the eight liturgical hours included the recitation of a Psalm. The great English poet and preacher, John Donne, celebrated the power of the Psalms in a sermon in 1625. He proposed that the Psalms were like the manna that had fed the Israelites on their long wandering in the desert. As Donne put it: "The

Psalms minister instruction and satisfaction to every man in every emergency and occasion." Written by anonymous scribes but attributed to David by tradition, the 150 Psalms were considered a universal guide to human conduct, a sacred refuge in time of trouble, and a set of texts that brought the experience of divinity closer.

Over 1,500 years ago, Saint Augustine said that the Psalms hold a mirror up to human nature. Despite their sources in an ancient Jewish culture, the Psalms became indispensable to Christian worship, preaching, and song. Divided into five sections, the Psalms reach to every dimension of human life—prayer, repentance, history, anger, love, memory, and prophecy. The psalmist begs for protection from the wicked, confesses the weaknesses of his own soul, enumerates God's abundant gifts, pleads to be delivered from suffering, and demands that the whole creation praise the Lord.

The Puritans thought they had a special relationship to the promises of the Bible, and they felt especially close to the eloquence of the Psalms. As they patiently built their godly settlement in the wilderness, their preachers and historians constantly invoked biblical precedent. For example, the harassment they endured from the English king is like the pursuit of David by Saul, and the pain of separation caused by the departure from Old England recalls the sorrow felt by David and Jonathan. Through all sorts of linkages the Puritans adapted Bible stories and heroes for their own enterprises. Their journey across the ocean is a latter-day exodus. The New World is a frightening wilderness but can also become the Promised Land. Their heroes were likened to Moses leading the new nation of Israel out of the Babylon (sometimes the Egypt) of Old World depravity.

The Puritans dealt with their history as if it were a sort of third testament fulfilling the promises of both the Old and New Testaments and approaching the end of secular history. Given their own interpretation of their role in the Christian story, the Puritans wanted to make the Psalms a centerpiece of their worship. Rejecting all previous translations, including the graceful phrases of the King James version, they aspired to accuracy: a plain translation, in the words of the preface, the verbal equivalent of an unpolished altar.

They did succeed in leaving aesthetic criteria behind. Whatever their fidelity to the Hebrew originals, the individual poems in the *Bay Psalm Book* are awkward and frequently tongue-tied. Comparison with the King James Bible will illustrate the difference. I take as an example the opening verses of the 23rd Psalm, perhaps the text best known and loved by modern readers regardless of their religious beliefs:

> The Lord is my Shepherd; I shall not want. He maketh me to lie down in green pastures: he leadeth me beside the still waters. He restoreth my soul: he leadeth me in the paths of righteousness for his name's sake. Yea, though I walk through the valley of the shadow of death, I will fear no evil: for thou art with me; thy rod and thy staff they comfort me.

The wonderful dignity and quietly powerful reassurance of these lines are thrown into bold relief by comparison with the singsong couplets in the *Bay Psalm Book*: The Lord to me a shepherd is, want therefore shall not I.

> He in the folds of tender grass, doth cause me down to lie: To waters calm me gently leads. Restore my soul doth he: he doth in paths of righteousness: for his name's sake lead me. Yea though in valley of death's shade I walk, none ill I'll fear: because thou art with me, thy rod, and staff my comfort are.

These are the consequences of approaching the Psalms as Scripture rather than poetry.

The King James version of the Psalms has invaded our language with so many phrases that we no longer realize the source: sweeter than honey, whiter than snow, my cup runneth over, the heavens declare the glory of God, make a joyful noise, and many others. No such list could be compiled from the *Bay Psalm Book*. On the contrary, as the passages I read a few moments ago illustrate, the level of a typical line in the Puritan text ranges from clumsy at best to unreadable at worst. Just as an aside, we might also wonder why John Cotton and his collaborators thought that clunky English rhymes provided a literal version of Hebrew poetry.

Despite its evident weaknesses, the *Bay Psalm Book* remained in use for over a century. Subsequent editions improved somewhat on the verse, but the main motive remained unchanged: to provide the faithful with a literal account of the Word of God. That singleminded commitment to a certain version of the truth could not and did not survive. Ultimately, the descendants of the Puritan settlers would accommodate themselves to the less dogmatic requirements of a rapidly expanding, heterogeneous society. Nonetheless, that fierce original sense of mission became part of the Puritan legacy, a worldview that continued to influence American ideas for generations. Nathaniel Hawthorne, one of the greatest novelists in our literature, is unthinkable apart from his Puritan ancestors. In the "Custom House" essay that serves as preface to *The Scarlet Letter*, Hawthorne itemizes the sins and failures of the Puritans. At the same time, he was irresistibly attracted to their moral seriousness, which he contrasted to the superficiality of his own time. He refused to consent to the 19th-century belief in progress. Instead, he shared with the Puritans a conviction that human beings are fundamentally flawed. Hope is a comforting dream rather than a realistic appraisal of life. Long after Hawthorne's explorations of the New England past, echoes of Puritan ideas can still be heard in the nation's public speech. Politicians routinely invoke the image of the United States as "a city on a hill." Beyond that, the Puritans encouraged later Americans to intermingle the public and private and to insist that daily life be measured by the yardstick of religious conviction. The *Bay Psalm Book*, though it is no longer read, remains a potent symbol of that long-term, shaping spirit.

Lecture Three
Common Sense

Scope: Thomas Paine's pamphlet *Common Sense* was published in the first weeks of 1776, inexorably changing the course of the debate over independence. It is widely considered one of the most important political pronouncements in Western history. Paine would later state that his motive in writing *Common Sense* was "to rescue man from tyranny and false systems and false principles of government, and enable him to be free." Paine's influence was critical in shaping the discourse of the Revolution; he organized a powerful antimonarchy thesis in *Common Sense*, bolstered by a procommoner sentiment and economic and military rationales for independence. Just seven months after the publication of *Common Sense*, Colonial delegates met in Philadelphia to sign the Declaration of Independence, marking the beginnings a new democracy. Paine insisted that America's invention of a new kind of government would have a resounding impact on the rest of the world. Later, Paine's absolutist inclinations led him to become a major voice in defense of French revolution, but imprisonment, near execution, and poverty marked his final years.

Outline

I. In 1776, representatives of the 13 colonies, angered by the abusive behavior of the English king, met in Philadelphia and resolved to liberate their countrymen.

   A. Large economic and cultural forces, as well as the voices of individual people, shaped the events of this time. No one played a more critical role than Thomas Paine, sometimes called the father of the American Revolution.

   B. Born in England (in rural Norfolk) in 1737, Paine had little formal education but was an enthusiastic student of science. He was influenced primarily by Newton and developed a rational and critical attitude toward the big political and social questions of the day.

C. Paine lived for a few years in London, where he counted Benjamin Franklin among his friends. Franklin encouraged Paine's radical ideas and would encourage Paine's writings about American independence.

D. Paine arrived in Philadelphia in the fall of 1774, with only two letters of introduction from Franklin as an entrée into the New World. Philadelphia was at this time the largest city in America, the center of Colonial commerce, culture, and politics.

   1. Paine immediately adopted the most radical of views, attracting notice for his candor and eloquence in stating them.

   2. At this time the notion of revolution was not in widespread favor, and Paine's writings helped shift the colonists' hopes and expectations toward independence.

II. *Common Sense* was published in January of 1776, with the author only identified as "an Englishman" in the first edition. The 46-page pamphlet caused an instant sensation; it sold upward of 500,000 copies in a population of fewer than 4 million.

   A. Historian Bernard Bailyn noted the importance of pamphlets to political communication in the Revolutionary era.

      1. Pamphlets were easier to produce than books and more durable than newspapers and posters; they were the preferred form for political debate.

      2. Bailyn remarked that it was in pamphlets that "the basic elements of American political thought of the Revolutionary period appeared first."

   B. *Common Sense* was the most prominent example of this genre. It was remarkable for the boldness of its ideas and the exceptional power of its style.

      1. Paine begins with an inquiry into the sources of legitimate government, rather than a list of miscellaneous complaints.

      2. He concludes that hereditary monarchy is obsolete and illegitimate and that modern men are capable of deciding laws and structures of authority for themselves.

   C. Paine appeals to the democratic instincts of his readers by coupling his repudiation of monarchy with praise for the commoner: "Of more worth is one honest man to society and in the sight of God, than all the crowned ruffians that ever lived."

D. Once he has established this underlying position, Paine then responds to particular issues and answers the counterarguments.

  1. He writes, "I challenge the warmest advocate for conciliation to show a single advantage that this continent can reap by being connected with Great Britain."

  2. America's economy had been stifled by unfair laws that reduced Colonial commerce and manufacturing prospects. Paine declares himself an early advocate of free trade rather than exclusive deals with British merchants at fixed prices.

  3. In military affairs, Paine argues that Britain provides no real protection for America and instead has provoked wars and ruled only out of self-interest, not benevolence.

  4. Paine asserts that geography itself demands independence, as he says that, "there is something very absurd in supposing a continent to be perpetually governed by an island."

III. Paine's arguments were strong, though he was not a systematic philosopher. Others were advancing similar demands, but it was Paine's straightforward style and inspirational rhetoric that made *Common Sense* both remarkable and accessible to the common person.

  A. The pamphlet reaches prophetic heights when Paine insists on the far-reaching importance of America's aspiration for liberty.

   1. In these passages, Paine proposes a version of what came to be called American exceptionalism: the idea that what happens in America would have resounding global consequences.

   2. By creating a new system of democratic government, America would shake the foundations of hereditary privilege in the rest of the world.

  B. Seven months after the publication of *Common Sense*, the Colonial delegates met in Philadelphia, where they would author, sign, and publish the Declaration of Independence.

  C. Thomas Paine's writings in service to his adopted country continued after *Common Sense*, and as the war progressed he published a series of additional pamphlets, *The American Crisis*.

IV. In the last decade of the 18th century, Paine's prophetic and absolutist inclinations led him to France, where he became a major voice in defense of the French Revolution.

A. Paine was imprisoned for his objections to the homicidal excesses of the Terror, and he was nearly executed. During his time in jail, Paine wrote *The Age of Reason*, a repudiation of organized Christianity and the Bible.

B. When Paine returned to America in 1802, his bitterness and atheist beliefs condemned him to a life of loneliness and poverty. The first international revolutionary, Thomas Paine was nearly forgotten by the time he died in 1809.

Suggested Reading:

Larking, *Thomas Paine and the Literature of Revolution.*

Liell, *46 Pages.*

Questions to Consider:

1. Paine concedes no value to the counterarguments against independence. What weaknesses do you see in his polemic defense of independence? What arguments could be made on the side of continued loyalty to the British Crown?

2. Paine had been a resident of the American colonies for only a few months when he wrote *Common Sense*. Is it significant that this most influential of all arguments for Colonial separation from Great Britain was formulated by a recent immigrant? How did his experience in England prepare him for his great rhetorical task?

Lecture Three—Transcript
Common Sense

In 1905, Henry James, then living in England, returned to the United States for his first visit in two decades. He stayed for nearly a year, traveling from New England to the West Coast and recording his impressions in a book called *The American Scene*. When he visited Philadelphia, he made a tour of Independence Hall. He admired the elegant architecture and concluded that the high ceilings and large windows provided just the right setting for the events that had taken place there. This is how James phrased it:

> One fancies, under the high spring of the ceiling and before the great ... window sashes of the principal room, some clever man of the period, after a long look round, taking the hint. "What an admirable place for a Declaration of something! What could one here—what couldn't one really declare?" And then after a moment: "I say, why not our Independence?—capital thing always to declare."

James is, of course, making a small joke, but behind the joke lies an important issue. To put it simply: Looking back on the events of 1776, we are inclined to take them for granted. The past assumes an atmosphere of inevitability. Representatives of the 13 colonies, angered by the abusive behavior of the English king, met in Philadelphia and resolved to liberate their countrymen from the tyrant's oppression. Having done so, they appointed George Washington to lead their armies to a shining victory out of which automatically came a new nation.

Hindsight is always misleading, perhaps never more so than in the case of the American Revolution. Nothing that happened was inevitable; everything could have turned out differently. As the British novelist Leslie Hartley once remarked: "The past is a foreign country: They do things differently there." So it was with the year 1776. To be sure, large economic and cultural forces shaped events, but the unpredictable choices of countless men and women also mattered. No individual played a more critical role than Thomas Paine, a man sometimes called the father of the American Revolution.

Three decades after the War for Independence, John Adams had this to say about Paine: "I know not whether any man in the world has had more influence on its inhabitants or affairs for the last 30 years than Tom Paine. ...

Call it [said Adams] the Age of Paine." Adams did not intend his remark as a compliment: In his old age, he had become disillusioned with the course of the new American republic and bitter about the course of the Revolution in France. He blamed Paine for many of the excesses he deplored on both sides of the Atlantic.

Nevertheless, whether he spoke as a friend or an enemy, Adams was conceding the remarkable influence that Paine had exerted on the course of American and European history in the last decades of the 18th century. Paine's writing, and in particular his pamphlet, *Common Sense*, published in the first weeks of 1776, changed the course of the debate over independence in the English-speaking New World. It has often been proposed that *Common Sense* was one of the two most important political pronouncements in modern Western history; the other was Karl Marx's *Communist Manifesto*. In my own view, given the course of events in the past several decades in the United States and around the world, *Common Sense* deserves the higher rank. Paine's remarkable pamphlet occupies a unique place in political history.

Of all the men and women who made the American Revolution, Paine was among the least likely. Born in England in 1737 in the rural county of Norfolk, Paine had only arrived in Philadelphia in the fall of 1774. He never occupied a seat in the various congresses that debated the colonies' future, never led a military unit in the War for Independence, nor did he ever serve in the new American government. He exerted his influence exclusively with his pen. Not very much is known about Paine's 37 years in England. He pursued several occupations, all without success. He failed at corset making, his father's trade, and failed again as a sailor, a teacher, and a merchant. Perhaps most important in shaping his revolutionary views, he suffered the loss of a government job as a tax collector, victimized by what he saw as the arbitrary and unfair behavior of middle-level bureaucrats. That experience provoked him to write his first dissenting political pamphlet, a satirical fiction called *Farmer Short's Dog Porter*, in which a farmer and his dog are both sentenced to hang for the crime of voting against a trio of corrupt judges. The pamphlet is funny in a crude sort of way, but it expressed Paine's genuine outrage at a system in which power was reserved for the wellborn and the well-connected, and in which commoners were treated as less human than aristocrats.

Although he had little formal education, Paine was an enthusiastic student of science. Growing up in the mid-18th century in the wake of Newton's monumental achievements, Paine absorbed a rationalist and skeptical attitude toward all of the big political and social questions of his day. Faced with any doctrine or dogma, his first response was always to ask: "Why?"

He was, in short, a son of the Enlightenment—that loosely organized philosophical movement that swept across all of northern Europe in the 18th century. Central to Enlightenment ideas were a critical response to virtually every established institution and a commitment to the power of human reason. Here was the key to modernity: the substitution of rational inquiry and scientific experiment for older forms of reliance on belief and received opinion. The argument from authority, for centuries the strongest of proofs, now retreated to be replaced by the argument from facts. The power of belief remained strong, and I will have more to say about that in a few minutes. But the standard of evidence in science and in the management of social and political affairs shifted from the invisible to the visible world.

Paine lived for a few years in London and counted among his friends Benjamin Franklin. Franklin, who was living in London as a representative of American Colonial interests, was himself a leading Enlightenment figure and one of the most celebrated scientists of the day. He encouraged Paine's radical opinions. It was Franklin who would eventually propose that Paine write down his ideas about American independence. When Paine came to America, he owned almost nothing beyond the clothes on his back. However, he carried two letters of introduction from Franklin, which gave him entry into Philadelphia's intellectual and mercantile society. At this time, Philadelphia was the largest city in the New World—the center of Colonial commerce, culture, and politics. Along with 30 bookshops, the city supported two-dozen printing presses and half-a-dozen newspapers, which reported the constant and lively debates about the present situation and future course of the colonies.

Paine immediately adopted the most radical of the arguments, and he attracted notice for his candor and for the colorful eloquence with which he expressed his views. Resistance to the British government had been going on for over a decade, but it was almost always constrained by the basic assumption that Americans were British citizens. While they chafed under the weight of an escalating taxation that they considered unjust, most colonists instinctively thought of themselves as loyal subjects of the king. They sought reform within the imperial status quo. It seems clear that only a minority wanted independence. Tensions mounted in the mid-1770s.

The king's ministers rejected all of the colonists' demands for relief from taxes. Anger led to violence.

On April 19, 1775, British troops exchanged fire with ragged bands of Colonial militiamen at Concord and Lexington, two small towns outside Boston. Fifty men died on the Colonial side, along with 73 British soldiers. The skirmishes proved to be the opening battles in the American War for Independence. Many years later, Ralph Waldo Emerson would famously describe the first salvo at Concord as "the shot heard 'round the world." However, the significance of those encounters was not self-evident at the time.

War now seemed unavoidable, but many on both sides would have described it as a civil war, conflict between two regions of a single country. Only gradually did American public opinion shift toward a more radical understanding of the struggle.

As Paine himself put it in the early years of the Revolution: "Independence was a doctrine scarce and rare even toward the conclusion of the year seventy-five. All our politics had been founded on the hope or expectation of making the matter up." In other words, most Americans still wanted to find some way of reconciling the dispute between Britain and the colonies. This is where Thomas Paine's writing proved decisive: He redefined those hopes and expectations.

Common Sense was published in January of 1776, the author identified only as "an Englishman" in the first edition. The 46-page pamphlet caused an instant sensation. In less than a year, it was reprinted in at least 25 new editions and sold upwards of 500,000 copies, including pirated versions: this in a population of fewer than 4 million. As remarkable as they are, those numbers surely underestimate the pamphlet's circulation. Copies were passed from hand to hand, and the text was read out loud in whole or part in coffee houses and other gathering places. The pamphlet was literally read to tatters as it moved swiftly from one reader to another. By July of 1776, a substantial proportion of Colonial adults had surely come in contact with Paine's arguments. As Paine himself put it—exaggerating, but only a little—*Common Sense* had enjoyed what he called "the greatest sale that any performance ever had since the use of letters."

Historian Bernard Bailyn has shown how important pamphlets were to political communication in the revolutionary era. Books were expensive; magazines and newspapers carried news of only local and passing interest; broadsheets and posters were used for announcements and were then discarded. Pamphlets were easier to produce than books and more durable than newspapers and posters. They were the preferred form for political debate. In Bailyn's words, it was in pamphlets that "the basic elements of American political thought of the Revolutionary period appeared first.

Common Sense was simply the most prominent example of this genre, a document marked by the boldness of its ideas and the exceptional power of its style. Paine would later say that his motive in writing *Common Sense* was "to rescue man from tyranny and false systems and false principles of government, and enable him to be free." If this sounds grandiose, it is also an honest expression of Paine's commitments. He was more interested in human freedom than America's independence. He was a Libertarian ideologue, not an American nationalist. He felt connected to the cause of republican government, not to the patriotic idea of the American nation that inspired so many of his contemporaries. As we shall see, he would pursue the same political goals in France and England after the American Revolution was concluded. Paine's priorities explain the way he organized the pamphlet. Rather than opening with a list of grievances against Britain, he shrewdly begins with an inquiry into the sources of legitimate government. He invokes first principles, in other words, not simply miscellaneous complaints. Those principles lead him to conclude that hereditary monarchy is obsolete and illegitimate. In the first of many quite brilliant rhetorical strokes, Paine acknowledges that the power of kings and aristocracy may once have been useful—but only in what he calls "dark and slavish times," when men were not capable of deciding for themselves what laws and structures of authority made sense. The modern age in Paine's view has no need for this sort of tyranny. Only custom and habit could explain the willingness of human beings to subordinate themselves to tyrants. As Paine says: "A long habit of not thinking a thing wrong, gives it a superficial appearance of being right." That insight is important and general.

As we will see when we discuss *Uncle Tom's Cabin*, even an institution as morally repulsive as slavery had many defenders. Some of these advocates were motivated by self-interest, to be sure, but slavery was an ancient and universal practice. People all over the world had developed what Paine calls "a long habit of not thinking" that it was wrong. So, too, with monarchy, which was the most venerable and commonplace of political arrangements, and which had therefore acquired an aura of legitimacy. For centuries, the majority of subjects all over the Western world even subscribed to the notion that kings ruled by divine right, that kings were the representatives of God on earth. In *Common Sense* Paine sets out to correct that error and to make his readers think for themselves about traditional arrangements that have held them hostage for too long. As he says at one point, employing a dry irony: "When we are planning for posterity, we ought to remember that virtue is not hereditary.

In addition to his condemnation of monarchy as an abstract principle, Paine repeatedly launches personal attacks on King George III. A dangerous tactic, which could have brought charges of treason, these insults were also unusual. It had been customary for opponents of British behavior to target Parliament and royal ministers, mostly exempting the king from blame. Polite fiction separated the monarch from his policies. Many colonists continued to think of themselves as children of a royal father. Paine knew that this bond of affection had to be dismantled. Referring to William the Conqueror, Paine reminded his readers that the origin of British kingship could be traced to a "French bastard landing" in Britain hundreds of years earlier accompanied by a royal gang of armed bandits. As to royal paternity, Paine declared: "Even brutes do not devour their young, nor savages make war upon their own families." Monarchy is evil in itself; hereditary monarchy is worse. Reform is irrelevant. The king is nothing but "the chief among plunderers," in Paine's phrase. Appealing to the democratic instincts of his readers, Paine cleverly couples his denigration of the king with praise for the common man, and he says: "Of more worth is one honest man to society and in the sight of God, than all the crowned ruffians [who] ever lived." The only course for America is independence. "Reconciliation is now a fallacious dream," Paine insists, and he vividly adds: "Every thing that is right or natural pleads for separation. The blood of the slain, the weeping voice of nature cries, 'tis time to part.

Once he has established this underlying position, Paine then responds to particular issues and answers the counter-arguments. He writes: "I challenge the warmest advocate for reconciliation to show a single advantage that this continent can reap by being connected with Great Britain." America's economy has been stifled by unfair laws that have reduced Colonial commerce and manufacturing to second-class status. Paine declares himself an advocate of free trade, insisting that Americans should be able to sell their raw materials and finished products to the highest bidder. Instead, they are obliged to sell exclusively to British merchants and at fixed prices. In military affairs, says Paine, Britain provides no real protection for America. On the contrary, the king's imperial ambitions have provoked ruinous wars, fought on American soil, costing American blood and treasure. Great Britain's king and Parliament have acted from self-interest, not benevolence. In Paine's summary epigram, England has never protected us "from our enemies on our account, but from her enemies on her own account.

Beyond that, England is simply too small and too far away to have custody over America: "There is something [says Paine] very absurd in supposing a continent to be perpetually governed by an island. Geography itself, in other words, demands independence. Paine's arguments were strong, but he was not a systematic philosopher. His ideas were a combination of erratic reading, the debates he heard in the coffee houses of London and Philadelphia, and his own instinctive preference for human liberty. Others were advancing some of the same ideas that he was. Indeed, John Adams would later complain that Paine got more credit than he deserved for propositions that Adams had been putting forward for several years. There was some truth in that claim. Adams, however, was a trained lawyer, and his political prose often smelled of the library and the reading lamp. Paine's style was vigorous and engaging, reaching from the plain talk of the street to the rhapsody of poetry. "I offer nothing more than simple facts, plain arguments, and common sense," he famously says in opening his attack on the king. Much of the pamphlet proceeds at just this straightforward level. Paine wanted to reach a wide audience, including not just the elite but people with little education, who were unlikely to embrace an abstruse dissertation filled with technical, philosophical, or legal vocabulary— common sense for common people.

But Paine also wanted to inspire his readers. From time to time, and especially as he nears the conclusion, he reaches to a heightened and often memorable rhetoric. "The cause of America is in a great measure the cause of all mankind," he states at one point, making a remarkable assertion. From the viewpoint of Europe, the strife in the American colonies was marginal turbulence in a barely civilized territory on the edges of the map, a map that located Europe at the very center of the world.

On the contrary, Paine insists on the far-reaching importance of America's aspiration for liberty. In one of the most famous passages in *Common Sense*, he declares:

> The sun never shone on a cause of greater worth. 'Tis not the affair of a city, a country, a province, or a kingdom, but of a continent. … 'Tis not the concern of a day, a year, or an age; posterity are virtually involved in the contest, and will be more or less affected even to the end of time by the proceedings now. Now is the seed time of continental union, faith, and honor.

Using a wonderful metaphor, a name carved on a tree's bark, Paine warns his readers that if they prove too weak to act, their failure will be visible into the distant future. He writes: "The least fracture now will be like a name engraved with the point of a pin on the tender rind of a young oak. The wound will enlarge with the tree, and posterity read it in full-grown characters." Paine's prose reminds us that political rhetoric depends as much on style as logic. In these passages, Paine proposes a version of what came to be called "American exceptionalism." What happens in America has consequences for the rest of the world. In Paine's exulted view, America will invent a new kind of government, and in so doing will shake the foundations of hereditary privilege everywhere. Paine is here reaching back to John Winthrop, who had told his Puritan followers 150 years earlier that the Massachusetts Bay colony was "a city upon a hill." Near the end of *Common Sense*, Paine assumes the tone of a prophet:

> O! ye that love mankind! Ye that dare oppose not only tyranny but the tyrant, stand forth! Every spot of the Old World is overrun with oppression. Freedom hath been hunted round the globe. Asia and Africa have long expelled her. Europe regards her as a stranger and England hath given her warning to depart. O! receive the fugitive and prepare in time an asylum for mankind.

This soaring passage has echoed down the centuries.

When Abraham Lincoln, in the midst of the Civil War, described America as "the last, best hope of Earth," he was following Paine's lead. So, too, was Emma Lazarus when she welcomed the world's "wretched refuse" in a poem now inscribed on the pedestal of the Statue of Liberty. America has not always lived up to its claim that it will be "an asylum for mankind," but Paine's words capture an enduring and cherished national conception.

Seven months after the publication of *Common Sense*, Colonial delegates meeting in Philadelphia authored, signed, and published the Declaration of Independence. What had been barely thinkable a year earlier now became official policy. The famous opening words belong to Thomas Jefferson, but they were inspired at least in part by Paine's example: "We hold these truths to be self-evident, that all men are created equal, that they are endowed by their Creator with certain unalienable Rights." Jefferson probably also reached back to Paine when he charged George III personally with over two-dozen "crimes and usurpations," and when he accused him of "cruelty … scarcely paralleled in the most barbarous ages."

Thomas Paine's service to his adopted country did not end with *Common Sense*. As the war progressed, he published a series of additional pamphlets, *The American Crisis*. He wrote the first of these in the dark days of

December, 1776, when the Continental Army was staggering under early defeats. The opening lines have become a permanent part of America's rhetorical heritage:

> These are the times that try men's souls. The summer soldier and the sunshine patriot will, in this crisis, shrink from the service of their country; but he that stands it now, deserves the love and thanks of man and woman.

George Washington ordered that this essay be read out to his troops on Christmas Eve, as they prepared to cross the Delaware River from Pennsylvania to New Jersey, where they would win their first victories. Paine was rewarded for his contributions with appointment as Secretary to the Committee on Foreign Affairs of Congress, a long title that meant simply that he was paid to continue to write in defense of the revolutionary cause.

His essays and reports included a dozen more pamphlets on the American Crisis, in which he continued to savage the king, ridicule the British aristocracy, and cheer the patriotic sacrifices of America's fighting men. Indulging his unquenchable anger against his native country, Paine declares in one of these later pamphlets that Great Britain is "the greatest and most ungrateful offender against God on the face of the whole earth [whose] national account with heaven must some day or other be settled." Those invocations of God and heaven were commonplace in Paine's political writing. Though he was personally an enemy of all religions and churches, he sprinkled his text with biblical quotes and references to God. He knew that most Americans, regardless of their particular affiliations, were steeped in the Bible and regarded it as an authoritative text. Paine deliberately borrowed scriptural images to elevate his prose and to insinuate his argument with readers and listeners. Beyond that, his invocations of divine providence and heavenly design place young America squarely on God's side.

In the last decade of the 18th century, Paine's prophetic and freedomloving inclinations led him to France, where he became a major voice in defense of the French Revolution. British statesman Edmund Burke, in his *Reflections on the Revolution in France*, had launched a broad-scale attack on the excesses of revolutionary violence. In response to Burke's arguments on behalf of hierarchy and tradition, Paine published *The Rights of Man*, dedicated to George Washington. He demanded a fundamental break with the past. "It is an age of revolutions [he wrote] in which everything may be looked for.

Although he spoke almost no French, Paine was elected to the Revolutionary Convention in 1792. Eventually, when he expressed his own reservations about the homicidal excesses of the Terror, Paine found himself imprisoned and condemned to execution, which he barely avoided. He used his year in jail to compose *The Age of Reason*, a root-and-branch repudiation of organized Christianity and the Bible. In the end, Paine returned to America, but his bitterness and his reputation for atheism condemned him to loneliness and poverty. In the town of New Rochelle, he was ostracized and not permitted to vote. Scholar Mark Philp has nicely summarized Paine's sad last years: "He was outlawed in Britain in 1792, nearly guillotined in France in 1794, and anathematized as an infidel in America on his return in 1802." The first international revolutionary, Paine was almost completely forgotten by the time he died in 1809. Only six people attended his funeral in New York City.

Lecture Four
The Last of the Mohicans

Scope: In the years during which James Fenimore Cooper published his five Leatherstocking Tales, including *The Last of the Mohicans* in 1826, the United States was an emerging independent nation. Although growing industries and rapid westward expansion were transforming the young nation, America had yet to contribute significantly to the sciences, arts, and literature, with minor exceptions. James Fenimore Cooper was the nation's first bestselling novelist, writing three dozen novels and becoming an internationally celebrated author. Cooper's Leatherstocking Tales featured a common heroic figure, Natty Bumppo—known as Hawkeye in *The Last of Mohicans*—a brave and resourceful woodsman, a founding figure in American mythology. The book takes place in 1757, during the Seven Years' War between the French and the English; it is both an adventure story and an extended commentary on American values. Despite the novel's accomplishments, Cooper is no longer regarded as a writer of major importance.

Outline

I.   The United States was a young and expanding nation in 1820, the year James Fenimore Cooper published his first novel. The republic had grown from 13 states to 22, and the westward march that would continue to expand the nation's boundaries had begun.

   A. The new nation was essentially an agrarian society at this time, although the advent of technological change was visible. Canals and railroads increased the movement of goods and produce across the continent.

   B. Politically, the nation was robust and confident, with marked pride in its differences from the Old World of monarchy and inherited privilege.

   C. Culturally, the young nation had not achieved the same successes in the arts, science, or literature. American writing was predominantly political pamphlets and manifestos, with a few noted exceptions.

II. James Fenimore Cooper was the nation's first bestselling novelist.

    A. Born in 1789, Cooper was brought up in Cooperstown, New York, which was part of his father's vast landholdings.

    B. Cooper was expelled from Yale University after only two years; he subsequently spent time in the navy before inheriting his father's fortune at just 20 years old.

    C. He married Susan De Lancey, also the child of a landowning family, a few years later.

    D. In a bet with his wife that he could write as good a work of fiction as those from England, he published his first book, *Precaution*, a poor attempt at satirizing Jane Austen's novel of manners. The rest of his novels were primarily tales of the sea or American history, and he would go on to achieve international renown as an author.

III. Cooper's major achievement can be found in his five Leatherstocking Tales, a series that included *The Pioneers* (1823), *The Last of the Mohicans* (1826), *The Prairie* (1827), *The Pathfinder* (1840), and *The Deerslayer* (1841).

    A. These books tell the story Natty Bumppo, a brave and resourceful woodsman who established himself as a founding figure in American mythology.

    B. In *The Last of the Mohicans*, Natty is called Hawkeye. Like the other Natty characters, Hawkeye is a woodsman of uncommon skill and courage, at home in the wilderness, armed with an unerringly lethal long rifle.

    C. Hawkeye lives in a rough harmony with weather and animals; he is deeply learned in the arts of nature but contemptuous of book learning. This reflects Cooper's own suspicion of abstract intellect and his preference for practical problem solving.

IV. The novel's setting is Upstate New York in 1757, during the Seven Years' War. An English commander of Fort William Henry, Colonel Munro, has come under French siege, while his two daughters Cora and Alice have set out to rejoin him. They travel under the protection of a British major, Duncan Hayward, and their guide is a Huron Indian named Magua.

A. The plot is driven by a simple rhythm: danger and escape. With implausible scenarios and heightening tensions, Cooper helps to invent the modern cliffhanger, where suspense is maximized before resolution.

B. Cooper's liberties with reality are in part reflection of the romanticism that rose against the triumph of reason in the 18th century. The novel is best understood as a romantic allegory.

C. There are many memorable descriptions of natural beauty and its discovery throughout the novel. Like his European predecessors, Cooper was attracted to nature's glories just as they were disappearing. The gains of civilization were paid for by the loss of the natural world.

V. Hawkeye's closest affiliations are with Chingachgook and Uncas, his Mohican friends. Like the natural world they inhabit, the Indians are doomed.

    A. The novel's final scenes, the death and burial of Uncas, symbolize the gradual elimination of Native Americans from the land.

    B. Cooper's characterizations of Indians both stereotype in his demonization of Magua and also elevate their possibilities as characters. Uncas is graceful, fearless, even noble, and his behavior confirms his virtue.

        1. Hawkeye insists that Indian souls are equal in value to white souls and that both races will find themselves sharing the afterlife.

        2. In the book's last scene of mourning, Hawkeye's devotion and friendship to Chingachgook is underscored, and Hawkeye sheds his only tears in the novel.

VI. Despite the serious subject matter explored in *The Last of the Mohicans*, Cooper is no longer regarded a writer of major importance. How do we explain this decline?

    A. The language of Cooper's fiction is a heightened, formal rhetoric that sounds obsolete to modern readers, especially in dialogue.

    B. In 1895, Mark Twain published an essay called "Fenimore Cooper's Literary Offenses" that ridiculed the plots and characters of the entire Leatherstocking series. He declares that Cooper breaks the rules of fiction, where language and dialogue should be recognizable, relevant, and relatable.

C. More recent generations of readers have found Cooper's myth of the New World lacking, the vision essentially only that of a man's world, wherein physical (and often violent) action define the quality of men.

Suggested Reading:

Person, *A Historical Guide to James Fenimore Cooper.*

Ringe, *James Fenimore Cooper.*

Questions to Consider:

1. Hawkeye feels bonds of affection and even kinship with his Mohican allies. At the same time, he frequently and proudly insists that he is "a man without a cross," that is, a full-blooded white man with no mixture of Indian blood. How are Hawkeye's apparently contradictory views best explained? What are the implications of his ambivalence for the novel as a whole? How does the novel treat the affectionate feelings that Uncas has for Cora?

2. In the novel, the wilderness is a place of both safety and danger. Follow Cooper's descriptions as the novel proceeds and select those that best convey his understanding of the natural world and the many different roles it plays in human lives.

Lecture Four—Transcript
The Last of the Mohicans

Let's begin with a glance at the United States in 1820, the year in which James Fenimore Cooper published his first novel. Although it had been more than two centuries since English settlers had landed at Jamestown, the United States as an independent nation was less than 40 years old. John Adams and Thomas Jefferson, the second and third presidents, were still living. Signs of rapid growth were everywhere. The country's fifth president, James Monroe, presided over a republic that had almost doubled in the number of states, from 13 to 22. The population had more than doubled, from 4 million to 10 million, including 1 million slaves. Mainly as a result of the Louisiana Purchase, the nation's boundaries had also expanded enormously. What had been a necklace of narrow seacoast settlements now reached across much of the continent, to Oregon in the northwest, and to Texas in the southwest. The westward march that would continue throughout the 19th century was well underway.

This young United States was essentially an agrarian society. Most of its working people were engaged in farming. At the same time, the advent of technological change was already visible. Eli Whitney had invented the cotton gin, which provided the mechanical basis for a greatly expanded cotton industry (and an increased demand for slaves) in 1793. Just a few years later, the first canals were built, enabling goods and produce to move more rapidly across the nation's interior. Railroads, which would transform the continent, began to appear in the 1820s. Cities were beginning to experience the growth that would ultimately change the nation into an urban society 100 years later.

Politically, the new nation was robust, confident, and proud of its separation from the Old World of monarchy and inherited privilege. European visitors were shocked by the familiarity of people toward each other, the absence of formal social rituals, the raucous backslapping, the universal use of first names. Aristocratic titles had been eliminated. Status did not come automatically with birth; It had to be earned in battle, in business, or through the ballot box. Most Americans viewed all these differences from their European ancestors with satisfaction.

Culturally, on the other hand, young America felt much less secure. After nearly 200 years as a Colonial outpost, the nation's arts and letters seemed crude, imitative, and frankly second-rate. Europe was the place of great architecture, painting, and literature. England had been the home of Chaucer, Shakespeare, and Milton. In 1820, the English critic Sidonie Smith wrote an essay that would become a famous summary of America's cultural shortcomings. Smith asked: "In the four quarters of the globe, who reads an American book, or goes to an American play, or looks at an American picture or statue?" The answer Smith expected was: no one. Americans, he said, were an industrious and ingenious people. However, he concluded, "during the 30 or 40 years of their independence, they have done absolutely nothing for the Sciences, for the Arts, or for Literature.

This was not completely fair. As we saw in the last lecture, Americans had produced writing that was widely read, both domestically and abroad. The Declaration of Independence, and Tom Paine's *Common Sense* and *The Crisis*, had inspired reformers and revolutionaries across Europe. *The Federalist Papers*—produced by Alexander Hamilton, James Madison, and John Jay—exerted an influence on both sides of the Atlantic. Admittedly, these were political pamphlets and manifestos, less significant as literature than as statements of ideological purpose. But Smith also ignored Washington Irving, who had already gained a wide audience for his imaginative writing.

Irving's work was miscellaneous, frequently humorous, and typically satirical. His *Knickerbocker's History of New York* is, in the words of one scholar, "a monument of mock erudition," piling up false documents and invented characters in a long and quite funny parody of the historian's craft. Irving's best-known works are two stories, both from a volume called *The Sketch Book of Geoffrey Crayon*, published in that significant year of 1820. "Rip Van Winkle" and "The Legend of Sleepy Hollow" have remained popular since the day they appeared, now almost two centuries ago. You probably recall the plots of the two stories. Rip Van Winkle falls asleep just before the Revolution. When he wakes up 20 years later, he finds that he is the citizen of a new nation. Providing the comic details of Rip's confusion in this changed world, Irving also makes a set of ironic observations on the distance between individual lives and grand political arrangements.

In "The Legend of Sleepy Hollow," set in the last years of the 18th century, the schoolmaster Ichabod Crane competes with the town bully, Abraham Van Brunt—known as Brom Bones—for the hand of Katrina Van Tassel, who is the only daughter of a wealthy farmer. Late one night, after a party, Ichabod is pursued through the woods by a headless horseman (Brom Bones in disguise). The terrifying experience persuades him to flee the town, leaving Brom Bones to marry Katrina. Although most of Irving's work has disappeared, in Rip Van Winkle and Ichabod Crane he created characters that have endured for nearly two centuries. They are among the first and most popular inventions in America's long tradition of comic writing, known even to millions who have never read the original stories. One of the great comic actors of the 19th century, Joseph Jefferson made a fortune playing Rip Van Winkle for 40 enormously successful years. Even today, revivals of Rip Van Winkle will occasionally turn up, demonstrating the long-lasting appeal of Irving's character and perhaps also suggesting the continued general relevance of a story about a man who sleeps through the most important events of his lifetime.

If Washington Irving was America's first successful man of letters, James Fenimore Cooper was the nation's first bestselling novelist. Cooper was born in 1789, the year of George Washington's inauguration as president. He was brought up in Cooperstown, New York, a town that was part of the vast landholdings of his wealthy father, William. Cooper completed two years at Yale, before being expelled for bad behavior. The details are not certain. There was talk of an explosion in a student room and rumors about a donkey placed on a professor's chair. Cooper then spent several years in the navy. He was just 20 years old when he inherited his father's fortune. A few years later, he married Susan De Lancey, also the child of a land-owning family. Cooper would never have to write for money. He took up novel writing almost by accident, to win a bet with his wife that he could write as good a work of fiction as most of those imported from England.

In 1820, he published his first book, a novel of manners called *Precaution* that rather badly imitated the work of Jane Austen. Despite its defects, that first fictional step led to a remarkable career. By the time Cooper died in 1851, he would write three-dozen more novels—most of them tales of the sea or American history. He became an internationally celebrated author. At a New York City memorial service a few months after his death, the tributes included messages from Emerson, Hawthorne, Longfellow, and Melville. Europeans, including Tolstoy and Balzac, also acknowledged their admiration.

What was the source of Cooper's immense success? By almost universal agreement, his major achievement can be found in his five Leatherstocking Tales, which appeared over the course of nearly two decades. The series began with *The Pioneers*, continued with *The Last of the Mohicans*, *The Prairie*, *The Pathfinder*, and concluded with *The Deerslayer*. These books tell the story of Natty Bumppo, a brave and resourceful woodsman who established himself as a founding figure in American mythology. Sir Walter Scott provided part of Cooper's source and inspiration. If *Precaution* imitates Austen, the Leatherstocking Tales recall Scott's hugely popular novels: *Waverly*, *Ivanhoe*, *The Lady of the Lake*, and others—sagas of Scottish and early English history. Not surprisingly, Cooper found himself referred to as "the American Scott" by contemporaries. Equally unsurprising, given Cooper's pride, he resented the phrase since he disliked being considered imitative, and he also insisted on his patriotic credentials as an American.

Cooper's hero, Natty Bumppo, is called by different names in the different books. He is by turns Leatherstocking, Deerslayer, Hawkeye, and Pathfinder. He is a woodsman of uncommon skill and courage, far more at home in the wilderness than in villages and towns. His long rifle, called "kill deer," is unerringly lethal, and he uses it to defend his friends, both whites and Indians. He has never been to school, but he knows everything he needs to survive in the nation's vast forests. Living in a rough harmony with weather and animals, Hawkeye is a child of the woods, deeply learned in the arts of nature and its creatures, and contemptuous of book learning.

Cooper's suspicion of abstract intellect, and his preference for practical problem-solving, would remain a feature of American cultural life for generations. The historian and political scientist Richard Hofstadter once famously described American society as "anti-intellectual." The claim is too sweeping, but Cooper exemplifies a deep-seated native preference for doing over debating. Though the term "pragmatism" was not part of Natty Bumppo's vocabulary—or Cooper's for that mater—it captures something of the practical, problem-solving attitude that the Leatherstocking novels embrace. Natty is called Hawkeye in *The Last of the Mohicans*, the second of the Leatherstocking novels and probably the best. The passage that introduces him into the novel emphasizes his nobility. Natty is first seen by the light of a flaming torch, an entrance that heightens the drama:

> The strong glare of the fire fell full upon his sturdy, weatherbeaten countenance and forest attire, lending an air of romantic wildness to the aspect of an individual who, seen by the sober light of day, would have exhibited the peculiarities of a man remarkable for the strangeness of his dress, the ironlike flexibility of his frame, and the singular compound of quick, vigilant sagacity, and of exquisite simplicity.

The novel's setting is upstate New York in 1757 during the Seven Years' War between the French and English. Both armies had treaties with various Indian tribes, who provided manpower—especially in the form of guides and warriors. The main distinction to keep in mind about these tribes is that the Hurons, who had migrated from Canada to upstate New York, were allied with the French, while the Mohicans, who had probably moved from the western territories, made alliances with the English.

The Last of the Mohicans can be read both as an adventure story and as an extended commentary on American values and beliefs. Cooper anticipated the formulas that would help to sell millions of adventure novels in the next two centuries: Along with many scenes of largescale battle and hand-to-hand combat, he includes a romantic plot involving the two daughters of an English colonel, a man named Munro. The sisters, the dark-skinned Cora and the fair Alice, set out to rejoin their father, commander of Fort William Henry, which has come under a French siege. They are joined by a religious singing master named David Gamut, and they travel under the protection of a British major, Duncan Hayward. Their guide is a Huron Indian named Magua, who proves treacherous and who plans to lead the British party into ambush. By a happy accident, the group encounters Hawkeye, who is accompanied by his Mohican friends: Chingachgook and his son, Uncas. They rescue the daughters, Gamut, and Major Hayward and take them to a secluded cave. On the following day, Magua and a band of Hurons attack the cave and take Cora, Alice, Gamut, and Hayward captive.

In the next episode, Hawkeye and the Mohicans rescue the captives yet again, kill all the Hurons except the arch-villain Magua, and lead the British travelers to Fort William Henry. Shortly after the reunion of father and daughters, Colonel Munro surrenders the fort to the French commander, General Montcalm. Despite Montcalm's assurances, the British soldiers and civilians are massacred by Indians as they march out of the fort. Once again, Magua captures Cora, Alice, and David Gamut. Once again, Hawkeye and the Mohicans pursue Magua and rescue Alice and Gamut. Cora, however, is murdered by one of Magua's allies, and Uncas is killed trying to avenge Cora's death. Hawkeye settles the score by shooting Magua. The book closes with the solemn funeral ceremony, mourning both Cora and Uncas, the warrior who is the last of the Mohicans.

The plot, as you can see, is driven by a simple rhythm: danger and escape followed by more danger and another escape. Many of the devices are utterly implausible, in particular the repeated last-second rescues against all odds. Captives are bound, tomahawks are raised, and fatal blows are about to land—when suddenly, a well-placed rifle shot turns the tables. Cooper was helping to invent the modern cliffhanger, in which suspense rises to a maximum of intensity before resolving itself. If the events are unlikely, the excitement is undeniable. Cooper's inventions routinely defy reality. In one extended episode, Hawkeye is able to infiltrate the Huron camp by clothing himself in a bearskin and imitating a bear's movements. There is absolutely no chance that Indians would actually have been fooled by such a preposterous trick, but Cooper never allows realism to interfere with a good yarn.

Here, again, he anticipates the whole library of adventure tales, in which the demands of non-stop action always trample on mere logic. But the liberties that Cooper takes with probability should also remind us of the fact that he did not set out to write a realistic novel. *The Last of the Mohicans* is best understood as a romantic allegory—that is, a story in which setting, and plot, and character represent a collection of ideas. The novel brought to its New World subject matter a cluster of attitudes that had been shaped in Europe, especially in Germany and England. Romanticism represented a reaction against the triumph of reason that had distinguished the 18th century, from Newton's scientific achievements early in the century to the rise of republican politics and the Industrial Revolution at the end. The romantics chaffed under the mechanical dominion of rationality. They sought relief in alternatives: the innocence of childhood, the unpredictable world of dreams, and the beauties of unspoiled nature.

Cooper is the American heir to this discovery of nature. His forests and lakes are places of primal mystery and profound beauty. Many of the most memorable scenes in *The Last of the Mohicans* are devoted to descriptions of the natural scene: the vast extent of the forests, the silence that is broken only by birdsong or the rustling of animals, the clarity of the air and water, and the sublime grandeur of mountains and waterfalls. Like his European predecessors, Cooper was attracted to nature's glories at just the moment when they were disappearing. As Americans advanced irresistibly into every remote corner of the primitive landscape, they brought with them the inevitable degradation of nature's age-old beauty. The gains of civilization were paid by the loss of the natural world. In a vivid phrase, Cooper said that the woods around his own hometown had been badly "lacerated" by the white habitation.

A similar response can be found in the work of the country's earliest landscape painters, Thomas Cole and the other members of the Hudson River School. Beginning in about 1825, just as Cooper was unfolding his fictional versions of America's vanishing wilderness, the painters took on the same task. America's mountains and forests are portrayed as sacred places threatened by the assault of human expansion and technological progress.

Scholars have described this transformation as the entry of the machine into the garden: the invasion of the natural world by the instruments of settlement and technology. Thomas Cole made that assault quite explicit in a painting called *River in the Catskills* in 1843. A small figure stands in the foreground, with his back to us, representing the viewer. He contemplates a scene of natural beauty: a winding, sunlit river in the near foreground, behind that a grove of trees, and mountains in the distance. However, a railroad train speeds across the vista, literally cutting the landscape in half. In his journals, Cole complained about the hurry and noise of railroad travel. He worried that the locomotive would take control of both nature and man, who would be made to serve what he called a "merciless and tyrannical" machine. Like Cole, Hawkeye speaks for nature, which he says "is sadly abused by man, when he once gets the mastery."

Cooper created his most famous image of man's abuse of nature in another Leatherstocking novel, *The Pioneers*. Basing the episode on historical fact, Cooper recalls the flocks of pigeons that once crossed back and forth over the New York frontier, millions of birds that stretched as far as the eye could see and actually darkened the daytime sky. It became a sport for the men of the region to slaughter the birds in vast numbers—not for food or use, but merely for the excitement of the kill. "This comes of settling a country," says Hawkeye, who refuses to take part. He foresees a divine retribution for the cruel destruction: "The Lord won't see the waste of his creatures for nothing, and right will be done to the pigeons, as well as others, by and by.

In this scene, Cooper has created a prophetic environmental parable. Human greed will eventually lead to crisis. Hawkeye's condemnation confirms that he is an outsider in his own civilization. In *The Last of the Mohicans*, his closest affiliations are with Chingachgook and Uncas. Like the natural world of which they were the original inhabitants, the Indians are doomed.

The novel's final scenes, the death and burial of Uncas, symbolize the gradual elimination of Native Americans from the land. The novel's ending is an elegy to an entire way of life. The book's last speech is given to Tamenund, a frail and aged chief who predicts the sad fate that has overtaken the Indians: "The pale faces [says Tamenund] are masters of the earth, and the time of the red men has not yet come again. My day has been too long."

Tamenund's sad testimony was, of course, anchored in historical fact. For 300 years, from the beginnings of European settlement in the early 17th century through the ending of the Indian wars in the late 19th century, Native Americans were displaced, oppressed, and murdered by white soldiers and civilians. They were attacked by traders, trappers, pioneers, and simple criminals. Sometimes the whites used guns, in other cases dishonest diplomacy. Treaties were signed and then invariably broken. In *The Last of the Mohicans*, the narrator concludes that whites have been the "usurpers" of the Indians' ancient territories. Explaining that reality to the naïve Major Hayward, Hawkeye says: "'Tis a long and melancholy tradition, and one I little like to think of; for it is not to be denied, that the evil has been mainly done by men with white skins." In 1838, at the midpoint of the Leatherstocking series, the Cherokee nation was compelled to turn over all of its lands east of the Mississippi. As part of President Andrew Jackson's notorious Indian removal policy, the Cherokees were forced to march hundreds of miles to the Oklahoma Territory. This devastating experience—which killed 4,000 men, women, and children in an original group of 15,000—has become known as "The Trail of Tears." Similar acts of genocide were commonplace, often sanctioned by the U.S. government.

This brutality was authorized by a view of Indians that denied their humanity. In the popular imagination, Indians were savages, not entitled to the respect that the whites extended to persons of their own color.

Cooper is capable of that sort of prejudice. Some of the Indians in the novel are described as thievish and untrustworthy. The villainous Magua, in particular, is quite literally demonized: At one point he is compared to Satan. On the other hand, Cooper also reserves his deepest admiration for Indian characters. When Uncas is first introduced, the narrator refers to him as graceful, fearless, dignified, and even noble. Uncas's subsequent behavior confirms his virtue. To be sure, there is still some stereotyping at work here: Uncas and Chingachgook are idealized as children of nature, which is another way of subtracting from their humanity. But whatever the limits of Cooper's vision, the Indians in this and his other novels consistently exhibit more courage, fortitude, and loyalty than either their white allies or their white enemies. The narrator says that they behave with what he calls "an elevation of breeding that many in a more cultivated state of society might profitably emulate."

Hawkeye is not inclined to theological discussion, but he insists on several occasions that Indian souls are equivalent in value to those of whites, and that both races will find themselves sharing whatever afterlife God has devised. In the book's last scene, as Chingachgook mourns the death of Uncas, Hawkeye assures him of his friendship, and the two men clasp hands and weep together. These are the only tears that Hawkeye sheds in the novel.

As I have tried to suggest, *The Last of the Mohicans* explores serious subjects: the course of U.S. history and the conflicts that it brought between settlers and nature and between whites and Indians. If Cooper is no longer regarded as a writer of major importance, how do we explain the decline in Cooper's reputation? I want to offer two explanations. First, the language of Cooper's fiction presents a nearly insurmountable obstacle for most modern readers. He resorts to a heightened, formal rhetoric—especially in the dialogue—that sounds obsolete and undermines his characters and their predicaments. To give a single example, after the massacre at Fort William Henry, Hawkeye has this to say while surveying the field of dead bodies:

> Nothing but vast wisdom and unlimited power should dare to sweep off men in multitudes … for it is only the one that can know the necessity of the judgment; and what is there short of the other, that can replace the creatures of the Lord?

It took me two or three readings to sort that one out.

In 1895, Mark Twain published a savage essay called "Fenimore Cooper's Literary Offenses." The specific subject was *The Deerslayer*, but the entire Leatherstocking series was the target. Twain ridiculed Cooper's plots and characters and devoted an unforgettable paragraph to the language of Leatherstocking:

> The rules of fiction [Twain wrote] require that when the personages of a tale deal in conversation, the talk shall sound like human talk, and be talk such as human beings would be likely to talk in the given circumstances, and have a discoverable meaning, also a discoverable purpose, and a show of relevancy, and remain in the neighborhood of the subject at hand, and be interesting to the reader, and help out the tale, and stop when the people cannot think of anything more to say. But this requirement has been ignored from the beginning of [Cooper's novel] to the end.

Cooper has never recovered.

If Cooper's language places a barrier between his novels and modern readers, his values have also come to seem obsolete. A hundred years after the first of the Leatherstocking novels appeared, the English novelist D. H. Lawrence, in his *Studies in Classic American Literature*, called Cooper's books "the true myth of America." He identified Cooper's hero, Natty Bumppo, as "the very intrinsic-most American." In effect, Lawrence affirmed Cooper's stated ambition: to speak to and for a new nation, which was still defining itself. Americans were eager to embrace a homespun hero who seemed to embody their aspirations toward democracy. Hawkeye represented at least some of the virtues that the citizens of the new United States cherished: self-reliance, pragmatism, loyalty, and courage. More recent generations of readers have noted the severe limits that mar Cooper's myth of the New World. It is essentially a man's world, indifferent to the concerns and tasks of women. It is also a world in which physical action— often violent action—defines the quality of a man. In consequence, the institutions of civilized society, the mechanisms of deliberation and compromise, are neglected and diminished. In short, the same qualities that brought the Leatherstocking Tales their popularity now helped to explain their undeniable decline in esteem. The arc of Cooper's reputation reflects the nation's constantly evolving understanding of itself. *The Last of the Mohicans* is certainly not the final word in our national debate—but it was among the first.

Lecture Five
Uncle Tom's Cabin

Scope: Harriet Beecher Stowe intended to intervene directly in the debate over slavery, and her outrage over the Fugitive Slave Law of 1850 was the direct impetus to her writing *Uncle Tom's Cabin*. It was the bestselling American novel of the 19th century, and likely the first American book to sell over a million copies. Praised and attacked by newspapers, clergymen, and politicians all over the country, *Uncle Tom's Cabin* put a human face on the institution of slavery. The novel depicts the journey of Tom, a slave sold from a Kentucky farm into a life of deep uncertainty and danger, who is emboldened by his abiding faith. It is this Christian belief in an afterlife that allows him to forgive his final slave master's torture. In the end of the novel, Stowe intends Uncle Tom to die a martyr's death, though the ending has provoked much controversy and debate for the 150 years it has been in print. No other text in American literary history has combined popularity, notoriety, and influence in the same measure, and as such *Uncle Tom's Cabin* remains a permanent part of the nation's culture.

Outline

I. America's argument over slavery was only a trickle of dissent beginning in the 17th century.

   A. In 1696, a group of Philadelphia Quakers announced their support for abolition in Pennsylvania.

   B. A few years later, famous Puritan diarist Samuel Sewall produced the first antislavery tract published in New England.

   C. Despite demonstrations of antislavery sentiment, the slave trade flourished. In 1776, as continental delegates gathered in Philadelphia to declare their independence, slavery was legal in all 13 colonies.

II. In the first several decades of the 19th century, the division between North and South over slavery grew; most observers knew that slavery was the principal threat to national union.

   A. For their part, slaves resisted slavery in a variety of ways, and escaped when they could.

B. The division between the North and the South grew more profound and dangerous.
  1. Southerners claimed that slavery was authorized by the U.S. Constitution.
  2. Southerners also insisted that the entire Southern economy had come to depend on slavery.
  3. Southern preachers utilized a Bible defense of slavery, which relied on scriptural support found therein.
  4. Slavery's defenders also appealed to their version of the law of nature.

C. Abolitionism grew in strength and numbers despite long odds. Rooted in the Enlightenment idea of an essential human dignity, abolitionism began in the northern states.

D. The event that galvanized both sides in the slavery debate was the passage of the Fugitive Slave Law of 1850.

III. To people in the North, including Harriet Beecher Stowe, the Fugitive Slave Law was brutal proof of "the slave power conspiracy."

A. Stowe was born in Connecticut in 1811, the daughter of Lyman Beecher.

B. Educated and gifted, she began writing for publications as a teen and continued writing after her marriage to Calvin Stowe.

C. Outraged by the Fugitive Slave Law, Stowe began to write *Uncle Tom's Cabin.*

D. *Uncle Tom's Cabin* was an instant success, with 10,000 copies of the novel sold in the first week and 300,000 in the first year.

IV. The novel is the story of Uncle Tom, a slave from a Kentucky farm, sold when the farm's owner falls into debt. He is purchased along with Harry, the young son of Eliza, Mrs. Shelby's maid. While Eliza and Harry escape and eventually find safety in Canada, Uncle Tom is shipped down the Mississippi River to a slave market.

A. On the journey, Tom rescues a young white girl named Eva, who has fallen overboard. In gratitude, Eva's father buys Tom and brings him to New Orleans.

B. The bonds of affection that grow between the white family and Tom are nurtured by their shared Christian faith.

       1. Eva grows ill, and before she dies, she reveals that she has had a vision of Jesus in heaven; she also urges her father to emancipate Tom.

       2. Although Eva's father wishes to free Tom after his daughter's death, he is killed before he can do so.

  C. Tom is sold to a brutal planter named Simon Legree, who abuses his slaves mercilessly.

       1. Legree develops a special hatred for Tom, who refuses to whip another slave when Legree orders him to.

       2. Tom's faith is tested with his new master's brutality but is restored when he has visions of Eva and Jesus. He continues to bear Legree's torments with patience.

  D. Tom's courage defines Stowe's "Victory," the title of the final chapter, in which Tom expires under a final beating. His faith in the afterlife is what propels his ability to forgive Legree and die a martyr's death.

V. The Christian devotion that sustains Eva and Tom is central to Stowe's purposes. The political and economic implications of slavery were secondary to the central point: Slavery was unforgivably wrong, a sin against nature and God.

  A. Stowe insisted that true Christianity required abolition; she often suspended the story to point to its moral and religious significance.

  B. She did not intend to write a great American novel; she wrote out of anger and despair, wanting to do what she could to end slavery.

  C. Her storytelling borrowed from all kinds of sources: slave narratives, pious sermons, abolitionist press clippings.

VI. Reaction to *Uncle Tom's Cabin* was unprecedented. Stowe became internationally famous overnight, and she received an enormous reaction from both those praising and vilifying her.

  A. Critics of the book abounded, many expressing shock and outrage, fueled not only by her abolitionist views but also by her gender.

  B. Other Stowe critics insisted her account of slavery was inaccurate, that it exaggerated the evils and understated the moderation and benevolence of the South's "peculiar institution." In response, Stowe published a companion volume, *A Key to Uncle Tom's Cabin*.

C. The effect of *Uncle Tom's Cabin* on mass culture was seen in its unprecedented sales and its appearance in the form of songs, toys, playing cards, figurines, and the like.

    1. The novel was translated into dozens of languages and sold all over Europe and South America.

    2. It was also adapted dramatically on American stages more often than any work aside from the plays of Shakespeare in the latter half of the 19th century.

D. If *Uncle Tom's Cabin* aroused the opposition of many contemporaries, then the novel has also faced powerful objections in the years since.

    1. Stowe's narrative techniques, her direct appeals to the reader, her preference for simplicity over complexity, and the novel's sentimentalism and melodrama all combined to repel some readers.

    2. Other readers objected to Stowe's treatment of her African American characters.

E. Some recent feminist scholars have proposed that Stowe's point of view embodied a revolutionary effort to replace patriarchal conventions with a more humane set of standards. Other scholars have reasserted Stowe's pioneering influence by reexamining the connections between the African American and women's fights for equality.

Suggested Reading:

Hedrick, *Harriet Beecher Stowe.*

Tompkins, *Sensational Designs.*

Questions to Consider:

1. Some critics have argued that Stowe's emphasis on Christian salvation may weaken her antislavery message. The novel insists, for example, that Uncle Tom wins the "victory" of a heavenly reward by dying at the hands of his slave master. Does this religious conviction diminish the novel's political message?

2. Gender plays an important role in this novel. Consider the main characters and the extent to which concepts of masculinity and femininity shape their attitudes and responses. In particular, Tom has been described as a man who responds to his trials with stereotypical feminine patience and fortitude.

Lecture Five—Transcript
Uncle Tom's Cabin

In 1862, Harriet Beecher Stowe visited President Abraham Lincoln at the White House. "So," Lincoln said by way of introduction, "you're the little woman who wrote the book that made this great war." The book, of course, was *Uncle Tom's Cabin*, or *Life Among the Lowly*, which Stowe had published a decade earlier. It was the bestselling American novel of the 19th century and was probably the first American book to sell over a million copies. Lincoln's remark was a friendly exaggeration, but it contained an element of truth. Stowe had intended to intervene directly in the debate over slavery, and she had succeeded far beyond her expectations. Praised and attacked by newspapers, clergymen, and politicians all over the country, *Uncle Tom's Cabin* put a human face on the institution of slavery. As we shall see in the course of this lecture, the novel is still widely read, and it remains a focus of controversy to this day.

America's argument over slavery goes back to its earliest Colonial history, long before the nation declared its independence from Great Britain. The first Africans were imported into Virginia in 1619, the beginning of a traffic that would continue for almost 200 years. Opposition to slavery, at first only a trickle of descent, also began in the 17th century. In 1696, a group of Philadelphia Quakers announced their support for abolition in Pennsylvania. A few years later, in 1700, Samuel Sewall produced a pamphlet called *The Selling of Joseph: A Memorial*. This was the first anti-slavery tract published in New England; Sewall based his argument on appeals to common sense and natural law. Despite these and other early demonstrations of anti-slavery sentiment, the slave trade continued without interruption. In 1776, as continental delegates gathered in Philadelphia to declare the nation's independence, slavery was legal in all of the 13 colonies.

Thomas Paine—whose pamphlet, *Common Sense*, we looked at in an earlier lecture—was among the many observers who ridiculed the contradiction between the glorious rhetoric of the Declaration of Independence, which insisted that "all men are created equal," and the shameful reality of slavery. Abigail Adams made similar observations and also noted the exclusion of women from those men who were created equal. In 1787, Benjamin Franklin, now in his 80s, was elected president of the Pennsylvania Society for Promoting the Abolition of Slavery. Two years later, Franklin presented the first anti-slavery petition to the United States Congress. Like

Tom Paine and Abigail Adams, Franklin had become convinced that the continued existence of slavery was an ugly stain on the fabric of America's democratic aspirations.

The moral contradiction was sharpened in 1793, with the invention of the cotton gin. This machine made it possible to process cotton at a much faster rate, which in turn propelled the demand for more slaves. In the first half of the 19th century, the economies of the Southern states grew to depend more and more on slave labor. Most observers, North and South, knew that slavery was the principal threat to national union. In 1820, during the Congressional debate that led to the Missouri Compromise, the aging Thomas Jefferson wrote that slavery, "like a fire bell in the night, awakened and filled me with terror. I considered it at once as the knell of the Union." To his dying day, however, Jefferson never freed his own slaves. For their part, slaves resisted bondage in a variety of ways, including tool breaking and sabotage. They escaped when they could.

The men and women, black and white, who organized the Underground Railroad conducted thousands of slaves to free states or Canada. Almost every Northern city had at least one station on the Railroad: usually private homes in which escaped slaves found temporary refuge on their dangerous journeys. Other slaves and free blacks organized armed revolts throughout the South. Led by men such as Gabriel Prosser, Denmark Vesey, and Nat Turner, these rebellions failed, but they served as prophecies of the violence to come.

In the first several decades of the 19th century, the division between the North and the South grew more profound and dangerous. Southerners insisted on the legality of slavery, which was authorized by the United States Constitution itself. The Constitution did forbid the importation of slaves into the United States after 1808, but it carefully protected the rights of individual states to enact and enforce racial laws. For decades, Congress imposed a "gag rule," which prohibited even the discussion of slavery on the floor of the House or Senate. John Quincy Adams, sitting in Congress after his defeat as president, devoted years to speaking out against the gag rule. He found little sympathy among his Northern colleagues, and none from the South. In 1835, in an especially cowardly gesture of accommodation with Southern demands, the Postmaster General of the United States agreed to prohibit the delivery of any abolitionist material in the South—an incontestable violation of federal law. Along with their political and constitutional arguments, Southerners also insisted that the entire Southern economy had come to depend on slavery. To abolish slavery, they predicted, would destroy the economic well-being of the entire region, at least for its white inhabitants.

As the outcome of the Civil War would demonstrate, this argument was completely accurate. In 1860, when slaves were counted as property, the states of the Confederacy were among the wealthiest in the nation. After 1865, the devastated South would become the country's most impoverished section, a position it maintained for decades. In addition to law and economics, pro-slavery advocates invoked the law of God. Southern preachers perfected a theme widely known as the "Bible defense of slavery," which relied on scriptural support for slavery. Unfortunately, such support is not hard to find. According to Exodus 21:21: "the slave is the owner's property" and the Gospel of Matthew includes the declaration that "A disciple is not above the teacher, nor a slave above the master. Significantly, God, who is conspicuously absent from the United States Constitution, was included by name in the Constitution of the Confederate States of America.

Finally, slavery's defenders also invoked their version of the law of nature. African Americans were simply inferior and were not entitled to the legal rights of white citizens. Southerners could and did appeal to the racial prejudice of their Northern adversaries. An increasing number of Northerners might oppose slavery, but most of them shared the "colorphobia," as white racism was then sometimes called, of the South. The notion of equality between the races was virtually non-existent on both sides of the Mason-Dixon Line.

This is the conspiracy of law, prejudice, economics, religion, and custom against which the proponents of abolition struggled. Rooted in the Enlightenment idea of an essential human dignity, abolitionism grew in strength and numbers throughout the first half of the 19th century. Despite the long odds, the abolitionist campaign made substantial gains. The movement's early victories were local: By 1804, just two decades after the end of the Revolutionary War, slavery had been abolished in every Northern state. Thousands of black and white men and women, including some of the greatest orators and writers of the period, joined the cause. The white abolitionist Wendell Phillips published an important pamphlet, *The Constitution, A Pro-Slavery Document*, in 1842. Another white antislavery leader, William Lloyd Garrison, was jailed for calling a slave trader a murderer. Phillips and Garrison both advocated immediate emancipation. Garrison's magazine, the *Liberator*, established itself as the most influential of many anti-slavery periodicals. Extending Jefferson's metaphor, Garrison argued that to "go slow" in ridding the nation of slavery would be the same as going slow in saving one's house from the fire that was burning it down.

Garrison recruited other spokesmen for the abolitionist movement; the most prominent among them was Frederick Douglas. An escaped slave, whose autobiographical *Narrative* remains one of the major documents in America's literary and political history, Douglas quickly emerged as the most eloquent and effective leader in the anti-slavery campaign. Douglas's memoir brought the murderous experience of slavery to vivid life. Only *Uncle Tom's Cabin* would have a wider circulation in the years before the Civil War. The unforgettable descriptions of the beatings that Douglas endured, along with the daily humiliations and the unrelenting insults that he suffered, remain indelible and eloquent accounts of the crime of slavery.

The event that galvanized both sides in the slavery debate was the passage of the Fugitive Slave Law as a part of the Compromise of 1850. The so-called Compromise was actually a series of laws that attempted to find a middle ground between slave and free states. The most controversial element of the 1850 Compromise decreed that runaway slaves had to be returned to their masters, including escaped slaves who had reached free states. Any citizen who failed to assist in the capture and return of the slaves would be subject to arrest and imprisonment, and federal troops were dispatched to enforce the law.

All Americans, whether in the North or the South, were suddenly conscripted into participation in slavery. Slave catchers roamed across the country, sweeping up free blacks along with escaped slaves, motivated by the bounty of $10.00 for every African American they delivered. To people in the North, including Harriet Beecher Stowe, the Fugitive Slave Law was a brutal proof of what they called "the slave power conspiracy." Northern resistance was often fierce—federal officials attempting to enforce the law were frequently met with mobs and violence. More than any political event of the 1850s, the Fugitive Slave Law solidified Northern anger at Southern intransigence. The Supreme Court, led by Chief Justice Roger Taney, affirmed the law in a sweeping 1857 decision in the case of an escaped slave, Dred Scott. Taney's inflammatory judgment included the stunning assertion that African Americans "had no rights which the white man was bound to respect." One abolitionist paper called the Dred Scott decision the "death knell" of the Union. Compromise now seemed like a naïve and ultimately criminal evasion. Conflict loomed nearer each day.

For her part, Harriet Beecher Stowe said it was the Fugitive Slave Law that confirmed her decision to write in opposition to slavery. Stowe was born in Connecticut in 1811, the daughter of Lyman Beecher, an immensely popular evangelical preacher. She was educated and gifted and began writing for publication while still in her teens. She continued writing after her marriage to Calvin Stowe, contributing stories to such periodicals as *Godey's Lady's Book*. The Stowes had seven children, and their marriage lasted for 50 years. When one of her sons, 18-month-old Samuel Charles, died in a cholera epidemic in 1849, she wrote: "It was at his dying bed and at his grave, that I learnt what a poor slave mother may feel when her child is torn ... from her."

That emotional solidarity and her outrage at the Fugitive Slave Law impelled Stowe to start writing *Uncle Tom's Cabin*. Over the course of nearly a year, from the summer of 1851 through the spring of 1852, the novel appeared in serial installments in the abolitionist magazine the *National Era*. When it was published in book form, 10,000 copies were sold in the first week, 300,000 in the first year. Presses worked 24 hours a day turning out copies to meet the demand.

The novel opens on a Kentucky farm. The farm's owner, Arthur Shelby, has fallen into debt and has decided that he must sell some of his slaves. The purchaser is a vulgar slave trader named Mr. Haley, who buys Uncle Tom, a man with a wife and children; and Harry, the young son of Eliza, the woman who serves as Mrs. Shelby's maid. Eliza overhears the conversation and runs away with Harry in a desperate effort to escape. The next few chapters include one of the novel's most famous scenes, though it takes up just two paragraphs. Eliza manages to cross the icy Ohio River that separates Kentucky from the free North by leaping from one block of ice to another. She has, in effect, crossed the River Jordan and has entered the Promised Land. She finds her way to a Quaker family, where she is reunited with her husband, George Harris. Eventually, Eliza, Harry, and George will find safety in Canada.

While Eliza is escaping, Uncle Tom is shipped down the river, the Mississippi River, to a slave market. On the journey, he rescues a young white girl named Eva, who has fallen overboard. In gratitude, Eva's father, Augustine St. Clare, buys Tom and takes him home to New Orleans.

Another member of the St. Clare household is a young and mischievous black girl named Topsy. When Tom asks her about her parents, Topsy responds: "Never was born! ... never had no father, nor mother, nor nothin'.

I was raised by a speculator, with lots of others." The bonds of affection that grow between the white family and Tom are nurtured by their shared Christian faith. That faith sustains Eva when she grows ill. Her death is another of the novel's most familiar episodes. As Eva dies, she tells Tom and her father that she welcomes death because she has had a vision of Jesus in heaven. She also urges her father to free Tom. Shaken by his daughter's death and stung by his conscious, St. Clare decides to emancipate Tom—however, before he can do so, he is killed when he steps in and tries to settle a brawl. Tom is then sold to a brutal planter named Simon Legree, who abuses his slaves mercilessly. He exploits young females sexually. A woman named Cassy was made pregnant by Legree, but killed her child rather than see it sold away from her. Legree develops a special hatred for Tom, who refuses to whip another slave when Legree orders him to do so. Tom, discouraged by his hopeless situation and by the sufferings of the other slaves, slides toward unbelief. His faith is restored when he has visions of Eva and Jesus. He continues to bear Legree's torments with patience. Tom turns back Legree's threats with a courage engendered by his firm belief in the afterlife: "Mas'r Legree, I an't a grain afeared to die. I'd as soon die as not. Ye may whip me, starve me, burn me,—it'll only send me sooner where I want to go."

In a chapter that Stowe called "Victory," as Tom expires under a final beating, he forgives Legree and dies a martyr's death. Arthur Shelby's son, George, has made a perilous journey to Legree's plantation to buy Tom's freedom, but he arrives too late.

In the novel's final chapters, the Harris family moves to France and decides to settle in Liberia, the African country created by the United States government in the 1840s as a refuge for both free American blacks and slaves. George Shelby inherits his father's Kentucky farm and emancipates the slaves to honor Tom's memory. If the Harris plot holds out a kind of hope for America's slaves, Tom's death insists that for most African Americans in bondage, hope—at least in this life—is only a dream. The Christian devotion that sustains Eva and Tom is central to Stowe's purposes. The political and economic implications of slavery did not interest her. She saw slavery as unforgivably wrong, a sin against nature and God. She bravely attacked priests and ministers who defended slavery, insisting that true Christianity required abolition.

Repeatedly, the narrator interrupts *Uncle Tom's Cabin* to insert a religious comment on the events. Following one of Legree's acts of brutality, for example, the narrator says that Legree felt "one of those vivid flashes that often send the lightening of conscience across the dark and wicked soul. He understood full well that it was GOD who was standing between him and his victim, and he blasphemed him."

When Tom dies and Legree says he is pleased that the slave's mouth is finally shut up, the narrator makes the angry response: "Yes, Legree; but who shall shut up that voice in thy soul? that soul, past repentance, past prayer, past hope, in whom the fire that never shall be quenched is already burning!" As that outburst suggests, Stowe never hesitated to suspend her story and point to its moral and religious significance. She did not set out to write a great American novel; she wanted to do what she could to end slavery, and she wrote out of anger and despair. Barred from the pulpit by her sex, Stowe could be described as a female preacher, using her pen to deliver the message that she knew Americans needed to hear.

Early in the novel, when Eliza hears that her child, Harry, is to be sold and plans her escape, Stowe's narrator turns directly to the readers, specifically the mothers in her audience, and asks:

> If it were your Harry, mother, or your Willie, that were going to be torn from you by a brutal trader, tomorrow morning,—if you had seen the man, and heard that the papers were signed and delivered, and you had only from twelve o'clock till morning to make good your escape,—how fast could you walk? How many miles could you make in those few brief hours, with the dearling at your bossom,—the little sleepy head on your shoulder,—the small, soft arms trustingly holding on to your neck?

Stowe borrowed freely from all kinds of sources: slave narratives, sentimental stories, pious sermons, and reports of slaveholder brutality that she gleaned from the abolitionist press. She deployed every rhetorical device in the service of her message: melodrama, coincidence, furious chases, narrow escapes, and deathbed scenes. Whatever the novel's limits as literature, it quickly assumed an almost unique place in the history of American fiction. Stowe's characters may have been drawn with the simplicity of allegory, but they became synonymous with their virtues and vices. Innocent Eva, sanctified Tom, and the cruel Legree are among those rare fictional creations that have stepped out of their novel and become permanent residents of America's collective imagination.

The reaction to *Uncle Tom's Cabin* was swift and electrifying. Stowe became internationally famous overnight. She received thousands of letters, some praising her as a savior of African Americans, others laced with insults and obscenities. Henry Wadsworth Longfellow called the novel "one of the greatest triumphs in recorded literary history." Frederick Douglas said that "The word of Mrs. Stowe is addressed to the soul of universal humanity," and Leo Tolstoy called Stowe's novel a great work, "flowing from the love of God and man." The Southerner George Frederick Holmes, on the other hand, called Stowe a "foul-mouthed hag," and the South Carolina novelist William Gilmore Simms wrote: "Mrs. Stowe betrays a malignity so remarkable that the petticoat lifts of itself, and we see the hoof of the beast under the table." As that extravagant remark about Mrs. Stowe's petticoat suggests, the outrage that *Uncle Tom's Cabin* stirred up was fueled not only by her abolitionist views but also by her gender.

In an age when property rights and political leadership were reserved exclusively for men, a woman had stepped forward with an incendiary attack on the status quo. More than one Southern critic expressed shock that such indelicate subjects as torture and rape—whether the incidents were true or not—had been described by a woman. Stowe was fully aware of the disadvantages under which she labored as a woman. Her letters to family members often included complaints about the limited rights of women in American society. Ironically, even the royalty income she earned from *Uncle Tom's Cabin*—$10,000 in the first four months—was the property of her husband.

A favored tactic of Stowe's critics was to insist that her account was simply not accurate—that it exaggerated the evils of slavery and understated the moderation and even the benevolence of the South's "peculiar institution." (The word "peculiar" in that famous phrase, by the way, meant distinctive, not strange. Defenders of slavery, including South Carolina Senator John C. Calhoun used the term proudly.) In response, Stowe quickly assembled and published a companion volume, *A Key to Uncle Tom's Cabin*.

In this book, Stowe printed a vast collection of documentary materials, including the testimony of slave owners themselves. By any fair estimate, Stowe was far more often right than wrong. In addition to its unprecedented sales, *Uncle Tom's Cabin* was absorbed into mass culture in the form of songs, toys, playing cards, figurines, coffee mugs, and even wallpaper. Translations into dozens of languages brought the novel to readers in countries all over Europe and South America. The text also spread through the country in scores of dramatic adaptations. Aside from the plays of Shakespeare, no work appeared more often on American stages in the second half of the 19th century than one version or another of Stowe's story of slavery. Productions declined toward the end of the century, but according to one estimate, there were still four "*Uncle Tom's Cabin* Companies" on tour in the early 1900s. Ironically, in most of the performances, white actors in blackface played African American characters, just as they did in minstrel shows.

If *Uncle Tom's Cabin* aroused the opposition of slavery's defenders in its own day, the novel has also faced powerful objections in the years since. Some readers have been repelled by the book's sentimentalism and melodrama. Stowe's narrative techniques, her direct appeals to her audience, her preference for simplicity over complexity, have been taken as evidence of her primitive aesthetic standards. Other readers have objected to Stowe's treatment of her African American characters. To be sure, she shared many of the racial attitudes of her time and class. She insisted that black people deserved to be free, but she did not argue for social and intellectual equality. Her reaction to suffering African Americans alternated between anger on their behalf and pity that inclined toward condescension.

Some of the black characters—for example, George Harris—meet oppression with resistance. Others behave in stereotypical ways, insisting on their loyalty to white masters and mistresses, or contenting themselves with trivial amusements. Uncle Tom himself has borne much of this criticism. Stowe intended his patience and his ultimate martyrdom as honorable and even saintly. To many readers, however, Tom's dignity has felt like subservience and weakness. The phrase "Uncle Tom" has become a term of racial abuse, suggesting a black person who fails to demand his rights. One of the most unforgiving attacks on the racial politics of the novel can be found in James Baldwin's 1949 essay, "Everybody's Protest Novel." Baldwin attacked the book on both literary and ideological grounds. Comparing it to another bestselling novel in our course, Baldwin wrote that *Uncle Tom's Cabin* is "a very bad novel, having, in its self-righteous, virtuous sentimentality, much in common with *Little Women*." In Baldwin's opinion, Stowe's religious convictions led her into an ultimately destructive reduction of black people to self-hating actors in a white allegory. In Tom's death at the hands of Simon Legree, Baldwin sees racial suicide. This, he writes, is "the heritage of the Negro in America: 'Wash me,' cried the slave to his Maker, 'and I shall be ... whiter than snow!' For black is the color of evil."

To be saved, in Baldwin's reading of Stowe's novel, black people have to become white. In Baldwin's opinion, Stowe was "not so much a novelist as an impassioned pamphleteer." She was unable to understand or present the humanity of African Americans. Tom, Baldwin concluded, "has been robbed of his humanity and divested of his sex."

Baldwin's essay was not the last word on *Uncle Tom's Cabin*. Some feminist scholars have proposed that Stowe's point of view embodied a revolutionary effort to replace patriarchal conventions with a more humane set of standards. Reexamining the connections between the campaigns for African American rights and women's rights, other readers have reasserted Stowe's pioneering influence. The scholar Henry Louis Gates, Jr., for example, has said that he finds the novel far more "culturally capacious" than Baldwin's polemic would allow.

In short, over 150 years after its publication, *Uncle Tom's Cabin* continues to provoke debate and argument. No other text in American literary history has combined popularity, notoriety, and influence in the same measure. Whatever the ultimate decision about the book's aesthetic or political value—and surely there will be no ultimate decision—*Uncle Tom's Cabin* remains a permanent part of the nation's culture.

Lecture Six
Ragged Dick

Scope: Horatio Alger Jr. was and remains an exceptionally significant figure in America's cultural history. He published a long series of books that told the same story over and over again: An orphaned boy rises from poverty to affluence through a combination of luck and pluck. In 1868, the first of these books, and the most well-known, was called *Ragged Dick; or, Street Life with the Boot-Blacks*. While the books were poorly regarded as literature, Alger's "rags-to-riches" formula repeated successfully in nearly 100 books, selling millions of copies since the late 19th century. However, this single phrase didn't encompass Alger's intentions in writing the story of Dick Hunter in *Ragged Dick*, nor in any of his other similarly plotted books. Dick's goal is not wealth but respectability, a point he makes repeatedly in the novel. His motivation is a steady job that would provide for the chance to live as a respectable citizen. Despite some criticisms of Alger's idealized vision of American ideas of self-improvement, Alger has endured. His books are no longer widely read, but his name remains a durable emblem for an American success story.

Outline

I.   To understand Horatio Alger's importance, we must begin in the years following the Civil War, a turbulent era of national transformation.

   A.   The Civil War was the most lethal event in American history; more soldiers lost their lives than in all of the other wars in the nation's history combined.

   B.   Politically, the War was also a decisive turning point: The struggle over slavery was won, and the country would never again face the threat of secession.

   C.   The American economy was transformed by the Civil War. By stimulating the rapid growth of manufacturing in the North, the United States was catapulted into a position of world leadership in every category of industry and trade.

1. By the end of the 19th century, the United States was producing more coal, iron, and steel than any other country in the world, and almost 200,000 miles of railroad track crisscrossed the nation.
2. A manufacturing revolution was made possible by a host of inventions: high-powered drills to dig deeper for coal, a mechanized reaper, the Bessemer process, and ice-cooled rail cars.

D. New millionaires were created every day by this industry boom: businessmen, inventors, bankers, and speculators.
1. The gap between rich and poor reached unprecedented levels, and radicals attacked the men they called "robber barons."
2. Mark Twain called these years "the Gilded Age," a time of excess coexisting with widespread deprivation.
3. Social critic Thorstein Veblen coined the phrase "conspicuous consumption" to describe the limitless displays of wealth.

E. The vast discrepancies between the rich and poor at this time provoked furious debate.
1. A doctrine called social Darwinism defended inequalities in wealth, claiming success and failure in the marketplace were part of a natural competitive struggle.
2. Progressives and reformers fought for changes to improve conditions for the working man.
3. The plight of the poor was documented by journalist Jacob Riis in a series of landmark books published around the turn of the century.

II. Horatio Alger's contact with life in the nation's slums produced his bestselling novels, where he dramatized the opportunities the poor could seize to better their lives.

A. Born in Massachusetts in 1832, Horatio Alger was the son of a Unitarian minister. He held jobs as a teacher and a journalist, only to return to his alma mater, Harvard University, to earn a degree in divinity.

B. After moving to New York City, Alger found the subject that would make him of one of the most successful novelists of the 19th century: orphaned boy rising to achieve success.
1. Alger wrote nearly 100 books with the same premise, selling upward of 1 million copies in his lifetime, and millions more after his death in 1899.

2. Despite poor writing, plotting, and character development, the books found an audience with their formulaic approach and appeal to the self-improvement spirit.

III. *Ragged Dick* (1868) was the first and most well-known of these books. Dick Hunter, the title character, is a boy in his early teens who has been taking care of himself since he was orphaned at seven years old. He is living on the streets, making an occasional penny shining shoes.

    A. Despite his poverty, Dick is instinctively virtuous. On the book's first page he declares, "I wouldn't steal. It's mean." Despite ragged clothes and frequent hunger, Dick never steals, cheats, or lies.

    B. In an era of shady business dealings, when success was often the result of deceit, Alger's novels promote a moral world in which his boys and young men deserve their good fortune: Success follows merit.

    C. Hard work is another key element in Alger's equation. Dick is a fairly successful boot-black due to his rising early, working long hours, and giving excellent value.

    D. In both his honesty and effort, Dick is an idealized specimen of the thousands of boys who made their homes on New York City streets.

IV. The plot of *Ragged Dick* is a series of more or less exciting episodes, each of which gives Dick a chance to demonstrate his moral superiority.

    A. In one chance encounter, Dick is hired as a guide by a wealthy business man in exchange for a new suit of clothes. The walking tour that follows demonstrates Alger's vast and detailed knowledge of New York City.

    B. Alger's emphasis on the power of education was typically American. From its inception, the nation had invested its resources in an educational system to produce competent citizens.

        1. Dick is inspired to educate himself by one of his patrons and concludes that reading and study are the necessary ingredients of worldly success.

        2. By the end of the novel, he takes more pride in his ability to write a good business letter than in almost any other accomplishment.

C. Dick earns his success by thrift, honesty, and hard work, but Alger's formula is "luck and pluck," acknowledgment that no can be successful without the aid of good fortune.

    1. However, Dick is not motivated by money but rather by, in the narrator's words, "a new vision of respectability."

    2. Self-worth and self-respect are the greatest rewards of self-improvement.

V. The story of Ragged Dick's metamorphosis into the respectable Richard Hunter, Esq., was repeated again and again in Alger's subsequent books.

    A. Alger was not the first author to tap into American ideas of self-improvement; foremost among his predecessors is Benjamin Franklin, whose *Autobiography* also provided guidelines for achieving wordly success by a certain combination of hard work, intelligence, and occasional good luck.

    B. Both men have been targeted by critics for what is perceived as self-centered materialism. In Alger's case, his response to poverty was sympathetic, but he considered the poor responsible for their own fate.

Suggested Reading:

Scharnhorst, *Horatio Alger, Jr.*

Questions to Consider:

1. Horatio Alger's tales of Ragged Dick, Tattered Tom, and his other young heroes have sometimes been called Cinderella stories for boys. Does this seem like a plausible comparison? What is the source of Dick's rigorous moral code? What role do realism and symbolism play in Alger's books and in fairy tales generally?

2. In our discussion, we noted the consistently detailed nature of Alger's descriptions: *Ragged Dick* includes dozens of New York place names, including buildings, streets, and avenues. Does this technique contribute to the book's contemporary success? In what sense is the city itself a principal character in the novel?

Lecture Six—Transcript
Ragged Dick

With *Ragged Dick*, we take up the story of American bestsellers in the years following the Civil War. Like *Uncle Tom's Cabin*, Alger's novel takes for its subject what Stowe called "life among the lowly. Unlike Uncle Tom, on the other hand, *Ragged Dick* ultimately celebrates American opportunity rather than lamenting its limits. In the long run, Stowe is undoubtedly the more significant writer. At the same time, as I will try to show in this lecture, Alger deserves more recognition and attention than he often receives. In 1940, the American novelist, Nathanael West, had this to say about Alger: "Only fools laugh at Horatio Alger and his poor boys who make good. The wiser man who thinks twice about that sterling author will realize that Alger is to America what Homer was to the Greeks."

West undoubtedly had his tongue planted firmly in his cheek: Horatio Alger is not Homer, and his heroes are nothing like Achilles or Ulysses. But Alger was and remains an exceptionally significant figure in American cultural history. To understand Alger's importance, we have to begin with the world in which he wrote his novels, in the years following the Civil War—a turbulent era of national transformation. In human terms, the Civil War was the most lethal event in American history. More soldiers lost their lives to wounds and disease than in all of the other wars in the nation's history combined. Politically, the war was also a decisive turning point: The struggle to end slavery was won, and the country would never again face the threat of secession. In addition, the war transformed the American economy. By stimulating the rapid growth of manufacturing in the North, the war catapulted the United States into a position of world leadership in virtually every category of industry and trade.

Beginning in the 1860s, American manufacturing expanded at an astounding rate. By the end of the century, the United States was producing more coal, iron, and steel than any other country in the world. By 1900, almost 200,000 miles of railroad track crisscrossed the nation. The United States remained an agricultural colossus, but it had simultaneously become the largest industrial and manufacturing economy in the world.

A host of inventions made the manufacturing revolution possible: high-powered drills to dig deeper for coal; a mechanized reaper, which opened vast new fields to the cultivation of wheat; the Bessemer process, which reduced the time to finish a ton of steel from several hours to five minutes; and ice-cooled rail cars, which permitted long-distance shipment of fresh meat and produce. (We will return to those rail cars in a later lecture, when we discuss Upton Sinclair's *The Jungle*.) New millionaires were created every day: businessmen, inventors, bankers, and speculators. At the same time, countless Americans subsisted on low wages, and many lived in poverty. The gap between rich and poor reached unprecedented levels, and radicals attacked the men they called "Robber Barons."

Mark Twain called these years "The Gilded Age," a time of excess and ostentation that coexisted with widespread deprivation and misery. The rich competed with each other in displays of wealth. Enormous mansions lined New York's Fifth Avenue, symbols of the limitless resources of the Astors, the Vanderbilts, the Morgans, and the Rockefellers. Social critic Thorstein Veblen coined the phrase "conspicuous consumption" to describe these elaborate structures and the fabulous art collections and imported furnishings they housed. In Veblen's disenchanted view, these palaces were not intended as places to live in. On the contrary, they were gargantuan trophies through which the wealthy competed with each other for bragging rights. The discrepancies between the lives of the rich and poor provoked a furious debate. On the one side, spokesmen for the status quo invoked a doctrine called "Social Darwinism" to defend inequalities in wealth. In this view, success and failure in the marketplace were allegedly part of a natural competitive struggle. The idea of the survival of the fittest, in other words, applied to human relations as well as biology.

In a Sunday school talk, John D. Rockefeller assured the listening children that his own success was part of the natural order.

> The American Beauty Rose [said Rockefeller] can be produced in the splendor and fragrance which bring cheer to its beholder only by sacrificing the early buds which grow up around it. This is not an evil tendency in business. It is merely the working out of a law of nature and a law of God.

The billionaire as botanist. On the other side, progressives and reformers fought for changes that included better working conditions, healthcare, and old-age pensions. The first large-scale union movement, the Knights of Labor, emerged in these years. In the Midwest, the Populist movement erupted, with calls for a poor peoples' revolution. Marxian socialists, many of them immigrants, argued for state control of the means of production and a more equitable distribution of income.

The plight of the have-nots was documented by journalist Jacob Riis in a series of landmark books: *The Children of the Poor*; *The Battle With the Slum*; and especially the first, *How the Other Half Lives*, published in 1890. Riis forced his middle-class readers into closer contact than they had ever had with the festering slums of Bottle Alley, Five Points, and Mulberry Bend. His prose was straightforward but memorable, as he reported on the suffering of the million people crowded into the dilapidated tenements of the Lower East Side. The worst season was summer, as this passage from Riis's book indicates:

> With the first hot night in June, police dispatches that record the killing of men and women by rolling off roofs and window-sills while asleep, announce that the time of greatest suffering among the poor is at hand. It is in hot weather, when life indoors is well-nigh unbearable with cooking, sleeping, and working … that the tenement expands, reckless of all restraint. … In the stifling July nights, when the big barracks are like fiery furnaces, their very walls giving out absorbed heat, men and women lie in restless, sweltering rows, panting for air and sleep.

Riis's exposés scandalized the city's officials and sparked a period of reforming legislation. Theodore Roosevelt called Jacob Riis the most useful citizen in New York. There were several reasons for the impact of Riis's work, but the most important was the illustrations included in his books. Carrying his primitive and cumbersome camera equipment from one tenement or alley to another, he took his own pictures—dozens of images of blighted lives and ruinous buildings. Some were reproduced as facsimile drawings, but others were printed as Riis took them. His photographs were among the pioneering works of American documentary realism, and they have endured as indelible scenes of urban poverty.

Horatio Alger, Jr., also had close contact with life in the nation's slums, but his response was far more optimistic. He was less interested in social reform than the possibilities of self-improvement. In a series of bestselling novels that he wrote over two decades, Alger dramatized the opportunities that the poor could seize to better their lives and circumstances. In a sense, Alger built a bridge between the progressive and conservative sides of the debate: He acknowledged and deplored the sufferings of the poor, but he insisted that the have-nots could become haves themselves. His books were essentially fantasies, but they were rooted in the genuine excitement and anxieties of their time. Sales in seven figures document the link between Alger's fiction and the daydreams of countless young Americans.

Alger was born in Massachusetts in 1832, the son of a Unitarian minister. After graduating with honors from Harvard, he found jobs as a teacher and journalist and then returned to Harvard to earn a degree in divinity. Just before the Civil War, he published several melodramatic novels with titles such as *Manson, the Miser* and *The Mad Heiress*. Bad eyesight kept Alger out of the army. He traveled in Europe and supported the Union side with poems and stories. As the war ended, he started writing children's fiction because, in his words: "It would pay me better." At about the same time, he was dismissed from a Unitarian pulpit in Massachusetts for sexually molesting boys in his congregation. He was never again accused of indecency, but he frequently boasted of his gift for friendship with boys; he sought them out everywhere he lived. After moving to New York, Alger found the subject that would make him one of the most successful novelists of the 19th century. Recycling and embellishing the stories he heard from street children, he published a long series of tales that told the same story over and over—an orphan boy rises from poverty to affluence through good fortune and hard work. It was a combination that Alger famously called "luck and pluck. Alger managed to repeat this formula in nearly a hundred books, which sold upwards of 1 million copies in his lifetime and millions more after he died in 1899.

The books are consistently bad: filled with one-dimensional characters, stilted dialogue, preposterous plots, and fumbling descriptions—yet, they are also consistently entertaining, as Alger plays variations on the same material in dozens of different ways. They obviously spoke to some need or desire in at least part of the reading public. It is not possible at this distance to determine how seriously any of those original readers took Alger's stories and his calls to upward mobility, but his tales codified several of the culture's leading themes with simplifying clarity.

The first of these books and the most well-known was called *Ragged Dick; or, Street Life with the Boot-Blacks*, published in 1868. The title character, Dick Hunter, is a boy in his early teens who has been taking care of himself since he was orphaned at seven years old. He has no home, sleeps in wooden boxes or on the backs of delivery wagons, and scratches out a precarious livelihood shining shoes. Despite his poverty, Dick is instinctively virtuous. In a conversation with a porter on the book's first page, he declares: "I wouldn't steal. It's mean." His clothes are rags, and he sometimes goes hungry, but he never steals, cheats, or lies. Demonstrating a personal affection for his own creation, Alger says early in the novel: "Dick was frank and straightforward, manly and self-reliant. His nature was a noble one, and had saved him from all mean faults. I hope my young readers will like him as I do."

Such intrusions are fairly common in Alger's novels. He never hesitates to stop the action, step forward, and share his opinion of his characters. Dick's unshakable goodness is an essential part of Alger's message. In an era of shady business dealings and sharp practice, when success was often the result of deceit, his heroes are relentlessly honest. Alger's novels promote a moral world in which his boys and young men deserve their good fortune: Success follows merit. Hard work is another key element in Alger's equation. Compared to most other boys, Dick is a fairly successful boot-black. He gets up early each morning, works long hours, and gives excellent value. Certain customers seek him out because of their respect for his skill and dependability. In case we readers miss the point, Alger makes it explicit: "Now, in the boot-blacking business, as well as in higher avocations, the same rule prevails, that energy and industry are rewarded." The implication is that the playing field is level, and everyone has a chance.

In both his honesty and effort, Dick is an idealized specimen of the thousands of boys who made their homes on New York City streets. In addition, Dick is unusual in his intelligence. He has a native quickness and a great capacity to learn from experience. He is also good-humored and optimistic. He is never discouraged. He is perfectly aware that he has nothing, but he keeps sorrow at a distance with a smile. He plays a facetious game in which he pretends that his raggedy clothes were handed down by the Emperor of France, Louis Napoleon. He enjoys boasting facetiously that his friends include the city's mayor and other dignitaries, and that he is merely waiting for his inheritance to arrive. Although he can't read or write, he is naturally curious and has learned much about the world by listening to his customers' conversations.

The plot of *Ragged Dick* is a series of more or less exciting episodes, each of which gives Dick a chance to demonstrate his moral superiority, his good sense, and his courage. When one of his customers sends him into a store to get change for a two-dollar bill, the crooked clerk falsely accuses Dick of trying to pass counterfeit currency. Dick bravely stands his ground. The clerk is exposed and fired, and Dick pockets a handsome tip.

In the next episode, after a chance encounter, Dick is hired by a wealthy businessman to guide his nephew, a young man named Frank, around the city. In exchange, the man gives Dick a new suit of clothes, the first he has ever had. The walking tour that follows demonstrates Dick's impressive knowledge of New York. In this scene and throughout the novel, Dick moves through dozens of the city's neighborhoods, providing detailed and accurate information about the streets and buildings. Literally scores of places are named and described: the Astor House, City Hall, Barnum's Museum, the Old Bowery Theater, the Custom House, the New York Hospital, the famous statue of George Washington in Union Square, Central Park, and many other sights. Alger's devotion to the city had a patriotic dimension. When Dick shows Frank the new and opulent Fifth Avenue Hotel, Frank suggests that even Queen Victoria would be content to live there. Alger immediately barges in to correct his character's statement:

> Though Frank did not know it [Alger confides to us], one of the queen's palaces is far from being as fine a looking building as the Fifth Avenue Hotel. St. James's Palace is a very ugly-looking brick structure, and appears much more like a factory than like the home of royalty. There are few hotels in the world as fine looking as this democratic institution.

Comment like this doesn't do much to advance the plot, but it typifies Alger's exuberant belief in the superiority of everything American. Lingering over New York's panorama of memorable places, Alger is in effect introducing the rest of the country to the great metropolis. Whatever its dangers for a poor young boy, Alger knew that New York also symbolized America's stupendous growth and its opportunities. One character says of Taylor's Saloon, a new and elegant restaurant: "It reminds me of Aladdin's palace." In the years after the Civil War, New York was booming. With a sharply rising population—many of the new inhabitants were immigrants—the city's domination of American finance, trade, and culture was already firmly established. The country was still an agrarian society, but the nation's cities were growing at a breathtaking rate. Boys from small towns and villages all over the country were leaving the farms and narrow horizons of their homes to try their luck in the cities.

Thomas Hovenden's painting *Breaking Home Ties*, 1890, is a wonderful sentimental memorial to that human drama. In the center of the large picture, a tall young man stiffly accepts his mother's farewell embrace. An older woman, probably the boy's grandmother, sits stoically at a rough table. To the left, a faithful dog looks on sadly. In the rear, the young man's father carries his luggage through a door. Like thousands of others, the boy is leaving home to seek the wider set of chances he can only find in the city. (By the way, at the great Columbian Exposition in Chicago in 1893, this painting was voted the favorite of the millions of people who attended.)

Although Alger's heroes find themselves in the city by accident at birth, they hope to act out the same journey: from neediness to affluence. Character, as Alger repeatedly insists, is the first prerequisite.

Each of Dick's adventures illuminates his high quality. When his savings passbook is stolen, he and a friend set an ingenious trap for the thief. When the local bully tries to pick a fight, Dick casually beats him up. In the book's final episode, Dick jumps into the East River to save a young girl from drowning. As it happens, she is the daughter of a prosperous merchant, who shows his gratitude by giving Dick a job in his firm. The starting salary is good, and the chances for advancement are better. Dick is ready to take the job because he has learned how to read and write. Although he quit after two days when he first went to school, he gradually realizes that education is indispensable to his plans. He makes friends with a boy named Henry Fosdick who becomes his tutor. Slowly and at first painfully, Dick learns to read and write, talents he knows he will need if he is going to leave his shoe shine kit behind him.

Alger's emphasis on the power of education was typically American. From its earliest beginnings as a British colony, the nation has invested its resources and its belief in an educational system that can produce competent citizens. Reading has always been seen as the gateway to a useful life. As I mentioned in an earlier lecture, the original settlers of Massachusetts established common schools within a few years of founding their first towns. *The New England Primer*, first published in 1688, instructed thousands of children in the rudiments of their language. The *Primer* included a famous set of rhymes to help boys and girls memorize the alphabet. Many of them also reinforced religious and moral propositions: "A, In Adam's fall we sinned all; T, Time cuts down all, both great and small; W, whales in the sea God's voice obey."

In the 19th century, *McGuffey's Readers*, which provided a standardized introduction to literacy, were among the bestselling books in American history. The *Readers* were anthologies of literary excerpts that were used to illustrate the rules of grammar and rhetoric. The books also aimed to instruct students in the virtues of hard work, honesty, good behavior, and religious orthodoxy. It is estimated that over 100 million copies of *McGuffey's* were sold between the 1830s and 1950s, making it second only to the Bible in sales over those years. To give just one historical example of the enormous importance of literacy in American society, consider the life of African American abolitionist Frederick Douglass. In his *Narrative*, the autobiography he first published in the 1840s, Douglass proudly tells of the great risks he took to learn his letters. At a time when educating blacks was illegal, Douglass knew that he could never provide leadership in the struggle for equality without the tools of reading and writing. He studied the alphabet one letter at a time, then studied some of the great writers of the past, and as I described in the last lecture, he went on to become one of the country's most eloquent spokesmen for the eradication of slavery.

Dick Hunter's career illustrates the same thesis. He is inspired to educate himself by one of his patrons, a man named Mr. Whitney. Mr. Whitney tells him about his own first job in a printing office. More than the salary he earned, Whitney tells Dick, he valued the taste for reading and study that he acquired in that shop. Dick draws the right conclusion: Reading and study are the necessary ingredients of worldly success. By the end of the novel, he takes more pride in his ability to write a good business letter than in almost any other accomplishment.

Dick earns his success by his thrift, and honesty, and hard work, but he is also lucky. He meets his benefactors by chance and inadvertently finds himself in promising situations. The aspiring boy must be able to take advantage of whatever comes his way, but he has no control over what those opportunities will be. Alger's formula, we recall, is "luck and pluck." Alger was acknowledging that no one can be confident of success without the aid of good fortune. What does success mean for Ragged Dick and the heroes of Alger's other books? Horatio Alger's name is often associated with a single phrase: "rags to riches." However, this misrepresents his views. Dick's goal is not wealth but respectability, a point he makes repeatedly in the novel: "I'm afraid I'm a pretty rough customer, but I ain't as bad as some. I mean to turn over a new leaf, and try to grow up 'spectable." As he begins to earn enough money to set up a savings account, he is motivated, in the narrator's words, by "a new vision of respectability." He is, in fact, not motivated by money and certainly has no interest in becoming rich. Instead, he wants to have a steady job, enough money to buy decent clothes and food, and the chance to live as a good citizen.

In the last scene of the book, the narrator summarizes Dick's happy new situation. He is making a salary of $10.00 a week, ample if not extravagant. He will save about half of it; his savings will steadily increase:

> It was [says the narrator] indeed a bright prospect for a boy who, only a year before, could neither read nor write, and depended for a night's lodging upon the chance hospitality of an alley-way or old

wagon. Dick's great ambition to "grow up 'spectable" seemed likely to be accomplished after all.

The story of Ragged Dick's metamorphosis into the respectable Richard Hunter, Esq., was repeated again and again in Alger's subsequent books. The titles make up a catalog of alliterative, interchangeable nouns and adjectives: *Slow and Sure*; *Mark, the Match Boy*; *Strive and Succeed*; *Phil, the Fiddler*; *Brave and Bold*; and—my own favorite—*Strong and Steady*, with its unforgettable subtitle: *Paddle Your Own Canoe*.

Horatio Alger was not the first author to tap into American ideas of self-improvement. Foremost among his predecessors is Benjamin Franklin, whose *Autobiography* also provided guidelines for achieving worldly success. Franklin was the only one of the Founders who actually began life as a poor boy. By combining hard work, intelligence, and occasional good luck, he rose to become more than respectable: a relatively wealthy man who retired from his printing business at 42 years old and devoted himself to a long list of scientific and humanitarian enterprises. Franklin's devotion to upward mobility, like Alger's, has provoked quite a bit of resistance. Both men have been the targets of critics who see them as spokesmen for a selfcentered materialism. Certainly it is the case that Alger's attitude toward corporate power is more conciliatory than antagonistic.

His response to poverty was sympathetic, but he considered the poor at least partly responsible for their own fate. As Mr. Whitney says to Dick: "You know in this free country poverty in early life is no bar to a man's advancement. ... Remember that your future position depends mainly upon yourself." The most memorable assault on the views that Franklin and Alger embrace is probably embodied in F. Scott Fitzgerald's *The Great Gatsby*. Gatsby is a parody of the selfmade man. He has literally invented himself, changing his name, making up most of his biography, and hiding his criminal activities behind a veneer of—here is Alger's favorite word— "respectability. He climbs from rags to wealth, but only through crime. Murdered by an outraged husband for a homicide he did not commit, Gatsby is a deeply disillusioned comment on the American dream.

Despite the criticisms, Alger has endured. His books are no longer widely read, but his name remains an emblem for a still-popular point of view. We can find some version of the phrase "a career out of Horatio Alger" in any day's newspaper story about some successful man (or, nowadays, woman). In 1947, a group of Alger enthusiasts founded the Horatio Alger Association of Distinguished Americans, which confers membership on what the Association calls "outstanding individuals in our society who have succeeded in spite of adversity." The first class elected included Charles Wilson, president of General Motors; and Robert Young, chairman of the New York Central Railroad. More recent inductees have included Howard Schultz, chairman of Starbucks; and newsman Tom Brokaw.

In a later lecture, I shall return to the American idea of success, when I discuss Dale Carnegie's *How to Win Friends and Influence People*. In that lecture, I shall also document how the American Dream has persisted through every sort of cultural change from the 17th century to the 21st, from Puritanism to postmodernism.

Lecture Seven
Little Women

Scope: Louisa May Alcott's *Little Women*, published in 1870, became one of the bestselling novels of the 19th century, and it continues to hold a special place among readers nearly 150 years later. The emergence and domination of women writers during this period took place within the context of women's evolving political and economic rights, turbulent topics of debate in the 19th century that were part of everyday conversation in the Alcott household. These themes emerge in her novel about the four March daughters, Meg, Jo, Beth, and Amy. Alcott accomplishes in *Little Women* a reproduction of the typical experiences of adolescent girls, and one of the novel's main themes is the resulting tension between impulse and propriety. The girls' progression toward adulthood responsibility is seen through the girls' various courtships and eventual marriages in part 2, which reveals a shift toward more conventional perspective on gender. An overarching central theme of the entire novel is religion and the twin virtues of hard work and pious faith.

Outline

I. By the mid-19th century, women not only made up the majority of fiction readers, but they also enjoyed great prominence as fiction writers.

   A. Some of the biggest bestsellers in the early republic were novels by and about women. Professor Nina Baym, in her important book, *Woman's Fiction*, includes three bestselling debut women authors in the single year of 1854: Ann Sophie Stephens, Mary Jane Holmes, and Mary Virginia Hawes.

   B. The success of women writers was not appreciated by their male contemporaries, nor was their work regarded highly as serious literature.

      1. Over the following decades, reading lists established by academics and critics of major 19th-century fiction would include Hawthorne, Melville, Twain, and others, but no women writers.

      2. As the line between serious literature and popular literature was further defined and policed, women writers' accomplishments were given little due.

C. The debate about women writers took place in the context of an even larger controversy over women's political and economic rights, or the "woman question," as it was often called. The debate over women's rights and capabilities would continue for generations.

    1. In 1776, the year of independence, Abigail Adams noted the irony of liberty for only men, and in a famous letter asked her husband John to "remember the ladies."

    2. By the end of the century, women on both sides of the Atlantic were becoming more vigorous in their demand for equal rights.

II. Louisa May Alcott grew up in a family where lively debate over the status of women and other current topics was part of everyday life.

A. Alcott's mother, Abigail May, was the daughter of a prominent Boston family. Her father, Amos Bronson Alcott, was a self-taught philosopher and teacher who became a member of the Transcendentalists.

B. Poverty defined Louisa May Alcott's early years, along with constant movement from home to home, resulting in erratic schooling.

C. As a young woman, Alcott developed strong abolitionist views and worked briefly as a nurse in a Washington DC hospital where she was infected with typhoid fever.

III. Alcott's early years as a writer produced all sorts of fiction, from sensational tales to romance melodrama to serious novels. In need of income, she accepted a request in 1867 to write a girls' book.

A. In a few months, she had finished part 1 of *Little Women*, which was published as a separate volume.

B. In response to excellent sales, part 2 quickly followed, and the single-volume version we know appeared in 1870.

IV. The "little women" are the four March daughters, but it is Jo who is closest in temperament to Louisa May Alcott. Her portrayals reproduce the typical experiences of adolescent girls, and each of the girls emerges as a differentiated character.

A. Alcott's attitude toward the March girls is undisguised affection, as she reveals their ability to enjoy life despite their relative poverty. Throughout the book, the narrator takes liberties to make edifying commentary, emphasizing the importance of pious behavior.

B. On Christmas morning, the girls feed a nearby family of poor German immigrants with their own Christmas breakfast. Afterward the girls rehearse a play they write and produce themselves.

   1. The play introduces one of the novel's main themes: the tension between impulse and propriety; a girl's desire to act naturally versus the demands of convention.

   2. The physicality required to play male parts delights Jo, as do the artistic endeavors for each girl.

C. One of the early chapters also includes a well-known scene that teaches the importance of humility: Amy brings a package of pickled limes to school, which the teacher has forbidden.

D. Much of part 1 explores the friendship between the Marches and their wealthy neighbors, the elderly James Laurence and his grandson and ward, Laurie.

   1. Mr. Laurence warms under the cheerful attention of the March girls, eventually becoming their benefactor.

   2. Laurie, a handsome and decent young man, befriends all the sisters, but develops a special affection for Jo.

E. Part 1 of *Little Women* concludes with two emotional climaxes that change the tone and direction of the book.

   1. Beth contracts scarlet fever after visiting the poor German family and holding their dying baby. Beth nears death, but recovers.

   2. Mr. March's return alters the family dynamic, which had been defined by female responsibility and spontaneity. Shortly after the father's return, Meg marries a young tutor.

V. In part 2, the novel's shift away from female autonomy implies that feisty independence are parts of a girl's childhood and that adulthood necessarily brings with it more conventional outcomes.

A. A major theme throughout part 2 is courtship and marriage for all the girls, except Beth.

   1. Jo refuses Laurie's proposal and later marries an older man, Fritz Bhaer. Amy spends time with Laurie in Europe, and eventually they fall in love.

   2. Beth has a relapse of scarlet fever, grows weaker, and dies peacefully in a passage wherein the experience of grief becomes a pious celebration.

B. Beth's death is given its meaning by her faith. Religion, and specifically the Christianity of New England Protestantism, is central to the entire novel.

    1. The novel's preface is a quote from *Pilgrim's Progress*, John Bunyan's 17th-century allegory of the sanctified life. It is Beth's favorite book, and she turns to it for comfort as she lies dying.

    2. In Alcott's mind, this religious commitment and the necessity of hard work were the basic tenets of a life of virtue.

C. In the novel's final chapter, "Harvest Time," Jo and Fritz set up a school for boys, and she bears two sons of her own. At a family reunion, the three March sisters and their mother agree they have realized their childhood dreams.

Suggested Reading:

Baym, *Woman's Fiction.*

Saxton, *Louisa May.*

Questions to Consider:

1. In the nearly century and a half since *Little Women* was published, the place of women in American society has changed substantially. The novel offers valuable insight into gender relations in the mid-19th century. To what extent does it also retain contemporary relevance? What is the role and meaning of the several marriages in the novel?

2. Are the four sisters intended as individuals or types, or both? Does each of them represent some distinctive aspect of female life and opportunity in 19th-century America? How do they differ from each other, and what do they have in common?

Lecture Seven—Transcript
Little Women

Little Women was originally published in two volumes. The first appeared in the same year as Horatio Alger's *Ragged Dick*. The second volume came out just a year later, and the complete novel in the year after that. Without pressing too hard, it might be said that *Ragged Dick* and *Little Women*, emerging almost simultaneously after the Civil War, stand as the quintessential boys' book and girls' book of the 19th century. We have seen how Alger's tale resonated with its cultural context. In this lecture, I'll try to trace some of the same connections for Louisa May Alcott's novel, *Little Women*.

The book opens with one of the most famous lines in American literature: "'Christmas won't be Christmas without any presents,' grumbled Jo, lying on the rug." Along with its familiarity, the sentence looks forward to the novel's domestic and Christian focus. It also hints at the special role that Jo will play in the story. When *Little Women* was published, the Civil War lay just a few years behind. The nation was still counting its dead and trying to come to terms with a radically changed world. Slavery had ended; Abraham Lincoln had been assassinated; the South had been almost literally destroyed. The optimism that Horatio Alger urged coexisted with widespread anxiety. In part because it provided a message of reassurance, *Little Women* became one of the bestselling novels of the 19th century. It has continued to hold a high place among readers nearly 150 years later. The book has been adapted as a film at least four times and has also been turned into a play, an opera, a musical, and an animated television feature. The 2006 Pulitzer Prize went to a novel called *March*, based on *Little Women's* idealistic husband and father, Robert March.

Looking back from the 21st century, it may seem surprising that such enormous esteem should have come to a 19th-century novel by a woman that has women and girls as its subjects. In fact, by the mid-19th century, women not only made up the majority of fiction readers, but they also enjoyed great prominence as fiction writers.

Indeed, some of the biggest bestsellers in the early republic were by and about women: Susanna Rowson's *Charlotte Temple* and *The Coquette* by Hannah Foster. Both are tales of seduction, in which naïve girls squander their virginity, fall into despair, and die. Over the next several decades, many other women published novels that did quite well in the American marketplace. Catherine Maria Sedgwick specialized in historical romances. Mrs. E. D. E. N. Southworth published almost 20 novels in the 1850s, which earned both considerable notoriety and substantial royalties. Susan Warner's *The Wide, Wide World* tells the story of a young orphan, Ellen Montgomery, who grows into adulthood through a series of difficult and dangerous episodes. The book went through 14 editions in its first two years.

Many other women writers found a large audience in the mid-19th century. Professor Nina Baym in her important book, *Woman's Fiction*, includes three who all began important careers and published bestselling first novels in the single year of 1854: Ann Sophia Stephens, Mary Jane Holmes, and Mary Virginia Hawes. In short, women not only competed in the fiction marketplace, they dominated it. Not everyone was delighted by this development. In 1855, in a famous letter to a friend, Nathaniel Hawthorne complained quite bitterly about the situation: "America," he wrote, "is now wholly given over to a damned mob of scribbling women, and I should have no chance of success while the public taste is occupied with their trash— and should be ashamed of myself if I did succeed."

In a sense, Hawthorne won the argument. Over the following decades, critics and academics established reading lists of major 19th-century American fiction in which Hawthorne held a high place—along with Herman Melville, Mark Twain, and Henry James—and women were not included. As the line between serious literature and popular literature was defined and policed with increasingly grim vigilance, women writers were pushed aside, lumped together as minor and ultimately dispensable.

I would wager that everyone in this lecture's audience has heard of (and has probably read) *The Scarlet Letter*, *Moby Dick*, *The Portrait of a Lady*, and *Huckleberry Finn*. Very few of you, on the other hand, have read (or even heard of) Catherine Sedgwick's *Hope Leslie*, E. D. E. N. Southworth's *The Lost Heiress*, or Mary Jane Holmes's *Tempest and Sunshine*. Not to worry, I would know nothing about these books, either, if I didn't read American literature for a living, but these were the novels that American women, who made most of the book purchases, were buying and presumably reading in hundreds of thousands of copies.

There were a couple of male novelists who were immensely popular with American readers in the early and mid-19th century, but they were both British: William Thackeray and especially Charles Dickens. Because English books were not yet protected by copyright, they were often brought out in pirated editions that sold for mere pennies. When Dickens toured the United States in 1842, he was greeted by swarms of enthusiastic admirers. The enthusiasm cooled somewhat when he accused his audience of being pirates who owed him and other English writers a great deal of money.

Among books produced by American writers, all of the bestselling novels of the 1850s were by women. In that decade, there were only two bestselling titles by American men, and both were nonfiction memoirs: Phineas T. Barnum's *Struggles and Triumphs* and Donald Grant Mitchell's *Reveries of a Bachelor*. The debate about women writers took place in the context of an even larger controversy over women's political and economic rights. The "woman question," as it was often called, had been discussed for generations. In 1776, the year of independence, Abigail Adams noted the irony of a liberty that would benefit only men. In a letter that has become famous, she wrote to her husband, John, asking him to "remember the ladies" and reminding him that "all men would be tyrants if they could. Abigail's plea was ignored, but the chorus of demands grew, as women on both sides of the Atlantic became more vigorous in demanding their rights.

At the end of the 18th century, Mary Wollstonecraft published *A Vindication of the Rights of Women*, an influential argument on behalf of female equality with men. Though Wollstonecraft was British, her book was widely discussed and debated in America. In 1848, 300 people, including 40 men, gathered in upstate New York for a two-day meeting "to discuss the social, civil, and religious condition of women." Known as the Seneca Falls Convention, this historic meeting is usually identified as the formal beginning of the movement to secure votes for American women. Elizabeth Cady Stanton drew up a Declaration of Sentiments, modeled on the Declaration of Independence. The suffrage movement was a long, slow, and often frustrating sequence of events that did not reach its conclusion for 70 years: Women would not secure the franchise until 1920, with the ratification of the 19th Amendment to the Constitution.

Louisa May Alcott grew up in a lively, talkative family in which arguments about the status of women—along with every other topic of debate in the 19th century—were part of everyday conversation. Her mother was Abigail May, daughter of a prominent Boston family. Her father was Amos Bronson Alcott, a self-taught philosopher and teacher who became a member of the Transcendentalists. This group, which included Ralph Waldo Emerson and Margaret Fuller, believed that divinity resided in the world, and that each human being participates in that divinity. In Emerson's famous declaration in his essay "The American Scholar": When America adopts the transcendental worldview: "A nation of men will for the first time exist, because each believes himself inspired by the Divine Soul." Acting on such opinions, in 1843 Bronson Alcott established a model socialist community he called "Fruitlands," to which he moved his entire family. Alcott imposed a vegetarian diet and cold-water baths; his venture quickly collapsed under the weight of its own extreme integrity. Years later, Alcott's daughter, Louisa, wrote a book called *Transcendental Wild Oats*, a parody of her father's scheme. In the book, Fruitlands is turned into "Apple Slump," an eccentric haven for theorizing men and hardworking women.

As this brief background suggests, Louisa May Alcott's childhood was not lived in the idealized circle of love and stability she created for the March family in *Little Women*. Poverty defined her early years, along with constant movement from one temporary home to another. Her schooling was erratic, though she did have the undeniable advantage of conversations with Thoreau and Emerson. As a young woman, she developed strong abolitionist views, supported the Union cause in the Civil War, and worked briefly as a nurse in a Washington DC hospital until she was infected with typhoid fever. Out of that experience came one of Alcott's earliest books, *Hospital Sketches*, published in 1863, which features a nurse named Tribulation Periwinkle. Alcott earned over $600 in that year from her writing, an impressive sum at a time when laborers worked for wages of $1 a day. Over the years that followed, Alcott wrote all sorts of fiction—from sensational tales, to romance melodramas, to more serious novels.

In fall of 1867, a publisher wrote to her, asking for a girl's book. This was the initiative that led to *Little Women*. Alcott later said she accepted the assignment only because she needed the money. In a few months, she had finished part one of the book, which was published as a separate volume. In response to excellent sales, part two quickly followed, and the single-volume version we know appeared in 1870. The novel enjoyed prodigious sales and has never been out of print. It is still read by children (mostly girls) and adults (mostly women) in America and around the world in scores of translations. The "little women" of the title are, of course, the four March daughters. When the story opens in the early years of the Civil War, Margaret (usually called Meg), the oldest, is 16. She is, the narrator tells us, "plump and fair, with large eyes, plenty of soft brown hair, a sweet mouth, and white hands." Meg is serious and mature, qualities she needs as the senior child in this remarkable and boisterous family.

Next is 15-year-old Jo (she intensely dislikes her real name, Josephine). The narrator tells us that Jo is "very tall, thin and brown ... with sharp gray eyes, which appeared to see everything." Jo is the closest character and temperament to Louisa May Alcott, and she is the most restless of the girls. She's not quite happy with being a girl, and she's quite unhappy about becoming a woman. She envies the freedom and the opportunities that automatically go to boys. Elizabeth, known to everyone as Beth, is a bright-eyed girl of 13; she is painfully shy and seems "to live," the narrator says, "in a happy world of her own." The youngest of the daughters is Amy, whose pretty head is covered in blond curls; Amy is willful and still enjoying life at the center of everyone's attention. Mrs. March, known as "Marmee," presides over this household with love and abundant patience. The girls' father is absent from part one. Mr. March, though too old for soldiering, has volunteered to serve as a Union chaplain. This is a perfectly plausible plot choice, and it also gives Alcott the chance to emphasize Mr. March's patriotism and courage. As Meg says: "I think it was so splendid in Father to go as a chaplain when he was too old to be drafted, and not strong enough for a soldier."

Alcott's own commitment to the Union cause shines through here and elsewhere in the novel. One morning while she is shopping, Marmee meets an elderly man whose four sons have all gone into the army. Two of them have been killed in battle, another has been seriously wounded, and the fourth is being held in a Confederate prison camp. When Marmee tells him that he has done a great deal for his country, the old man responds proudly: "Not a mite more than I ought, ma'am. I'd go myself, if I was any use; as I ain't, I give my boys, and give 'em free." Alcott's major accomplishment in *Little Women* is to reproduce the typical experiences of adolescent girls. The ordinary triumphs and defeats of each day were made to seem authentic and significant by the affectionate skill with which they are presented. Furthermore, each of the girls receives enough time and space in the narrative to emerge as a differentiated character. Jo is obviously Alcott's favorite, but she devotes equal narrative energy to all four sisters. Tolstoy once famously said: "Happy families are all alike; every unhappy family is unhappy in its own way." *Little Women* works to disprove that overrated remark. Happy families each have their distinctive stories, the particular burdens and challenges out of which they construct communities of solidarity and trust. The Marches face reversals, including death, but these obstacles knit them more closely together. Alcott believed in the possibilities of family life, despite the disappointments of her own childhood.

If it was a fiction, then she held tight to it as a necessary fiction. Late in the book, Jo bursts out that "families are the most beautiful things in all the world!" Alcott's attitude toward her girls is undisguised affection. At one point, Jo declares that the four March sisters have full lives despite their relative poverty—she says: "I don't believe fine young ladies enjoy themselves a bit more than we do." To this, the narrator adds: "And I think Jo was right." Alcott never hesitates to interject an edifying comment or pious sentiment. *Little Women* is committed to teaching readers about the importance of virtuous behavior.

The Christmas morning that opens the novel provides the first occasion for the March family to demonstrate its values and its generosity. Marmee tells the girls about a nearby family of poor German immigrants who will not even have enough to eat for breakfast. All the girls immediately agree to carry their own food to the other family. For the rest of the day, the girls rehearse a play, a bombastic tragedy that they write and produce themselves. In part, the spectacle is Alcott's satire against the prevailing theatrical conventions of her period, but the episode also captures the playful intensity with which adolescents approach this sort of experience. Although they have a lot of fun, they are also anxious to do it as well as they can. In addition, the play introduces one of the novel's main themes: the tension between impulse and propriety, between a girl's desire to act naturally and the demands of convention. Jo, in particular, enjoys the play because it gives her the chance to assume a number of male parts and to run, and jump, and brandish a sword. Alcott invents a whole series of adventures for her heroines, each accompanied by a moral that she thought would be suitable for young readers.

One of the early chapters includes a well-known scene that teaches the importance of humility. Amy brings a package of pickled limes to school, which the teacher, Mr. Davis, has expressly forbidden. She wants to share the limes with her classmates in order to advance her social standing and popularity, especially with children who come from wealthier homes than hers. Instead, she is found out and punished. Mr. Davis strikes her across the hand with a ruler and then makes her stand on a platform in front of the class.

Alcott points out two lessons from Amy's humiliation. The first, somewhat predictably, is that "pride goes before a fall." Despite the truth of that adage, however, Marmee reaches a second conclusion: that corporal punishment is wrong. Without excusing Amy's behavior, Marmee reserves her greater anger for Mr. Davis.

A considerable portion of part one is taken up with the friendship that develops between the Marches and their wealthy neighbors, the elderly

James Laurence and his grandson and ward, Theodore, known as Laurie. Though he has a reputation for gloom and unfriendliness, Mr. Laurence warms up under the cheerful attentions of the March girls. He also becomes their benefactor, discreetly providing gifts and money to them to get them through some tight spots. Laurie—a handsome, intelligent, and decent young man—befriends all the March sisters, but he begins to develop a special affection for Jo. Three of the girls demonstrate a distinctive artistic aptitude. Amy is a gifted painter, Beth plays the piano skillfully, and Jo possesses a talent for writing. Eventually, she wins a contest sponsored by a local magazine. The recognition and the $100.00 prize confirm her desire to live by her pen if she can. Typically, she spends the money on a vacation for Beth and Marmee. Jo's fictional principles, like those of her creator, are moral and didactic. At several points in the novel, Alcott ridicules the contemporary writers—especially the women—who pander to the public's taste for sensation. Among others, she parodies the highly successful Mrs. E. D. E. N. Southworth, whom I mentioned earlier, under the name Mrs. S. L. A. N. G. Northbury.

Part one of *Little Women* concludes with two emotional climaxes. In the first, Beth contracts scarlet fever when she visits the poor German family and holds their dying baby. After sinking near to death, Beth recovers, though she remains weakened. As she is regaining her strength, Mr. March returns from the hospital in Washington, where he also has been near death from an illness. If Mr. March is a tribute to Alcott's father, he is—as I suggested earlier—altogether idealized. He is far more admirable and reliable than Bronson Alcott. Marmee says of him: "He never loses patience—never doubts or complains—but always hopes, and works and waits so cheerfully that one is ashamed to do otherwise before him."

Despite his many virtues, Father's sudden appearance changes the tone and direction of the novel. His enlistment had done more than prove Alcott's support for the Northern cause. Sending Mr. March off to the war also removed him from the domestic scene. Alcott was then able to create a specifically female world within the house. Relations between and among the girls, and between all of them and Marmee, are unaffected by a dominant male presence. When Mr. March reenters the home, he takes his place as head of the family. Though Marmee and the girls are relieved and delighted by his safe return, he alters the set of family relationships, which had been defined by female responsibility and spontaneity. Shortly after Father's return, Meg marries a young tutor named John Brooke. He is a poor but honorable man, and Mr. March and Marmee both approve of him.

Part two of *Little Women* begins three years after part one. Mr. March's patriarchal role is reaffirmed in an early chapter:

> To outsiders [the narrator says], the five energetic women seemed to rule the house, and so they did in many things; but the quiet man sitting among his books was still the head of the family, the household conscience, anchor and comforter; for to him the busy, anxious women always turned in troublous times, finding him, in the truest sense of those sacred words, husband and father.

Except for Jo, each of the girls moves toward more traditional conceptions of their gender as the novel progresses. Alcott says of Meg in the years following her marriage and the birth of her first child: "Meg had spent the time in working as well as waiting, growing womanly in character, wise in housewifely arts, and prettier than ever; for love is a great beautifier." The novel implies that independence and a feisty indifference to convention are part of a girl's childhood; adulthood brings more familiar tasks.

Along with this shift away from female autonomy, the novel reaffirms a more conventional treatment of gender roles. The chapters are crowded with events, including travels to Europe and New York, but the major theme that runs through part two is courtship and marriage. Jo refuses Laurie's proposal and eventually marries an older man, a German scholar named Fritz Bhaer, whom she meets while working as a governess in New York. Amy spends time with Laurie in Europe, and eventually they decide they are suited to each other. In counterpoint to these romantic complications, Beth has a relapse, grows weaker, and dies. Jo sits with Beth for weeks, providing whatever comfort she can. Consoled by her family and by her firm religious beliefs, Beth dies peacefully.

It is the novel's most famous scene, and it exemplifies the vision of salvation that pervades the whole book. The chapter's final paragraph turns grief into a kind of pious celebration:

> When morning came, for the first time in many months the fire was out. Jo's place was empty and the room was very still. But a bird sang blithely on a budding bough, close by, the snowdrops blossomed freshly at the window, and the spring sunshine streamed in like a benediction over the placid face upon the pillow—a face so full of painless peace that those who loved it best smiled through their tears, and thanked God that Beth was well at last.

As these sentences suggest, Beth's death is given its meaning by her faith. Religion, and specifically the Christianity of New England Protestantism, is central to the entire novel. In one of her early conversations with Jo, Marmee tells her to put all her confidence in God:

> My child, [she says] the troubles and temptations of your life are beginning, and may be many; but you can overcome and outlive them all, if you learn to feel the strength and tenderness of your Heavenly Father. ... His love and care never tire or change.

The novel's preface is a quote from *Pilgrim's Progress*, John Bunyan's 17th-century allegory of a sanctified life. This remarkable book was among the most loved and read by Christians on both sides of the Atlantic for centuries. In the story, a man named Christian travels from the City of Destruction to the Celestial City—that is, from this life to the next. Along the way, Christian encounters characters who help and hinder him: Mr. Worldly Wiseman, for example, who counsels Christian to seek salvation in the law rather than Christ, versus Faithful, who urges Christian to stay on the path that leads to salvation. *Pilgrim's Progress* is quoted repeatedly in *Little Women*. Indeed, Bunyan's book is mentioned more frequently than the Bible. Clearly, Alcott intends her young readers to take it as a model of the good life, in the same way that Meg, Jo, Beth, and Amy do. Most memorably, Beth turns to Bunyan as she sinks toward death. The narrator says that she "looked among the books on her table, to find something to make her forget the mortal weariness that was almost as hard to bear as pain, as she turned the leaves of her old favorite, *Pilgrim's Progress*.

In Alcott's mind, this religious commitment is a requirement for a life of virtue. The other necessity is work. Marmee tells her daughters: "Work is wholesome, and there is plenty for every one; it keeps us from ... mischief; is good for health and spirits, and gives us a sense of power and independence better than money or fashion." Belief and work, along with the love and trust that bind the Marches together, formed the basis of Alcott's view of a productive and valuable life. In the novel's final chapters, Jo and her husband set up a school for boys—mostly poor, but including rich boys who need moral guidance. Over the next several years, she has two boys of her own. At a family reunion, the three March sisters and their mother agree that they have realized the dreams of their childhood. The concluding chapter, which bears the symbolic title "Harvest Time," ends with Marmee gathering children and grandchildren around her. Her voice full of what Alcott calls "motherly love, gratitude, and humility," she says: "Oh, my girls, however long you may live, I never can wish you greater happiness than this." As a portrait of domesticity, Alcott's *Little Women* has few equals in our literature. At the same time, the book is neither as sentimental nor as secluded from reality as its reputation sometimes suggests. The Marches work hard at their happiness, and they confront absence, illness, and death as the years go by. If the book seems out of touch with the more disabling pathologies that can also invade the home, it nonetheless stands as an enduring testament to the shared aspirations that can guide a humane family life.

Lecture Eight
The Adventures of Huckleberry Finn

Scope: By the mid-1880s, Mark Twain was among the most popular writers in the country. *The Adventures of Huckleberry Finn*, intended as a sequel to *The Adventures of Tom Sawyer*, proved to be Twain's bestselling novel. What Twain achieved in *Huckleberry Finn* were the literary possibilities of colloquial American speech. Insisting that the path to what Twain called "the soul of the people, the life of the people" could only be found in everyday language, his prose is not simply an imitation or transcript of vernacular speech, but a selective, perfected new version of it. His genius for expression reached its highest level in *Huckleberry Finn*. Twain's most important choice is to make Huck the narrator; Huck's voice, one of the principal literary achievements of the American 19th century, evokes a world that is both earthy and mythic, a world in which the nation's democratic promises stand in judgment of racial inequality. The journey that Huck and Jim, an escaped slave he befriends, take down the Mississippi is a voyage into American history.

Outline

I. Mark Twain was born in 1835 in a two-room cabin in small-town Missouri. His family moved to Hannibal when he was four years old, and it was this town perched on the border between frontier and society that would later be immortalized in his fiction.

   A. Missouri was a slave state; Twain was raised in an atmosphere accepting of slavery and segregation. Twain's own father, John Clemens, was a part-time judge who sent abolitionists to jail.

   B. As a child, Twain had a reputation for making people laugh, a characteristic that he would use later in life.

   1. He also loved to hear "tall tales" told by relatives and the family's slaves. One of those slaves, a kindly man called Uncle Dan'l, provided a major source for the character of Jim in *Huckleberry Finn*.

   2. Twain avoided school whenever possible, and he spent time around the Mississippi River, as the leader of a gang of boys who got into minor trouble.

C. At first Twain wanted to be a river pilot; he even earned his license in 1859 and spent what he called the happiest two years of his life as a pilot.

D. Twain traveled west, changing his name and establishing himself as a famed comic lecturer. He continued his travels, going on to Europe, North Africa, and the Middle East, seeing more of the world than most other early American writers.

    1. Though he wasn't the first to earn fame as a comic, Mark Twain was considered the best.

    2. Twain's popularity reached across the country and even the globe. On a tour of Asia, he reported that Mark Twain and George Washington were the only two American names the people in India recognized.

E. Twain's success as a lecturer aided his sales as a writer. His first books were nonfiction, based on his travels abroad and his time living in the Southwest.

    1. In 1876, Twain published *The Adventures of Tom Sawyer*.

    2. He immediately set to work on a sequel, but it took him eight years to finish his masterpiece, *The Adventures of Huckleberry Finn*.

II. In *Huckleberry Finn*, Twain's most important choice is to make Huck the narrator. He must reproduce more or less faithfully the speech and consciousness of an uneducated and often perplexed teenage boy while communicating the novel's serious themes.

A. Since *Tom Sawyer*, Huck's mother has died and his drunken father has vanished, so Huck lives with Miss Watson and Widow Douglas, who try to civilize him.

B. While *Huckleberry Finn* is heavy with motive and moral, the plot is almost nonexistent. The novel is a sample of picaresque, where the plot consists of a more or less unconnected series of adventures, usually dangerous.

C. Huck's first serious challenge is the reappearance of his drunken, abusive father. He escapes by faking his own death and makes his way to Jackson's Island, where he meets Jim, a runaway slave.

III. In terms of the novel's symbolic economy, Huck has found in Jim a new family to replace what he has run from. Both Huck and Jim have chosen to reinvent themselves, and a bond grows between the black man and white boy as they proceed down the river.

A. Jim frequently acts as Huck's protector and counselor, while Huck hides Jim from white men who approach their raft.

B. To avoid suspicion, they travel mainly by night and sleep during the day.

    1. One night, Huck and Jim climb aboard a wrecked steamboat called the *Walter Scott.*

    2. This selection was intentional; Scott was a bestselling novelist whose romanticization and idealization of the South had great impact.

C. As Huck and Jim float deeper into the South, Twain abandons the novel as he tries to resolve a simple question: Why would a runaway slave run south? It took him another seven years before he would finish the book.

    1. His solution to the question that stalled him was to take the power of initiative away from Huck and Jim, and to put others in control.

    2. Here Twain introduces two of the most comically sinister characters in American fiction: King of France and Duke of Bilgewater, both swindlers and thieves.

    3. The comedy turns into terror when the King and Duke sell Jim back into slavery for $40.

D. The book's moral center lies here: Huck wrestles with whether he should write a letter to return Jim to servitude or allow his humanity to best his socialization.

E. Huck and Tom Sawyer make several lame attempts to rescue Jim, though Tom's childish tricks are played at the cost of Jim's dignity as a human being, and the novel descends into farce.

IV. Huck's retreat and subservience to Tom's ridiculous schemes creates a moral confusion. Huck is the young man who has supposedly grown into ethical insight and has learned to treasure Jim's value. Huck's retreat bespeaks Twain's failure of nerve, or of clarity, and it has been a source of argument almost since *Huckleberry Finn*'s publication.

A. This is one of the reasons the book has been continuously controversial.

B. For his part, Twain knew the attacks would be good for sales, and they certainly were.

V. In subsequent decades, the book has continued to spark debate, less about its indelicacy than about its treatment of gender and especially its use of racially inflammatory language.

    A. Most readers have concluded that despite this, *Huckleberry Finn* is essentially an affirmation of human solidarity, a repudiation of suffocating conventions, and an exploration of a limited but generous heart.

    B. Above all, this is a novel that revealed to Americans the versatility, range, and unexpected precision that resides within their own language.

Suggested Reading:

Emerson, *The Authentic Mark Twain.*

Kaplan, *Mr. Clemens and Mark Twain.*

Questions to Consider:

1. *Huckleberry Finn* presents an exceptional mixture of comedy and violence, sometimes in the same episodes. Scenes of mistaken identity, slapstick, and verbal humor provide the comedy, while dead bodies, slavery, and angry mobs exemplify the violence. How does this remarkable intermingling of tones contribute to Twain's narrative and to his major themes?

2. Many critics have suggested that Jim eventually becomes a surrogate father for Huck. What are the strengths and weaknesses of that hypothesis? Can the links that undeniably bind the two characters overcome the fundamental differences of race, class, and servitude that divide them?

Lecture Eight—Transcript
The Adventures of Huckleberry Finn

"All modern American literature comes from one book by Mark Twain called *Huckleberry Finn.* ... it's the best book we've had. ... There was nothing before. There has been nothing as good since." That was Ernest Hemingway's famous opinion. It may sound a bit over the top: What about Hawthorne, Melville, and James—not to mention Hemingway's contemporaries, Fitzgerald and Faulkner? When he elevated *Huckleberry Finn* to the highest rank, Hemingway had a particular achievement in mind. In Hemingway's opinion, Mark Twain discovered—indeed he can be said to have invented—the literary possibilities of colloquial American speech. What Walt Whitman did for poetry, Twain did for fiction: He turned the language of ordinary men, women, and children into art. That achievement did much to shape the entire course of modern American literature. In 1938, in the preface to his great trilogy, *U.S.A.*, John Dos Passos said that: "Mostly, *U.S.A.* is the speech of the people." It was Mark Twain who first realized the truth of that statement. It was Twain who embraced the plurality of American experience and the countless dialects and variations through which that experience expressed itself in language. It is a deeply democratic instinct, an affirmation of the idea that all of the nation's people contribute to our culture. With some justice, Mark Twain has sometimes been called the Lincoln of our literature. Twain insisted that the path to what he called "the soul of the people, the life of the people," could only be found by listening to their speech. "There is no such thing as 'the Queen's English,'" he said. "The property has gone into the hands of a joint stock company and we own the bulk of the shares."

Twain had an uncanny ability to capture the swing and bite of ordinary talk, to reproduce its images, its vocabulary, and its rhythms, but his prose is not simply an imitation or transcript of vernacular speech. It is instead a selected, perfected new version. Sensitive to the numberless local differences in dialect, he famously said that every town and village should have its own novelist, in order that the whole mongrel panorama of American speech could be adequately preserved. As we will see, this genius for expression reached its highest level in *Huckleberry Finn.*

Twain was born in 1835 in a two-room cabin in small-town Missouri. When he was four years old, his family moved to Hannibal, where he grew up and which he would later immortalize in his fiction. It was a town straddling the border between the frontier and society. As such, Hannibal could be taken as a symbol for Twain's own intellectual and emotional identity: negotiating between the open but lawless wilderness and the civilized but constricting places of settlement. Missouri was a slave state. Twain was raised in slavery's segregated and sometimes brutal atmosphere. He later said that he never heard anyone condemn slavery. All the "good people," including the preachers, insisted that the South's "peculiar institution," as African American slavery was called, was approved by God. Twain's own father, John Clemens, was a part-time judge who earned the applause of his neighbors when he sent abolitionists to jail.

While Twain was still a child, he developed a reputation for making people laugh. He grew up hearing the tall tales told by his older relatives and by the family's slaves. One of those slaves, a kindly man called Uncle Dan'l, probably provided a major source for the character Jim in *Huckleberry Finn*. Twain avoided school as effectively as he could. He was the leader of a gang of boys who spent a lot of time on the banks and islands of the Mississippi River and continually got into trouble, mostly of a minor sort.

Here was some of the raw material that Twain would later transform into the stuff of his most famous fiction. When Twain was just 11 years old, his father died. The young boy was then apprenticed to an older brother, Orion. He discovered that he enjoyed reading and writing. By the time he was 16, Twain was publishing short items in his brother's newspaper. From Benjamin Franklin, through Mark Twain, to Ernest Hemingway and beyond, many of America's most important and most influential writers have served their apprenticeships in journalism. Not surprisingly, these are also among the writers who have placed their stamp most permanently on our literary speech.

For the next several years, Twain moved around the eastern half of the country, looking for work as a printer and reporter. He spent time in St. Louis, New York, Philadelphia, Washington, Cincinnati, New Orleans, and Keokuk, Iowa. This was an extraordinary amount of travel for someone in the first half of the 19th century, when transportation was typically primitive, slow, and dangerous. Although Twain didn't realize it at the time, he was also absorbing the diversity of America's various regions. Already a sprawling continental society, the United States had generated differences in habits, clothing, and food that defined the special character of each local place. Above all, Twain learned how Americans of all those regions and classes talked. Along with his childhood experiences in Hannibal, his journeys gave him an education in the diversity of American culture and the range of American speech.

At first, Twain wanted to be a river pilot, not a writer. Guiding a riverboat up and down the Mississippi was a job that offered good wages and considerable prestige. Twain was a funny man, but he was altogether serious about the high calling of the riverboat captain. He learned every bend and snag of the river, earned his license in 1859, and spent what he later called the two happiest years of his life as a pilot. He often referred to the master of a steamboat, only halfjokingly, as a kind of demigod. Beyond its satisfactions, the work brought him once again into contact with people from every walk of life, providing anecdotes and language patterns that he would store up for the career as a writer that still lay ahead of him. In these years, young Sam Clemens also chose the pen-name Mark Twain, the call that steamboat crews shouted to indicate 2 fathoms, or 12 feet, of water.

Twain enlarged his range of experiences further during the Civil War. After a couple of weeks' service in a raggedy unit of pro- Confederate irregulars, he traveled west with his brother, Orion, who had been made Secretary of the Nevada Territory. Here is where Twain's career began as a writer and a lecturer. Still only 30 years old, and now using the name Mark Twain exclusively, he established himself as a comic celebrity. He traveled further, this time to California and Hawaii—then to Europe, North Africa, and the Middle East. Only Herman Melville among earlier American writers would see as much of the world as Mark Twain. Within just a few years, Twain had lifted himself from near-poverty to substantial wealth. He made more money from his lectures than his publications, as he would continue to do throughout the rest of his life.

The 19th century—free for better and worse of telephones, radios, television, and Internet—was an age of non-stop talk and talkers, of orators, and preachers, and carnival barkers, and barroom philosophers, and traveling salesmen. Mark Twain was the finest talker—and the most attentive listener—in the country. Twain was not America's first successful comic lecturer. In his lifetime, the country's preferences in public speaking had changed. Prior to the Civil War, lyceum lecturers, including such distinguished intellectuals as Ralph Waldo Emerson, had instructed their audiences in moral philosophy, English poetry, and classical architecture. After the war, those edifying topics were swept away by the lowbrow entertainment provided by men such as James Whitcomb Riley, Artemus Ward, and David Ross Locke—who used the wonderful pseudonym Petroleum Vesuvius Nasby. Modern stand-up comedy can trace at least some of its origins to humorists like these. The best of these new performers, by unanimous consent, was Mark Twain. Shuffling on stage in his trademark white suit, clutching his half-smoked cigar, he mesmerized audiences with his unmatched sense of timing, and the precarious balance he maintained between worldliness and innocence.

In an essay called "How to Tell a Story," Twain said that the "humorous story is told gravely; the teller does his best to conceal the fact that he even dimly suspects ... there is anything funny about it." Following his own directions, Twain delivered his "snappers," as he called them, deadpan, and he always seemed surprised by the commotion they caused. Some of his material was political: "Suppose you were an idiot. And suppose you were a Congressman. But I repeat myself." Or this: "It is by the goodness of God that in our country we have those three unspeakably precious things: freedom of speech, freedom of conscience, and the prudence never to practice either of them. Europeans received a good deal of Twain's comic attention. He made a particular target of the French. He often said that: "Man is but little lower than the angels. ... He is between the angels and the French." He also decided that: "France has neither winter nor summer nor morals—apart from these drawbacks it is a fine country." Of a recently deceased friend he said: "I didn't attend the funeral, but I sent a nice letter saying that I approved of it." Of humanity in general, he suggested that: "Man was made at the end of the week's work—when God was tired."

Twain's popularity reached across the country and indeed the globe. On a tour of Asia, he reported that Mark Twain and George Washington were the only two American names the people in India recognized. Twain's success as a lecturer aided his sales as a writer. His first books were nonfiction: *The Innocents Abroad*, based on his travels in Europe and in North Africa, and *Roughing It*, a collection of funny episodes, which drew on his years in the Southwest. A steady stream of stories and books followed, including *The Adventures of Tom Sawyer*, which introduces the contrasting characters of Tom, a mischievous but ultimately respectable boy, and his friend Huck Finn, a more complex and disreputable figure. Eight years later, Huck moved to the center of Twain's masterpiece, *The Adventures of Huckleberry Finn*, published in 1884 and one of the bestselling novels of its generation. In fact, Twain had begun the book in 1876, almost immediately after the publication of *Tom Sawyer*, and planned it as a sequel. We will take a look at the reasons behind the long delay as we discuss the novel.

Twain's most important choice was to make Huck the narrator of his own story. He manipulates Huck's point of view brilliantly. He reproduces, more or less faithfully, the speech and consciousness of an uneducated and often perplexed teenage boy and at the same time communicates the novel's serious themes. Huck's voice, one of the principal literary achievements of the American 19th century, evokes a world that is both earthy and mythic, a world in which the nation's democratic promises stand in judgment of its racial inequality, its sentimental hypocrisy, and its indifference to the plight of the poor and the dispossessed. The journey that Huck and Jim take down the Mississippi is a voyage into American history.

The novel's first lines connect the story directly to its predecessor: "You don't know about me," says Huck, "without you have read a book by the name of *The Adventures of Tom Sawyer*, but that ain't no matter. That book was made by Mr. Mark Twain, and he told the truth, mainly." Since Huck's mother has died and his drunken father has vanished, he lives with Miss Watson and the Widow Douglas, who do what they can to civilize him. "Don't put your feet up there, Huckleberry ... don't scrunch up like that, Huckleberry ... why don't you try to behave?" It is a hopeless project. When the Widow warns Huck that he needs to reform if he wants to get to heaven, he thinks to himself: "Well, I couldn't see no advantage in going where she was going, so I made up my mind I wouldn't try for it." This is more than a comic line. As the novel proceeds, Huck will confront a crisis of conscience and will eventually have to choose between his society's heaven and hell.

In a "note" that serves as preface to the novel, Twain warned: "Persons attempting to find a motive in this narrative will be prosecuted; persons attempting to find a moral in it will be banished; persons attempting to find a plot in it will be shot." One-third of that comic threat is close to the truth: *Huckleberry Finn* is heavy with motive and moral, but the plot is almost non-existent. The novel is a sample of picaresque. In a picaresque novel— the term comes from the Spanish word *picaro*, or "rogue"—the plot consists of a more or less unconnected series of adventures, usually dangerous, sometimes comic. The shape of picaresque could be likened to a road or river, which leads by twists and turns from one perilous encounter to the next. The hero is typically less than conventionally heroic: The noble but deluded title character of *Don Quixote* is an early example. While they don't resemble the Knights of the Round Table, picaresque protagonists often possess enormous native skill and an instinct for virtue.

Huck's initial adventures are harmless. Tom Sawyer organizes a band of young highwaymen who will steal and pillage throughout the neighborhood. There is much swearing of oaths, and plotting, and flapdoodle. But it's all pretend: Tom has gotten his information from boys' books and doesn't understand half of what he reads. Twain is having a bit of fun with outlandish juvenile behavior. Huck's first serious challenge comes with the reappearance of his father. Pap Finn is filthy, sadistic, and drunk whenever he can afford it. He kidnaps Huck, locks him in a dirt-floored cabin, and periodically beats him. Huck escapes, covers his tracks by killing a pig and using the blood to fake his own death, and makes his way to Jackson's Island, midway between the Missouri and Illinois shores of the Mississippi. On the island, Huck meets Jim, who has escaped from the Widow Douglas and intends to be free. In terms of the novel's symbolic economy, Huck has found a new family to replace what he has run from. Both Huck and Jim have chosen to reinvent themselves, and for the next several chapters a bond grows between the black man and the white boy as they proceed down the river.

Jim frequently acts as Huck's protector and counselor. In one episode, he warns Huck away from a dead body because he recognizes that the dead man is Huck's father. For his part, Huck hides Jim when white men approach too close to their raft. To avoid suspicion, they travel mainly by night and sleep during the day. One stormy night, Huck and Jim climb aboard a steamboat that has been wrecked against a boulder. They discover a robbery in progress and barely manage to escape by stealing the lifeboat. The name of the steamboat is the *Walter Scott*, a deeply premeditated choice on Twain's part. As I mentioned in discussing *The Last of the Mohicans*, Scott was the author of some of the 19th century's bestselling novels—historical romances that summoned up a medieval civilization of valor and beauty. In Twain's opinion, as he put it in a lecture some years after *Huckleberry Finn*, Scott did immense harm, especially in the American South, by persuading Southerners to fall "in love with dreams and phantoms." According to Twain, it was Scott that made "every gentleman in the South a Major or a Colonel, or a General or a Judge, before the war; and it was he, also," said Twain, "that made these gentlemen value these bogus decorations."

From *Ivanhoe* to the Ku Klux Klan, Scott stands accused of nurturing the Southern obsession with the destructive fairy tales of chivalry and caste, along with a narrowly defined and violent sense of honor. These are the attitudes that compelled the male members of the Shepherdson and Grangerford families to feud with each other for 30 years over an insult that none of them can even recall. Twain takes his argument all the way up to the Confederate rebellion: "Sir Walter," he wrote, "had so large a hand in making Southern character, as it existed before the war, that he is in great measure responsible for the war." In short, the wreck of the steamboat *Walter Scott* signifies the wreck of the Southern society that had found the material for its illusions in Scott's romances.

Huck and Jim have been planning to reach Cairo, the southernmost town in Illinois. From there, Jim could travel up the Ohio River and seek freedom. They reach Cairo in the novel's 16th chapter, then drift past it in a fog and find themselves floating deeper into the South. At that point, Twain abandoned the novel for seven years. The question he could not resolve was simple: Why would a runaway slave run South? On more than one occasion over the next several years, Twain threatened to burn his manuscript in frustration. His solution, partial solution, was to remove the initiative from Huck and Jim and put others in control. Enter the preposterous King of France and the Duke of Bilgewater, two of the most comically sinister characters in American fiction. Swindlers and thieves, there is a kind of exuberance in their self-confidence and their steady commitment to whatever criminal opportunity comes their way.

In one of their first escapades, the King takes over a religious revival in the town of Pokeville, telling the crowd that he is a reformed pirate who has decided to spend the rest of his life converting other pirates to the Gospel's truths. He collects $87.75 and a jug of whiskey. Twain's exasperated comedy is directed at the good citizens of Pokeville, surrogates for Americans high and low who are easily taken in by hucksters and fakers.

Note that in episodes like this, Huck and Jim have been reduced essentially to the role of bystander. That is also the case in the chapters that follow—some of the novel's darkest pages, in which Colonel Sherburn, the chief man in a tiny Arkansas town, murders a helpless drunk named Boggs in cold blood over an insult. Twain's satiric purpose here is two-fold. Sherburn represents another specimen of the South's brutality and misplaced sense of integrity. Boggs insulted Sherburn; Boggs dies. Beyond that, Twain skewers the cowardice of the townspeople. They threaten Sherburn with vigilante justice and lynching, but they back down when he confronts them and tells them there isn't a brave man in the whole crowd. The King and Duke engineer one crackbrain scheme after another. They give a performance of Shakespeare that ends in rotten eggs and cabbages. They show up at the funeral of a man named Peter Wilks, claiming to be the long-lost relatives and heirs. The comedy congeals into terror when the King and Duke sell Jim back into slavery for $40.00 This, in turn, precipitates an internal debate in which Huck blames himself for having helped Jim escape.

In the context of his culture, Huck knows that he ought to feel shame for depriving Miss Watson of her lawful property:

> The more I studied about this, the more my conscience went to grinding me, and the more wicked and low-down and ornery I got to feeling. ... I was stealing a poor old woman's [slave] that hadn't ever done me no harm.

Here is the book's moral center. Huck's Christian duty is clear: He must write to Miss Watson and apologize for his conduct. He wrestles with his obligation; he tries to pray; he finally writes the letter that will ensure Jim's return to servitude, but then he reflects on the friendship and loyalty that he and Jim have shown each other, and how they have protected each other:

> I got to thinking over our trip down the river; and I see Jim before me, all the time, in the day, and in the night-time, sometimes moonlight, sometimes storms, and we a floating along, talking, and singing, and laughing ... somehow I couldn't seem to strike no places to harden me against him. ...

Ultimately, Huck's humanity gets the better of his training:

> It was a close place. I took [the letter] up, and held it in my hand. I was a trembling, because I'd got to decide, forever, betwixt two things, and I knowed it. I studied a minute, sort of holding my breath, and then says to myself: 'All right, then, I'll go to hell'— and tore it up.

Unfortunately, from this high point the novel declines into slapstick and moral confusion. Tom Sawyer suddenly shows up, brandishing a cockeyed scheme to rescue Jim from the farm in which he is being held. The entire enterprise is further compromised by Tom's knowledge that Miss Watson, who died two months earlier, has already set Jim free in her will. The silliness that Tom had orchestrated in the early chapters returns. Now, however, the childish tricks are played at the cost of Jim's dignity as a human being. He is made to suffer through a series of increasingly melodramatic escapades, none of which has any bearing on his freedom. For three weeks, Jim suffers one humiliation after another, and the novel descends into farce.

Tom Sawyer's behavior is inexcusable, but Tom is a marginal character in this novel. Far more importantly, it is Huck's willingness to defer to Tom that damages the novel's moral authority. Huck is the young man who has supposedly grown into ethical insight and who has learned to treasure Jim's value. Huck's retreat bespeaks Twain's failure of nerve, or of clarity, and it has been the source of argument almost since *Huckleberry Finn* was published. Even Hemingway, whose high praise I quoted at the beginning of this lecture, went on to warn readers that they shouldn't read the last third of the novel. This is just one of the reasons why the book has been continuously controversial.

The *Boston Advertiser* complained about Twain's "coarseness and bad taste." Louisa May Alcott, whose *Little Women* we discussed in an earlier lecture, said: "If Mr. Clemens cannot think of anything better to tell our pure-minded lads and lassies, he had best stop writing for them."

In 1885, the Concord Massachusetts Public Library announced that it would refuse to circulate the book to patrons because of its bad language and dubious attitudes. One of the library's directors told a reporter that *Huckleberry Finn*

> deals with a series of adventures of a very low grade of morality ... and all through its pages there is a systematic use of bad grammar and an employment of rough, coarse, inelegant expressions ... The whole book is of a class that is more profitable for the slums than it is for respectable people.

For his part, Twain knew that the attacks would be good for sales. He wrote to a friend:

> The Committee of the Public Library of Concord, Mass., have given us a rattling tip-top puff which will go into every paper in the country. They have expelled Huck from their library as 'trash & suitable only for the slums.' That will sell 25,000 copies for us sure.

The prediction was an underestimate. *Huckleberry Finn* proved to be Twain's bestselling novel. In part, the large sales followed from Twain's established reputation as a humorist. By the mid-1880s, he was among the most popular writers in the country, but the controversy about the novel's alleged indecency undoubtedly contributed to the book's success.

Over the subsequent decades, the book has continued to spark debate—less about its indelicacy than about its treatment of gender, and especially its use of racially inflammatory language. Most readers have concluded that *Huckleberry Finn* does indeed exhibit some of the blinkered beliefs of its time. Nonetheless, the novel deserves its high place because of its affirmation of human solidarity, its repudiation of suffocating conventions, and its exploration of a limited but generous human heart. The novel also tests the boundary between high art and popular culture. Above all, to return to my opening remarks, this is the novel that helped Americans understand the versatility, range, and unexpected precision that presided within their own language. In one way or another, all of American writing has been changed by the example of *Huckleberry Finn*.

Lecture Nine
The Virginian

Scope: The Western genre has proved to be one of the most important American cultural creations of the 20th century. When Owen Wister published *The Virginian* in 1902, he invented the Western novel at the very moment that the world he described had disappeared. This was the novel that established almost all of the conventions that would define the Western novel for the generations. It also captured a particular tone: The Virginian, the title character, remains in complete control, commanding quiet strength. *The Virginian* was based on a romanticized conception of men Wister had actually met in Wyoming and other Western territories, and the novel develops two main plot lines. The first follows the Virginian through a series of perilous adventures culminating in a final gunfight, and the second is the romance with an Eastern schoolteacher called Molly. The novel's narrator is a soft young man from the East, a tenderfoot, never named (like the Virginian), who will become the student to the Western master.

Outline

I.   A decade before *The Virginian* was published, the U.S. census of 1890 famously declared that the frontier had closed. The march of settlement had reached the Pacific, and the peopling of the continent was proceeding at an unstoppable rate.

   A. In 1893, the American Historical Association held its annual meeting in Chicago. The historians had gathered at the World's Columbian Exposition, a huge world fair organized to celebrate the 400th anniversary of Columbus's first landing.

   1. Frederick Jackson Turner, a young historian at the University of Wisconsin, delivered a lecture called "The Significance of the Frontier in American History." This 40-page essay would have a profound and permanent influence on how American scholars and citizens view history.

   2. In Turner's view, the disappearance of the continuous frontier "mark[ed] the closing of a great historic movement."

B. The turn of the 20th century saw a profound transformation in American life.

    1. Cities were growing at an unprecedented rate.

    2. The populations of those cities were increasingly made of immigrants and their children.

    3. Cities of a million or more inhabitants created concentrations of people, and such crowding was another stimulus to the lure of the open skies and wide spaces of the Old West.

C. In the second chapter of *The Virginian*, the narrator contrasts the beauties of unspoiled nature with the contamination of human occupation.

    1. The imagery Wister evokes is religious: The grandeur of the West embodies God's own handiwork; the mountains, sky, and plains are religious symbols.

    2. In the novel, the people of these open spaces are also superior beings.

D. The places and the people Wister celebrates are disappearing. Already by 1900, the most visible remnant of the cowboy's life was the Wild West shows that toured the country.

II. *The Virginian: A Horseman of the Plains*, the novel's full title, is Wister's elegy to America's heroic past.

A. Wister had not grown up anywhere near the Old West.

    1. Wister was the son of affluent Philadelphia parents: His father was a successful physician, and his mother was a poet.

    2. Educated in private schools and at Harvard, Wister intended to practice law. However, he traveled repeatedly to Wyoming, finding the setting and its people irresistible.

B. The novel's narrator is from the East, a young man who represents the sort of soft and feminized men bred in the nation's new urban civilizations.

    1. The narrator has come west to visit an old friend, the owner of a large ranch called Sunk Creek.

    2. The Virginian meets the narrator at the train station to guide him to the ranch, and the description of the Virginian is the narrator's enraptured admiration.

C. The Virginian's remarkable qualities and mastery as a horseman are apparent. He is a man of uncommon ability and courage, with an instinctive sense of justice and the skill to master almost any dangerous situation.

D. The novel has two central figures: the cowboy-teacher, who has the knowledge and skills that define the Old West at its best, and the narrator-student, who grows out of his Eastern flabbiness into an appreciation of the Virginian's exceptional merits.

III. The novel follows two main plot lines.

    A. In the adventure plot line, the Virginian alternately prevails with his wits and good humor or with violence.

        1. From the card game with a nasty cowboy named Trampas in the first chapter, Wister makes it clear that the antagonizing relationship between Trampas and the Virginian must eventually end with a duel.

        2. Acting as a surrogate for the reader, the narrator reacts with shock and terror when the Virginian sentences two men to hang for stealing cattle.

    B. This conjunction of self-governance and the courage of individual characters lies at the core of the novel's ethical framework.

    C. Between the hanging scene and the climactic scene with Trampas, Wister develops the second major plot line, a romance between the Virginian and a young schoolteacher from Vermont.

        1. Mary Stark Wood, or Molly, is a feisty, independent woman who has left New England after refusing to marry a man simply for his name and money.

        2. Their courtship involves a reciprocal exchange of ideas and values: He teaches her how to ride and read the Western sky; she gives him books that he diligently reads.

    D. Despite Molly's attempts to persuade the Virginian to avoid confrontation with Trampas, the outcome is a foregone conclusion.

        1. Within hours of the duel, Molly and the Virginia are married.

        2. This union symbolizes the honorable civilization of the East joining together with the self-reliance and strength of the West. Here, the sharp divide that has separated the nation's two halves is moderated, and perhaps even dissolved.

IV. *The Virginian* has had a remarkable afterlife.

    A. It established all the conventions that would later define the Western novel. Wister brought together the open spaces and endless sky, the strong yet soft-spoken hero, the tenderfoot companion, the Eastern schoolteacher love interest, and the final gunfight.

    B. The Western's cultural reach has been even greater in movies than in print. The first Western film was produced just one year after Wister's novel, and *The Virginian* has been filmed at least five times.

        1. Some of the nation's most iconic films have been Westerns: *Stagecoach* (1939), *My Darling Clementine* (1946), and *Fort Apache* (1948).

        2. The stars of Western films—actors such as John Wayne and Gary Cooper—established themselves as Hollywood's preeminent male attractions.

    C. In recent decades, the flaws of Wister's novel have attracted a great deal of critical attention. As a document in cultural history, however, the novel remains indispensable.

Suggested Reading:

Payne, *Owen Wister.*

Questions to Consider:

1. Wister's novel established the popularity of the Western as a distinctive American literary genre. At the same time, *The Virginian* shares certain characteristics of plot and character with other sorts of fiction, including the detective story. What are some of those similarities? Do these resemblances suggest more general insights into American culture?

2. *The Virginian* is considerably more romantic than its reputation as a portrait of a Western strong man would predict. Much of the novel is taken up with the courtship between the main character and his eventual wife, Molly Wood. What is the role of gender in this novel, and how does it shape the book's conception of masculinity?

Lecture Nine—Transcript
The Virginian

As we saw in the last lecture, *Huckleberry Finn* examines the contrast between settled life and the freedom of life on the move. At the end of that novel, Huck tells the reader that he is going to light out for the territory; he has seen more than enough of civilization and its constraints. Less than two decades later, Owen Wister explored a variation on that theme in the novel, *The Virginian*. In one of the book's early scenes—it was once among the most familiar episodes in American literature—we find ourselves watching a poker game in a saloon. One of the players, a nasty-looking cowboy named Trampas, frowns at the Virginian and sneers: "Your bet, you son-of-a—. In response, the narrator tells us:

> The Virginian's pistol came out, and his hand lay on the table, holding it unaimed. With a voice as gentle as ever, the voice that sounded almost like a caress, but drawling very little more than usual, so that there was almost a space between each word, he issued his orders to the man Trampas: 'When you call me that, smile!' He looked at Trampas across the table. Yes, the voice was gentle. But in my ears it seemed as if somewhere the bell of death was ringing; and silence, like a stroke, fell on the large room.

"When you call me that, smile." The line would become famous, a signature of manly strength on the frontier, where there was no law but the gun and insults often led to homicide. It also captured a particular tone: The Virginian remains in complete control, speaking in a gentle voice that nevertheless echoes like the bell of death. Here is the progenitor of Hollywood's classic Western heroes, men whose bravery is never loud-mouthed or angry. Like the Virginian, they command with quiet strength. *The Virginian*, which was the bestselling novel of 1902, invented the genre of Western fiction at the very moment that the world it described had disappeared. A decade earlier, the U.S. census of 1890 had famously declared that the frontier had closed. America still contained vast empty spaces, as it still does, but the march of settlement had reached the Pacific. The peopling of the continent was proceeding at an unstoppable rate. By a grisly coincidence, the year 1890 also saw the last major battle between the U.S. Army and Native Americans. The massacre at Wounded Knee, South Dakota, took place on December 29. Five hundred troops killed upwards of 150 members of the Lakota Sioux, most of them in cold blood.

In 1893, just three years later, the American Historical Association held its annual meeting in Chicago. The historians had gathered at the World's Columbian Exposition, a huge international affair organized to celebrate the 400th anniversary of Columbus's first landing in the Americas. Frederick Jackson Turner, a young historian at the University of Wisconsin, delivered a lecture called "The Significance of the Frontier in American History." This 40-page essay would have a profound and durable influence on the way in which American scholars and citizens understood their history. Turner proposed that American development is explained by what he called the "existence of an area of free land, its continuous recession, and the advance of American settlement westward." The disappearance of that continuous frontier, in Turner's view, "mark[ed] the closing of a great historic movement." The Turner Thesis, as it was usually called, has been challenged repeatedly over the past 100 years. Nonetheless, it expressed in vivid language a widely held view of the trajectory of American experience.

The great historian Henry Adams said that "history broke in halves" in 1900. If he exaggerated, it was not by much. The years around the turn of the 20th century saw a profound transformation in almost every corner of American life. As Turner predicted, the first major changes were demographic. Cities were growing at an unprecedented rate. From its founding and through the 19th century, the United States was an agrarian society. By 1920, another census report would declare that more than half of all Americans now lived in cities. In addition, the population of those cities was increasingly made up of immigrants and the children of immigrants. Beginning in 1880 and continuing through the early years of the First World War, unprecedented numbers of newcomers arrived in America.

To give just a single example, upwards of 1.25 million immigrants came to this country in 1907, when the country's entire population was about 75 million. Cities of a million or more inhabitants created concentrations of people that had never been seen before in the United States. In 1900, it was estimated that the Lower East Side of New York had a greater density of men, women, and children than Calcutta or Bombay. Such crowding was another stimulus to the lure of the Old West, with its open skies and wide spaces.

In the second chapter of *The Virginian*, the narrator contrasts the beauties of unspoiled nature with the contamination of human settlement. He declares that the West is enveloped in what he calls "a pure and quiet light, such as the East never sees; [it could be] the air of creation's first morning." Imitating the worst of civilized society, the crude shacks of a town like Medicine Bow, Wyoming, the narrator tells us:

stood, rearing their pitiful masquerade amid a fringe of old tin cans, while at their very doors began a world of crystal light, a land without end, a space across which Noah and Adam might come straight from Genesis.

The language here is worth pausing over for a moment: creation's first morning, a space that might have been home to Noah and Adam. Wister is making mythic claims for the American landscape. The grandeur of the West embodies God's own handiwork; the mountain, skies, and plains are religious symbols. Like Emerson in the previous century, but even more energetically, Wister identifies the world of nature with the world of divinity. This reverence for the land had by 1900 become a common response, and indeed as we have seen can be traced back to the novels of Cooper and the paintings of Thomas Cole. The people of these open spaces are also superior beings. With only a few exceptions—the villainous Trampas is one—the narrator tells us that

> there was scarce a face among them that had not in it something very likable. ... Daring, laughter, endurance—these were what I saw upon the countenances of the cowboys. ... In their spirit sat hidden a true nobility, and often beneath its unexpected shining their figures took on heroic stature.

These are the sorts of men who were given enduring visual expression in the paintings and sculptures of Wister's friend, Frederick Remington. (Remington also provided illustrations for later editions of this novel.) All this, the places and the people, is slipping away even as Wister celebrates it. He included a short introduction to the novel, which makes this point emphatically. He writes that his subject, specifically the Wyoming Territory between 1874 and 1890, "is a vanished world," and the horseman has vanished as well. He was, says Wister, "the last romantic figure upon our soil. He will never come again. He rides in his historic yesterday." With his disappearance, something of the poetry and indeed the magic has gone out of American life.

Already by 1900, the most visible remnant of the cowboy's life was the Wild West shows that toured the country. Setting up shop in cities and small towns, shows like Buffalo Bill's Wild West and Congress of Rough Riders entertained audiences with parades of horses, imitation Indian attacks, and shooting contests—Annie Oakley was a favorite in this department.

The Wild West Show was one of the most popular attractions at the Columbian Exposition. While Professor Turner gave a theoretical commentary on the closing of the frontier, Buffalo Bill acted out the consequences just a few blocks away. Owen Wister despised these traveling circuses. *The Virginian: A Horseman of the Plains*, to give the book its full title, is his elegy to America's heroic past. Wister had not grown up anywhere near the Old West. On the contrary, he was the son of affluent Philadelphia parents. His father was a successful physician. His mother, a poet, was the daughter of the great Shakespearean actress Fanny Kemble and Pierce Butler, a wealthy Southern planter. Wister was educated in private schools and at Harvard, from which he graduated in 1882 with highest honors. After studying music in Europe, Wister returned to the United States with the intention of practicing law. However, he traveled repeatedly to Wyoming, first to recover from an illness, but then because he found the setting and its people irresistible.

As the narrator of *The Virginian* puts it, in a high-falutin' passage: "No lotus land ever cast its spell upon man's heart more than Wyoming had enchanted mine." Wister started writing stories about the West in the 1890s, which he published in *Harper's* and other good magazines. They earned a considerable reputation. *The Virginian* was Wister's greatest success. The novel's narrator, is a young man from the East, a tenderfoot, never named, who represents the sort of soft and feminized men who were bred in the nation's new urban civilization. He makes a symbolically appropriate entrance in the novel's first chapter, arriving by train from what the narrator calls "the far shores of civilization" and discovering that his luggage has been lost. The train represents the intrusion of technology and commerce into the natural landscape. The lost luggage signifies the narrator's initiation into the harsh, demanding world of Wyoming: Stripped of his civilized furnishings, he is forced to start over.

The narrator has come west at the invitation of an old friend, the owner of a large ranch called Sunk Creek. The Virginian, also never named, has come to meet the narrator at the Medicine Bow station to guide him to the ranch. Looking down into a corral from his coach window, the narrator has his first glimpse of the cowboy before he even gets off the train. He sees a muscular and handsome man who tames a colt that the other men around him cannot even rope.

When he gets a closer look at the cowboy, the narrator's admiring response is—there is no other word for it—gushing:

> Lounging there at ease against the wall was a slim young giant, more beautiful than pictures. His broad, soft hat was pushed back;

a loose-knotted, dull-scarlet handkerchief sagged from his throat; and one casual thumb was hooked in the cartridge belt that slanted across his hips. He had plainly come many miles from somewhere across the vast horizon, as the dust upon him showed.

His boots were white with it. His overalls were gray with it. The weather-beaten bloom of his face shown through it duskily, as the ripe peaches look upon their trees in a dry season. But no dinginess of travel or shabbiness of attire could tarnish the splendor that radiated from his youth and strength.

There is more than a little hero worship in lines like these, as well as a personal attraction that is barely concealed.

Watching the tall Virginian tease an older man who is about to marry, the narrator tells us: "Had I been the bride, I should have taken the giant [Virginian], dust and all." The horse-roping episode and the Virginian's mastery of Trampas in the card-playing scene immediately establish his remarkable qualities. He is a man of uncommon ability and courage, with an instinctive sense of justice. He has the skills to master almost any dangerous situation. He is, as a bystander who watches him rope the pony says, a man who "knows his business."

As the novel unfolds, we learn that the Virginian's business reaches beyond the stereotypical tasks of the cowboy. He can do those things superlatively well, but he is also master of the social skills needed to lead other men and women. He is usually quiet, but when he speaks he is eloquent. He can entertain, persuade, and even seduce when the need arises. The Virginian's relationship with the narrator is an important element of the book. As they travel together, the narrator becomes the Virginian's student, learning the skills that a man needs to survive on the frontier: how to ride a horse, shoot a gun, travel light, and even how to tell the tall tales that cowboys use to get through long nights. Despite its title, in other words, the novel really has two central characters: the cowboy-teacher who has the knowledge and skills that define the Old West, and the narrator-student, who grows out of his Eastern flabbiness into an appreciation of the Virginian's exceptional merits.

When he was asked why the Virginian remained unnamed, Owen Wister explained: "It was by design [that] he continued nameless, because I desired to draw a sort of heroic circle about him … and thus if possible create an illusion of remoteness." *The Virginian* was based on a romanticized conception of men Wister had actually met in Wyoming and other Western territories. He also has literary antecedents, the most important of whom is Hawkeye, the main character in James Fenimore Cooper's Leatherstocking Tales, such as *The Last of the Mohicans*, which we discussed in an earlier lecture.

The Virginian includes two main plot lines. The first follows the cowboy hero through a series of perilous adventures. He is given the job of managing the delivery of a trainload of cattle to Chicago and then returning to Sunk Creek Ranch with all his men. In these chapters, the Virginian is constantly tested. His men, provoked by Trampas, are always on the edge of mutiny or desertion. In this case, the Virginian prevails with his wits and good humor, talking the men around without resorting to violence. In a genuinely funny sequence, the Virginian regains the allegiance of his men by telling a better tall tale than Trampas. Reaching back into the traditions of Western humor, the Virginian spins a yarn about the huge money that has recently been made in frog farming. He assures his wide-eyed listeners that bidding wars between leading New York restaurants has made millionaires of frog farmers. He also tells of the frog wars that have broken out as the passion for frogs has spread across the nation. When Trampas falls for the joke, the other cowboys declare that the Virginian has won this verbal duel. "Rise up, liars, and salute your king," yells one of them.

However, the rhetorical contest is a foreshadowing of the more lethal actions that lie ahead. From the card game in the first chapter, Wister makes it clear that Trampas and the Virginian must sooner or later end their duel with violence. That encounter comes in two extended episodes in the second half of the book. In the first, which is based on historical events, the Virginian sets out to capture rustlers who have been stealing and re-branding cattle belonging to the Sunk Creek Ranch. Two of the outlaws are caught. Sadly, one of them is a friend of the Virginian's named Steve, a man who had always seemed reliable and honest, but Steve has fallen under the influence of Trampas. Despite his affection for Steve, the Virginian— serving as prosecutor, jury, and judge—decides that both men must hang. Acting as a surrogate for the reader, the narrator reacts with shock and terror. The prospect of the hanging frightens him. He confesses:

> Dead men I have seen not a few times, even some lying pale and terrible after violent ends, and the edge of this wears off; but I hope I shall never again have to be in the company with men waiting to be killed. By this time to-morrow the gray flannel shirt would be buttoned round a corpse.

When the hanging actually occurs, the narrator clutches a blanket over his head, saving himself and us from the sight.

Beyond the killing itself, the narrator is instinctively revolted by the idea of vigilante justice. Here, too, he expresses the objections that most readers feel. Wister makes it clear that the Virginian suffers enormous emotional anguish from the execution, but he also insists that the sentence had to be carried out. The Virginian is not acting out of anger or the desire for personal vengeance. On the contrary, at least in his own mind, he is enforcing justice in a place where violence and anarchy are the norm. Judge Henry, a well-educated man and a pillar of the community, defends the Virginian's act when he says:

> In Wyoming the law has been letting our cattle-thieves go for two years. We are in a very bad way, and we are trying to make that way a little better until civilization can reach us. ... Call this primitive, if you will. But so far from being a defiance of the law, it is an assertion of it—the fundamental assertion of self-governing men, upon whom our whole social fabric is based.

This conjunction of self-governance and the courage of individual characters lies at the core of the novel's ethical framework. Wister dedicated the book to President Theodore Roosevelt, a friend from Harvard and one of the novelist's heroes. Roosevelt, in his turn, read the book within a few days and sent a complimentary note. It's not surprising that Roosevelt, the Rough Rider president, found the book's message appealing. Like Wister, Roosevelt was an Eastern patrician who cherished both the beauty and the immensity of the West. He shared Wister's view that the urban society of the East was a less manly, less independent environment.

Recall that Roosevelt was the author of a book called *The Strenuous Life*, published in 1900, just a couple of years before *The Virginian*.

> I wish to preach [said Roosevelt in that book], the doctrine of the strenuous life, the life of toil and effort, of labor and strife; to preach that highest form of success which comes, not to the man who desires mere easy peace, but to the man who does not shrink from danger, from hardship, or from bitter toil, and who out of these wins the splendid ultimate triumph.

Wister's *Virginian* stands for all those men who choose duty over convenience, and danger over peace. Hanging his friend for cattle theft represents just such a duty—necessary, if sad. Between the hanging and the climactic scene with Trampas, Wister develops the novel's second major plot line, the romance between the Virginian and a young woman who has come to Wyoming from Vermont as a schoolteacher. Mary Stark Wood of Bennington, always called Molly, is descended from a long line of distinguished citizens. She is a stubborn, independent woman who has left New England because she refuses to marry a man simply for his name and his money. She also has what the narrator approvingly calls "a craving for the unknown."

She is introduced to the Virginian when he rescues her from an overturned stagecoach. The courtship that follows involves a reciprocal exchange of ideas and values. He teaches her how to ride and read the signs in the sky that forecast weather. She gives him books that he diligently reads: Walter Scott's historical novels and George Eliot's *The Mill on the Floss*. The Virginian studies Shakespeare so attentively that he can quote passages from memory. The two plots, call them the adventure plot and the romance plot, converge late in the novel. The Virginian is gravely wounded by Indians—almost the only appearance of Native Americans in the book, by the way. By a nice coincidence, Molly rides by shortly afterward and is able to carry him to her cabin. As she nurses him back to health, the last of her resistance fades. The two make plans to marry. Fearful for his safety, and also repelled by frontier violence, Molly tries to persuade the Virginian not to confront Trampas, but Trampas has challenged the Virginian's honor by spreading lies about his honesty and courage. In the moral calculus of the frontier, an insult to a man's honor has to be avenged in blood. Even the local bishop consents to the duel.

As the narrator tells us, employing a vocabulary of deliberately archaic machismo: "It had come to that point where there was no way out, save only the ancient, eternal way between man and man. It is only the great mediocrity that goes to law in these personal matters." The outcome is a foregone conclusion. Despite her deepseated resistance to the male code of violence, Molly's passion overcomes her abstract principles. Within hours of the duel in which the Virginian kills Trampas, she and the cowboy are married. The union has obvious symbolic implications, both for gender and for national culture. When Molly chooses the Virginian, despite her reservations about his values, the narrator says: "At the last white-hot edge of ordeal, it was she who renounced, and he who had his way."

In short, this is on its face a novel about male dominance and female submission. At the same time, gender relations may be a bit more complicated than the book's reputation might suggest. Professor Melody

Graulich, in a wonderfully provocative essay titled "What If Wister Were a Woman?" discovers a more complex statement of the roles of men and women. Molly is presented from her first appearance in the novel as a woman of strong views, and it is clear that she will continue to voice them as the Virginian's wife. Beyond that, the structure of the novel's conclusion also complicates its themes. In the marriage of the Virginian and Molly, the civilization of the East, in its most articulate and honorable form, is joined to the self-reliance and strength of the West. The sharp divide that has separated the nation's two halves is moderated and perhaps even dissolved.

That outcome may explain why Henry James, whose literary tastes were quite different from those of Theodore Roosevelt, also praised the novel. What he most admired, James wrote Wister, was the way in which the Virginian developed. This was, he said:

> so clearly and finely felt by you, I think, & so firmly carried out ... to the last intimacy of the man's character, the personal & moral complexion & evolution, in short of your hero. ... You have made him live with a high, but lucid complexity.

The Virginian has had a remarkable afterlife. There had been tales of the Wild West before Wister's—dime novels of adventure and derring-do—but this was the book that consolidated almost all the conventions that would define the Western novel for generations. Wister brought together the open spaces and endless sky; the strong, soft-spoken hero; the tenderfoot companion; the Eastern schoolteacher who provides a love interest; and the final gunfight. The Western genre proved to be one of the most important American cultural creations of the 20th century. The Western's reach has been even greater in movies than in print. The first narrative film made in the United States was, you may recall, Edwin S. Porter's *The Great Train Robbery*, a Western produced just one year after Wister's novel. *The Virginian* itself has been filmed at least five times, and some of the nation's iconic films have been Westerns: *Stagecoach, Destry Rides Again, The Ox-Bow Incident, My Darling Clementine*, and *Fort Apache*, to name only a few. The stars of those Western films—actors such as John Wayne, Gary Cooper, and James Stewart, among others—established themselves as Hollywood's preeminent male attractions. In part, those movies were simply tapping into the American fondness for adventure stories, often laced with violence, but they were also a tribute to a myth—a myth of individual integrity, barely surviving in a world of compromise.

In a classic essay, the film critic Robert Warshow made large claims for the Western hero:

> He fights not for advantage ... but to state what he is, and he must live in a world that permits that statement. The Westerner is the last gentleman, and the movies which over and over tell his story are probably the last art form in which the concept of honor retains its strength.

The Virginian stands at the head of that tradition. In recent decades, the flaws of Wister's novel have attracted a great deal of critical attention. The book's problematic embrace of white supremacy and manifest destiny, and its romantic views of self-justifying violence, have quite properly alienated many readers. As a document in cultural history, on the other hand, the novel remains indispensable. Looking back at the 19th-century Western past, Owen Wister did much to invent the 20th-century American imagination.

Lecture Ten
The House of Mirth

Scope: Edith Wharton's second novel, *The House of Mirth*, was published in 1905. Unlike her first, however, *The House of Mirth* was an immediate bestseller, and it established Wharton's reputation as an astute and often funny critic of the American moneyed class. The book centers on Lily Bart, a beautiful, unmarried woman who has enjoyed a prosperous childhood, only to be reduced to shabby gentility after her father goes bankrupt and dies. The novel's plot traces an arc that leads slowly but inevitably downward. Banished from the highest levels of society, Lily is pushed down the social ladder until her eventual decline into poverty, underpaid labor, and death. Wharton uses Lily's fate as a vehicle for satirizing the society in which she lives and dies. In doing so, Wharton explores the meaning of success, the demands of gender, and the limits of human freedom. The novel's success helped to boost Wharton's own independence: It sold 140,000 copies in the first year alone, making it one of the bestselling novels of the beginning of the 20th century.

Outline

I. Wharton, born Edith Newbold Jones, grew up in a world of privilege, money, and leisure. She was the youngest child of affluent parents with a well-established lineage, George Frederic Jones and Lucretia Rhinelander.

   A. The family lived in the fashionable upper reaches of old New York; the world in which young Edith resided was dominated by "the 400," allegedly the number of people who could fit into Mrs. William Astor's ballroom.

   B. Wharton's material advantages coexisted with years of insurmountable frustration. She always felt an insatiable appetite for reading and ideas, and she wanted to write. Her mother demanded, however, that her daughter keep within the respectable conventions of society. She was to debut at the earliest possible age and then marry someone of her class.

      1. Wharton's mother orchestrated her daughter's marriage in 1885 to Edward Wharton, a man with no intellectual or cultural interests to attract his new wife. The marriage, though a failure, persisted for almost three decades.

      2. Divorce incurred terrible social consequences, and Wharton knew from personal experience the price that resistance to old order would entail. This would become the subject of much of her strongest fiction, beginning with *The House of Mirth*.

II. The novel follows the life of Lily Bart, a beautiful, unmarried woman on the verge of 30 years old—a perilous age in the marriage market. After her father bankrupts the family and dies, Lily must use her beauty and wits to find a rich mate.

    A. A sequence of eligible and wealthy men come close to proposing, though in each case Lily does or says something unconventional or daring and finds herself deserted.

    B. Banished from the highest levels of society, and unfit for the sorts of work that women could find in the early 20th century, Lily is reduced to service as the companion of rich women.

      1. Treated as property by herself and others, Lily is undeniably complicit in her own undoing.

      2. She is held captive to the values she despises, unable to find or even to imagine an alternative for herself.

    C. The novel's title is taken from the biblical book of Ecclesiastes, which captures much of its thematic intention: "The heart of the fool is in the house of mirth." Wharton provides a relentless satire on the cruelly vacuous world of high New York society.

III. In 1899, Thorstein Veblen published *The Theory of the Leisure Class*, an influential analysis of American behavior and attitudes. He coined the phrase "conspicuous consumption," which, as Veblen explains it, involves the purchase and display of material possessions on a scale far beyond life's necessities.

    A. In Wharton's upper-class world, a rich man's most conspicuous ornament is his wife.

    B. One of the principal themes of Wharton's novel is to satirize the distorted values of the wealthy.

C. Many of the funniest episodes in the book provide case studies in the confusion between integrity and possessions that marks the upper-class inhabitants of the "house of mirth." For example, to Lily's prim Aunt Peniston, "the mere idea of immorality was as offensive … as a smell of cooking in the drawing room."

IV. Underlining its emphasis on pretence and performance, *The House of Mirth* is a notably theatrical novel. The grand houses are stage settings on which men and especially women present themselves as beautiful objects.

A. This motif reaches a visual and thematic climax in the tableaux vivants episode: an entertainment at the conclusion of a huge party in which the novel's various women dress in imitation of old master paintings.

B. The highlight of the evening is Lily Bart's appearance in the guise of *Mrs. Lloyd*, a famous full-length portrait by Joshua Reynolds. While the crowd is dazzled, the narrator implies that this event capsulizes Lily's entire career: reduced to an object of visual gratification.

V. One of the spectators at the tableaux vivants is Lily's most constant male companion throughout the novel, a bachelor lawyer named Lawrence Selden.

A. Selden has strong negative opinions about the wealthy men and women in Lily's circle, but he lacks the ambition and courage to act on his disapproval.

B. He scolds Lily for her interest in material pleasure, ignoring the fact of her poverty and his middle-class comfort.

    1. In particular, he lectures her on what he calls "the republic of the spirit."

    2. This idealized and naive conception of freedom has no relevance to a single woman without financial support.

VI. Lily's fate is narrated in the vocabulary of Darwinian evolution. She is frequently described in terms that connect her to her circumstances through a kind of adaptation.

A. Lily's dilemma is a comment on the limits of freedom, and especially on the constraints that a single, financially dependent woman faced at the turn of the 20th century.

B. While *The House of Mirth* is not an overtly political novel, the career of its heroine dramatizes some of the economic and social discrimination against which women were protesting in those years.

C. As she sinks more deeply into poverty, Lily finds that she needs sleeping pills to get any rest. One night—accidentally or deliberately, the novel does not make clear—she takes an overdose and dies.

Suggested Reading:

Lee, *Edith Wharton.*

Lewis, *Edith Wharton.*

Questions to Consider:

1. How much freedom of choice does Lily Bart have? To what extent is she a victim of circumstance, and to what extent the author of her own tragedy? More generally, what does the novel have to say about gender, about the role and identity of women in the society of New York at the turn of the 20th century?

2. Gerty Farish and Nettie Struther stand outside the society that dominates *The House of Mirth*. What is the narrator's attitude toward these women? What contribution do they make to the novel's inquiry into manners and morals?

Lecture Ten—Transcript
The House of Mirth

Just a few years after Owen Wister, in *The Virginian,* offered his romantic view of American life on the unpeopled frontier, Edith Wharton brought her larger talents to bear on the manners and morals of life in the crowded city. Aside from a shared friendship with Theodore Roosevelt, Wharton and Wister had little in common. At the same time, both created influential images that mapped something of the range of American experience. In particular, they explored the tension between social constraint and individual freedom. This was a perennial theme that had taken on a new urgency as the frontier closed and cities grew by leaps and bounds.

Wharton served a long literary apprenticeship. Born in 1862, she was 40 years old when she published her first novel, *The Valley of Decision.* Set in 18th-century Italy, the book is a historical romance. The novel is filled with gorgeous trappings, handsome furniture, grand buildings, and a sun-drenched landscape. In fact, the furniture and buildings are far more convincing than the plot. That authenticity can be traced to Wharton's lifelong fascination with architecture and interior design. Her nonfiction writing included her first book, *The Decoration of Houses.* Another of her books, *Italian Villas and Their Gardens,* includes brilliant illustrations by the painter Maxfield Parrish.

The Valley of Decision was a false start. Henry James wrote Wharton a letter combining admiration with skepticism. On the one hand, he saluted her obvious talent. On the other, he advised her to leave the European past behind and take up the New York society that had surrounded her from childhood. He argued in favor of what he called "the American Subject." In a wonderful Jamesian outburst, he admonished her: "Don't pass it by—the immediate, the real, the ours, the yours, the novelist's that it waits for. Take hold of it … keep hold, and let it pull you where it will. … *Do New York!*" Wharton might have chosen New York with or without James's splendid advice. In any case, three years after *The Valley of Decision,* she published her second novel, *The House of Mirth,* which has endured as one of New York's great stories.

The book was an immediate bestseller, and it established Wharton's reputation as an astute and often funny critic of America's moneyed classes. Looking back on her novel years later, Wharton recalled how close she had been to her material. "There it was before me," she said of New York's upper crust of wealth and prestige, "in all its flatness and futility, asking to be dealt with as the theme most available to my hand, since I had been steeped in it from infancy."

Wharton, born Edith Newbold Jones, had indeed grown up in a world comfortably upholstered with money and leisure. She was the youngest child of affluent parents, George Frederic Jones and Lucretia Rhinelander, who combined a solid investment income with the confidence of a well-established lineage they could both trace back before the Revolution. These were the actual Joneses, it has sometimes been said, up with whom all of us try to keep. Throughout her childhood, Edith lived in the fashionable upper reaches of Old New York. The family spent winters in Paris, summers in Newport, and the months that were called "the season" in Manhattan. The world in which young Edith resided was dominated by "the four hundred," allegedly the number of people who could fit into the ballroom of Mrs. William Astor's mansion, which dominated the corner of Fifth Avenue and Thirty-Fourth Street. In their own view, at least, these were the only people who mattered. The four hundred are long gone, but the phrase survives as a shorthand marker for social prestige.

Wharton's material advantages coexisted with years of insurmountable frustration. From her earliest childhood, she felt an insatiable appetite for reading and for ideas, and she wanted to write. Her mother, on the contrary, insisted that her daughter prepare herself for what was expected of her: a debut at the earliest possible age, followed by a suitable marriage to someone of her own class.

As part of her maternal campaign, Mrs. Jones quite ruthlessly opposed her daughter's literary aspirations. In a book called *A Backward Glance*, the memoir she published when she was past 70, Wharton could still feel the sting of her mother's disapproval. In a famous anecdote, she recalls her first effort at writing a novel. The opening sentence sets the scene: "'Oh, how do you do, Mrs. Brown?' said Mrs. Tompkins, 'If only I had known you were going to call I should have tidied up the drawing-room.'" The 11-year-old Edith showed the manuscript to her mother, who responded with crushing irrelevance: "Drawing rooms are always tidy." It is a small but significant episode, which Wharton repeated to friends for decades. She saw it as an emblem of an entire worldview. Her family and friends treated her with puzzled contempt when she talked about novels or ideas, a proof in her eyes of the anti-intellectualism that governed the upper classes. She regarded New York's high society as a cultural desert. She always enjoyed the comforts of affluence and was never slow to admit it, but she refused to pay the price that social conformity seemed to entail, especially for women.

Wharton's mother rejected Edith's desire to marry a young man whom she actually loved and more or less orchestrated her daughter's marriage in 1885 to Edward Wharton, a slow-witted man with no intellectual or cultural interest whatsoever. "Teddy," as he was called, devoted himself exclusively to horses, dogs, hunting, alcohol, and other women. The marriage, which was evidently a failure from the first night, persisted painfully for almost three decades. The couple separated after several years, but Edith avoided divorce for decades because the social consequences that women paid were so high. Impropriety or even the appearance of irregularity was punished. Wharton knew from personal experience the pain that resistance to old orders can inflict, and this would become the subject of much of her strongest fiction, beginning with *The House of Mirth*.

The novel follows the life of Lily Bart—a beautiful, unmarried woman on the brink of 30, a perilous age in the marriage market. Lily had enjoyed a prosperous childhood, but she and her mother were reduced to shabby gentility after Lily's father went bankrupt and then died when Lily was still a child. Guided by her single-minded mother, Lily is reduced to using her beauty and her wits to find a rich mate. At first, she seems assured of success. A sequence of eligible and wealthy men is attracted to her, and several come close to proposing. In each case, however, Lily does or says something unconventional, or daring, or merely unexpected, and in each case she finds herself deserted. By temperament and breeding, Lily is unfit for the sorts of paid work that women could find in the early 20th century. She is not going to become a teacher, or a nurse, or a social worker. Unmarried and unable to support herself in the style to which she has become accustomed, she is obliged to attach herself as a companion to rich women. These presiding matrons of society provide Lily with hospitality in exchange for small personal services. Her assignments include playing bridge for money, an occupation that simply adds to her debts.

When she naively accepts investment advice from a repulsive, rich man, she becomes entangled in scandal, despite her innocence. His sexual intriguing is apparently obvious to everyone except Lily. The novel's plot traces an arc that leads slowly but inevitably downward. Banished from the highest levels of society, Lily finds a place a rung or two lower on the fashionable ladder—then eventually declines into poverty, underpaid labor, and death. Treating herself as property, and treated as property by those around her,

Lily is both user and used. Morally, she is the most attractive major character in the book, but she is undeniably complicit in her own undoing.

Captive to the values she simultaneously despises, she is trapped by her inability to even imagine an alternative for herself. Wharton uses Lily's fate as a vehicle for satirizing the society in which she lives and dies. In doing so, Wharton explores several large questions about the meaning of success, about the demands of gender, about the limits of human freedom.

The novel's title, which is taken from the biblical book of Ecclesiastes, captures much of its thematic intention: "The heart of the wise man is in the house of mourning, but the heart of the fool is in the house of mirth." With a combination of relish and anger, Wharton provides a relentless satire on the cruelly vacuous world of New York society: Overweight men and overdressed women wallow placidly in a gilded wasteland, finding their satisfactions in gambling, sexual intrigue, pointless travel, and extravagant display. All values are calculated in dollars and more dollars.

In 1899, just a few years before *The House of Mirth* appeared, the social critic Thorstein Veblen published *The Theory of the Leisure Class*. I mentioned Veblen in our discussion of Horatio Alger, Jr., and he will come up again when we talk about Sinclair Lewis and *Main Street*. You recall that Veblen coined the famous phrase "conspicuous consumption" in his influential analysis of American behavior and attitudes. As Veblen explained it, such consumption involves the purchase and display of material possessions on a scale far beyond the necessities of life. For Wharton's characters, as indeed for many of the current Masters of the Universe on Wall Street, the most conspicuous of all objects in a rich man's collection is his wife. She must be carefully selected from the right background. She must be enveloped in the most expensive clothing and jewelry, and she must preside over the most elaborate parties and dinners. She is also expected to remain faithful to her husband, but she will only be punished if her indiscretions are exposed.

In *The House of Mirth* the narrator tells us that: "The pitiless code of Lily's world decreed that a woman's husband should be the only judge of her conduct. She was technically above suspicion while she had the shelter of his approval." Moral standards, in other words, had been replaced by expediency and a frantic devotion to respectability.

The House of Mirth offers a sustained indictment of these deformed values, often narrated with Wharton's trademark irony. When a daughter of the Van

Osburghs—the wealthiest of the novel's families—is married, the wedding, in the narrator's acid description:

> was celebrated in the village church near the paternal estate on the Hudson. It was the "simple country wedding" to which guests are convoyed in special trains, and from which the hordes of the uninvited have to be fended off by the intervention of the police.

> While these sylvan rites were taking place in a church packed with fashion and festooned with orchids, the representatives of the press were threading their way, notebook in hand, through the labyrinth of wedding presents.

Calling this a "simple country wedding" bespeaks the same self-satisfaction and the same smug indifference to decency that led the Vanderbilts and Belmonts to build their gargantuan mansions in Newport and call them "cottages.

Wharton returns to this moral confusion in many of the novel's episodes. In one passage, the narrator describes the misplaced rectitude of Lily's wealthy and straight-laced aunt, Mrs. Julia Peniston, with whom Lilly is forced to live after her mother dies. Aunt Julia hears rumors that Lily may be misbehaving. The mere suggestion that Lily may have done something or other that sounds indelicate, even though it is never specified, leaves Mrs. Peniston horrified. We are told that:

> Mrs. Peniston had kept her imagination shrouded, like the drawing-room furniture. … The idea that any scandal could attach to a young girl's name, above all that it could be lightly coupled with that of a married man, was so new to her that she was as much aghast as if she had been accused of leaving her carpets down all summer or of violating any of the other cardinal laws of housekeeping.

As she continues to brood on the indeterminate allegations against Lily, she cringes at the "fast" behavior of modern girls:

> The modern fastness appeared synonymous with immorality, and the mere idea of immorality was as offensive to Mrs. Peniston as a smell of cooking in the drawing-room; it was one of the conceptions her mind refused to admit.

This is simultaneously comic and sinister. In her shrunken, scolding person, Mrs. Peniston embodies the reduction of human choices to conformity and convention. She represents a society that no longer knows the difference between unethical behavior and drawing-room codes of conduct. In an earlier lecture, I mentioned that the Puritans sometimes had trouble distinguishing between large and small moral questions. Mrs. Peniston, a descendant of those Puritan ancestors, exhibits the same trouble. The consequences are ultimately lethal. Despite promises that Lily will be her chief beneficiary, Mrs. Peniston changes her will before her death and cuts off Lily's last chance at financial independence.

Portraying a world that is obsessed with surfaces and performance, *The House of Mirth* is a theatrical novel. Its houses and rooms are stage settings on which costumed men and women play the parts assigned to them. This dimension of the novel reaches its climax in a famous scene at one of the book's great parties. The grand event is hosted by Mr. and Mrs. Wellington Bry. The Brys are a rich but slightly insecure couple that intends to climb up the ladder of status by providing the most memorable entertainment of the season. The Brys decide to organize a series of *tableaux vivants*, living pictures in which a dozen women agree to exhibit themselves in a series of poses that imitate famous paintings. One of the women appears as a Titian, another as a Van Dyck, another as a Watteau, and so on. The highlight of the evening is Lily Bart's appearance in the dress and pose of *Mrs. Lloyd* by Joshua Reynolds. The pale, gauzy draperies in which she is dressed accentuate the long curves of her body. After reporting the pleased comments of the women and especially the men in the gilded audience, the narrator comments: "It was as though [Lily] had stepped, not out of, but into, Reynolds's canvas." The seeming compliment is actually frightening in its implications. Lily has been transformed into an aesthetic object, and her identity has become coextensive with the other beautiful things—the paintings, and sculpture, and furniture—that adorn the houses of the rich.

Her theatrical self-presentation resembles an act of self-extinction. She lives only as a desirable commodity, dependent on the approval and ultimately the financial power of others. One of the men watching Lily Bart is Lawrence Selden, a moderately successful lawyer who loves her in a timid sort of way. The novel also begins and ends with scenes in which Selden is looking at Lily, a repeated action that tells us much about his character. He doesn't have the nerve to declare his feelings—and she in any case regards him, at least at first, as insufficiently wealthy to meet her needs. By the time he decides to break through his reserve, on the last pages of the novel, it is too late. Throughout *The House of Mirth*, Selden offers a critique of the vulgar materialism that defines the rich and the richer. He lectures Lily repeatedly on the higher values of plain living and hard work. Selden proposes that Lily abandon her efforts to find residence in the "house of mirth." She should join him in what he calls the "republic of the spirit." This is a place in which conventional ideas of success are replaced by a devotion to freedom.

When Lily asks whether he means freedom from worry, Selden grandly replies: "[Freedom] From everything—from money, from poverty, from ease and anxiety, from all the material accidents." This is not a philosophy; it is mere talk. Note the self-consuming language in which he articulates his vision: freedom from both money and poverty, freedom from both ease and anxiety. Above all, Selden's smug rhetoric has no relevance to Lily Bart, a woman shaped from the day of her birth to play the role imposed on her. Selden, like so many of the male characters in Wharton's stories, is a moral trifler. Wharton knew that fine sentiments, like Selden's talk about the "republic of the spirit," come more readily to the well-fed.

Wharton was a masterful maker of images and metaphors. She deploys them repeatedly throughout the novel, using the language of biology to underscore the powerful forces that control Lily's fate. In the first chapter, Selden observes that "In judging Miss Bart he … always made use of the 'argument from design.'" Underneath this small joke is a deep structure of significance. As I mentioned in our discussion of *Ragged Dick*, almost from the day *The Origin of Species* was published in 1859, Darwin's influence was pervasive—touching virtually every cultural and intellectual domain. Whether it was understood properly or not, and it was usually not, Darwin's conclusions encouraged a widespread use of scientific vocabulary in efforts to explain human actions.

The literary naturalism that emerged in the second half of the 19th century on both sides of the Atlantic produced fictions in which characters were compelled to their choices by the combination of heredity and environment. This is precisely the language that Wharton uses in describing Lily Barton. Late in the novel, as Lily sinks into poverty and despair, she spends sleepless nights wondering about the extent of her own responsibility for her bad choices. When Lily decides that she is perhaps not so much to blame, the narrator adds that she was perhaps even less to blame than she believed. This is followed by an extended biological analogy:

> Inherited tendencies [the narrator tells us] had combined with early training to make her the highly specialized product she was: an organism as helpless out of its narrow range as the sea-anemone

torn from the rock. She had been fashioned to adorn and delight; to what other end does nature round the rose leaf and paint the hummingbird's breast?

What holds our interest is that Lily simultaneously recoils from her fate and rushes to embrace it. She knows the emptiness of the lives that her rich acquaintances pursue, but she cannot conceive of any other. In the narrator's phrase, Lilly "had been brought up to be ornamental," a comment that summarizes her predicament and also recalls one of the novel's working titles: *A Moment's Ornament*.

Lily's advances and retreats provide the novel's primary rhythm. One of her only genuine friends, a woman named Carry Fisher, tries to explain Lily's self-destructive behavior. "I think," says Mrs. Fisher, "it's because, at heart, she despises the things that she's trying for. And it's the difficulty of deciding that makes her such an interesting study." As Lilly says herself, later in the novel: "it was easy enough to despise the world but decidedly difficult to find any other habitable region."

Lily Bart's fictional career is a comment on the limits of human freedom, but more specifically on the restraints placed on women's freedom. When *The House of Mirth* was published, votes for women were still 15 years in the future. Millions of women were working outside the home, but most at traditionally female occupations at the bottom of the wage scale. Birth control was unreliable, often illegal. Divorce was relatively rare, and—as Wharton's own life demonstrated—it brought substantial penalties to women. In every one of these areas, women were organizing in ever-larger numbers to demand their rights.

In 1898, just a few years before *The House of Mirth* appeared, the feminist writer Charlotte Perkins Gilman published her influential polemic, *Women and Economics*. In it, she attacked the customary division of labor by gender. Very little of this tumultuous political context is visible in Wharton's novel. Instead, the question of a "woman's place," as it was often called, is acted out in social terms. For women in Wharton's world, the rules were strict and unbending.

Lily's fist conversation with Lawrence Selden takes place in his comfortable bachelor apartment. She looks around at the modest but fully adequate spaces and thinks above all about the privacy they provide. She exclaims: "What a miserable thing it is to be a woman." She means, quite simply, that her gender has provided her with just two alternatives: She can choose independence and accept poverty, or elect marriage and achieve security at the cost of her autonomy. She says of marriage: "There's the difference—a girl must, a man may if he chooses." Marriage to a wealthy man will provide not only the end of worry over money, but also the additional security of respectability.

We might take a moment and compare Lily's situation with the main characters in a couple of the other novels we have discussed. Several of the male heroes in those fictions also found themselves in hard places. Like Lily Bart, Huckleberry Finn and Ragged Dick are both orphans and both initially at the mercy of others. But they can exert themselves on their own behalf. Huck can light out with Jim and light out again at the end of his story for the wide-open spaces. Dick can work his way from poverty to prosperity. No woman at the turn of the 20th century could plausibly occupy the same space or follow the same path as these two young men.

Perhaps Lily could have demonstrated greater strength of purpose, but the odds against her are long by any accounting. Trapped by a combination of choice and circumstance, she is reduced to a job trimming hats in a fashionable shop whose customers include her former friends. Hunger and worry keep her awake through the nights, when she comes to rely on a drug to get any sleep at all. Near the novel's end, in a famous and controversial scene, Lily takes an overdose of the medicine and dies. A suicide or an accident? Wharton deliberately leaves the question unanswered and unanswerable. On her final night, Lily has decided that she will need to take more of the drug if she is to have any sleep. She knows there is some risk, but her need for sleep is paramount. The narrator tells us:

> She did not, in truth, consider the question very closely—the physical craving for sleep was her only sustained sensation. Her mind shrank from the glare of thought as instinctively as eyes contract in a blaze of light—darkness, darkness was what she must have at any cost.

Dreaming of the child she will never have, Lily falls into a sleep from which she never awakens. The following morning, described with rather unsubtle irony as spring-like and sunny, with a promise of summer in the air, Lawrence Selden comes to her. Intending at last to make his feelings known, he finds Lily's body. The ending is more than slightly melodramatic, but Wharton wanted to emphasize the penalty of suppressing and even denying love. At a time when literary realism was engaged with the plight of the poor—think of Stephen Crane's *Maggie: A Girl of the Streets* or Theodore Dreiser's *Sister Carrie*—Wharton was sometimes belittled for devoting her attention to the wealthy classes. Defending her choice of subject matter, she later wrote: "A frivolous society can acquire dramatic significance only through what its frivolity destroys." The city that Edith Wharton evokes in *The House of Mirth* is as full of danger for a woman as Crane's tenement blocks or Dreiser's saloons.

Somewhat ironically, the novel gave a substantial boost to Wharton's own independence. The book was initially published in installments in *Scribner's Magazine*, and she was paid the then high price of $5,000 for the serial rights. She earned far more when the book appeared in hard covers. One hundred and forty thousand copies were sold in the first year, making it one of the bestselling novels of the first several decades of the 20th century. Wharton was also pleased that Henry James called it "altogether a superior thing." The book's continued popularity has several probable sources. The plot is colorful and entertaining; the questions of gender that the novel raises continue to be timely; and Wharton's remarkable prose joins descriptive skill and ironic humor in rare combination. Above all, Lily Bart—perhaps precisely because of her limitations—has proven to be an endurably and, indeed, irresistibly attractive heroine.

Lecture Eleven
The Jungle

Scope: During a time when new investigative journalism poured out in response to corporate power, Upton Sinclair's *The Jungle* was muckraking's masterpiece. Published in February 1906, it is a brutal exposé of the meatpacking plants in Chicago at the turn of the century. Based on Sinclair's personal observations in the meatpacking plants, the novel presents a catalog of suffering, injustice, and despair. The hopes and lives of the workers, many of them immigrants, are mutilated by the knives of the slaughterhouses and the greed of the big business owners. In Sinclair's world, life is a jungle, particularly for the poor. A socialist who rejected social Darwinism, Sinclair looked forward to a socialist revolution in which the workers would control the means of production, and strife would be replaced with harmony. *The Jungle* was an international sensation. Even President Roosevelt responded to the book and promised reform of the meatpacking industry; however, the socialist manifesto that Sinclair intended it to be had little impact, and the political message for "the workingmen of America" was largely ignored.

Outline

I. Social Darwinism is the pseudoscientific notion that economic competition is an inevitable and natural extension of the evolutionary process.

   A. In Sinclair's view, Rockefeller and his fellow titans of industry were ruthless predators in a jungle of exploitation and abuse. This was no a law of nature or of God; rather, humans designed it for the benefit of the few at the expense of the many.

   B. Sinclair had come to socialism only a few years before writing *The Jungle*.

      1. The son of an alcoholic father and a religious mother, Sinclair grew up in near poverty with little formal schooling.

      2. He became a prodigious reader and gained admission to City College of New York at just 14 years old.

C. Previously, Sinclair had written novels proposing that the evils of mankind could be alleviated by an immersion into beauty. He quickly abandoned this idealistic thesis and moved toward politics.

D. Even in its prewar heyday, socialism was always a marginal movement in America, practically wiped out by the nationalism and xenophobia that came with World War I.

E. Opposition to the concentrated power of big business impelled radicals and progressives alike; dark suspicions of corporate power were informed by an outpouring of investigative journalism.

    1. The muckrakers had a few predecessors in the Gilded Age, but there was no precedent for the scale and tenacity of this new journalism.

    2. The muckrakers were the most influential collection of newspaper and magazine writers the nation has ever produced; they turned over every corporate and government stone in search of corruption and conspiracy.

F. *The Jungle* is widely considered muckraking's propagandistic masterpiece.

II. Sinclair's novel was actually the product of a commission. After Sinclair wrote a series of articles for *The Appeal to Reason*, America's most important socialist newspaper, its editor challenged Sinclair to work his material into a novel.

A. *The Jungle* was initially published in installments; the first chapters began appearing before Sinclair finished the book.

B. The book opens with the wedding of Jurgis Rudkis and his 15-year-old bride. Rather than signs of good fortune, premonitions of disaster hover over the wedding scene.

C. The narrator leads his characters through a sequence of unrelieved calamities, each one worse than the one before. On several occasions, the narrator likens himself to Dante, guiding readers through a landscape of despair.

D. Packingtown is described in a vocabulary intended to summon hell, and Jurgis will spend the next several years in this vast wilderness of smoke and filth.

III. Chicago's meatpacking industry was made possible by two new technologies: the invention of the refrigerated railroad car and the assembly line.

    A. In the meat slaughterhouses, each worker has a specific job in a grim choreography of death.

        1. Sinclair's emphasis on the brutality pushes toward metaphors, likening the worker's conditions to those of the animal.

        2. This is the novel's central point: Workers have little more control over their lives and deaths than do the pigs and cattle on which they use razor-sharp knives.

    B. Jurgis assumes that hard work will ensure his livelihood and advancement. He slowly realizes that no one rises by honesty or hard work solely, and that victims of the system also prey on each other.

    C. The horrors of the factory are repeated in the homes and streets of Packingtown. After being forced to have sex with her manager, Jurgis's young wife, Ona, begins working in a brothel to earn money.

        1. When Jurgis beats Connor in revenge, he is thrown into jail for 30 days.

        2. Prison is the ironic site of Jurgis's salvation. In part, the novel is an exercise in education, for both Jurgis and the reader.

    D. Sinclair's motive here is to expose the powerful men and agencies far beyond Packingtown; he patiently lays out the conspiracy that crushes the workers and their families.

        1. The conspiracy includes the intimate relationships between corrupt owners and meat inspectors, all of whom are protected by corrupt politicians and police.

        2. It also includes a Democratic boss named Mike Scully who presides over a profitable empire of graft and vice.

    E. Jurgis continues to suffer after leaving prison; he is blacklisted and can't find work.

        1. With no money for a doctor, Ona dies in childbirth, and Jurgis's only child drowns in a pool of water caused by unpaved roads outside of their house.

        2. After resorting to begging and petty crime, Jurgis begins work as a goon and strikebreaker for Boss Scully, emphasizing how far he has fallen.

IV. Jurgis ultimately finds the answer in socialism; the last few chapters of the novel survey his conversion to this doctrine.

  A. Once more, Jurgis undergoes an education, this time into the doctrines and writings of socialism. His tutor is a Russian tailor named Ostrinski.

    1. Sinclair suspends the novel's action for an entire chapter so that Ostrinski can instruct Jurgis—and the reader—in socialist economic and political theory.

    2. Jurgis understands finally that he and his family have not been victims of fate or bad luck, but of organized greed.

  B. Jurgis becomes a socialist and union organizer. The novel concludes with Sinclair's excited report of the 1904 election results and the gains that socialist candidates have made all over the country.

V. The sensation that *The Jungle* caused certainly impacted the meat industry and had far-reaching effects.

  A. Within a few months, Congress created the Food and Drug Administration, an agency with strong authority to regulate the quality of the nation's food.

  B. It was a triumph, but Sinclair felt that *The Jungle*'s political message was lost almost completely. The socialist revolution he called for never happened.

Suggested Reading:

Mattson, *Upton Sinclair and the Other American Century.*

Scott, *Upton Sinclair, the Forgotten Socialist.*

Questions to Consider:

1. It is obvious that Sinclair failed in the intention he declared in writing *The Jungle*: The workers of America did not rise up and establish a socialist state. Leaving that historical outcome to one side, how persuasive and how logical are the arguments that he makes in favor of socialism in the novel? Which parts, if any, of his critique of capitalism are compelling?

2. How well do the characters and plot of the novel support Sinclair's political thesis? Is there tension between the polemical ideas and the realism of *The Jungle*'s events? More generally, do "propaganda novels" necessarily suffer from their nonliterary motives?

Lecture Eleven—Transcript
The Jungle

In the last lecture on *The House of Mirth*, we looked at Edith Wharton's representation of American society near the top of the economic ladder. In this lecture, we will discuss a book published just one year later, which dramatizes life at the bottom. Few pairings better illustrate the sheer diversity of experience in the United States in the tumultuous years around the turn of the 20th century. With all their differences, however, Upton Sinclair resembles Wharton at least in this—his alienation from prevailing assumptions and his interest in the limits that social circumstances impose on human freedom. Let's begin with the famous title: *The Jungle*. While Sinclair's novel is less widely read today than it was 100 years ago, the title has remained indelibly inscribed on the national memory. Life is a jungle, particularly for the poor—a ceaseless struggle for survival in which the strong prey on the weak. As the narrator says late in the novel, the "world of civilization" was "a place of brutal might, an order devised by those who possessed it for the subjugation of those who did not."

When we discussed Social Darwinism in connection with Horatio Alger's *Ragged Dick*, I quoted, among other passages, John D. Rockefeller's comment that the growth of American business was like the growth of an American Beauty rose. Small buds must be snipped to permit the largest blossom to flourish. Upton Sinclair was repelled by Social Darwinism. For him, Rockefeller's image of a tidy greenhouse was a misleading metaphor intended to legitimize the oppression that the wealthy imposed on the people below them. In Sinclair's view, Rockefeller and his fellow titans of industry were not gardeners but ruthless predators in a jungle of exploitation and abuse. The tragic and intolerable situation was not a law of nature or god. On the contrary, Sinclair believed that human beings designed it, for the benefit of the few at the expense of the many, and human beings could change it. Sinclair's alternative was cooperation rather than competition. He looked forward to a socialist revolution in which the workers would control the means of production and strife would be replaced by harmony.

Visions of human solidarity have a long history in the Western world. Utopias of one sort or another have tantalized the imagination of discontented artists and philosophers back to the Greeks. In the early 20th century, those seductive dreams were often absorbed into some version of socialist theory. Sinclair had come to socialism only a few years before he wrote his famous novel. The son of an alcoholic father and a demanding, religious mother, he grew up in near-poverty, with little formal schooling. In spite of that, he became a prodigious reader and managed to gain admission to City College in New York when he was just 14 years old. He graduated in 1897, harboring ambitions to become a man of letters who would also improve the world in some unspecified way.

His literary models included the romantic poet Percy Shelley, who—a century earlier—had combined art with a commitment to human liberation. (It was Shelley, you may recall, who described poets as "the unacknowledged legislators of mankind.") Sinclair's first novels, now forgotten, proposed that the evils humanities faced could be alleviated by an immersion in beauty. He soon abandoned this somewhat idealistic thesis and moved toward a more active engagement with politics. In 1902, he joined the Socialist Party of America. In the late 19th and early 20th centuries, the Socialist Party enjoyed more success than ever before or since. By no coincidence, those years corresponded to the most violent period of labor unrest in the nation's history. Bloody warfare in the Pennsylvania coalfields was followed by the brutal Pullman Strike in the Midwest in 1894. The year 1905 was a year of revolution in Russia, and there was revolutionary talk in the United States as well.

The Industrial Workers of the World—the I.W.W., or "Wobblies," as they were called—was a union established on explicitly radical terms in 1905. Among other things, the Wobblies offered membership to African Americans at a time when most American unions were rigorously segregated. In the decade before the First World War, the Wobblies battled police and national guardsmen in the timber regions of the Pacific Northwest. Running for president on the Socialist Party ticket, Eugene V. Debs received 100,000 votes in 1900, half-a-million in 1904 and 1908, and a million in 1912, almost 6 percent of all the ballots cast.

In 1910, Victor Berger of Milwaukee was the first person elected to Congress on a Socialist ticket, and 100 other Socialists won local offices. As Berger's case demonstrates, support for Socialist candidates and their ideas reached from Eastern cities across the Midwest. For just a moment, socialism achieved a status of near-respectability. This proved to be the high point of American socialism as a political force. Even in its heyday, it is clear socialism was always a marginal movement in this country. The Socialist Party was more or less erased by the nationalism and xenophobia that accompanied the First World War. Nonetheless, its advocates shared with less-militant Americans a growing discontent about the state of the nation. In particular, they worried that large corporations seemed to exercise unsupervised control over the quality of life. The biggest companies and their leaders were indifferent to government regulation and contemptuous of public opinion.

Even mainstream politicians insisted on change. Theodore Roosevelt was called the "trust buster" for successfully breaking up nearly 50 corporate monopolies during his seven years in the White House. Instead of revolution, American politicians in the first decade of the 20th century embraced a cycle of reform: the Progressive Era, as it is still called. Progressives aspired to replace political machines with professional managers. They supported greater protection for workers and consumers, a 10-hour or 8-hour workday and restrictions on child labor. Progressives called for a graduated income tax and specific electoral reforms, such as the recall of elected officials and the direct election of U.S. Senators. They were generally indifferent to racial discrimination, but many of them did endorse voting rights and protective legislation for women.

Opposition to the concentrated power of big business impelled radicals and progressives. Their dark suspicions of corporate power were informed by an outpouring of investigative journalism. The "muckrakers," as they were called, had a few predecessors among 19th-century critics of the Gilded Age, but there was no precedent for the scale and tenacity of the new journalism. They were the most influential collection of newspaper and magazine writers the nation has ever produced. They earned a reputation for influence and integrity that remains unblemished today, a century after they did their work.

Making an index of American institutions, the muckrakers turned over every corporate and government stone they could find in search of corruption and conspiracy. They found what they were looking for. Just to read the titles of the many books and articles they produced is to gather some idea of the scope of their investigations: Ida Tarbell's *History of the Standard Oil Company*, Edward Bok's "Patent-medicine Curse," Lincoln Steffens's *The Shame of the Cities*, G. W. Galvin's "Our Legal Machinery and Its Victims," Thomas Lawson's *Frenzied Finance*, Robert Hunter's "Children Who Toil," David Graham Phillips's "The Treason of the Senate," Louis Brandeis's "Greatest Life Insurance Wrong," and Charles Edward Russell's *Lawless Wealth*. A number of magazines dedicated their articles and editorials to reform, among them *Cosmopolitan*, *McClure's*, and *The Masses*.

The Jungle was muckraking's fictional masterpiece. Based on Sinclair's personal observations in the meatpacking plants of Chicago and his interviews with Chicago workers, the novel presents a catalog of suffering, injustice, and despair. The hopes and lives of the workers, many of them immigrants, are mutilated by the knives of the slaughterhouses and the greed of the owners.

Unlike any other book on our reading list, *The Jungle* was the product of a commission. In 1904 and 1905, Sinclair had written a series of articles for a magazine called *The Appeal to Reason*, America's most important socialist journal. Published weekly in the town of Girard, Kansas, the *Appeal* charged just twenty-five cents for an annual subscription. Readers found a variety of radical material in each issue. Excerpts from Tom Paine's *Common Sense* and chapters from the works of Marx and Engels shared space with articles and speeches by Jack London, Eugene Debs, and "Mother" Jones, the fiery trade union organizer.

The low price and the national appetite for political argument attracted an estimated 500,000 subscribers. No radical journal, whether on the right or the left, has ever reached that many readers. The *Appeal*'s editor, impressed by the power of Sinclair's reports on the stockyards, challenged him to turn his material into a novel. *The Jungle* was initially published in installments. The first chapters began appearing before Sinclair had finished the book. This may help to explain some of the stylistic and structural problems that I will refer to a little later. The novel opens with a wedding. Jurgis Rudkis and his 15-year-old bride, Ona, are both new immigrants from Lithuania. The ceremony is followed by a traditional Old World celebration, which features hours of dancing and drinking. In a sentimental novel, marriage symbolizes stability and hope for the future. In the well-worn phrase, the bride and groom will live happily ever after.

In *The Jungle*, on the contrary, premonitions of disaster hover over the wedding scene. Most of the guests are too poor to contribute to the collection that goes to the newlyweds, and during the reception they share stories of their brutal lives in the packinghouses and other industries of Chicago. From this first chapter, for the next two-thirds of the novel, one misfortune follows another. The narrator leads his characters through a sequence of unrelieved calamities, each one worse than the one before. On several occasions, the narrator likens himself to Dante, guiding readers through a landscape of despair.

Packingtown is repeatedly described in language that summons hell, as in this passage:

> half a dozen chimneys, tall as the tallest of buildings, touching the very sky—and leaping from them half a dozen columns of smoke, thick, oily, and black as night. It might have come from the center of the world, this smoke ... a black pall as far as the eye could reach.

In these yards, 8 to 10 million animals—cattle, pigs, and sheep—are turned into food each year. "For the odors in these ghastly charnel houses," the narrator says, "there may be words in Lithuanian, but there are none in English." Jurgis will spend the next several years in this vast wilderness of smoke and filth. Chicago's meatpacking industry was made possible by two new technologies. The first was the invention of the refrigerated railroad car in the 1870s. Ranchers could now send their herds of cattle and other animals to a single destination instead of selling them in small lots to buyers who traveled across the plains. Now the cattle and pigs traveled to their fate on their own legs in great herds or on train cars. We saw a cattle drive like this in Owen Wister's *The Virginian*.

After they reached Chicago, the animals were cut into portions of various sizes and shipped across the country as processed meat. Beef and pork production was transformed from a nationwide collection of small transactions into a vast mechanized and centralized business. The second new technology that made the meatpacking industry possible was the assembly line. Henry Ford is often identified as the man who brought the assembly line to industrial manufacturing. However, scholars of technology have pointed out that the Chicago slaughterhouses were the pioneers in this innovation. Though their task was disassembly, taking apart rather than putting together, the methods were the same: Labor was divided into specialized tasks, and production moved swiftly.

Animals went down a chute on one end of a building. They were killed and impaled on a hook that carried their carcasses past a sequence of workers. Each worker had a specific job in a grim choreography of death. One man cut the large carcass in half; those next in line sliced off particular portions of the animal. By the end of the bloody journey—a matter of minutes—nothing was left. "It ways," says the narrator, "pork-making by machinery, pork-making by applied mathematics." One of the novel's famous lines declares: "They use everything about the hog except [its] squeal."

As he lingers over the brutality of the killing, Sinclair repeatedly pushes his descriptions toward metaphor. The men who work in these foul-smelling, filthy, cold, damp, dangerous factories are themselves not far removed from the animals they slaughter. This, in fact, is the novel's central argument: Workers have little more control over their lives and deaths than the pigs and cattle on which they use their razor-sharp knives. Ironically, Jurgis is initially dazzled by the sheer scale and efficiency of what he sees. He is eager to find a job and begins as a shoveler, who continuously shovels the blood and entrails from each animal into a huge pit. The work is barbaric, but it pays Jurgis enough to cover his rent and the cost of his meager food. He works every day to the point of exhaustion. Each time the family needs extra money, Jurgis announces: "I will work harder." Jurgis assumes that his hard work will ensure his livelihood and advancement. He slowly realizes that no one rises by way of honesty or hard work. Graft and payoffs define all employment transactions. Promotions are bought, not earned through honest labor. Beyond that, and one of the bitterest lessons Jurgis learns, the victims of the system also prey on the other victims.

Managers steal from the workers, and the workers steal from each other. The narrator tells us:

> from top to bottom the place was simply a seething cauldron of jealousies and hatreds; there was no loyalty or decency anywhere about it, there was no place in it where a man counted for anything against a dollar.

The novel's early chapters reproduce the realities of the slaughterhouse in abundant and often nauseating detail. Diseased animals are routinely passed by corrupt or lazy inspectors and added to the meat-making process— tubercular steers, hogs already dead of cholera, cattle covered with boils that explode with filth when the workers cut them open.

The most notorious parts of the novel comprise a nightmare of injury, stench, and suffering. The narrator tells us that each type of workplace was a separate little inferno, each with its own peculiar disease. The men in the pickle room, for example, worked with an acid that could literally eat away their fingers. Among the butchers, the narrator says, "you could scarcely find a person who had the use of his thumb; time and again, the base of it had been slashed, till it was a mere lump of flesh." Other men had no fingernails: "they had worn them off pulling hides." The men in the cooking rooms contracted tuberculosis within two years. Those in the chilling room suffered from rheumatism. The hands of the wool pluckers, the narrator tells us, "went to pieces even sooner than the hands of the pickle men, and the men who worked at the stamping machine almost always had parts of their hands cut off."

The litany of misery culminates with the novel's most famous passage. The narrator describes the fate of the men who worked in tank rooms covered with blinding steam:

> Their peculiar trouble [says the narrator] was that they fell into the vats; and when they were fished out, there was never enough of them left to be worth exhibiting—sometimes they would be overlooked for days, till all but the bones of them had gone out to the world as Durham's Pure Leaf Lard!

Some of my former students have told me, years after we've discussed the book, that this is the only episode in *The Jungle* that they still recall with complete clarity. After a century, it remains the classic emblem for the pathological distortions of the early industrial workplace. The horrors of the factories are repeated in the homes and streets of Packingtown. Jurgis's young wife, Ona, is forced to have sex with her thuggish manager, a man named Connor, to save her job. Then, judging herself ruined, she starts working in a brothel to earn money for the family. When Jurgis beats Connor in retaliation, he, Jurgis, is thrown into jail for 30 days. Ironically, it is in prison that Jurgis begins to learn the truth. In part, the novel is shaped as an exercise in education, both for Jurgis and the reader. As he learns more about the causes of the dreadful conditions, so too, do we. In the jail, he hears other men explaining how the system of injustice works, how socialism would provide an alternative.

Jurgis begins to understand the dimensions of organized corruption. Here, in what the narrator calls a "Noah's ark of the city's crime," he realizes that most of the men have been incarcerated for the crime of being poor. They were, says the narrator, "swindlers and thieves of pennies and dimes, and they had been trapped and put out of the way by the swindlers and thieves of millions of dollars." Sinclair, like other progressives and radicals, knew that the conditions in the stockyards could not exist without the cooperation of powerful men and agencies far beyond Packingtown.

He patiently lays out the conspiracy that crushes the workers and their families: the intimate relationships that bind corrupt owners to corrupt meat inspectors, all of whom are protected by corrupt politicians and corrupt police. A Democratic boss named Mike Scully presides over a profitable empire of graft and vice. As the narrator says in a summary comment, all the agencies of crime were linked in blood brotherhood with the politician and the police; more often than not they were one and the same person—the police captain would own the brothel he pretended to raid, and the politician would open his headquarters in his saloon.

After he leaves prison, Jurgis continues to suffer. He is blacklisted and can't find work. Ona dies in childbirth, in part because Jurgis has no money for a doctor. His only child, a son named Antanas, drowns in a pool of muddy water that has settled in a dangerous hole in the unpaved street outside their shabby house. Sunk in despair, Jurgis takes to the road as a tramp. When he returns to Chicago, his decline continues. He works for a while as one of the thousands of laborers digging tunnels for telephone wires, but winds up seriously injured and hospitalized. Begging and petty crime follow. His next job, working as a goon and strikebreaker for Boss Scully, emphasizes how far Jurgis has fallen.

In our discussion of *Huckleberry Finn*, I described the rhythm of the picaresque novel, a narrative structure in which the hero faces a sequence of threats, each of which leads to escape. Instead of a cumulative unfolding of cause and effect, each episode is a more or less self-contained adventure. *The Jungle* is constructed as a parody of that picaresque rhythm. Jurgis is confronted with a long sequence of threats, each one of which leads to disaster rather than escape. In the end, Jurgis finds the answer in socialism. The last few chapters of the novel survey his conversion to this lifesaving doctrine. He attends a socialist rally and is transfixed by the charisma and eloquence of the speaker, a speaker who captures all the pain and suffering that Jurgis and other laboring men and women endure.

The speaker shouts that the workers are "bound in the service of organized and predatory Greed!" The houses and factories in which they spend their lives are prisons, dungeons, tombs. Sinclair poured all of his contempt for the capitalist system into this long, inflammatory speech. After reviewing the crimes committed against ordinary people by the powerful, the socialist speaker calls on his audience to take what is rightfully theirs:

> To you, the toilers, who have made this land, and have no voice in its councils! To you, whose lot … is to sow that others may reap, to labor and obey, and ask no more than the wages of a beast of burden, the food and shelter to keep you alive from day to day. It is to you that I come with my message of salvation, it is to you that I appeal.

The term "salvation" requires a comment. The rhetoric of early 20th century American socialists was typically steeped in religious vocabulary. Socialism was presented as a new creed, a system of belief and commitment that would lead to a transformation in human affairs little short of miraculous.

Christ was often invoked as a pioneer socialist, a heroic figure who spoke for the meek and the poor and preached the virtues of generosity and sacrifice. The narrator makes the point explicitly: the Socialist movement, he says, "was the new religion of humanity—or you might say it was the old religion, since it implied but the literal application of all the teachings of Christ." Once more, Jurgis undergoes an education—this time into the doctrines and writings of socialism. His tutor is a Lithuanian-speaking tailor named Ostrinski. Sinclair suspends the novel's action for an entire long chapter so that Ostrinski can patiently instruct Jurgis—and, of course, the reader—in socialist economic and political theory.

The pages bulge with abstract and numbing details, but for Jurgis they lead to a single overwhelming insight: He and his family have not been victimized by fate or bad luck but by the organized greed of capitalism. Jurgis becomes a socialist and a union organizer. The novel concludes with Sinclair's excited report of the 1904 election results, and the gains that socialist candidates made all over the country.

In the concluding scene, the socialist orator offers an apocalyptic prediction: The workers will unite and become an irresistible force for change. The famous final line is a rising shout of triumph: "We shall bear down the opposition, we shall sweep it before us—and Chicago will be ours! Chicago will be ours! CHICAGO WILL BE OURS!"

The Jungle was an international sensation. Published in February 1906, the book appeared almost immediately in a British edition. Over a dozen translations followed. Sinclair was launched into an epic controversy over the accuracy of his charges; several independent investigators supported his allegations. The most celebrated response to the book came from President Theodore Roosevelt. After he read the novel, he invited Sinclair to the White House. Mr. Dooley, a fictitious bartender invented by Finley Peter Dunne, imagined Roosevelt's reaction. I will not try to reproduce the Irish brogue:

> Teddy was toying with a light breakfast an' idly turning over the pages of the new book with both hands. Suddenly he rose from the table, and cryin': "I'm poisoned," began throwing sausages out of the window. ... Since then the President, like the rest of us, has become a vegetarian.

Mr. Dooley overstates the public response only by a little. For six months, newspapers reported the rising popularity of meatless diets all over the country.

Roosevelt was immune to Sinclair's argument for socialism, but he promised reform of the meat-packing industry. Aside from the dangers to health posed by contaminated beef and pork, the economic arguments were compelling. International sales of American meat products dropped by an estimated 50 percent in the year following *The Jungle*'s publication. Within a few months, Congress passed legislation creating the Food and Drug Administration, assigning the new agency strong authority for regulating the quality of the nation's food. It was a triumph, but Sinclair felt that he had been defeated. He often said he had aimed for the public's heart and hit its stomach instead. The president and the nation's citizens had reacted swiftly and decisively to protect themselves from tainted meat, but they had ignored *The Jungle*'s political message almost completely. The novel was dedicated to "the workingmen of America," and Sinclair's socialist manifesto was spelled out in excruciating detail. Jack London compared Sinclair to Harriet Beecher Stowe and said that "what *Uncle Tom's Cabin* did for black slaves, *The Jungle* has a large chance to do for the wage slaves of today." But the socialist revolution never happened.

What about the nation's food? In February 2008, 102 years after the publication of *The Jungle*, the United States government recalled 143 million pounds of tainted beef from a company named Westland/Hallmark. It was the largest recall of meat in U.S. history.

Lecture Twelve
Main Street

Scope: Several of the books discussed so far in this course have exemplified the shift toward the city, both in the nation's social history and in its imaginative life. The turmoil and anxieties that accompanied America's industrial and urban transformation provoked a divided response: Some writers returned to the country's agrarian and small-town past with feelings of affection and nostalgia. Sinclair Lewis, however, developed an entire social analysis of rural America in *Main Street*. The novel offered the definitive satire of small-town America. The reviews were almost uniformly ecstatic, and the sales matched this enthusiasm. Part of the book's popularity was evidently the deflation of mythic small-town America. The novel follows the journey of Carol Milford, and it is her experiences that provide the scenes for satiric treatment of small-town American life. A decade after the publication of *Main Street*, Lewis won the Nobel Prize in Literature. He was the first American to receive the prize in the three decades of the awards.

Outline

I. As one group of writers reacted to America's urban and industrial transformation with sentimental evocations of the small town, another group of writers mounted a campaign against what they believed was the darker reality of rural life.

    A. This "revolt against the village" was a central feature of American literature in the first two or three decades of the 20th century.

    B. Two of the most influential of the dissenting writers were the poet Edgar Lee Masters and the novelist Sherwood Anderson.

        1. Masters and Anderson chose to emphasize the psychological penalties that small towns inflict on their residents. The fragmentary nature of their works serves as a metaphor for the fate of their characters.

        2. Sinclair Lewis, on the contrary, developed a fuller social analysis of rural America in *Main Street*.

II. The novel is set in Gopher Prairie, Minnesota, a town based on Sauk Centre, where Lewis had grown up. Sauk Centre was perched on the edge of the prairie, isolated by climate and distance. Here, Lewis felt misplaced early in life and relished the role of outsider.

   A. Lewis's father, Edwin, was a physician and a practical man, displaying little interest in his son's eccentricities or writing. Lewis's mother, a teacher, died when he was just six; his stepmother encouraged Lewis's avid reading.

   B. Lewis attended Yale, where despite being a rather mediocre student he became editor of the *Yale Literary Magazine*, in which he published a number of stories.

   1. In the decade following graduation, Lewis combined journalism with fiction writing.

   2. His first five novels did little to predict the enormous success he would earn with *Main Street*.

III. In the first scene, the novel's main character, Carol Milford, is standing on a Minnesota hillside, looking over the Mississippi River. Lewis insists on the symbolic significance of this moment: As she lifts her arms up to the sky, Carol enacts the impatience and ill-defined expectations of youth.

   A. Carol wants intellectual stimulation, and she spends a year studying library science in Chicago, where she throws herself enthusiastically into the cultural and social life of a major city.

   B. Carol marries a young doctor, Will Kennicott, and moves with him to the town of Gopher Prairie. She is motivated in part by her marriage and in part by her urge to bring civilization to people she thinks of as crude and benighted.

   C. These early scenes establish distance between Carol's perspective and her husband's: Where she sees only ugliness and aesthetic poverty, he sees the prosperity that fertile acres and hard work have brought.

   D. *Main Street* has a story, but not much of a plot. Lewis is more interested in the messages he wants to convey than in his characters or narrative.

   1. Aside from Carol and Will, most of the book's men and women are thin caricatures.

      2. The sequence of events merely provides a mechanism for disclosing the moral and intellectual deficiencies of Gopher Prairie.

    E. Despite admiring the scale of the western landscape and the dignity of farmers, Carol finds herself stifled by the atmosphere of Gopher Prairie.

      1. The narrator describes her as "a woman with a working brain and no work."

      2. Throughout the novel, Carol is moved to improve the town and its inhabitants. But each scheme fails, defeated by the combination of inertia and provincialism that defines this small town.

IV. Carol reads modern writers such as Theodore Dreiser, Sherwood Anderson, and H. L. Mencken. She shares their opinions about rural American life, and the preconceptions she brought with her to Gopher Prairie are reinforced by her experiences there.

    A. Despite the novel's antagonism toward traditional heartland complacency, *Main Street* bears little trace of sustained ideological inquiry.

    B. The novel's focus remains social and domestic, and Carol's marriage becomes the barometer of her discontent.

      1. Although she loves Will, she also finds herself repelled by his identification with the town.

      2. She invests much of her affection in her son, but harbors vague longing for more.

    C. Carol's frustration eventually prompts her to leave her husband and move to Washington DC with her son.

      1. There she finds work in a government office and enjoys her newfound autonomy.

      2. After a year, however, Will shows up, provoking both Carol's renewed affection and her sense of obligation.

      3. She returns to Gopher Prairie, presumably to accept the fate she has been trying to escape.

    D. Despite Carol's eventual surrender, and the limits on her perceptions, the narrator consistently treats her with generosity. She is the only major character that escapes satiric treatment.

E. Carol has lived through some of the most tumultuous years in American social and political history, when the debate over values ran wide and deep. Carol faces an inevitable confusion: She knows that Gopher Prairie belongs to the past, but she cannot envision the future.

V. In the years following the tremendous success of *Main Street*, Lewis published a series of novels that explored what he perceived as America's prevailing pathologies.

    A. In 1930, Sinclair Lewis became the first American to win the Nobel Prize in Literature.

        1. Some critics and journalists welcomed the honor as Europe's recognition of American writers.

        2. Others complained that Lewis had been singled out because his fiction ratified European stereotypes of American mediocrity.

    B. In the decades since, Lewis's critics have come to outnumber his supporters. Many of the issues he engaged remain relevant, but Lewis's simplified characters, repetitive stories, and broad satiric techniques no longer attract the audience they once enjoyed.

Suggested Reading:

Lingeman, *Sinclair Lewis*.

Questions to Consider:

1. The phrase "village virus" has become a byword for the satire that Lewis directs toward the American small town. However, the reality of life in Gopher Prairie seems to be more complicated than this simplifying phrase implies. What are some of the positive elements that *Main Street* explicitly or implicitly includes?

2. Gender plays an important role in the novel. Why does Lewis choose Carol Kennicott as his central character and point of view rather than a male character? Does the narrator's attitude toward Carol change through the course of the novel? More generally, what stereotypes and expectations are associated with femininity, and how do those ideas strengthen or weaken the novel's themes? Do Carol's opinions and choices seem obsolete, or do they remain relevant?

Lecture Twelve—Transcript
Main Street

In our discussion of *The Virginian*, I mentioned the landmark United States census of 1920, which announced that the majority of Americans now lived in cities. Several of the books we have discussed so far in this course have exemplified the shift toward the city, both in the nation's social history and in its imaginative life. Horatio Alger's *Ragged Dick*, Upton Sinclair's *The Jungle*, and Edith Wharton's *The House of Mirth* are altogether different novels in their themes and techniques. However, each recorded the rise and increasing importance of the American city in the second half of the 19th century and the first decades of the 20th. The turmoil and anxieties that accompanied America's industrial and urban transformation provoked a divided response. On the one hand, numerous writers returned to the country's agrarian and small-town past with feelings of affection and nostalgia. The slower pace and stronger communities of village life seemed to offer an antidote to the speed and loneliness of cities. *The Wonderful Wizard of Oz*, to give a well-known example, published by Frank Baum in 1900, contrasted the fake magic of an Emerald City with the genuine values of a home that is identified with the heartland. In the end, Kansas may be less glamorous than Oz, but it is a much friendlier place.

Eleanor Porter's *Pollyanna*, which appeared in 1912, fondly idealizes both childhood and the small town as it enumerates the unlikely adventures of its orphaned and impoverished title character. Young Pollyanna Whittier is an irrepressible child who spreads joy wherever she goes. Her virtues and her ultimate triumph over adult gloominess exemplify the wholesomeness and stereotypical integrity of rural America. Meredith Nicholson's *A Hoosier Chronicle*, published in the same year as *Pollyanna*, describes the small towns of Indiana as "comfortable and cheerful and busy ... with lots of old-fashioned human kindness flowing round. ... And I guess it's always got to be that way, out here in God's country."

That notion of the village and small town as "God's country" has had a long and robust life in the American imagination. It survives to this day, affecting everything from our political choices to our holiday plans. At the same time, against these sentimental evocations of the small town, another group of writers mounted a campaign against what they believed was the darker reality of rural life. This "revolt against the village," as it was called, was a central feature of American literature in the first two or three decades of the 20th century. Two of the most influential of these dissenting writers were the poet Edgar Lee Masters and the novelist Sherwood Anderson.

Masters, who practiced law in Chicago to support himself as a writer, published the *Spoon River Anthology* in 1915. This long poem presents a set of free-verse monologues, spoken by men and women who are dead and buried in the hilltop cemetery overlooking the town of Spoon River. Over 200 of these dead souls talk about their lives, mainly about their thwarted ambitions and their failures. The collective self-portrait that emerges from these candid, sometimes harrowing, confessions contradicts the illusions that provide hope's foundations, and they undercut the idea of the small town as a cozy, peaceable haven. Petit the Poet says he missed his artistic chance by contenting himself with "little iambics, / While Homer and Whitman roared in the pines." Knowlt Hoheimer died in the Civil War, one of "the first fruits of Missionary Ridge." He lies under a patriotic Latin inscription, which ironically he cannot even understand.

Like Petit and Hoheimer, many of Spoon River's dead citizens are trapped in the eternal contemplation of lives cut short or wasted, ounce by ounce, in futility. These individual confessions add up to an even more depressing whole than its parts. Taken together, the *Spoon River* sketches strip away the façade of trust and tranquility that supposedly govern human relations in a small town. On the contrary, these are tales of long-nurtured anger, sexual repression, mutual suspicion, and petty jealousies.

As one of the dead woman [Flossie Cabanis] says: "In all this place of silence / There are no kindred spirits." *Spoon River Anthology* had a far-reaching influence on both poets and fiction writers. Masters had found an effective way of letting the inhabitants of an American village speak for themselves. He had also invented a structure in which separate poetic statements could be read alone or in groups, and in almost any order. The unifying qualities were the cemetery setting and the shared tone of regret.

Sherwood Anderson claimed that he didn't much like *Spoon River*, but he learned a great deal from it. He, too, wanted to knit together a sequence of individual stories into a coherent narrative. Anderson was fascinated by the experiments of modernism, both in the painting of Cézanne and Gauguin, and in the writings of James Joyce and Gertrude Stein. He once wrote that life "is a loose, flowing thing," not a narrative governed by conventional plots. (In England, Virginia Woolf would say much the same thing.)

Anderson's experiments eventually led to *Winesburg, Ohio*, published in 1919, which remains an indispensable testament to the vanishing life of small-town America. The two dozen sketches that make up *Winesburg* are held together by their shared setting in the little Ohio town of the title; by the character of George Willard, who will eventually escape the town and seek his future in the city; and by a pervasive tone of loneliness and suppressed desire. Communication has become virtually impossible in Anderson's fictional world. Talk is difficult, and touch is dangerous.

Though they live in close proximity, the men and women of Winesburg are divided by impenetrable barriers. Many of the stories take place in twilight or in dimly lit rooms: a pervasive symbol of the darkness that shrinks connections between the town's people. Anderson rewrites the myth of the small-town peaceable kingdom, showing us instead a series of parallel but unshared tragedies.

Edgar Lee Masters and Sherwood Anderson chose to emphasize the psychological penalties that small towns inflict on their residents. The fragmentary nature of their works serves as a metaphor for the fate of their characters. In *Main Street*, on the contrary, Sinclair Lewis developed an entire social analysis of rural life. Published, by a nice coincidence, in 1920, the year of that urban census, the novel offered the definitive satire of small-town America. *Main Street* is set in Gopher Prairie, Minnesota, a town based on Sauk Centre, where Lewis had grown up.

Founded only 30 years before he was born, the town was perched on the edge of the prairie, isolated by climate and distance. Wood-frame buildings barely sheltered the few thousand residents from brutal cold in the winter and scorching heat in the summer. Lewis later claimed that he hated the place from his earliest memories. A skinny boy, awkward, with a face blotched by acne and a head full of bright red hair, he felt misplaced in Sauk Centre and relished the role of outsider.

His father, Edwin Lewis, was a physician and a practical man who was embarrassed by his son's eccentricities and had no interest in his writing. Lewis's mother, a teacher, died when he was just six. His father remarried within a year, and his stepmother did what she could to soften Dr. Lewis's rigorous discipline with compassion. She encouraged young Sinclair's reading, in writers from Dickens and Goethe to Kipling and Tolstoy. Lewis attended Yale, where he reaffirmed his commitment to writing. One of his teachers, the legendary William Lyon Phelps, later said that Lewis "was not disliked but was regarded with amiable tolerance as a freak. ... He was a complete and consistent individualist." Lewis would continue to be described in about those terms for the rest of his life. Although he was a mediocre student, Lewis did become editor of the *Yale Literary Magazine*, in which he published a number of apprentice stories. In the decade following graduation, he combined journalism with his own fiction writing. Along with inventing his own stories, he sold plots to Jack London, the self-proclaimed socialist and the famous author of such novels as *The Call of the Wild* and *The Sea- Wolf.* Lewis's first five novels, forgotten books with titles like *Our Mr. Wrenn* and *The Trail of the Hawk*, did little to predict the enormous success that he would earn with *Main Street.*

The reviews of the novel were almost uniformly ecstatic, and several other major writers also praised the book. H. L. Mencken said it was "excellent work." F. Scott Fitzgerald called it "the best American novel" he had ever read. Sales were extraordinary. In 1925, five years after the book's publication, the trade paper *Publishers Weekly* estimated that *Main Street* was the bestselling novel of the entire quarter-century between 1900 and 1925. Lewis's biographer, Richard Lingeman, tells the story of a British visitor to the United States, who remarked to a friend:

> You never entered a railroad car or a trolley car or a restaurant without seeing people reading *Main Street*. When you arrived in a place the reporter did not inquire "What do you think of our city?" but "Have you read *Main Street*?" It was the eternal topic of conversation over the donuts and coffee.

What made the book so popular? Apparently, many Americans were eager to see the myth of the small town deflated. Lewis declares the satiric point before the novel even begins. "This is America," he announces in the first words of a prefatory note. According to Lewis, Gopher Prairie is merely typical, a continuation of Main Streets everywhere. Then, in a famous litany of scorn, Lewis defines *Main Street* as

> the climax of civilization. That this Ford car might stand in front of the Bon Ton Store, Hannibal invaded Rome and Erasmus wrote in Oxford cloisters. What Ole Jenson the grocer says to Ezra Stowbody the banker is the new law for London, Prague, and the unprofitable isles of the sea; whatsoever Ezra does not know and sanction, that thing is heresy, worthless for knowing and wicked to consider.

> Our railway station is the final aspiration of architecture. Sam Clark's annual hardware turnover is the envy of the four counties which constitute God's Country.

As these introductory sentences suggest, there is nothing subtle in the way Lewis goes about dismantling the pretensions of Gopher Prairie. The novel's main character is a young woman named Carol Milford. In the first scene, in 1912, she is standing on a Minnesota hillside, looking over the Mississippi River. Lewis insists on the symbolic significance of the moment. Carol is rebellious but confused. As she lifts her arms up to the sky, she enacts the impatience and ill-defined expectations of youth. She wants more intellectual stimulation than she can find at Blodgett College, a backwater place that is still busy, in the narrator's words, "combating the heresies of Voltaire [and] Darwin." Carol wants to be useful, but she doesn't know how. After graduating from college, she spends a year studying library science in Chicago. Here she throws herself enthusiastically into the cultural and social life of a bustling major city.

When she returns to St. Paul, a slow-moving minor city, she is soon stultified by the tedious routine that comes with her job as a librarian. Carol accepts a proposal of marriage from a young doctor, Will Kennicott, and moves with him to the town of Gopher Prairie. She is motivated in part by her attraction to Will, and in part by her urge to bring civilization to people she thinks of as crude and benighted. On the train ride to the town, Carol is dismayed by the people who will be her neighbors. The narrator says, staying with Carol's point of view: these people

> do not read; apparently they do not think. They wait. ... A soiled man and woman munch sandwiches and throw the crusts on the floor. ... The smell grows constantly thicker, more stale. [One of the passengers is] an old woman whose toothless mouth shuts like a mud-turtle's, and whose hair is not so much white as yellow like moldy linen.

These early scenes also establish the distance between Carol and her husband. Where she sees only ugliness and aesthetic poverty, he sees the prosperity that fertile acres and hard work have brought.

She is still attracted to his confidence and optimism, but she worries that she has married a stranger. Between them, Carol and Will occupy symbolic positions that contrast with almost allegorical precision. Romantic idealism confronts pragmatic realism, a contest that is deeply embedded in the American grain.

As a number of readers have pointed out, *Main Street* has a story but not much of a plot. Lewis is more interested in the messages he wants to convey than in his characters or his narrative. Aside from Carol and Will, most of the book's men and women are thin caricatures. The sequence of events does little more than provide a mechanism for disclosing the moral and intellectual deficiencies of Gopher Prairie. When Carol takes her first tour of the town—a journey of exactly 32 minutes, the narrator tells us—Lewis devotes several pages to an itemized, painstakingly detailed inventory of all the town's sad and disappointing buildings. As she walks down Main Street, Carol passes Dyer's Drug Store, with its "greasy marble soda fountain" and "pawed-over heaps of toothbrushes"—black and overripe bananas in the window of Howland & Gould's Grocery; the "reek of blood" that oozes from Dahl & Oleson's Meat Market; a saloon buzzing with fat, black flies; a clothing store displaying men's suits which, the narrator says, were "flabbily draped on dummies like corpses with painted cheeks."

A significant part of the novel's strength lies in the sheer malicious energy that informs passages like this. Every adjective presses down on Carol's consciousness. Each image adds its symbolic weight to the total. Over time, Carol does discover some of the attractions of her new situation. She finds much more to admire in the countryside around the town. She is moved by the scale of the western landscape and by the dignity of the farmers. In making this contrast between settled place and wilderness, Lewis is once again writing in the American tradition. Since James Fenimore Cooper and the painter Thomas Cole, whom we've discussed, the country's unspoiled but shrinking open land has always served as an emblem of the losses that civilization that brings. Eventually, Carol makes a couple of friends with whom she can share her interest in books and ideas. With her husband's permission, she redecorates the living room of their house. Despite her efforts, however, Carol continues to find herself stifled by the atmosphere of Gopher Prairie. She finds the townsfolk to be "a savorless people, gulping tasteless food ... listening to mechanical music, saying mechanical things about the excellence of Ford automobiles." The pious widow, Mrs. Bogart, pays a call and brings her "Good Influence," capital G, capital I, with her. Not the acid kind of "Good Influence," the narrator tells us, but "the soft, damp, fat, sighing, indigestive, clinging, melancholy, depressingly hopeful kind" of Good Influence.

Once again, Lewis makes his likes, and especially his dislikes, exuberantly clear. In addition to her distaste for the village, Carol is bored. Her small duties as the town doctor's wife occupy only a little of her time. The narrator says that, "she was a woman with a working brain and no work." Her attempts to fit into the trivial bridge games and sewing circles with which the town's women fill their time compound her discontent. The women also do little to conceal their disapproval of her attitudes and behavior. Even her long-suffering husband treats her with a little bit of condescension. He reminds her that the townspeople are his patients, and that she should not offend them.

Throughout the novel, Carol keeps trying to improve the town and its inhabitants. Each scheme fails, defeated by the combination of inertia and provincialism that defines Gopher Prairie. When she proposes a new town hall to the wives of the most prominent men, she is confronted by conflicting schemes: One woman tells Carol that her husband would prefer a church, another dreams of a new school, while yet another would like to see a National Guard armory. Later, when she tries to organize a dramatic society, the results are disastrous. The town's women fall into bickering over who will get which part. Appointed to the library board, Carol quickly realizes that there is nothing she can do to make it better. Worn down by the recalcitrance of the town's opinions, Carol makes repeated if halfhearted efforts to adjust herself better to her neighbors' expectations. She sometimes criticizes herself for treating the citizens of Gopher Prairie with contempt. In the end, however, she cannot adapt to the demands of conformity. In a famous passage two-thirds of the way through the novel, Carroll concludes that the American small town is sunk in what she calls

> an unimaginatively standardized background, a sluggishness of speech and manners, a rigid ruling of the spirit by the desire to appear respectable. It is contentment ... the contentment of the quiet dead, who are scornful of the living for their restless walking. It is negation canonized as the one positive virtue. It is the prohibition of happiness. It is slavery self-sought and self-defended. It is dullness made God.

We have been told that Carol reads modern writers such as Theodore Dreiser, Sherwood Anderson, and H. L. Mencken. She also shares their opinions about rural American life. The preconceptions she brought with her to Gopher Prairie are reinforced by her experience. Rather than community, the village creates a nest of busybodies, especially the women, everyone minding everyone else's business. Nasty gossip provides much of the daily ration of conversation. Will tells Carol, "there's nothing in this town that you don't do in company with a whole lot of uninvited but awful interested guests."

In one of the novel's most celebrated passages, a neighbor of Carol's, a man named Champ Perry, quite cheerfully admits that he is a victim of the disease that afflicts everyone who spends too many years in a town like Gopher Prairie. "I have," he confesses, "the Village Virus." "It sounds dangerous," Carol responds. "It is," says Champ, half-facetiously but half-seriously.

> More dangerous than the cancer that will certainly get me at fifty unless I stop this smoking. The Village Virus is the germ which ... infects ambitious people who stay too long in the provinces ... people who have a glimpse of the world that thinks and laughs but have returned to their swamp.

The phrase "Village Virus" quickly entered the vocabulary of social critics. Despite the novel's antagonism toward traditional heartland complacency, *Main Street* bears little trace of sustained ideological inquiry. The novel brushes up against political issues only once, in the character of the town's handyman, Miles Bjornstam. Miles is a self-professed radical, a reader of Byron and Thorstein Veblen, who simply doesn't care for the opinions of the town's small-minded leading citizens. But Miles does nothing to act on his views. Although his neighbors insult him with the nickname "the Red Swede," the radicalism that Miles represents reaches only to a debate over taste, with no hint of engagement in the affairs of the real world. Much of the novel's action takes place during the First World War. That conflagration forms mainly a distant backdrop to the town's self-absorption. On one occasion, Carol attends church, expecting to hear a sermon on the war. Instead, the preacher talks only about the evils of Mormonism and alcohol.

The novel's focus remains social and domestic. Carol's marriage becomes a barometer of her discontent. She loves Will and often feels pride in his work, but she also finds herself repelled by his identification with the town. She invests much of her affection in her son but harbors vague longings for something more. Carol's frustration eventually prompts her to leave her husband and move to Washington DC with her son. There she finds work in a government office and enjoys the satisfaction of a new-found autonomy. She even takes part in protests for women's suffrage and spends the night in jail. After a year, however, Will shows up, provoking both Carol's renewed affection for him and her sense of obligation. She returns to Gopher Prairie, presumably to accept the fate that she has spent several years trying to escape. Carol's ultimate surrender may imply that her revolt against the village coincides with a good deal of romantic naiveté, but I think the conclusion is more complicated than that.

The narrator consistently treats Carol with generosity, despite the limits that constrain her perceptions. She is the only major character who escapes satiric treatment. In part, this is a matter of gender. In *Main Street* and several other novels, Lewis tried to deal sympathetically with the situation of American women. At one point, Carol says to one of her few close friends:

> I want you to help me find out what has made the darkness of the women. Gray darkness and shadowy trees. We're all in it, ten million women with good prosperous husbands, and business women in linen collars, and grandmothers that gad out to teas, and wives of under-paid miners, and farm wives who really like to make butter and go to church.

Carol has lived through some of the most tumultuous years in American social and political history. Even a partial list of the revolutionary developments in the first two decades of the 20th century would reach from the relativity of Einstein, which overturned centuries of stability in physics, to the advent of cubism and other disruptive developments in art, to the earthquakes of the First World War and the Russian Revolution. In American politics, the 19th Amendment, for which Carol spent a night in jail, was ratified in time to give women the vote in the presidential election of 1920.

While some Americans embraced the prospect of change, others yearned for "a return to normalcy," the campaign slogan on which Warren Harding was elected president in that 1920 campaign. The '20s would prove to be a predominantly conservative temperament, as Calvin Coolidge and Herbert Hoover followed Harding in the White House. The politics of progressivism and populism that had flourished in the pre-war years evaporated. Membership in the Ku Klux Klan surged to record levels.

In short, the debate over values ran wide and deep. Carol has found herself in a completely different but conflicted world, and her confusion about her place is almost inevitable. She knows that Gopher Prairie belongs to the past, but she cannot yet envision the future. Nor does she have the vocabulary to articulate what she wants. After complaining about the darkness in which women find themselves, she can only add: "I think perhaps we want a more conscious life. We're tired of drudging and sleeping and dying. … All we want is—everything and for all of us!" Carol's appeal to "everything" is a cry of frustration, not a program for change, but that frustration is deeply understandable. In the years following the tremendous success of *Main Street*, Lewis published a series of novels that explored what he thought of as America's prevailing pathologies. *Babbitt*, whose title character instantly became a byword for the hustle and materialism of businessmen, appeared in 1922. *Arrowsmith*, published in 1925, opposes an idealistic doctor to a lazy and self-serving medical profession. *Elmer Gantry*, 1927, dedicated to H. L. Mencken, exposes the hypocrisy of a small-time preacher.

In the fall of 1930, Lewis won the Nobel Prize in Literature. He was the first American to receive the prize in the three decades the awards had been given. Some critics and journalists welcomed the honor as Europe's recognition that American writers were now to be regarded as equals. Others complained that Lewis had been singled out because his fiction ratified European stereotypes of American mediocrity. After all, the Swedish Academy had neglected Mark Twain, Henry James, and Theodore Dreiser. In the decades since, Lewis's critics have come to outnumber his supporters. Many of the issues he engaged remain relevant—the ethics of business, the national tendency toward anti-intellectualism, the unsettled question of women's opportunities. A few phrases have proven durable: Main Street, Babbitt, the Village Virus. But Lewis's simplified characters, his repetitive stories, and his broad satiric techniques no longer attract the audience they once enjoyed. Nevertheless, his books, and especially *Main Street*, repay our reading, and they remain valuable documents in American social history.

Lecture Thirteen
The Maltese Falcon

Scope: Mystery stories can be traced back to the ancient world, but most scholars locate the beginnings of the modern literary genre in the work of Edgar Allan Poe in the early 19th century. Several of Poe's stories offered innovative devices that would be copied and repeated by generations of writers, including most prominently Arthur Conan Doyle and Agatha Christie. However, in the years after the First World War, a new, "hardboiled" version of the mystery story emerged, most notably in the work of Dashiell Hammett and Raymond Chandler. These were writers who, in the words of Chandler, describing Hammett, "gave murder back to the kind of people who commit it for reasons." Hammett's *The Maltese Falcon* remains one of the classics in this field. The plot involves a search for the falcon, which leads to a long series of betrayals and murders. It falls to Sam Spade, Hammett's famous private detective, to recover the bird and bring the murderers to justice.

Outline

I. Almost all novels raise questions that involve mysteries, often of an everyday sort. The mystery novel places a question, usually of a more lethal sort, at the center of its plot.

   A. By common consent, the pioneer mystery author was Edgar Allan Poe. Three of Poe's stories provided the template for many subsequent tales of detection: "The Murders in the Rue Morgue," "The Purloined Letter," and "The Mystery of Marie Roget."

      1. All three feature a brilliant French detective, C. Auguste Dupin, who is not part of the regular police and who uses his deductive power to solve each crime.

      2. The narrator of these stories is a less gifted friend who serves as a surrogate for the reader, a man whose admiration for the genius sleuth mirrors our own.

   B. Poe's descendants make a long list, among them Wilkie Collins and Charles Dickens. Arthur Conan Doyle remains the best known of these writers; his sleuth, Sherlock Holmes, is among the best-known fictional characters ever created.

II. The rise of the detective novel coincided with the emergence of the huge and crowded 19th-century city.

    A. An exciting place, the new city was also a place of mystery and danger—especially at night. Detective stories offered a momentary refuge from the perils of urban life.

    B. Regular police forces may not be capable of protecting us from the anonymous criminals that lurk in dark urban places, but we can depend on the intervention of the independent genius who can and will solve every mystery, no matter how difficult.

III. The conventions of traditional detective stories became so predictable that scholars have called them examples of formula fiction. However, following the First World War, a number of writers, principally in America, began to explore a different sort of mystery book.

    A. Led by Dashiell Hammett and Raymond Chandler, these writers developed what would be called the "hardboiled" school of detective fiction. The first examples appeared in "the pulps," cheap magazines such as *Black Mask* that featured large doses of sex and violence.

    B. According to Chandler, Hammett "gave murder back to the kind of people that commit it for reasons, not just to provide a corpse." Chandler also insisted that Hammett's characters spoke in a realistic language, not the artificial style of melodrama.

    C. Hammett, Chandler, and the other tough-guy writers wanted to transform the mystery story by joining it to the great realist tradition. Where the older detective conventions provided reassurance that reason could triumph over evil, the new variant pulled the reader deeper into the murky underside of modern urban life.

IV. Dashiell Hammett brought the right background to his mystery writing.

    A. A high school dropout, he took on a series of odd jobs as a teenager before joining the Pinkerton Detective Agency in 1915.

    B. He spent three years as a Pinkerton operative before joining the army near the end of the First World War.

        1. He never got to Europe but contracted a nearly fatal case of influenza in the worldwide epidemic that followed the war.

        2. While recovering, he contracted tuberculosis, which would weaken him for the rest of his life.

C. When he decided to devote himself full-time to writing, he chose the detective genre, in part because his background provided the expertise he needed.

V. *The Maltese Falcon* was Hammett's second novel. An immediate success in its own day, it was also the first crime novel to be included in the Modern Library series.

    A. *Falcon* is set in San Francisco, and the action takes place over a few days in December 1928.

    B. The story's hero, Sam Spade, would become one of the best-known characters in American fiction. Spade exerts an effortless control over every situation in which he finds himself.

    C. The book opens in the office that Spade shares with his partner, Miles Archer.

        1. A beautiful woman who calls herself Miss Wonderly hires them, allegedly to rescue her sister from a predatory man.

        2. That night, Archer is shot and killed. From that point, the novel's plot involves a series of intertwined mysteries: Who killed Miles Archer, and what is the connection between that murder and a mysterious black statuette?

        3. In the course of the novel, Wonderly—real name Brigid O'Shaughnessy—will form a romantic attachment.

    D. Spade's search for answers leads him into dangerous contact with an entire rogue's gallery of big-time gangsters and small-time hoodlums.

        1. The most colorful is Casper Gutman, a witty, unscrupulous, and enormously fat man.

        2. He is the one who tells Spade the statuette's background: a jewel-encrusted, golden treasure sent as a gift in the 16th century from the Maltese Knights of Saint John to Emperor Charles V.

    E. Playing one gangster off against another, Spade ultimately solves the mysteries and delivers the criminals to the police.

    F. Having figured out that O'Shaughnessy was Archer's killer, he turns her over as well, despite her appeals to his love for her.

        1. In a famous concluding speech, he also explains the elementary code of justice that motivates his behavior.

        2. In the shrunken morality of the modern world, this personal loyalty is as deep a commitment as Spade can make.

Suggested Reading:

Johnson, *Dashiell Hammett.*

Symons, *Dashiell Hammett.*

Questions to Consider:

1. The novel's famous final scene, in which Sam Spade refuses to protect Brigid O'Shaughnessy from justice, has provoked a good deal of critical discussion. Does Spade's explanation seem plausible? More generally, does his behavior in this scene seem consistent with his character throughout the rest of the novel? In what sense, if any, can Spade be considered a heroic figure?

2. There are just three important female characters in *The Maltese Falcon*: Brigid O'Shaughnessy, Effie Perine, and Iva Archer. What aspects of gender does each of these women represent? Are they defined in strictly stereotypical terms, or do any of them receive a more complex treatment?

Lecture Thirteen—Transcript
The Maltese Falcon

Almost all novels have an element of mystery built into them. Think about the interesting word "plot." On the one hand, it signifies the story line of a novel or play. On the other hand, "plot" can refer to a conspiracy, whose unknown purpose only gradually becomes clear. That double meaning is built into the art of fiction. Jane Austin's novels, to give a well-bred example, are shrewd anatomies of the customs and manners of life in early 19th-century provincial England, but they are also carefully plotted. We read them not just for the local pleasures of Austin's language, but also to see how they turn out. We want to learn: Who will marry whom? The mystery genre takes the portion of suspense that inhabits almost all fiction and puts it into the foreground. In this case, the plots are literally the plots, if I may put it like that. Some readers, among whom I count myself, love them. Others, to put it mildly, don't. The esteemed critic Edmund Wilson didn't. In 1945, Wilson wrote an essay with the provocative title, "Who Cares Who Killed Roger Ackroyd?" The reference was to Agatha Christie's celebrated mystery novel, *The Murder of Roger Ackroyd*. The answer Wilson offered to his own rhetorical question was: Nobody should care who killed Roger Ackroyd. As Wilson put it:

> How can you care who committed a murder which has never really been made to take place, because the writer hasn't any ability of even the most ordinary kind to persuade you to see it or feel it? How can you probe the possibilities of guilt among characters who all seem alike, because they are all simply names on [a] page?

A few paragraphs later in the essay, Wilson described the reading of mystery fiction as "a kind of vice that, for silliness and minor harmfulness, ranks somewhere between smoking and crossword puzzles." (Wilson didn't yet know how bad smoking was.)

If mystery stories are a vice, they have proven to be an extremely addictive bad habit. Scholars have estimated that as many as 1 out of every 10 novels published in the United States today can be categorized as a mystery of some sort. The appetite that these books feed is apparently insatiable, and it is by no means exclusively American. Georges Simenon, a Belgian, published at least 400 titles, sometimes working on several stories at once. Messengers ran back and forth between his apartment and his publishers' offices. Englishwoman Agatha Christie's crime stories have sold an estimated 1 billion copies. The works of both of these writers have been translated into over 50 languages, suggesting the global reach of this addiction. Why have these sorts of books been so popular? For some possible answers, we need to look back briefly on the history of the genre. While mysteries can be found in texts reaching from classical Greece and Rome through the 18th century, the formal beginnings of the modern detective story are usually traced to Edgar Allan Poe.

Almost all of Poe's fiction contains elements of the mysterious or uncanny. However, in the course of his brief career, he produced three stories that specifically anticipate the mystery tale as it would develop over the 19th century: "The Murders in the Rue Morgue," "The Purloined Letter," and "The Mystery of Marie Roget." All these tales feature a French detective named C. Auguste Dupin. In his first appearance in Poe's fiction, he is called in to investigate the brutal murder of two women in a flat on the Rue Morgue in Paris. There seems to be no way for a murderer to get in or leave the shabby apartment. Nor did the women murder each other. If you don't know the solution to this puzzle, I encourage you to read Poe's story. Our interest is not in the answer, but in the character of the detective, and the means he takes to solve the crime. Dupin foretells the mystery story's typical sleuth. He is a brilliant polymath, a mathematician of considerable power who, says the narrator, "is fond of enigmas, of conundrums, of hieroglyphics." He is an outsider who uses his genius to earn his living. Most important, Dupin is intellectually superior to the regular police forces of Paris and uses his sheer deductive power to dominate their plodding procedures. These qualities will also attach to his fictional successors. Along with the typical detective, Poe also invented a narrative strategy that would prove quite influential. Dupin does not tell of his own exploits. Instead, the unnamed narrator of the Dupin stories is a companion, a far less-gifted man who stands as surrogate for the general public and specifically for the reader. The narrator's gasps of amazement at the detective's brilliant deductions are those the reader is supposed to share.

Poe's first major descendants were English: writers such as Wilkie Collins in *The Moonstone*, and Charles Dickens, whose last unfinished novel was *The Mystery of Edwin Drood*. Fabricating an ending for *Edwin Drood*, by the way, has become a veritable cottage industry. Dozens of writers—if not scores of writers—have tried their hand, producing serious books, comedies, parodies, and travesties by turns. This more than century-long obsession is another proof of the mystery story's wide appeal.

But it was, above all, Arthur Conan Doyle who brought the apparatus of the detective story to maturity. Similarities between the works of Poe and Doyle are extensive. Sherlock Holmes, like Dupin, is a man of superior intellect, who uses the limitless power of his reasoning to solve crimes that consistently baffle Scotland Yard. His adventures are recorded and published by his friend and colleague, the fiercely loyal but rather slow-witted physician, John H. Watson. As several scholars have pointed out, the rise of the detective story coincided with the emergence of an urban and machine-driven society. Beginning in Europe in the late 18th century, the Industrial Revolution transformed human experience. The powers that were unleashed—first by steam, later by electricity—were both awesome and mysterious. The consequences were profound, especially for inhabitants of the vast new cities that industrialism engendered. Cities were exhilarating but also frightening places. On the one hand, they were associated with the art, and music, and culture that really defined civilization, but they were also identified with crowding, dirt, and crime. So many pickpockets, thieves, and hooligans with so many places to hide. In the 19th century, the English writer James Thomson published a celebrated poem called *The City of Dreadful Night*, which summarizes the theme of the poem pretty well. It was in London, at that time the largest city in the world, that Robert Peel in 1829 organized the first modern police force. In other words, while Poe's Auguste Dupin, Doyle's Sherlock Holmes, and their various imitators provided entertainment, they also perhaps enacted a widespread desire for security from the dangers of modern life. The conventional forces of law and order may fail to protect us from our adversaries, but we might find safety through the intervention of an individual genius.

Confronted by mysteries that reduce ordinary mortals to terrified confusion, the detective demonstrates the irresistible power of logic and reason. It may only be a dream of the triumph of good over evil, but it has proven to be a seductive dream. Although the classic detective is an outsider, he is reliably benevolent. Sherlock Holmes could have chosen to live isolated and comfortable in his own furnished rooms. Instead, he is committed to the defense of society and order. To be sure, he earns a good living from his trade, and he derives a good deal of satisfaction from the chase, but the money and the chase are ultimately less important than the abolition of evil. Holmes occasionally breaks the law, but only in pursuit of justice. As many readers have pointed out, there is something godlike about the way Holmes stands above ordinary legal considerations.

Arthur Conan Doyle was once asked if Poe had influenced him. He answered immediately: "Oh, immensely! His detective is the best detective in fiction." Like Dupin, Holmes is preternaturally intelligent, and his deductions seem miraculous to his less-brilliant companion, Watson. Doyle, in his turn, influenced dozens of later writers, who reproduced many of the same techniques and devices. Perhaps the most familiar was a cluster of authors who dominated what is sometimes called "the golden age" of detective fiction in the 1920s and '30s: along with Agatha Christie, a group that includes Dorothy Sayers, Margery Allingham, Josephine Tey, John Dickson Carr, and Ellery Queen. These writers have differences, to be sure, but they all produced versions of the same story. A body is found—in the drawing room, in the garden, in the conservatory—the police are helpless. The amateur sleuth gathers the clues, sorts them out while discarding the red herring, and announces the identity of the murderer in the last chapter— amazement and applause all around. Scholars have called these kinds of detective stories examples of formula fiction. The formulas persist because they provide readers with dependable points of reference. The expectations that readers bring to a classic mystery story are well-defined, and writers violate those expectations at their peril.

In 1928, Ronald Knox, a mystery writer and a theorist of the form, actually laid out 10 rules for detective stories: no supernatural agents, no clues concealed from the reader, no more than one secret passage per story, and so on. Knox was only partly serious, but his list did gather together the conventions that governed most detective fiction. It was all good fun, and for millions of readers it continues to provide entertainment and escape. However, in the years after the First World War, a number of writers, especially in the United States, pushed the detective story in a different direction. Chief among them were Dashiell Hammett and Raymond Chandler, whose work defined a new style in mystery writing—what became known as the "hard-boiled" school. The younger Americans published many of their stories in "the pulps," as they were called, cheap magazines printed on pulpy paper and having sale prices of a dime or 15 cents. *Black Mask* was the most celebrated, a monthly founded in 1920 that featured action, violence, proletarian heroes and villains, and generous helpings of sexual titillation. (Sex had been scrupulously excluded from the classic puzzle mystery.)

The hard-boiled writers took their jobs seriously. In a famous essay called "The Simple Art of Murder," Raymond Chandler said that his friend, Dashiell Hammett:

gave murder back to the kind of people that commit it for reasons, not just to provide a corpse; and with the means at hand, not with hand-wrought dueling pistols, curare, and tropical fish.

He put these people down on paper as they are, and he made them talk and think in the language they customarily used for [the] purposes. He had style, but his audience didn't know it, because it was a language not supposed to be capable of such refinements. They thought they were getting a good meaty melodrama written in the kind of lingo they imagined they spoke themselves. It was, in a sense, but it was much more.

Chandler's sneering references to "hand-wrought dueling pistols" and "tropical fish" are intended to contrast Hammett's realism to the contrived artifice of country-house mystery writers, such as Agatha Christie and Dorothy Sayers. The bodies that Hercule Poirot and Lord Peter Wimsey deal with are mere stage properties, riddles to be solved. Hammett's bodies, on the contrary, are the corpses of human beings, shot or strangled for genuine and often sordid human motives. Beyond that, Chandler's emphasis on speech sounds familiar. In an earlier lecture in this course, I referred to Mark Twain's attack on James Fenimore Cooper. As you may recall, Twain's chief complaint was directed at Cooper's language. The laws of fiction, Twain wrote, "require that when the personages of a tale deal in conversation, the talk shall sound like human [beings] talk, and be talk such as human beings would be likely to talk in the given circumstances." Twain was making the same charge against Cooper that Chandler was lodging against the authors of the classic detective novel—that is to say, both Twain and Chandler were arguing for literary realism. Where the older puzzle mystery offered escape from life's dangers and insecurity, the hard-boiled story pulled the reader deeper into the murky underside of modern urban life. The point was not to evade the threats that hovered over daily experience but to confront them.

This, in turn, required a different sort of detective. Sam Spade and Philip Marlowe, and the dozens of others who followed them, share a couple of qualities with their more elegant predecessors. They are typically loners, and they usually, if not always, line up with the forces of justice. But they are not supermen nor even particularly heroic. They are flawed, fallible, and frequently outsmarted, at least temporarily. They suffer violence, and they don't hesitate to dish out violence in return. As Chandler's compliments suggest, Hammett was the first major practitioner of the new fiction. Several of the stories Hammett published in *Black Mask* in the '20s featured a fat, unnamed agent called simply the Continental Op, or "operator." The Op embodies Hammett's exploration of a new kind of detective: cynical, opportunistic, not too far removed from the criminals he tracks down. He says on several occasions that he hunts gangsters and murderers simply because he enjoys it. Encouraged by the success of his stories, Hammett published five novels in just five years, beginning with *Red Harvest* in 1929, and concluding with *The Thin Man* in 1934. The tough-guy tone of the books is evident on the first page of *Red Harvest*, when the Continental Op checks out a city street:

> The first policeman I saw needed a shave. The second had a couple of buttons off his shabby uniform. The third stood in the center of the city's main intersection—Broadway and Union Street—directing traffic, with a cigar in one corner of his mouth.

Hammett came by his detective credentials honestly. He had dropped out of high school in Baltimore after one semester, and then moved through a series of odd jobs to help the family. In 1915, he signed on with the Pinkerton Detective Agency. He worked as a Pinkerton operative for three years, leaving to join the army near the end of the First World War. He never got to Europe, but he almost died in the great influenza epidemic that followed. As he recovered from the flu, he contracted tuberculosis, which would weaken him for the rest of his life. Living precariously on a military pension and the small checks he could earn cranking out advertising copy, Hammett turned to writing, and he chose detective fiction because he knew something about the business. *The Maltese Falcon* was Hammett's second novel, and the one that remains the best known. Among its other distinctions, *Falcon* was the first crime novel to be reprinted in the Modern Library, and it has also been included more recently in the prestigious Library of America series. Hammett wrote a preface for the Modern Library edition, which consists mainly of connections between the book's characters and people Hammett had known in his Pinkerton years. The identifications may or may not be true, and they don't help much in reading the novel. The point of the exercise was to demonstrate Hammett's experience and expertise.

The book's success was also attested by Hollywood's repeated use of the material. *The Maltese Falcon* was adapted three times in the 10 years after it was published. The third version—produced by Warner Brothers in 1941 and starring Humphrey Bogart, Mary Astor, Sydney Greenstreet, and Peter Lorre—is universally acknowledged as a superlative example of American film noir.

Falcon takes place in San Francisco, over a few days in early December 1928. Sam Spade, the detective, has much more physical appeal than the Continental Op. Hammett said that Spade was the man private detectives would like to be: attractive to women, quick with a smart remark, "a hard and shifty fellow, able to take care of himself in any situation." Over the decades since the publication of *Falcon*, Spade has become one of the best-known characters in American fiction. The story commences with a meeting between Spade and a woman named Brigid O'Shaughnessy, who calls herself Miss Wonderly. For 200 dollars, O'Shaughnessy hires Spade and his partner, Miles Archer, to follow a man named Floyd Thursby, who she claims has more or less kidnapped her younger sister. Archer, who has spent the interview leering at Wonderly, takes the assignment. At two o'clock in the morning, Spade receives a call from the police: Archer has been found shot dead, with his gun still in his pocket. Spade immediately goes to warn Archer's widow, Iva, with whom he has been having an affair, that the cops will soon be arriving. If she shot Miles, he tells her, she had better prepare her story. The rest of the novel revolves around two intertwined mysteries: who killed Miles Archer, and what is the connection between the murder and a mysterious black statuette that O'Shaughnessy wants to find. She tells Spade about it, after confessing that her name is not Wonderly. She also admits that she lied about Thursby, which provokes one of the book's famous exchanges. Spade assures her: "We didn't exactly believe your story. ... We believed your two hundred dollars."

When she tells Spade her new version, a ripping yarn that leads from an exiled Russian aristocrat to the docks of Hong Kong, Spade says he suspects that at least some of it is probably true. At about this point, Hammett also introduces the novel's longest digression. Spade tells O'Shaughnessy about a case he had worked on some years earlier. A man named Flitcraft, a successful real estate salesman in Tacoma, disappeared back in 1922. His wife hires Spade to find her husband. When Spade tracks him down, five years later, Flitcraft is living in Spokane under a new name, remarried, selling cars, and making a decent wage. He tells Spade that he had disappeared after a peculiar accident. Walking down a Tacoma street, he was nearly killed when a beam fell off a building and narrowly missed him. He said, according to the narrator, "He felt like somebody had taken the lid off life and let him look at the works." Life, he concluded, is a series of random, unexplainable events. So, Flitcraft decided to behave accordingly.

The story seems to be a diversion, but the thematic implications are altogether relevant. Flitcraft's narrative exemplifies the idea that life is not arranged in neat causal patterns. Instead, things happen, sometimes for reasons, sometimes not. Hammett is deliberately introducing into his novel a rebuke to the moral assumptions of the classic detective story. Rationality will not always ensure solutions. There is an intractable and real mystery lying underneath the entertaining and fictional mysteries of a novel.

Spade's search for the statue leads him into dangerous contact with a whole rogue's gallery of big-time gangsters and small-time hoodlums. Returning from a meeting with O'Shaughnessy, Spade discovers a small, perfumed man, Joel Cairo, searching his office. Cairo points a gun at Spade, who simply takes it away, beats Cairo up, and manages to gather a bit of information about the black bird, and about a mysterious man named Gutman. In the next major scene, Spade has both Cairo and O'Shaughnessy in his apartment. As they argue, Lieutenant Dundy and Sergeant Polhaus arrive, demanding entry. Spade refuses, but they push their way in when Cairo calls for help. The cops ask their questions, Dundy telling Spade he is a liar for denying his affair with Iva Archer. Frustrated by Spade's refusal to cooperate, Dundy punches him, and Polhaus has to step in to keep Spade from hitting back. The episode is thematically important, emphasizing the tension between the private detective and the police. That antagonism had been built into the traditional mystery story, but it had been playful and ultimately superficial. On the contrary, Dundy and Spade genuinely despise each other. The hostility between them symbolizes Hammett's contempt for the official forces of law and order. A private agent like Spade, with his mixed motives and his eccentricity, is a better protector of justice than the San Francisco Police Department.

The following day, Spade meets the novel's chief bad guy and its most colorful character. Casper Gutman is witty and unscrupulous, several hundred pounds of flesh wrapped in elegant clothes.

> His eyes [the narrator says] made small by fat puffs around them, were dark and sleek. Dark ringlets thinly covered his broad scalp. He wore a black cutaway coat, black vest, black satin Ascot tie holding a pinkish pearl, striped grey worsted trousers, and patent-leather shoes.

Gutman looks like a clown, but he is lethal. The first meeting between the two men is inconclusive. The next day, Gutman summons Spade to his hotel again. In a long and famous set piece, he tells Spade the Falcon's history. It is a fabulous black statuette made of gold and encrusted with precious gems. It was created in the 16th century as a gift from the Maltese

Knights of Saint John to the Emperor Charles V. The foot-high statue went missing on its journey to the emperor. Seized by a pirate who took it to Algiers, it has moved from one owner to another for 400 years. The value of the object is almost literally incalculable.

Spade lies that O'Shaughnessy has the bird and that he can deliver it, and he and Gutman negotiate over terms. But at that point, Spade realizes that his drink has been drugged, and he falls unconscious to the floor. He gets back to his apartment, sleeps for a couple of hours, then goes to the District Attorney's office for an informal conversation. Once again, Hammett underlines the distance between Spade and the authorities. Angry at the hectoring to which he is subjected by the DA and his assistant, Spade tells them: "I've had trouble with both of you before. As far as I can see, my best chance of clearing myself of the trouble you're trying to make for me is by bringing in the murderers—all tied up." In the novel's final chapters, Spade does indeed bring in the murderers. He learns that O'Shaughnessy has gone to meet the ship *La Paloma*, arriving from Hong Kong. Before Spade can follow, a giant man walks in, carrying a package, and falls dead, a knife in his back. Spade will learn that he is Captain Jacobi. The package, wrapped in sheets of newspaper, is the statuette. Spade checks the bird into a storage facility, mails the key to a post office box, and returns to his apartment for the climactic showdown. All the main characters are present. Spade points out that both he and Gutman need a fall guy, somebody to give to the police for the various murders. Spade nominates Gutman's bodyguard, a sociopath named Wilmer, and Gutman agrees. With the pressure rising, the group waits till morning, when Spade calls his secretary, Effie, with instructions on how to retrieve the package. When Effie arrives with the bird, Gutman scrapes away a portion of the black paint and finds only lead underneath. The statue is a fake. Undaunted, Gutman announces that he will now travel to Istanbul to continue the search.

At this point, the novel takes its last turn. Spade tells O'Shaughnessy that he knows she killed Miles Archer. When she confesses, he tells her that he is going to turn her over to the police. Appealing to the relationship that has developed between them, O'Shaughnessy pleads with Spade for protection. She gets him to admit that Archer was no good. Spade repeats that he is going to send her over, and his explanation articulates a kind of code. "Listen. When a man's partner is killed he's supposed to do something about it. It doesn't make any difference what you thought of him. He was your partner and you're supposed to do something about it." Spade's speech doesn't reach to the high abstraction of concepts like justice or truth. Rather like Hemingway, Hammett had grown skeptical of such words. His detective makes his peace with the world's inevitable disorder by working within the rules of his small terrain. He had a partner who was killed, and it is his job to do something. In the shrunken morality of the modern world, that is as deep a commitment as he can make.

The Maltese Falcon has had a long afterlife. Hammett's mean streets and skeptical moral attitudes do not express the whole of 20th-century America's imagination. But the plots, themes, and above all the world-weary tone of both narrator and characters undeniably captured some portion of a disillusioned modern sensibility.

Lecture Fourteen
The Good Earth

Scope: Pearl S. Buck's second novel, *The Good Earth* (1931), was foreign in concept and culture to mainstream America. Told chronologically, the novel follows the trials and tribulations of a Chinese farmer named Wang Lung from his wedding day until his death, while connecting his story to the larger framework of Chinese history. Buck's unique perspective sets the novel apart, that of an author who lived most of her life in China as a racial minority but whose firsthand experience imbued the novel with authenticity. While Buck's literary techniques were generally conventional, her subject matter and her stance toward her material was nearly revolutionary, and her portrait of rural China would prove to have a remarkable influence. *The Good Earth* was the first title to be named the bestselling American novel for two consecutive years. It also won the Pulitzer Prize and was the first American novel set in Asia to become a bestseller. In 1938, Buck became the third American, and first American woman, awarded the Nobel Prize in Literature.

Outline

I. Pearl S. Buck was born in West Virginia in 1892 to a Southern Presbyterian couple who were missionaries in China. She would spend most of her next 40 years in a number of cities and towns in the Yangtze Valley.

   A. Tutored from an early age in both English and Chinese, she was bilingual and, as she put it, "culturally bifocal."

   B. Buck would return to the United States to earn a college degree at Randolph-Macon Woman's College. She intended to remain in America but was needed back in China to nurse her mother through a final illness.

   C. She married her first husband, J. Lossing Buck, and lived with him among impoverished farmers in the rural Anhwei Province. These experiences provided material for many of Buck's stories and novels.

D. Up through the 1920s, Americans knew practically nothing of China, or Asia in general.

    1. In the early 1880s, the U.S. Congress passed the Chinese Exclusion Act, driven in part by domestic labor opposition to immigrant competitors and cultural misconceptions.

    2. Prior to *The Good Earth*, American writers and readers had reduced Asian people to simplifying and insulting stereotypes.

II. Within such a framework of ignorance, Buck's *The Good Earth* was revolutionary in its attempt to portray Chinese characters as human beings, not simply caricatures. The novel's plot is simple but filled with events, following the life of its principal character, Wang Lung.

  A. The structure is chronological, and Wang Lung's triumphs and defeats map the encounter between traditional China and the revolutionary future.

  B. Wang Lung is a deeply traditional figure, shaped by the generations his family has lived on the land. Land constitutes the core of Wang Lung's identity and motives. Despite the famines, floods, locusts, and bandits that repeatedly victimize his family, Wang Lung knows that only the land endures.

  C. As the son of a poor farmer, Wang Lung must buy a slave for his wife. O-lan becomes the novel's most memorable character, imbued with great strength of character despite her difficulties.

    1. O-lan embodied realities Buck had observed firsthand growing up in China. Her appraisal of Chinese women's plight within a sexual caste system is personified in O-lan.

    2. O-lan works the land with Wang Lung every day, helping him to become affluent enough to purchase acreage from the corrupt House of Hwang.

  D. The sudden onset of a killing famine terminates Wang Lung's newfound success and reduces the entire countryside to misery and starvation.

    1. As things worsen, many women in the village resort to female infanticide. O-lan herself smothers a newborn baby girl.

    2. The drought drives thousands of farmers off the land; these refugees, including Wang Lung and his family, flee to Nanking to seek relief.

E. By staying close to Wang Lung's perspective, Buck sympathetically recreates the limits of an uneducated and illiterate peasant consciousness.

    1. Revolutionaries and missionaries confound Wang Lung; for him, the abstractions of politics and religion are meaningless.

    2. He only knows hunger and poverty, and his single ambition is to return to his land.

III. In the next sequence of chapters, blind chance once again intervenes, this time restoring Wang Lung's fortunes. And yet his rise in status is mirrored by his fall from integrity.

  A. O-lan discovers a hidden cache of jewelry while swept up with a looting mob; she brings it to Wang Lung and the sale of the jewels allows the family to return to their land.

  B. When Wang Lung's wealth grows, he buys the great house of the Hwangs, a symbolic affirmation of the scale of his success. He begins to behave like a rich man, however: more interested in pleasure than work.

    1. He criticizes his loyal wife, O-lan, and her plain appearance while lavishing his mistress, Lotus, with attention and gifts.

    2. Wang Lung's punishment for his extravagance comes when he discovers his eldest son is also visiting Lotus. He banishes the young man, thereby threatening the family's stability.

  C. Wang Lung's moral decay is underscored by O-lan's death: Her life of duty and fidelity contrasts sharply with his decline.

  D. The family, central to Wang Lung's conception of his own identity, becomes instead a cause and emblem of his anxieties and regrets.

  E. The novel's final section is a kaleidoscope of natural calamity and political turmoil.

    1. An epic flood destroys his farms; then his house is taken over by the revolutionary army.

    2. Wang Lung survives, but a prophecy of disaster is embedded in his final scene with his two eldest sons. As he begs his sons not to sell the land that defines them as a family, it is clear that they are contemptuous of their peasant father and his traditional values.

IV. Although Buck's literary techniques were generally conventional and even old-fashioned, her subject matter and the stance she took toward her material were close to revolutionary.

    A. *The Good Earth* became the first volume of a trilogy. The direct sequel, *Sons*, was published in 1932. The third volume, *A House Divided* (1935), follows the family through its third generation, emphasizing the disintegration of Wang Lung's legacy.

    B. Buck's other works included other novels and a number of political essays, some of which attacked British imperialism and American racial discrimination.

        1. She was an outspoken activist on many different issues, including the plight of displaced and handicapped children.

        2. In her activism, Buck consistently displayed the instinctive sympathy for others that she had demonstrated in *The Good Earth* and her other novels about China.

Suggested Reading:

Conn, *Pearl S. Buck.*

Spencer, *The Exile's Daughter.*

Questions to Consider:

1. One of the novel's central concerns is the status and role of women in Chinese society. In what respects is *The Good Earth* a feminist book? In what respects does it seem to endorse traditional values? Why is the novel told from the point of view of the main male character, Wang Lung? Why does O-lan die little more than halfway through the story?

2. *The Good Earth* exerted a decisive influence on Western perceptions of China for several decades following its publication in 1931. What did readers infer about Chinese society from the novel? Do the cultural themes still seem relevant?

Lecture Fourteen—Transcript
The Good Earth

One of the tasks that novels have frequently performed is to take readers to places they have never been, where they can learn about people they would not otherwise know. Among the books we have discussed, several could be described in these terms. *The Last of the Mohicans* and *The Virginian* give us homebodies access to a vanished frontier life. When we read *Huckleberry Finn*, we share for a while in the bygone world of the Mississippi River in the great age of the steamboat. *The Jungle* compels us to share in the miseries of abused workers in settings that I assume few of us have visited except through the workings of Upton Sinclair's imagination, and even *The Maltese Falcon* introduces us to a stylized but unforgettable underworld of shadow and sudden death.

Pearl Buck's *The Good Earth* can claim a similar accomplishment. The novel is set in a part of the world that most of her readers, especially in the first half of the 20th century, had never seen. Her achievement was to make an unfamiliar culture approachable and accessible to Western readers, almost literally for the first time. Pearl Buck was nearly 40 years old when she published her first novel, *East Wind, West Wind*, in 1930. That book earned friendly but lowkey reviews and sold a not-too-bad few thousand copies. At the time, Buck remained an unknown person, living obscurely in the midsized Chinese city of Nanjing (Nanking as it was then called), thousands of miles away from the mainstream of American publicity and celebrity. That situation changed dramatically the following year, with the publication of Buck's second novel, *The Good Earth*. It was a main selection of the Book-of-the-Month Club, which helped its extraordinary sales. Indeed, on several occasions, the publisher had to borrow copies from the book club's inventory to meet bookstore demand. *The Good Earth* was the first work of fiction to be named the bestselling American novel for two consecutive years, 1931 and 1932. The book won the Pulitzer Prize in its year, and, in 1935, it won the William Dean Howells Medal as the best work of American fiction published in the first half of the 1930s decade. (Buck's competitors for the Howells Medal, by the way, included Hemingway, Dos Passos, and Faulkner.) *The Good Earth* has since sold tens of millions of copies, in English and in more than 70 translations. According to a United Nations survey conducted in the 1960s, Pearl Buck was at that time the most frequently translated of all American writers.

In the fall of 2004, Buck's novel returned to the bestseller list when it was featured on Oprah's Book Club. *The Good Earth* received exceptionally strong notices in every leading newspaper and magazine in the country. Many of the reviews paid particular tribute to the authenticity with which the novel presented its Chinese subject matter. To be sure, since most of those earlier reviewers had no firsthand experience in China, they were hardly authorities on the facts of Chinese society. What they more precisely meant was that *The Good Earth* presented its Asian characters as people who transcended stereotypes and behaved as recognizable and even ordinary men and women. *The New York Times*, for example, concluded that Pearl Buck had created "a China in which, happily, there is no hint of mystery or exoticism. There is very little in her book of the quality which we are accustomed to label 'Oriental.' "

The authority of *The Good Earth* was anchored in Buck's long, firsthand experience in China. Her parents were a badly matched pair of Southern Presbyterians named Absalom and Carie Sydenstricker. The dogmatic Absalom would ultimately spend over 50 years itinerating around the Chinese countryside, preaching an alien gospel to farmers who rarely expressed the slightest interest. Having traveled to China with her evangelizing husband, Carie Sydenstricker found herself trapped in loneliness and sadness for the rest of her life. Both parents exerted considerable influence on their remarkable daughter. Pearl would inherit her father's fierce determination, though she would leave his Christian commitments behind. For her part, Carie's poignant example of unrewarded female self-sacrifice taught Pearl to insist on her own needs and priorities as a woman in a man's world.

Pearl was one of the three Sydenstricker children, out of seven, who survived to adulthood. She was born in Hillsboro, West Virginia, in 1892 when her parents were on a home leave. She was taken to China at three months and lived there most of the next 40 years, mainly in a number of cities and towns in the Yangtze Valley. Compared with the childhood of other Americans, Pearl's was extraordinary. Tutored from early childhood in both English and Chinese, she grew up bilingual and, as she liked to say, "culturally bifocal." In her 40 years in China, she was a firsthand witness to the making of modern Chinese history. She lived through the Boxer Uprising of 1900, the last days of the Qing Dynasty and the reign of the Dowager Empress, the 1911 Revolution that ended over 2,000 years of monarchy, the modernizing Science and Democracy Movement, the Nanking Incident of 1927, the early years of the civil war between

Nationalists and Communists, the Japanese invasion of Manchuria in 1931, and the Japanese bombing of Shanghai in 1932. After centuries of relative stability, China was convulsed by unprecedented change during the decades that Pearl Buck lived there.

In the midst of her long residence, she returned to the United States for four years to earn a degree at Randolph-Macon Woman's College. She had intended to remain in America, but returned to China immediately after graduation in 1914 to nurse her mother through her final illness. She married her first husband, the agricultural economist J. Lossing Buck, and lived with him for several years in rural Anhwei province. Her experience among the impoverished farmers of Anhwei provided the materials for many of Buck's novels, including *The Good Earth*. The book's exceptional popularity requires some comment. *The Good Earth* was the first American novel set in Asia to become a bestseller. Indeed, over 20 publishers had rejected Buck's first book, *East Wind, West Wind*, in large part because the market for Chinese material was believed to be non-existent. Up through the 1920s, Americans knew next to nothing about China—or any other Asian country. Travel was difficult, language barriers were insurmountable, and incomprehension prevailed—in both directions. For its part, China may have been, in the opinion of historian Warren Cohen, "the most ethnocentric people in the world." In the 18th century, the Ch'ien-lung Emperor famously declared: "Our celestial empire possesses all things in prolific abundance and lacks no product within its borders. There is therefore no need to import the manufactures of outside barbarians. America through most of its history has been equally insular and inward-looking. Europe figured in the American imagination mainly because Americans—many of them, most of them—traced their ancestry back to one or another European nation. Separated by a vast ocean from Asia, American politicians and public had little interest in acquiring knowledge of any Asian society. Not too many years before the Second World War, a Harvard survey concluded that most Americans couldn't identify China on an outline map. I hope that is not still true today.

Of the few interactions that occurred through the 19th century, most were hostile and merely emphasized the immense Pacific distance between East and West. In the early 1880s, the U.S. Congress passed the Chinese Exclusion Act, which effectively prohibited immigration from China. The law would be renewed and enforced for over 60 years. This act of discrimination was driven in part by domestic labor's opposition to immigrant competitors and in part by cultural misconceptions.

In 1900, American opinions were inflamed by reports of the Boxer Uprising, usually termed the Boxer Rebellion at that time, in which bands of Chinese Nationalists took up arms against Westerners, including missionaries. The suppression of the Chinese by a coalition of Western and Japanese armies, along with the punitive compensation that was imposed, further poisoned relations.

Literature tended to reflect the same prejudices as politics. Prior to *The Good Earth*, American citizens and writers alike had reduced Asian people to a cluster of simplifying stereotypes, most of them insulting. The Chinese were dishonest, cruel, and inscrutable. They were addicted to opium and delighted in bizarre tortures. Their society was backward and decadent. In the absence of accurate knowledge, Americans replaced Chinese reality with stick figures of vice and immorality, transforming Asians into caricatures, either villains like Fu Manchu or sly tricksters like a man named Ah Sin, the title character of Bret Harte's "The Heathen Chinee." Harte's Ah Sin was followed by such figures as Earl Derr Biggers's detective Charlie Chan, who made his debut in a thriller called *A House Without a Key* in 1925, and John P. Marquand's Japanese agent Mr. Moto, also popular in the years between the wars. It should be acknowledged that characters like Chan and Moto are not merely one-dimensional. Both are fearless and smart to the point of brilliance, certainly smarter than their various white antagonists. Chan is always a step ahead of the regular Hawaiian police, who are often reduced to comic relief. For his part, Moto is cosmopolitan, brave, and unerringly shrewd. Nonetheless, both characters are presented principally as vehicles for exotic entertainment. Chan is given to pseudo-philosophic utterances (a travesty of Confucius), and his patience is always being tried by a sequence of numbered sons, each one more bumbling than the next.

Mr. Moto is a conglomeration of stereotypes, from his imperturbable demeanor and gold-filled teeth to his pseudo-Japanese name and his fluent but sing-song English. Everything is either very, very nice or not so nice. Within that framework, the cultural significance of Pearl Buck's *The Good Earth* becomes more or less self-explanatory. Hers was the first attempt to represent Chinese characters neither as idealized paragons of humanity nor as dangerous agents of the yellow peril, nor as figures of comedy, but simply as human beings responding to their choices and troubles in recognizably human ways.

The Good Earth is set in a rural landscape identical to the Anhwei village where Buck and her first husband, Lossing, had spent the early years of their marriage. The novel's plot is simple but filled with events, following the life of its principal character, the Chinese farmer Wang Lung, from his wedding day to his old age. The structure is strictly chronological. That helped to make the book a page-turner, but it also and more seriously secured the connection between this individual story and the unrolling of Chinese history. Wang Lung's triumphs and defeats map the encounter between imperial China and the revolutionary future. Wang Lung is a deeply traditional figure, shaped by the generations his family has lived on the land. Land constitutes the core of Wang Lung's identity and motives. The soil that he farms, on which his ancestors have worked for countless years, is thin and unforgiving. Nevertheless, he cannot conceive of any other safe haven in a universe that seems to be completely untrustworthy. Despite the famines, floods, locusts, and bandits that have repeatedly victimized the family, Wang Lung knows that only the land endures.

The village in which he grows up is isolated, impoverished, and primitive. Survival comes at the cost of endless, monotonous, crushing physical labor. Village life is based on an ancient hierarchy that venerates patriarchal values. Because he is the son of a poor farmer, Wang Lung has few options in choosing a wife. To save money, his father has directed him to buy a slave from the House of Hwang, the leading family in the region. In such a society, there is a bitter irony in the novel's famous opening line: "It was Wang Lung's marriage day." The woman he buys, O-lan, is the novel's most memorable character. Toughened by her life as a slave, which included beatings and sexual abuse, O-lan accepts her status and fate without complaint. She has made her accommodation with reality and buries whatever personal desires she might have in her tasks as wife, daughter-in-law, and mother. At the same time, she is portrayed as the story's moral center, a figure of courage, perseverance, and instinctive common sense. Both in herself and in her choices, O-lan embodies Pearl Buck's feminist sympathy for the damages that patriarchy inflicts on women.

The early chapters of the novel trace an upward trajectory, following Wang Lung's rise from poverty to prosperity. His first two children are male, a good omen in a society where boy babies are still called "big happiness" and girls are only a "small happiness." Despite her admiration for China's culture, Buck was quite clear-eyed about the second-class status to which girls and women have traditionally been reduced. O-lan embodied realities that Buck had been observing firsthand for decades. As a girl, she had herself grown up in a relentlessly patriarchal, Christian household, but she discovered that the Chinese girls and women she met were also trapped in a sexual caste system, even more punishing than the one she had seen at home. The endurance that these women demonstrated is personified in Buck's famous fictional character. O-lan works side by side with Wang Lung from dawn to dusk every day. Gradually, their efforts enable him to accumulate substantial parcels of land. He becomes affluent enough to buy acres from the rich but corrupt House of Hwang. This is the region's leading family, which has wasted much of its fortune in the purchase of expensive slave girls for the clan's patriarch and opium for his senior wife.

Wang Lung's success is suddenly terminated by the onset of a killing famine that reduces the entire countryside to misery and starvation. Whispers of cannibalism spread through the village, and women resort to the terrible practice of female infanticide. O-lan herself smothers a newborn girl baby. Wang Lung wraps the tiny body in a broken mat and places it next to an old grave. What follows is one of the most frightening scenes in the novel:

> He had scarcely put the burden down before a famished, wolfish dog hovered almost at once behind him, so famished that although he took up a small stone and threw it and hit its lean flank with a thud, the animal would not stir away more than a few feet. At last Wang Lung felt his legs sinking beneath him and covering his face with his hands he went away.

He knows that in this brutal world, the dead child will become food for the starving animal.

The drought drives thousands of farmers off the land. The refugees, including Wang Lung and his family, flee to Nanking seeking whatever relief they can find. His family shelters in a squalid hut propped against the city's wall. "He lived," says the narrator, "as alien as a rat in a rich man's house that is fed on scraps thrown away." O-lan teaches the children to beg, instructing them on how to cry out and attract pity from those who pass by. Wang Lung finds work pulling a rickshaw, becoming a beast of burden and destroying his body for a few pennies a day. O-lan even contemplates the agonizing possibility of selling one of her girl children.

Staying close to Wang Lung's point of view, Buck sympathetically re-creates the limits of an uneducated and illiterate peasant consciousness. When revolutionaries shout slogans that he does not understand, blaming poverty on the greed of the rich, the bewildered Wang Lung asks in complete sincerity: "Sir, is there any way whereby the rich who oppress us can make it rain so that I can work on the land?" He is equally puzzled when white missionaries preach about something called Christianity. For him, the abstractions of both politics and religion are meaningless. He only knows weariness, and hunger, and poverty, and his single ambition is to return to his land.

Buck creates a matching pair of wonderfully comic images to represent Wang Lung's distance from the ideological debates around him. Both the revolutionary orator and the Christian missionary have given him posters inscribed with Chinese characters. He can't read them, but brings them home. In both cases, O-lan uses the thick papers to fortify the soles of the family's threadbare shoes. Her sensible, practical response can be taken to represent Pearl Buck's impatience with the empty promises that both religion and politics extend to Wang Lung and his impoverished family.

In the next sequence of chapters, blind chance, which had pushed Wang Lung off his farm, restores his fortune. When O-lan is swept up by a mob looting a rich man's house, she discovers a hidden treasure of jewelry. The sale of the jewels allows the family to return to the countryside and start again. When his wealth grows large enough, he buys the great house of the Hwangs, an economic and symbolic affirmation of the scale of his achievement. However, Wang Lung's rise in status is mirrored by his fall from integrity. He begins to behave like a rich man, less interested in work than pleasure. He criticizes O-lan's fatigued and plain appearance and buys a sing-song girl named Lotus, whom he installs in a separate suite of apartments. Punishment first comes from inside his own family. When he discovers that his eldest son is also visiting Lotus, he banishes the young man, and in so doing threatens the stability of the family. At the same moment, his moral decay is underscored by O-lan's death. Her life of duty and fidelity offers a sharp contrast to his decline. As the household grows with the addition of more children, and grandchildren, and slaves, every day is marked by disputes over rank and privilege. The family, central to Wang Lung's conception of his own identity, becomes instead a cause and an emblem of his anxieties and regrets. The novel's final section is a kaleidoscope of natural calamity and political turmoil. Wang Lung's world is turned upside down.

A flood of epic proportions destroys his farms. Then his house is taken over and occupied by a unit of the revolutionary army. He survives these reversals, but a prophecy of disaster is embedded in the book's last scene. Now an old man, he has been reunited with his two eldest sons. As they look out over the family's acres, Wang Lung senses that once he is dead they will sell the land. He pleads with them to remember that the land is their most precious possession. It defines them as a family. As they reassure him, they exchange conspiratorial smiles behind his back. These are modern men, contemptuous of their peasant father and his antique values.

As I said earlier, there was no precedent in American fiction for the popularity of Pearl Buck's tale of two Chinese farmers and their family facing adversity in the distant provinces of north central China. Nevertheless, a few reasons can be offered in explanation. To begin with, Buck was a fine storyteller. The tale of Wang Lung is consistently engaging and often exciting. The novel's descriptive passages also communicate a fully rounded feeling of rural existence. Drawing on decades of experience and observation, Buck filled *The Good Earth* with the sights, and sounds, and smells of daily life on a Chinese farm: the landscapes and houses of a small village, the tools of the working men and women, the clothes the people wear, the food they eat, and the rituals of marriage and death. At the same time, the novel is told in a formal, quasi-biblical vocabulary, which is intended to confer a degree of dignity on the characters and events.

Many of the book's first reviewers admired the style, proposing that it lifted the story toward universality. Not all readers have agreed. Many have found the style portentous and stilted. In either case, the prose reflects Buck's deep democratic instincts. She believed that the trials and achievements of ordinary men and women deserved the same rhetorical respect as subjects conventionally considered more important. In addition, Buck's timing was fortunate. Underneath its alien details, the novel is a story of the land, a familiar American genre, and the formula that depicts the struggles of farmers on their soil had a particular appeal to Americans in the Depression. Beginning in 1929 and continuing through the 1930s, millions of farm families were pushed off their homesteads, victims of economic collapse and the natural disasters of drought and dust bowl. In those circumstances, it is not surprising that the suffering and endurance of farmers would become a favored fictional subject. Several of the bestselling novels of the 1930s dramatized one version or other of the plight of such people, including two that we will be discussing: *Gone with the Wind* and *The Grapes of Wrath*.

Beyond that, while Americans had historically evinced little interest in China, the publication of *The Good Earth* coincided with the Japanese invasion of Manchuria. Asian turmoil would become an increasingly unavoidable subject through the '30s. In the words of the historian John King Fairbank: "In 1931, when she published *The Good Earth*, Pearl Buck ran into history." Although Buck's literary techniques were generally conventional, and even old-fashioned, her subject matter and the stance she took toward her material were close to revolutionary. Her portrait of village China proved to have a remarkable influence. In the 1950s, a sociologist named Harold Isaacs published a book called *Scratches on our Minds*, a pioneering study of American attitudes toward the peoples of Asia. Isaacs asked a cross section of Americans where they acquired whatever images they had about Asia. He discovered that, and I quote Isaacs: "no single book about China has had a greater impact than ... *The Good Earth*. It can almost be said," he continued, "that for a whole generation of Americans [Pearl Buck] 'created' the Chinese, in the same sense that Dickens 'created' ... Victorian England."

The Good Earth became the first volume of a trilogy. The direct sequel, *Sons*, published in 1932, presents all three of Wang Lung's sons pursuing careers that repudiate their father's values. The first becomes a parasitic landlord, the second a mean-spirited moneylender, and the youngest a ferocious soldier. The third volume in the trilogy, *A House Divided*, follows the family through its third generation and emphasizes the final disintegration of Wang Lung's legacy, and the irrelevance of utopian theorizing to the lives of urban and rural poor. Along with these and other novels, Buck's publications in the 1930s included the first complete translation into English of the classic Chinese novel *Shui Hu Chuan* and biographies of both her parents, of her father in *Fighting Angel* and her mother in *The Exile*. She also published a number of political essays, attacking British imperialism and American racial discrimination. She exhorted women on both sides of the Pacific to claim a larger place in public life. Her articles, with titles such as "America's Medieval Women," appeared in *Harper's* and other leading magazines. When she gathered her feminist writing into a book called *Of Men and Women*, *The New York Times* likened Buck's insights to those of Virginia Woolf.

Buck's tireless efforts, over four decades, for African Americans and women, and for displaced and handicapped children, may have had their source in her own experience. She was, remember, the only major white American writer who grew up as a minority person. In her activist career, she displayed the instinctive sympathy for others that she had demonstrated in *The Good Earth* and her other novels about China. The film version of *The Good Earth* was released in 1937. Metro-Goldwyn-Mayer paid what was then the record price of $50,000 for the movie rights. The film, like the book, proved to be an immense commercial and critical success. It was seen by over 20 million people around the world and was nominated for several

Academy Awards. One of the stars, Luise Rainer, won an Oscar for best actress. In 1938, Buck was awarded the Nobel Prize for Literature, the third American (after Sinclair Lewis and Eugene O'Neill), and the first American woman to be so honored. She was also, at 46, one of the youngest recipients of the literature prize. It was assumed at the time, probably correctly, that the Academy had used the occasion of the award to make a political statement. At that moment, the Japanese, who had invaded Manchuria in 1931 and China proper in 1937, were continuing their apparently irresistible air and ground campaign against Chinese cities and major production areas. In Europe and Africa, various brands of fascism were ingesting countries and their citizens.

Against all this, Pearl Buck had established herself as a passionate opponent of totalitarian violence. Her speeches and fund raising in support of democracy found an answering response among progressive groups all over the world. *The Good Earth*, it turns out, was a powerfully political book after all, a manifesto on behalf of the rights of ordinary men and women— not just in China, but across the globe.

Lecture Fifteen
Gone with the Wind

Scope: Margaret Mitchell worked on *Gone with the Wind* for nearly 10 years, and the resulting manuscript was huge. Her publisher had to set the high price of $3 per copy, risky in the middle of the Depression. Within three months, however, over 500,000 copies had been sold, and it went on to become the bestselling novel of 1936 and 1937. As the novel unfolds across the years from 1861 to 1874, two stories are interwoven: the war and the devastation it inflicted on the South, and a turbulent romance between Scarlett O'Hara and Rhett Butler. Both narratives end in defeat; however, the heroine Scarlett discovers reservoirs of courage and self-reliance that help explain the book's popularity and longevity. *Gone with the Wind* received major reviews in every newspaper and magazine in the country, each one emphatically asserting the book's significance and achievement. Despite a contemporary perspective that rightfully places the book among others that belied that truth of slavery, and the reasons for which the South fought the war, *Gone with the Wind* quickly established itself as the bestselling work of fiction in American history.

Outline

I. When *Gone with the Wind* was published in 1936, the publisher could not have anticipated the behemoth success it would become. Indeed, even Margaret Mitchell herself pondered this.

   A. Mitchell was born in Atlanta in 1900 and lived most of her life there. Despite being a voracious reader, she resisted most formal education.

   B. Mitchell did her literary apprenticeship as a journalist with the *Atlanta Journal* in the 1920s; however, she gave up her newspaper work in 1926 after her second marriage.

   C. A few months later, she began work on *Gone with the Wind*, the only novel she would write.

II. The novel opens on the eve of the Civil War, introducing a 16-year-old Scarlett O'Hara living on a plantation called Tara, with her father Gerald, her mother Ellen, and the family's slaves.

   A. Despite rampant war talk, the early chapters evoke a life of comfort and abundance, in which the region's white families are nursed and cared for by their African American servants.

   B. Scarlett's concerns are primarily romantic: She declares her love for the aristocrat Ashley Wilkes, only to be rejected in favor of Wilkes's plainer cousin, Melanie Hamilton.

   C. War breaks out between the North and South, interrupting and ultimately transforming the domestic drama.

   1. Despite the attentions of the dashing, dark, and dangerous Rhett Butler, Scarlett marries Melanie's dull brother Charles, who dies of measles.

   2. The setting shifts to Atlanta, where Scarlett moves to be with pregnant Melanie. Here Rhett emerges as a daily presence in her life, simultaneously irritating and exciting her.

   D. During the scene depicting the burning of Atlanta, Scarlett delivers Melanie's child and they barely escape, with Rhett's assistance.

   E. Scarlett, abandoned by Rhett (who goes to join the Confederate army), makes her way back to Tara with Melanie and the baby.

   1. She finds nothing but disaster: Her mother has died, her father suffers from senile dementia, and her beloved Tara has been reduced to rubble.

   2. For Scarlett, this dramatic shift marks the major turning point in her life, where she transforms from the girlish Southern belle into a grimly determined and shrewd woman.

III. In the face of devastation, Scarlett discovers unknown reservoirs of courage and self-reliance. She begins to reclaim the land, working alongside her black servants to restore the plantation.

   A. In one of the novel's most famous passages, she vows to survive and persevere: "If I have to steal or kill—as God as my witness, I'm never going to be hungry again."

   B. Scarlett keeps her vow: In order to survive, she kills a Union soldier who threatens her, and she constantly devises plans to find money.

1. One such way is to marry storeowner Frank Kennedy, the fiancé of her sister Suellen. This helps resolve the debt owed on Tara, which is Scarlett's main goal—to preserve the land of her family.
2. Scarlett defies the conventions of respectable Southern womanhood, becoming a scandal for both her personal life and her business acumen.

C. Halfway through the novel, the narrator pauses to offer opinions about the state of the postwar South. The Reconstruction and the Freedmen's Bureau are perceived as vindictive and as feeding ex-slaves with unnecessary antipathy, and the plot now bends to the demands of this ideology.
1. Scarlett is attacked on a lonely road by two men, one white and the other black. The attempted robbery becomes a sexual violation.
2. The Ku Klux Klan takes revenge, depicted as Southern men defending their women from predatory blacks. Frank Kennedy is killed in the raid, leaving Scarlett a widow for the second time.

D. Scarlett and Rhett finally marry, although it quickly becomes clear that the passion that once attracted them has long vanished.
1. Their only daughter, Bonnie Blue Butler, is born, and Rhett adores the child even as his resentment toward a cool Scarlett grows.
2. When Bonnie is killed in a riding accident, Rhett's grief nears madness. The marriage is effectively over. But when Melanie dies, leaving Ashley available, Scarlett finally realizes that she in fact loves Rhett.

E. In the final scene, a desperate Scarlett is rejected by Rhett, who walks out of her life uttering the famous line, "My dear, I don't give a damn."
1. Despite the defeat, Scarlett recovers her will and confidence.
2. She resolves to return to her beloved Tara and plans to get Rhett back.

IV. Several weeks before the book appeared, *Publishers Weekly* printed an advance review of *Gone with the Wind* that suggested the book was "very possibly the greatest American novel." Although not every review was quite so emphatic, most made strong claims of a similar nature.

A. Above all, the book's enthusiasts insisted that *Gone with the Wind* was the greatest of all Civil War novels, and the one that best reproduced the truth of the war and postwar years.

    1. These historical assertions have proven fragile. In fact, Mitchell's depiction of the South is romantic and obsolete.

    2. The Southern "old ways" that Ashley holds so dear include, of course, slavery. For Mitchell's contemporaries and for generations of readers, *Gone with the Wind* validated and reinforced a deeply contemptuous view of African American humanity.

B. Just one year before *Gone with the Wind*, W. E. B Du Bois published his magisterial study *Black Reconstruction*. He argues that the historical truth of the postbellum American South has been held hostage to the ideology of white supremacy.

    1. The Civil War was not a noble enterprise in which sons of plantation owners fought for their honor, liberty, and womenfolk; it was a rebellion in defense of the crime of slavery.

    2. Today, 75 years after their publication, many of the positions Du Bois argued have become mainstream.

C. Despite the racial propaganda, which undoubtedly discounts Mitchell's claims to historical truth, *Gone with the Wind* remains a formidable achievement. Probably no other novel has occupied such a singular place in the American imagination.

Suggested Reading:

Pyron, *Southern Daughter*.

Questions to Consider:

1. Scarlett O'Hara has proven to be a durably fascinating character, both to male and perhaps especially to female readers. Aside from her personal qualities, her strengths and weaknesses, what symbolic role may she play in the novel? In what ways, if any, does she represent the power of tradition, and in what ways does she signal the advent of change and modernity?

2. Ashley Wilkes and Rhett Butler are juxtaposed with almost mathematical precision. What values does each represent? What is the novel's judgment on these two men and their choices?

Lecture Fifteen—Transcript
Gone with the Wind

The Good Earth, a story of the land, as I mentioned, was the bestselling novel of both 1931 and 1932. Hervey Allen's *Anthony Adverse*, a nearly forgotten three-volume blockbuster, followed as the bestselling novel of both 1933 and 1934. *Anthony Adverse* follows its title character across three continents and several decades of imaginative 19th-century history. It is the most conspicuous example I know of a novel that completely dominated bestseller lists in its own day, and then dropped more or less completely out of sight. The huge sales of *The Good Earth* and *Anthony Adverse* were impressive and even unprecedented. However, as commercial achievements, the two novels were quickly trumped by a book that was both a story of the land and a work of imaginative history. The phenomenal success of *Gone with the Wind* is a story almost as epic as the book itself.

Margaret Mitchell worked on the novel for 10 years, keeping the work-in-progress secret from almost everyone except her husband. When she delivered the gargantuan manuscript to her publisher, Macmillan, panic ensued. Because of its 1,037-page length, Macmillan needed to set the high price of $3.00 on each copy, a risky charge in the middle of the Depression. Macmillan's marketing managers ordered an initial print run of 10,000 copies, set an ultimate target of 27,500, placed some prominent ads, and crossed their fingers. No one could have predicted what happened next. After just three months, over 500,000 copies had been sold, a figure that rose to well over a million within six months. No previous novel, not even *Uncle Tom's Cabin*, had recorded those sorts of sales. *Gone with the Wind* was the bestselling novel of both 1936 and 1937, and it appeared on *The New York Times* bestseller list again in 1986 and 1991. Indeed, Margaret Mitchell's novel quickly established itself as the bestselling work of fiction to that point in American history. The book continues to enjoy strong sales today, more than seven decades after its publication.

Part of our task in this lecture is to ask why: Why did this book achieve such unprecedented popularity? As Mitchell herself confessed in a letter to a friend: "I cannot figure what makes the thing sell so enormously." In the same letter, Mitchell offered a clear-eyed estimate of her novel: "it is basically just a simple yarn of fairly simple people. There's no fine writing, there are no grandiose thoughts … nothing, nothing at all that have made other best sellers, best sellers. ... I can't figure it out." When Mitchell called her book a simple yarn, she was being candid, not modest. The elements of *Gone with the Wind* are mostly familiar and conventional. As the novel unfolds across the years from 1861 to 1874, two large stories are interwoven across its many chapters. The first is the history of the Civil War and the devastation that the war and the years following inflicted on the South. The second is a romance, in which the passions of a small group of men and women transform their lives. Both narratives end in defeat.

Margaret Mitchell was born in Atlanta in 1900 and lived most of her life in and around that city. She was bored by most of the formal education she was offered, though she did complete a single year at Smith College, and she was a voracious reader. Her favorite books were classic novels and Southern history. Mitchell did her literary apprenticeship as a journalist, writing scores of essays and reviews for the *Atlanta Journal* in the 1920s. She gave up her newspaper work in 1926, after her second marriage. A few months later, while recovering from an illness, she began work on her novel, the only one she would write. Apparently she spent about five years writing her big book, and five more revising it. The time, it would turn out, was well spent.

Gone with the Wind opens on the eve of the war. Scarlett O'Hara, a strong-willed and flirtatious 16-year-old lives on a plantation called Tara, with her father, Gerald, her mother, Ellen, and the family's slaves. The early chapters evoke a life of comfort and abundance, in which the region's white families are nursed and cared for by their African American servants. War talk is rampant, though Scarlett would prefer to talk about clothes and men. Precipitating the novel's first romantic crisis, Scarlett declares her love for a bloodless aristocrat, Ashley Wilkes. To her shock, Ashley rejects her in favor of a plainer and less-vivacious woman, his own cousin, Melanie Hamilton. Scarlett explodes with anger and slaps Ashley, who walks out. At that moment, enter the dashing, dark, and dangerous Rhett Butler, who instantly falls hard for Scarlett. The language the narrator uses to introduce Rhett stays close to Scarlet's point of view, and it teeters toward comedy as it reveals her overwrought romanticism. Rhett is a tall man, powerfully built. He reminds Scarlett, says the narrator, of a pirate, "and his eyes were as bold and black as any pirate's appraising a galleon to be scuttled or a maiden to be ravished." War breaks out between North and South, interrupting and ultimately overwhelming the domestic drama. Charles Hamilton, Melanie's dull brother, proposes to Scarlett before leaving for the front, and she accepts him—largely to spite both Melanie and Ashley. The marriage ends within a couple of months, when Charles dies of measles. Shortly thereafter, Scarlett gives birth to a son she names Wade.

The setting then shifts to Atlanta, when Scarlett goes to stay with the pregnant Melanie. Rhett re-emerges as a daily presence in her life, irritating her with his cynicism on the one hand, exciting her with his bad-boy swagger on the other. The next chapters relate a tumble of crises and adventures. The women in Atlanta get word that Ashley has been captured and imprisoned at Gettysburg. Melanie delivers her child, a son she calls Beau. The difficult delivery, which is almost botched by the incompetent Scarlett, is followed almost immediately by Sherman's destruction of Atlanta. Hardly a building is left standing. This is the novel's central set piece, in which Mitchell vividly describes the reduction of a major city to smoking ruin.

To get Scarlett and Melanie out of harm's way, Rhett hustles the women to safety in a horse-drawn wagon, and then leaves them to join a Confederate regiment. Scarlett keeps moving, driving the wagon through dangerous back roads and woods filled with renegade soldiers of both sides. She manages to get back to Tara, where she finds nothing but disaster. Her mother has died. Her father has declined into senile dementia. Tara has been reduced to rubble by pillaging Union soldiers. For Scarlett, this is the major turning point in her life. As the narrator says, describing the change:

> Never again could Scarlett lie down, as a child, secure beneath her father's roof with the protection of her mother's love wrapped about her. ...

> Somewhere along the ... road to Tara, she had left her girlhood behind her. She was no longer plastic clay, yielding imprint to each new experience. The clay had hardened, some time in this indeterminant day which had lasted a thousand years. Tonight was the last night she would ever be ministered to as a child. She was a woman now and youth was gone.

The war and its aftermath transform the girlish Scarlett into a grimly determined and shrewd woman. Stripped of her belongings and her family, she discovers reservoirs of courage and self-reliance that neither she nor the reader had known she possessed. Scarlett begins to reclaim and restore the plantation. Working alongside her black servants from dawn to darkness, she plants vegetables, mends fences, and clears debris. She insists that she will look forward, not back, and she vows in one of the novel's most famous speeches: "I'm going to live through this, and when it's over, I'm never going to be hungry again. No, nor any of my folks. If I have to steal or kill—as God is my witness, I'm never going to be hungry again." She does kill. When a Union soldier threatens her, she takes up a heavy pistol and shoots him. After a moment of stunned disbelief that she was capable of such an act, she is overtaken by exhilaration, a feeling that the narrator calls "a cool, tigerish joy." Scarlett has been redefined by her suffering and rage.

The end of the war brings the threat of further reversals. Poverty and despair loom over every town and village. The narrator offers the ironic comment that residents of the South, rich and poor, old and young, all had just two things in common: lice and dysentery. Predictably, as in all calamities, the losers prey on each other. A local politician named Jonas Wilkerson, once a hired hand at Tara, raises the taxes on the plantation, scheming to swindle the O'Haras out of their property and seize it for himself. Scarlett devises a plan to find the money. In defiance of the constraints on female behavior that had been bred into her from birth, she coolly decides that she will seduce Rhett in exchange for the cash she needs. Rhett has had a good war. Deeds of valor, combined with a lucrative career as a blockade-runner, have left him both admired and rich. Unfortunately, he has been imprisoned in a Union jail and is unavailable to Scarlett. Piling one calculation on top of another, Scarlett quickly turns her attention to a man named Frank Kennedy, who has become the prosperous owner of a general store. Ignoring the inconvenient fact that Kennedy is her sister Suellen's fiancé, Scarlett maneuvers him into marriage. The union is fruitful. Along with a second child, a daughter named Ella, Scarlett now has the funds to pay the debt on Tara. She invites Melanie and Ashley to join her there.

Scarlett also discovers a fine talent for commerce. Rhett, after bribing his way out of jail, advances the money that Scarlett invests in a profitable sawmill. Once again, Scarlett defies the conventions of respectable Southern womanhood, becoming a scandal both for her personal life and her business success. She also becomes morally callous: a sharp trader who doesn't flinch from using convict labor and driving hard bargains. Halfway through the novel, the narrator pauses to offer a set of opinions about the state of the postwar South. Scarlett, who has been too busy to pay much attention to anything outside her sawmill and plantation, now learns from Ashley that, as the narrator says: "the scourge of war had been followed by the worse scourge of Reconstruction. ... [The] South was being treated as a conquered province and ... vindictiveness was the dominant policy of the conquerors." Scarlett is only slightly disturbed by such comments, but the narrator moves away from her point of view to issue a more alarming analysis: "Scarlett did not realize that all the rules of the game had been changed and that honest labor could no longer earn its just reward." According to the narrator, the Freedmen's Bureau was:

> organized by the Federal government to take care of the idle and excited ex-slaves ... fed them while they loafed and poisoned their minds against their former owners. ...

> They kept the negroes stirred up with tales of cruelty perpetrated by the whites and, in a section long famed for the affectionate relations between slaves and slave owners, hate and suspicion began to grow.

The plot now bends to the demands of this ideology. In a sensational passage, Scarlett is attacked on a lonely road by two men—one white, the other black—or, in the words of the narrator: "a big ragged white man and a squat black negro with shoulders and chest like a gorilla." They want only her money, but the black man tears her shirtfront open to get it. The narrator says that "the black hand fumbled between her breasts, and terror and revulsion such as she had never known came over her." An attempted robbery has become a sexual violation. That night, the Ku Klux Klan takes revenge. The reader has already been told that: "It was the large number of outrages on women and the ever-present fear for the safety of their wives and daughters that drove Southern men to cold and trembling fury and caused the Ku Klux Klan to spring up overnight." Modeled in a crackbrained way on the knights of medieval romance, the Klan's vigilantes enforced a regime of terror across the African American South for generations. The ghost of Mark Twain hovers over these scenes, breathing his contempt for the pseudo-chivalry that deformed Southern conceptions of honor.

Frank Kennedy is killed in the Klan raid, which leaves Scarlett a widow for the second time. At this point, apparently in obedience to the laws of romance, Scarlett and Rhett finally marry and move into an ornate and ostentatious Atlanta mansion. However, it quickly becomes clear that the passion that once attracted them has apparently vanished. The marriage drifts toward loveless stalemate, cemented by Rhett's bitter belief that Scarlett's love for Ashley remains vital. The relationship is eased by the birth of a child, Bonnie Blue Butler. Rhett adores the child, but his resentment toward Scarlett continues to fester, especially when she decides to sleep alone. In another of the novel's most famous scenes, the drunken Rhett seizes Scarlett and carries her up the stairs to bed. She resists, but only momentarily. It is a rape, but one that the novel seems to authorize. Staying close to Scarlett's point of view, the narrator describes the scene in a vocabulary ripe with melodrama and female submission, the familiar language of the harlequin romance:

> She was darkness and he was darkness and there had never been anything before this time, only darkness and his lips upon her. She tried to speak and his mouth was over her again. Suddenly she had a wild thrill such as she had never known; joy, fear, madness, excitement, surrender. …

> For the first time in her life she had met someone, something stronger than she, someone she could neither bully nor break, someone who was bullying and breaking her. Somehow, her arms were around his neck and her lips trembling beneath his and they were going up, up into the darkness again, a darkness that was soft and swirling and all enveloping.

I can barely keep from blushing when I read it.

When the night is over, Rhett is gone. Shortly afterward, Bonnie Blue is killed in a riding accident, and Rhett is distracted by grief to the point of madness. The marriage is effectively ended. Scarlett's pain is made sharper by her realization that in fact she loves Rhett, not Ashley. When Melanie dies, making Ashley available, Scarlett decides that he was always an idealized figure, not a potential lover—too late. During a final interview, Rhett rejects Scarlett and walks out of her life. She pleads that he must stay: "If you go, what shall I do?" He departs on the immortal exit line, one of the two most-quoted sentences in *Gone with the Wind*: "My dear, I don't give a damn." Despite the defeat, Scarlett recovers her will and confidence. She will pause, plan, and get Rhett back. She assures herself that there has never been a man she couldn't get, once she set her mind upon him, but it will wait until tomorrow. After all, she tells herself, in the novel's other most-quoted sentence: "Tomorrow is another day."

Gone with the Wind received major reviews in every newspaper and magazine in the country. Several weeks before the book was published, *Publishers Weekly* printed an advance review proposing that the book was "very possibly the greatest American novel." The *New York Sun* compared Margaret Mitchell with Tolstoy, Hardy, and Dickens. J. Donald Adams, the editor of *The New York Times Book Review*, assigned *Gone with the Wind* to himself and pulled out the stops: "I would go so far as to say that it is, in narrative power, in sheer readability, surpassed by nothing in American fiction."

Not every notice went quite that far, but many of them made strong claims. Above all, the book's enthusiasts insisted that *Gone with the Wind* was the greatest of all Civil War novels, and the one that best reproduced the truth of the war and the postwar years.

These tributes brought Mitchell particular satisfaction, because she had spent several years diligently reading books, newspapers, diaries, and letters to ensure the historical accuracy of her novel. However, those historical assertions have proven exceptionally fragile. In fact, Mitchell's depiction of the South was romantic and obsolete. Where a writer like William Faulkner exposed the moral calamity that brought the South to its destruction, *Gone with the Wind* recycles the misty-eyed mythology of the Lost Cause. Gallant Ashley Wilkes, in a letter from the front to his wife Melanie, explains why he fights. He knows that he and his comrades have been betrayed by what he calls the "words and catch phrases, prejudices and hatreds" of their own leaders. His Southern patriotism has different routes. When he goes into battle, Ashley says:

> I see Twelve Oaks and remember how the moonlight slants across the white columns and the unearthly way the magnolias look, opening under the moon. ... And I see Mother, sewing there, as she did when I was a little boy. And I hear the darkies coming home across the fields at dusk, tired and singing and ready for supper. ... And there's the long view down the road to the river, across the cotton fields.

But all those images are only "symbols," Ashley tells Melanie, "symbols of the kind of life I love. For I am fighting for the old days, the old ways I love." Those "old ways," of course, included slavery. For Mitchell's contemporaries and for generations of readers, *Gone with the Wind* validated and reinforced a deeply contemptuous view of African American humanity—"darkies" and gorilla-like beasts. The loyal slave Sam is convulsed with happiness when he is reunited with Scarlett after the war. The narrator tells us that: "His watermelon-pink tongue lapped out, his whole body wiggled and his joyful contortions were as ludicrous as the gambolings of a mastiff. Appealing to a litany of defensive clichés, *Gone with the Wind* presents African Americans who are happily dependent in their bondage, sexually dangerous if not kept under restraint, and incapable of governing themselves, much less governing others. When blacks are emancipated and then quickly move into positions of authority, the resulting pandemonium quite appropriately elicits the terror of the Ku Klux Klan and the ensuing process of disenfranchisement—except that the pandemonium never happened.

By a coincidence of chronology, W. E. B. Du Bois published his magisterial study *Black Reconstruction* in 1935, the year before *Gone with the Wind* appeared. In 700 pages, Du Bois distilled the research he had been doing for over 30 years. His purpose was to rewrite the history that Margaret Mitchell—and most other white Americans, North and South—took for granted. The Civil War was not a noble enterprise in which the gallant sons of plantation owners fought for their honor, their liberty, and their womenfolk. It was a rebellion in defense of the crime of slavery. African Americans were neither brutes nor passive "Sambos," but human beings. They were disadvantaged by poverty and illiteracy, to be sure, but they responded quickly to the legal opportunities that emancipation brought. In 17 chapters, *Black Reconstruction* painstakingly sets out the economic and political circumstances of both blacks and whites in the Civil War and the postwar South. He traces the provisional triumphs of emancipated African Americans and the concerted racial opposition that ultimately defeated any possibility of an alliance between black and white workers. In particular, Du Bois defends the work of the Freedmen's Bureau, a special target of abuse in *Gone with the Wind* and in many other pro-Southern histories and fiction. Du Bois argues that the historical truth of the post-bellum American South has been held hostage to the ideology of white supremacy. For three generations, white portraits of Reconstruction, by professional historians and novelists alike, had become nothing more than an echo chamber droning with repeated anecdotes, unsupported claims, and downright lies.

Here is Du Bois's summary statement:

> In order to paint the South as a martyr to inescapable fate, … and to ridicule the Negro as the impossible joke in the whole development, we have in fifty years, by liable, innuendo and silence, so completely misstated and obliterated the history of the Negro in America … that today it is almost unknown.

Seventy-five years after its publication, many of the positions Du Bois argued in *Black Reconstruction* have become mainstream. At the time, however, as the popularity of *Gone with the Wind* proved, Du Bois faced a nearly united front of bigotry and preconception. The received view of Reconstruction as a period of wretched African American excess was further reinforced by the extraordinary success of the film version of Mitchell's novel. The movie, which won an unprecedented eight Academy Awards, is almost ritualistically invoked as an example of filmmaking during Hollywood's "golden age." Released in 1939, the making of the movie was attended with non-stop publicity and rising excitement across the country. The opening night in Atlanta was a glittering, legendary, and of course rigorously segregated affair. Like the novel, the movie also received commendations for the accuracy of its detailed historical representations. The burning of Atlanta, to give a single example, remains among the most celebrated sequences in Hollywood history. However, the racial message, while muted in the film, remains clear.

The black poet and critic, Melvin B. Tolson, writing in the *Washington Tribune*, itemized the conclusions that audiences around the world would draw when they saw the film:

> The North was wrong in fighting to free black men. The grand old Abolitionists were lunatics. Negroes didn't want to be free anyway. Slaves were happy. The greatest pleasure of the slave was to serve massa. Southern whites understand Negroes; that's the reason they treat them as they do. You need the Ku Klux Klan to keep Negroes in their place.

Despite this racial propaganda—which undoubtedly diminishes Mitchell's claim to historical truth—*Gone with the Wind* remains a formidable achievement. Probably no novel has occupied such a singular place in the American imagination.

To return to our opening question: Why? As I suggested in the first lecture in this series, we will never fully figure it out. Epic-length novels about the Civil War have been popular, but there have been literally hundreds of such books, and only one *Gone with the Wind*. Love affairs between full-blooded women and virile men, complete with bodice-ripping eroticism, have provided a favorite fictional subject, but there have been thousands of those books, and only one *Gone with the Wind*. Certainly the novel had a special relevance for its Depression-era readers. The whole of America was now experiencing something of the tribulations of the post-Civil War South: widespread unemployment, hunger, and a fear that things might not get better. Even the devastated landscape of Georgia and the other Confederate states found its analog in the drought that turned the middle of the nation into a vast dust bowl.

In both 1930s America and the post-bellum South, powerful and malevolent forces seemed to be in control, shrinking the range of human effort. Many readers in the Depression welcomed images of strength. Recall that Superman took his first comic book flight in 1938. This brings us to Scarlett. Her tenacity, her defiance of respectable conventions, and her determination to stand on her own feet against all obstacles and all odds, combine to make her a magnetic heroine. Mitchell's feminist portrait was altogether deliberate. In a letter to a friend at about the time she began writing the novel, Mitchell said: "I want to write a book about women. Every one has always told the men's stories; I want to tell the women's, and what it was like for them during the War." Throughout the book, the narrator emphasizes the authority of women despite the genteel cocoon in which Southern society tries to keep them. At one point, when Frank Kennedy is confused by Scarlett's shrewd business instincts, which far exceed his own, the narrator refers to Frank's "usual masculine disillusionment in discovering that a woman has a brain."

Margaret Mitchell was not the first writer to put a strong, independent, passionate, competent, and occasionally ruthless woman at the center of her story. Scarlett O'Hara has ancestors and foremothers in both English and American literature—but within that gallery of characters, Scarlett remains one of the most memorable.

Lecture Sixteen

How to Win Friends and Influence People

Scope: *How to Win Friends and Influence People* was the bestselling nonfiction book of the first half of the 20th century. Published during the Depression, and a descendant of Horatio Alger's novels, Dale Carnegie's book affirms the exceptional potential that characterizes ordinary men and women, and it celebrates the power of the individual to overcome long odds. Carnegie redefined the vocabulary of success and failure. In his world, success is built on personality. Talent and hard work matter, but personal appeal matters more. The key is to be likable. Whatever its distinctive message, *How to Win Friends* is anchored in a long history of American concern with success, and as America transformed itself into a consumer culture after 1900, advertising and marketing began to play increasingly large roles. This context helps to explain the popularity of *How to Win Friends*. Having grown up in near poverty, Carnegie learned early the importance of salesmanship and public speaking; ultimately, his major product was himself and his doctrine of personality.

Outline

I. *How to Win Friends and Influence People*, the bestselling nonfiction book of the first half of the 20th century, was published in the middle of the Depression. Dale Carnegie's tribute to individual competence and the possibilities of success found a responsive audience among citizens who were staggering under the burden of economic hardship.

    A. Carnegie redefined the meaning of success. Where earlier writers stressed hard work and commitment, *How to Win Friends*—from its title on—put the emphasis on personal appeal. The key is to be likable.

        1. Arthur Miller's *Death of a Salesman*, produced just a decade after Carnegie's book, illustrates the change.

        2. Willy Loman insists that the secret of success is to be liked. In his own view, he fails because people do not like him.

B. The lure of success lies near the heart of the American dream, and it has a long history.

1. In the 17th century, Cotton Mather taught his congregation that usefulness in worldly occupations was a religious obligation. The twin duties of religious citizenship entailed doing good for others while doing well for oneself.

2. In the middle of the 18th century, Benjamin Franklin published *The Way to Wealth*, which remains a byword for hard work and self-advancement.

3. The 19th century saw a flourishing of books that exhorted readers to achievement and provided instruction manuals on how to get ahead, including titles such as *Self-Made Men of America* and *Great Fortunes and How They Were Made*.

4. Henry Adams published a massive history of the United States. An introductory chapter called "American Ideals" summons up a romanticized vision of the man who embodies democratic possibility.

5. At the end of the century, the wealthy industrialist Andrew Carnegie injected a religious dimension into the subject in his book, *The Gospel of Wealth*.

6. Russell Conwell, a Philadelphia minister, delivered his sermon "Acres of Diamonds" to packed halls across the nation. As a book, it was among the most widely read of the 19th century.

7. *The Man Nobody Knows*, by Bruce Barton, was one of the bestselling books of the 1920s. It pushed the linkage between success and religion about as far as it could go.

8. One of the most popular magazines at the turn of the 20th century was called, simply and proudly, *Success*.

II. Following the First World War, the idea of success was transformed by the influence of psychology. The French scientist Èmile Coué invented a form of learned optimism, and his popularity marks a turning point in the idea of success.

A. Scholars note a shift in discussions of achievement from character to a concentration on personality. The change corresponds with the rise of marketing and advertising as major industries.

B. Despite the cynicism that advertising provoked, surveys indicated that a majority of citizens were in fact influenced by the claims made in advertisements.

    1. This background helps to explain the phenomenon of *How to Win Friends*.

    2. Where advertising used a primitive social science to sell products, Dale Carnegie sold himself and taught others how to sell themselves.

III. Born and raised in rural Midwestern poverty, Carnegie exhibited an early talent for public speaking.

  A. He went on to study oratory and debate in college.

  B. He took and lost a series of jobs—most of them in sales—before he realized that his skills as a speaker might provide him with a career.

  C. Beginning in 1912, he offered courses in elocution and public speaking to leading companies around the country. Out of these experiences, he ultimately distilled his landmark book.

IV. *How to Win Friends* has the look and feel of an instruction manual or textbook.

  A. The book's famous title proves to be quite scrupulously exact: You influence people by winning friends, and you win friends by following the advice Carnegie offers you.

    1. The book's purpose was not to overturn societal assumptions, or even to reform them.

    2. *How to Win Friends* offered "guaranteed" access to success and comfort.

  B. The lessons Carnegie teaches are repeated again and again, in a series of simple aphorisms.

    1. We should look at all our transactions from the other person's point of view. Instead of criticizing, offer praise. Be friendly. Above all, smile.

    2. This is probably the book's most famous axiom. Turn on a smile, not an insincere grin but "a real smile, a heart-warming smile … the kind of a smile that will bring a good price in the market place." If you don't feel like smiling, smile anyway.

C. Although it was often the target of critics and skeptics, Carnegie's book has remained an important and influential text. Continuing strong, the worldwide chain of Carnegie training schools, along with the long list of self-help Carnegie imitators that crowd bookstore shelves, document the permanence of *How to Win Friends* and its message.

Suggested Reading:

Cawelti, *Apostles of the Self-Made Man.*

Questions to Consider:

1. What is Dale Carnegie's definition of success? What is yours?
2. Continued sales of *How to Win Friends* and the proliferation of Dale Carnegie courses around the world indicate that both the book and the message remain resonant and popular. What is your explanation for that long-term phenomenon?

Lecture Sixteen—Transcript
How to Win Friends and Influence People

Gone with the Wind, the most popular American novel of the first half of the 20th century, was published in 1936. In the same year, Dale Carnegie published *How to Win Friends and Influence People*, the bestselling nonfiction book of the same period. This is nothing more than a coincidence. Nonetheless, there are a couple of tempting similarities: Both books testify to the uncommon potential that resides within commonplace men and women—and both, published in the depths of the Great Depression, ultimately celebrate the power of the individual to overcome long odds and win through to success. Whatever the explanation, the immense popularity these two books have enjoyed since the day each was published may testify to the insights they offer into the values that large numbers of Americans embrace. Whether they have read it or not, just about everyone has heard of Carnegie's book. Repeatedly revised and reprinted, *How to Win Friends and Influence People* continues to sell tens of thousands of copies each year. The title phrase has become synonymous with a particularly American brand of achievement. Dale Carnegie was undeniably one of Horatio Alger's descendants, and I will trace some of those connections in this lecture. However, as we shall see, Carnegie changed the formula for success. In his world, success is built on smiles. Talent and hard work matter, but personal appeal matters more. The key is to be likable.

Carnegie redefined even the vocabulary of failure. Arthur Miller's great play, *Death of a Salesman*, was produced just a decade after *How to Win Friends* was published. Miller's main character, Willy Loman, suffers one humiliation after another, and slides into reveries and fantasies from which he imagines himself a powerful and successful man. Willy repeatedly tells his son the secret of success. Willy is desperate to be liked. A man must be liked: The word tolls like a funeral bell throughout the play. In the end, Willy commits suicide to escape. He is ashamed. He has not been liked. He is a failure. In one newspaper account of *Salesman*'s opening night, a businessman was quoted as saying: "New England was always a tough territory." That may be, but Willy Loman's fate reaches much further than Yankee miserliness. A friend of mine, an authority on American drama, has argued that Willy is the quintessential hero—or better, anti-hero—for our time. If our course had room for plays, which don't quite fit into the category of "bestseller," the first choice would surely have been *Death of a Salesman*, which has earned enormous critical and commercial applause around the world for six decades. Arthur Miller's anatomy of failure serves as a perfect backdrop and antithesis to Dale Carnegie's formulas for success. Indeed, I would venture the proposition that America's public world still belongs to Carnegie. The rest of us just live there.

While Americans did not invent the idea of success, the concept has long had a particular association with the United States. It lodges at the heart of the American Dream, a term that has been defined in various ways but consistently evokes an America that is the land of opportunity, second chances, and self-made men and women. What is the source of this notion? Historians offer all kinds of hypotheses. Perhaps the nation was so vast that its frontier offered space for reinvention. Perhaps the population was upwardly mobile because the class structure was less oppressive in the New World. Or maybe the country's imagination was shaped by a particular version of the Protestant ethic, which puts a high value on striving and hard work. Or perhaps democracy encouraged competition for eminence. Whatever the merit of these and other explanations, the literature of success can be traced back to the Puritans and forward through Horatio Alger's novels to the self-help section of any contemporary bookstore. *How to Win Friends and Influence People* is perhaps the key 20th-century American text in this long tradition of American writing. In this lecture, I want to place the book in its historical context, and then suggest some of the reasons for its long-lasting popularity.

Nearly four centuries ago, the preacher Cotton Mather taught his congregation that usefulness in the world was a religious obligation. The duties of religious citizenship in the Massachusetts Bay Colony entailed doing good for others, while doing well for one's self. That link between worldly prosperity and virtue would prove to be influential over several centuries. Mather liked to call particular attention to the verse in Proverbs that a slack hand leads to poverty, "but the hand of the diligent maketh rich." In Mather's view, Christians needed to attend to both their heavenly and earthly callings. Worldly success could be considered a badge of divine favor.

Mather's 18th-century successor was Benjamin Franklin. In our discussion of Horatio Alger, we glanced at Franklin's importance to the American imagination. Unlike most of the other Founders, he started out poor. Through his own efforts, he earned enough to retire in his early 40s. In the genealogy of American success, no one occupies a larger space than Franklin. His famous pamphlet, *The Way to Wealth*, remains a byword for hard work and self-advancement. Poor Richard's aphorisms continue to be familiar after two and a half centuries, as these examples will suggest:

> If time be of all things the most precious, wasting time must be, as Poor Richard says, the greatest prodigality; since, as he elsewhere tells us, Lost time is never found again. ...

> Sloth makes all things difficult, but industry all easy; and He that riseth late must trot all day, and shall scarce overtake his business at night; ... Laziness travels so slowly, that Poverty soon overtakes him. ...

> [Surely the most famous] Early to bed, and early to rise, makes a man healthy, wealthy, and wise, as Poor Richard says.

The myth of America as a New World easily expanded to embrace the idea of the American as a new man. In a book called *Letters From an American Farmer*, Franklin's contemporary, Hector St. John De Crevecoeur, had famously asked: "What is this American, this new man?" His answer is contained in his question. The American is a new kind of individual, capable of extraordinary achievements. Unleashed by democracy, the American represents an unprecedented force in the world. Ralph Waldo Emerson labeled the years before the Civil War as the time of "the American newness.

The 19th century was awash in books and articles that urged young Americans to take advantage of their limitless opportunities, and to exert themselves on behalf of both profit and the public good. Self-improvement and self-invention were the two mandates of a democratic society. In 1848, John Frost published a book called *Self-Made Men of America*. Ten years later, Charles Seymour added a volume called *Self-Made Men*. A few years after the Civil War, James McCabe published *Great Fortunes and How They Were Made*, which carries the subtitle, *The Struggles and Triumphs of our Self-Made Men*.

In the late 1880s, Henry Adams published a massive history of the United States in the first two decades of the 19th century. An introductory chapter, called "American Ideals," summons up a romanticized vision of the man who embodies democratic possibility:

> Stripped for the hardest work, every muscle firm and elastic, every ounce of brain ready for use, and not a trace of superfluous flesh on his nervous and supple body, the American stood in the world a new order of man.

The Puritans, Franklin and Henry Adams, all had in mind an American who linked personal success with higher obligations, either to salvation or to the common good, or perhaps both. In a lecture he gave in the 1880s, the wealthy industrialist Andrew Carnegie—no relation to Dale—offered up a menu of practical advice:

> To summarize what I have said: Aim for the highest; never enter a barroom; do not touch liquor, or if at all only at meals; never speculate; never endorse beyond your surplus cash fund; make the firm's interest yours; … concentrate; put all your eggs in one basket and watch that basket; expenditure always within revenue.

Carnegie may have borrowed that remark about eggs from Mark Twain, by the way. In either case, a basket of eggs seems like a rather meager metaphor for Carnegie's vast fortune. Nonetheless, his wealth conferred authority on his opinions. So also did the religious vocabulary he tended to use. He compiled his thoughts on the subject of success in a book that he called *The Gospel of Wealth*, which he published in 1900. As the title suggests, stories of self-made men were sometimes treated with the reverence usually reserved for the scriptures. The theological inversion probably had part of its source in the biblical exhortation that Christians should put on the "new man." Furthermore, the preachments of earlier American ministers—such as Cotton Mather, whom I mentioned earlier—also legitimized prosperity by linking it to godliness. Russell Conwell, a Philadelphia minister, preached on behalf of success to packed halls across the nation. He's alleged to have delivered his most famous sermon, "Acres of Diamonds," 6,000 times. As a book, it was among the most widely read of the 19th century. "Dig in your own backyard," Conwell exhorted his listeners. You will find all around you the precious gems you are seeking.

One of the bestselling books of the 1920s pushed the linkage between success and religion about as far as it could go. Bruce Barton, the head of one of America's biggest advertising agencies, published a biography of Christ, which he called *The Man Nobody Knows*. If businessmen might resemble Jesus, the reverse could also be true: Jesus as businessman. Although several publishers hesitated to accept the book, which they understandably believed some pious souls would find irreverent, *The Man Nobody Knows* became the bestselling nonfiction book of 1925. In Barton's view, Jesus was "the founder of modern business," who took 12 ordinary men and "molded them into an organization which carried on victoriously."

One of the most popular magazines at the turn of the 20th century was called, simply and proudly, *Success*. Its pages were filled with biographies of the rich and famous, and it featured interviews between aspiring young journalists such as Theodor Dreiser and capitalist potentates, including Carnegie and J. P. Morgan. The magazine's founder, Orison Marden, published a book called, quite bluntly, *Pushing to the Front*. The book's title captures a defining characteristic of the period. So, too, do the novels of Horatio Alger, such as *Ragged Dick*, which we looked at in some detail earlier. All of this elevated rhetoric in defense of affluence and—frankly— greed is easy to caricature, and a good many American writers—including Mark Twain, Stephen Crane, and Henry James—did so.

When President Calvin Coolidge in the 1920s proposed that the business of America was business, he was lampooned for promoting a philistine materialism. Yet I suspect that Coolidge was closer to the mainstream of American opinion than most of his critics.

In the years following the First World War, the idea of success was redefined by the influence of psychology. The French scientist Émile Coué invented a form of learned optimism that he summarized in a famous phrase: On both sides of the Atlantic, millions of striving citizens told themselves, over and over: "Day by day, in every way, I am getting better and better." Coué's popularity marks a turning point in the idea of success. Several scholars have noted a shift from an earlier emphasis on character as the key to achievement to a concentration on personality. Success, which had been portrayed as the evidence of inherent superiority, now seemed to depend more on self-promotion. The transition was reflected in the emergence of the salesman as an iconic figure in American culture.

The years between the two world wars also saw the development of modern advertising: selling on a mass scale. Advertising has a long history, but it became a recognizably modern industry in the '20s. In the opinion of one contemporary, and I quote him: "the salesman and the advertising man were [the] agents and evangels" of Coolidge prosperity. Hundreds of millions of dollars were spent each year on marketing goods—from cigarettes, to automobiles, to food, to movies throughout the interwar decades. According to historian Roland Marchand, "advertising maintained a highly visible and nearly ubiquitous presence in all the popular media of the 1920s," a presence that continued through the 1930s, despite the hardships of the decade. Indeed, the anxieties and deprivations of the Depression enhanced the allure of advertising images, which typically offered access to upscale interiors, and cars, and adornments. These made up what one scholar has called a reassuring "iconography of abundance." Although many intellectuals pronounced on the phoniness of advertising, a survey in the late '30s indicated that "three out of four respondents, men and women, thought that advertising gave them better products. ... More than half believed that widely advertised products are usually the best." This background helps to explain the remarkable impact of *How to Win Friends and Influence People*. Where advertising used a primitive social science to sell products, Dale Carnegie sold himself, taught others how to sell themselves, and permanently altered the nation's culture into the bargain.

The book's gigantic sales might seem at first paradoxical: a triumphant celebration of success in the 1930s, the decade of America's most widespread failure. The paradox is more apparent than real. As many contemporary observers pointed out in the '30s, a commitment to self-reliance survived among large numbers of men and women throughout the Depression. A more critical view of corporate and financial failure coexisted with a continuing belief in the efficacy of initiative and hard work. In a time when up to a quarter of the workforce was idle, such a belief could engender enormous emotional pain. America had long nurtured a culture in which poverty gave some evidence of moral turpitude—a belief that was tested but not abolished by the Depression. Many of the Depression's victims reported feelings of "guilt and self-recrimination.

In doing the travel and research for his book, *My America*, published in 1938, Louis Adamic interviewed scores of people who felt personally responsible for their unemployment and impoverishment. Lorena Hickock, a journalist and friend of Eleanor Roosevelt, was hired to travel around the country and report on Depression conditions as she saw them. Writing back to her boss, Harry Hopkins, the head of the Works Progress Administration (the WPA), Hickock quoted a young woman who refused either aid or encouragement. The woman said: "Oh, don't bother. ... If, with all the advantages I've had, I can't make a living, I'm just no good, I guess."

Dale Carnegie spoke to this segment of the population, offering what he himself called "a formula" for success through the management of personal relations. Carnegie knew all about failure from his own experience. Born in 1888, he was raised on a pig farm in the little town of Maryville, Missouri, and attended a one-room school. His pious Methodist mother tried to push him toward the ministry, a career he never seriously considered. However, he gained his first experiences as a public speaker by reciting well-known temperance speeches, such as "The Saloon: Offspring of Hell." Carnegie pursued his interest in oratory at the State Teacher's College in

Warrensburg, Missouri, becoming one of the foremost debaters in his region. Like many restless young men of his generation, Carnegie drifted from job to job. He joined the International Correspondence Schools as a salesman. Failing in that, he tried selling pork products for Armour & Company. When that also failed, he took his speaking skills to New York and trained as an actor. After touring in a play called *Polly of the Circus*, he came back to New York and found a job as a salesman for Packard Trucks. At about that time, in 1912, Carnegie had his big idea. He convinced the management of the Young Men's Christian Association at 125th Street in New York to allow him to teach a course in elocution and public speaking. The course flourished and spread to other YMCA branches. Within two years, the poor boy from Missouri was earning nearly $2,000 a month, a substantial income for that time.

Carnegie hired assistants and continued to expand his locations throughout the 1920s and '30s. He organized training programs for some of the nation's leading corporations: Westinghouse, Sun Oil, and the New York Telephone Company among them. Along with his traveling and speaking, Carnegie began publishing articles for newspapers and magazines, spreading the news about the value of public speaking. In 1932, he wrote a moderately successful biography called *Lincoln the Unknown*. The book is trivial as a work of scholarship. Carnegie said in the preface that he wrote it "for the average busy and hurried citizen of today." For our purposes, the chief value of the Lincoln biography is the emphasis Carnegie puts on Lincoln's skills as a public speaker, especially in the famous debates with Stephen Douglas in 1858. Another of Carnegie's books, *Little Known Facts About Well Known People*, revealed his continuing fascination with eminent men. Two years later, Carnegie became one of those "well known people," with the publication and instant success of *How to Win Friends and Influence People*.

This is a book unlike any other on our list. Organized into six parts, five of which are subdivided into three or more chapters, *How to Win Friends* has the look and feel of an instruction manual or textbook, which is what it is. The book, as we shall see, combines predictable aphorisms and advice alongside more surprising material. Carnegie's method is to tell stories about people from all walks of life: Theodore Roosevelt and John D. Rockefeller share billing with dozens of lesser-known people, most of them alumni of the Dale Carnegie Institute of Effective Speaking and Human Relations. Their successes provide Carnegie with a series of vignettes that illustrate one or another of the principal points he wants to make. The book's famous title proved to be quite scrupulously exact: You influence people by winning friends, and you win friends by following the advice Carnegie offers you. The book's purpose was not to overturn societal assumptions, or even to reform them. On the contrary, *How to Win Friends* offered what Carnegie called "guaranteed" success and comfort squarely within the status quo.

The first part, which make Carnegie's attitude clear at the outset, is called "Fundamental Techniques in Handling People." The opening anecdotes, rather unpredictably, concern several gangsters, among them Al Capone, Dutch Schultz, and a murderer named "Two Gun" Crowley. It's a clever piece of rhetoric. No reader could put down the book without learning what relevance these famous criminals have to a respectable campaign of self-improvement. Carnegie wants to illustrate the point that all of these bad guys offered justifications for their actions, and thought of themselves as essentially good people. If they can labor under such opinions of themselves, what about the people you and I interact with every day? So the first lesson: Criticism is both useless and dangerous. "It wounds a man's pride," says Carnegie, "hurts his sense of importance, and arouses his resentment." No one will keep a friend or—this is the real point—a customer by insisting on that person's faults and weaknesses. The theme of the entire book is fully present in these early pages. Combining a homespun pragmatism with a common-sense view of human nature, Carnegie directs us to look at each of our transactions from the other person's point of view. Note that Carnegie's emphasis on this apparently generous empathy is strictly opportunistic. To recall the title of part one, this is your method of "handling people."

The second chapter expands on the first: Instead of criticizing, offer praise. Invoking one of Emerson's remarks, "Every man I meet is my superior in some way," Carnegie recommends that we take note of the other person's good points, and make our admiration of those points part of our conversation. If this sounds suspiciously like calculated flattery, Carnegie insists that it is merely good manners and good business. Part two of *How to Win Friends* is called "Six Ways to Make People Like You." The first method is to like them. Carnegie uses the little yellow-haired dog he had as a child to illustrate this point. Tippy simply liked young Dale, unreservedly. In reward, Dale liked the dog in return. The lesson: Be friendly, forget yourself, think of others. And so it goes: "Greet people with animation and enthusiasm." "Be a good listener." Call people by their name: "Remember that a man's name is to him the sweetest and most important sound in the English language." Above all, smile. This is probably the book's most famous axiom. Turn on a smile, not an insincere grin but "a real smile, a heart-warming smile … the kind of smile that will bring a good price in the market place." If you don't feel like smiling, smile anyway. This may have sounded a little fatuous to some of Carnegie's readers, but he quoted the great American psychologist William James in support of his view. The "sovereign path to cheerfulness," James had written, "if our cheerfulness be lost, is to sit up cheerfully and to act and to speak as if cheerfulness were already there." Something of the same insight underlies several contemporary cognitive therapies: a reminder that Carnegie's insights are frequently reliable. The popularity that *How to Win Friends* has enjoyed for over seven decades is not merely a function of shrewd marketing.

Carnegie was not the only popular figure who urged us all to smile in the Depression. Charlie Chaplin's film *Modern Times*, released in the same year as *How to Win Friends*, includes Chaplin's own composition as its theme song, "Smile.

The half-dozen ways to make people like you are followed by "Twelve Ways to Win People to Your Way of Thinking." Avoid arguments; admit your mistakes; try to start with a yes instead of a no; and let the other person do most of the talking. Part four contains "Nine Ways to Change People Without Giving Offense or Arousing Resentment," while part five provides an anthology of "Letters That Produced Miraculous Results." Not surprisingly, the letters were written by sales representatives and advertising agents who had taken the Carnegie Institute course in public speaking.

While the ancestry of *How to Win Friends* reaches back to the 17th century, and the book and its descendants remain strong sellers in the 21st, the volume also reflects the particular cultural values of its time and place. No section makes this more evident than the final part, called "Seven Ways for Making Your Home Life Happier." The assumption throughout this part, as it is throughout the book, is that the man is winning friends and influencing people while his wife is home busy with her domestic responsibilities. To be sure, wives and husbands are both warned against scolding and criticism. One of the seven ways to domestic bliss is the generally sensible advice: "Don't try to make your partner over," but the bulk of the suggestions in this part instruct husbands in how to manipulate their wives in exactly the same way they manage customers. Chapter four includes the observation: "Men should express their appreciation of a woman's effort to look well and dress becomingly. All men forget, if they have ever realized it, how profoundly women are interested in clothes." Likewise, Carnegie reminds men: "Women attach a lot of importance to birthdays and anniversaries—

just why, will forever remain one of those feminine mysteries." Like Sigmund Freud, Carnegie could never quite figure out what women wanted. If he was not progressive in his views of gender, Carnegie did take a fairly forward-looking position on sex. Referring to survey data on the sexual unhappiness of most wives, *How to Win Friends* places much of the responsibility on husbands, and the book ends, rather surprisingly, with a bibliography of 15 books of sexual advice.

Along with its unprecedented sales, Carnegie's book also attracted harsh criticism. In the *Saturday Review of Literature*, for example, James Thurber said that Carnegie's "disingenuities ... stand out like ghosts at a banquet." There was even a parody, Irving Tressler's *How to Lose Friends and Alienate People*.

The parodies and condescension inflicted little damage on Carnegie or his book. Now in its fourth edition, with a more gender-neutral and diverse vocabulary, *How To Win Friends*, and the worldwide chain of Carnegie "training schools," not to mention Carnegie's numerous self-help imitators, collectively document the permanence of the message.

Lecture Seventeen
The Grapes of Wrath

Scope: The Dust Bowl of the 1930s was one of the most profound environmental disasters in American history, and John Steinbeck's *The Grapes of Wrath* remains its unforgettable chronicle. The Joad family of *The Grapes of Wrath* belongs at once to history and to myth. Exiled from their failed Oklahoma farm by the collusion between the drought and the bankers, and straggling westward in search of a new life, they are representative figures of a dispossessed decade. At the same time, they are the last, unlikely pioneers in search of whatever still remains of the American dream. *The Grapes of Wrath* quickly sold 20,000 copies of its advance edition, and it went on to become one of the five bestselling novels of the 1930s. Steinbeck won the Pulitzer Prize, and the novel was immediately adapted as a hugely successful film. Despite disputes about its factual accuracy and the quality of its prose, Americans turn to Steinbeck's big novel for its indelible rendition of human solidarity and the possibilities of hope.

Outline

I. The calamity of the Dust Bowl had its origins in bad agricultural practices. For generations, farmers had turned over the region's grasslands to the cultivation of wheat and corn. That man-made process, coupled with the worst drought in U.S. history, stripped much of the growing soil from half a dozen states.

    A. By the end of 1934, *The Yearbook of Agriculture* estimated that 35 million acres of cropland had been completely destroyed and another 100 million acres had lost their topsoil.

    B. The dust storms of the decade were colossal events: Clouds of dirt, 2 and more miles high, carried millions of tons of dirt and debris at 50 miles an hour across hundreds of square miles.

        1. Hundreds of thousands of Americans—two-thirds of the 1930 population—clung to their homesteads and tried to survive.

        2. The other third, over a quarter of a million people, packed up their belongings and trekked west to find work or relief. It was the largest migration in U.S. history.

C. Despite marginal interventions by the government, the unprecedented scale of damage encouraged prophecies of doom.

D. Steinbeck was not the only writer to dramatize the plight of the Dust Bowl's victims; some of the most celebrated nonfiction books of the 1930s took the devastated land and its people as their subjects.

    1. Along with nonfiction books, several novels and stories also used Dust Bowl experience as fictional material, to great effect.

    2. Literary history, however, has made room for only one Dust Bowl novel, Steinbeck's *The Grapes of Wrath.*

II. John Steinbeck was born in California's Salinas Valley, grew up comfortably middle class, and studied at Stanford for several years. His first success as an author was with *Tortilla Flat* (1935).

A. Steinbeck remained a partisan of the marginal, the injured, and the disadvantaged throughout his career.

    1. His strike novel, *In Dubious Battle* (1936), fictionalizes a strike by lettuce workers near Salinas, California.

    2. With his next novel, *Of Mice and Men* (1937), Steinbeck turned from the public sphere of labor struggles to a more domestic subject. Poverty has much to do with the novel's tragedy, but the fate of Lennie Small expressed Steinbeck's belief that inhumanity has deeper sources than economic deprivation or class divisions.

B. Steinbeck found his greatest subject in the refugees from the Dust Bowl who migrated to California.

    1. He cared less about policy than he did about the Dust Bowl's victims.

    2. Moved to anger by the consequence of brutality during the Depression, Steinbeck determined to make a suitable, politically useful record.

III. The Joad family is exiled from its Oklahoma farm after the combined effect of bankers and the drought. They move westward in search of new life, and travel across half a continent to find what's left of their vision of the American dream.

A. Steinbeck attempted to enhance the authority of the novel by employing a multiplicity of voices.

    1. To reinforce the novel's larger significance, he regularly interrupts the Joad family's adventures with a series of "interchapters."

    2.   These are intended to broaden the novel's scope, generalize its themes, and confirm its documentary claims.

  B. The Joads are introduced as a family, like most others in the district, that has been run off its land. They are the victims of debt and drought.

  C. Conceived with monumental simplicity to illustrate the plight and the underlying integrity of America's victims, the Joads are memorable, if stereotypical, characters.

IV. The novel is divided into two long sections.

  A. The first is the Joads's journey west, and the trip is thick with cultural significance.

    1.   Throughout much of American history, ordinary men and women had followed the frontier in search of new spaces and opportunities.

    2.   *The Grapes of Wrath* is a text in the tradition of that repeated narrative.

  B. Steinbeck insists on the mythic dimensions of the Joads's quest: The family believes they are heading toward the Promised Land.

  C. The journey west is a story of repeated disappointments.

    1.   They get their first glimpse of what awaits them when they meet a man from California who is crazed with grief. He tells them that there is no work and that his wife and two children starved to death as a result.

    2.   Before they get to California, both Granma and Granpa die, and the Joads find themselves in "Hooverville," a squalid camp full of other hungry migrants.

  D. The novel's final chapters recount yet another series of catastrophes: Rose of Sharon's husband disappears, and her child is stillborn. Tom kills one of the deputies who are terrorizing the migrants. He joins a group of union organizers and dedicates himself to achieving justice, whatever the cost.

  E. Religion suffuses the book's last scene in the boxcar.

    1.   The Joads and a number of other migrants have taken refuge in a railroad boxcar, where they are threatened with a flood of almost biblical proportions.

    2.   A nameless old man is dying of starvation; Rose of Sharon saves his life by wordlessly nourishing him with the breast milk meant for her dead baby.

3. The novel ends with Rose of Sharon's silent, mysterious smile.

V. *The Grapes of Wrath* sold 10,000 copies a week for the first several months of its publication. Despite its bestselling status, the novel was denounced on the floor of the Senate and in the pulpits of the Midwest, reviled as a travesty by affronted Oklahomans, and banned in dozens of libraries.

   A. The controversy certainly added to the book's cachet among progressives.

   B. While Steinbeck's literary status remains problematic, his novel has accumulated a reputation as reliable history.
      1. There were also rebuttals to Steinbeck's depiction of migrant experience, most of them forgotten.
      2. The most memorable of these was Ruth Comfort Mitchell's novel *Of Human Kindness*.

   C. Today, seven decades after its publication, *The Grapes of Wrath* continues to attract readers and critical attention.

Suggested Reading:

Benson, *The True Adventures of John Steinbeck, Writer.*

Parini, *John Steinbeck.*

Questions to Consider:

1. *The Grapes of Wrath* opens in the midst of a drought and ends with a flood of epic dimensions. How do these framing scenes contribute to the meaning of the novel? More generally, what is the significance of nature in the book? Consider that certain animals—the steadfast turtle and the dog that is killed by a car—also play a part in defining both the facts and the symbolic value of the natural world.

2. In different sections of the novel, Casy, Tom, and Ma Joad all preach what might be called a gospel of humanity. Do they present similar or different proposals? Does the novel offer an intelligible and coherent set of ideas in response to the political and economic crisis of the Dust Bowl and Depression? To what extent has *The Grapes of Wrath* endured beyond its particular circumstances? Have the book's techniques and its themes become less pertinent as the 1930s recede further into the past?

Lecture Seventeen—Transcript
The Grapes of Wrath

The Dust Bowl of the 1930s—it was one of the most profound environmental disasters in American history, and John Steinbeck's *Grapes of Wrath* remains its unforgettable chronicle. For those who lived through it, the decade of drought and dust turned their lives upside down. By a lethal coincidence, the collapse of farming in the High Plains commenced shortly after the stock market crash and the onset of the Great Depression. For many Americans, the Dust Bowl rhymed with the Depression and became the symbol of an exhausted, defeated economy. Citizens of the Dust Bowl—mainly in Oklahoma, Kansas, Texas, and Colorado—faced a crisis they could neither resist nor even understand. The calamity had its origins in bad agricultural practices. For generations, Midwestern farmers had turned over the region's grasslands to the cultivation of wheat and corn. This eventually removed the thin ground cover of the plains. That manmade process, coupled with the worst drought in American history, stripped much of the fertile soil from half-a-dozen states. By the end of 1934, *The Yearbook of Agriculture* estimated that 35 million acres of cropland had been completely destroyed, and another 100 million acres—an area the size of Pennsylvania—had lost their topsoil. The dust storms of the decade were colossal events: clouds of dirt 2 and more miles high, carrying millions of tons of soil and debris at 50 miles an hour across hundreds of square miles. For days on end, the sun could not break through the clouds of dust. People had to tie cloths around their faces to avoid inhaling dust. They stuffed blankets under their doors and around their windows trying, usually without success, to keep the dust out. Dust sometimes darkened the skies of Chicago, hundreds of miles to the north, and occasionally reached the East Coast. Hundreds of thousands of men, women, and children—two-thirds of the 1930 population of that region—clung to their homesteads, and suffered, and tried to survive. The other third, over a quarter of a million people, packed up their belongings and trekked west to find work or relief. It was the largest internal migration in U.S. history.

The years of the Dust Bowl were, to quote the title of Timothy Egan's fine history of the period, "the worst hard time." Responses to the disaster were both political and technical. Franklin Roosevelt's administration responded with legislation that restrained bank claims on dispossessed farmers, and organized a Drought Relief Service. Despite these marginal interventions, the unprecedented scale of the damage encouraged prophecies of doom. To give one example, in 1936, Stuart Chase, an influential economist and a pioneer in regional planning, published an environmental history of America that he called *Rich Land, Poor Land*. Chase indicted the whole of American history as 300 years of accelerating waste. For him, the Dust Bowl was the most spectacular but only the most recent example of centuries of misuse. A section called "In the Year 2000" foresees an apocalyptic outcome. John Steinbeck was not the only writer to dramatize the plight of the Dust Bowl's victims. Some of the most celebrated nonfiction books of the 1930s took the devastated land and its suffering people as their subjects. Substantially improved cameras and printing technologies enabled Depression-era photographers to record the decade's experience in abundant visual detail. Several of the best-known books of the period combined photos and text to create a selective but powerful documentary history.

Margaret Bourke-White and Erskine Caldwell collaborated on *You Have Seen Their Faces*, whose sole purpose was to educate middleclass Americans about the appalling scale of the suffering in which the nation's poor were trapped. James Agee provided the text and Walker Evans took the pictures for *Let Us Now Praise Famous Men*. Dorothea Lange worked with her husband, labor economist Paul Taylor, on *An American Exodus*. Lange's photographs have remained perhaps the most famous images of the decade. In particular, the picture usually called "Migrant Mother" has endured as an emblem of the misery suffered by the Dust Bowl's involuntary migrants. The photograph is one of a series that Lange made of Florence Owens Thompson and her children in the early spring of 1936 in Nipomo, California. They had come to find work picking peas but ended up hungry and jobless. The picture gains much of its power from its derivative religious imagery. The migrant mother is posed in the manner of a Madonna, and thus becomes a latter-day symbol of suffering but saintly maternity. The woman is lifted out of the anonymous and topical, and her despair is suffused in the peculiar dignity of the religious past. As we will see, John Steinbeck also appealed to precisely this image in the conclusion of *The Grapes of Wrath*.

Along with nonfiction books, many novels and stories also used Dust Bowl experiences as fictional material. Perhaps the most notable was Josephine Winslow Johnson's novel *Now in November*, a fictional account of one family's destruction by the ruined land. The Haldmarnes leave an unnamed city and return to an unnamed countryside when Father loses a good job in a lumber mill and with it any hope of financial security for his wife, Willa, and their three daughters. By bad luck, however, their exodus coincides with the onset of the Dust Bowl. The mortgaged farm to which the family moves is quickly reduced to parched sterility in the killing drought. *Now in November* is told by one of the Haldmarne daughters, Marget, in a prose that combines hard-edged representations of daily life with impressionistic images of deprivation and despair. Overcome by misery, Marget asks at one point: "What use all this in the end? The hope worn on indefinitely ... the desire never fulfilled ... four o'clock and the ice-grey mornings. ... There seemed no answer, and the answer lay only in forgetting."

Even the family's few moments of happiness are bruised by their poverty. Father is a man made hard by toil and debt. Mother has practically vanished into her aging patience, the narrator says: "She lived in the lives of others as though she hadn't one of her own. Kerrin, Marget's older sister, likens her father to King Lear, but she goes mad herself, driven to suicide by disappointment and hate. The novel's central section, "The Long Drought," provides a day-by-day reckoning of the land's decay into baked and cracking clay. The deepening misery is doled out in sad anecdotes. Father reluctantly joins a milk strike, but it fails to raise prices. An aging man living by himself on a nearby farm breaks his hip in a fall, and almost literally shrinks into insensibility. Willa is burned in a fire that ravages the family's few surviving crops, and dies after a couple of months' lingering. The members of a neighboring family, African Americans named Ramsey, are victimized by a racist discrimination that is piled on top of the hardships they share with the poor whites around them, and each rainless day, as the fields scorch white, brings its added portion of anxiety and fear.

Now in November won the Pulitzer Prize before sinking from sight. The award was well deserved. Josephine Johnson's novel provides one of the most convincing and indeed hair-raising representations of the Dust Bowl in the writing of the 1930s. Literary history, however, has made room for only one Dust Bowl novel, Steinbeck's *The Grapes of Wrath*. Perhaps Johnson's gender and the fact that her main character is a woman also had something to do with the outcome.

John Steinbeck was born in California's Salinas Valley, grew up comfortably middle-class, and studied at Stanford University for several years. After a couple of false fictional starts, including a pirate romance, he found his subject and his first success with *Tortilla Flat*, a good-humored if rather one-dimensional portrayal of the allegedly carefree and picturesque *paisanos* of Monterey. Steinbeck remained a partisan of the marginal, the injured, and the disadvantaged throughout the rest of his career. The deep gulf between capitalism's winners and losers sharpened the edge of his social criticism, especially in the 1930s. At the same time, he was never willing to submit to the Communist Party and its ideological discipline. Like the communists, Steinbeck was given to moral simplification—but his was a homegrown variety, the sentimentality that has long attached itself to the plain people and the good land in the populist imagination. It is a version of that instinctive reverence for the land and its inhabitants that we have found in several of the earlier novels we've discussed, including *The Last of the Mohicans*, *The Virginian*, and *The Good Earth*. Enthusiastic advocacy typically played the role of explanation in Steinbeck's fictional world. *In Dubious Battle*, his strike novel, was mistakenly called Marxist by several critics. In fact, the book's sympathies are reserved exclusively for the untutored workers, migrant fruit and vegetable pickers. These are the obscure people whose courage and suffering transcend the mystifications of abstract systems. The book fictionalizes a strike by lettuce workers near Salinas, which, like the strike in the novel, failed when it met a sensational demonstration of violence by the owners and police.

With his next novel, *Of Mice and Men*, Steinbeck turned from the public sphere of labor strife to a more domestic and even intimate subject. George Milton is the friend and protector of the huge but feeble-minded Lennie Small. The two men work and share a modest but impossible dream of a little farm on which Lennie might raise rabbits. Despite his size and strength, Lennie is slow-moving and an easy target for ridicule. Poverty has much to do with the novel's tragedy; however, Lennie's fate expresses Steinbeck's belief that inhumanity has deeper sources than economic deprivation or class division. In a melodramatic sequence of events, Lennie more or less accidentally murders a woman who has been taunting him, and is then murdered by George to save him from a lynch mob. The pathos embodied in Lennie's death accentuates the unfair contest between humanity's claims and the deforming power of cruelty.

Steinbeck found his greatest subject in the refugees from the Dust Bowl who migrated to California. Although he had a detailed command of the economic and political background, he cared less about policy than he did about the Dust Bowl's victims. Steinbeck saw the harsh treatment of these families by police and businessmen as the saddest consequence of the Depression. Nature was cruel but indifferent. Men, on the other hand, had to choose their cruelty. Moved to anger by the brutality that scarred human relationships, Steinbeck determined to make a suitable and politically useful record. He first considered journalism, as he said in a letter of 1938: "I want to put a tag of shame on the greedy bastards who are responsible for this, but I can do it best through the newspapers." He did use newspapers, but then he reworked his reporting in *The Grapes of Wrath*. He produced the most controversial and influential novel of the 1930s.

Among earlier fictional works, only Upton Sinclair's *The Jungle* and Harriet Beecher Stowe's *Uncle Tom's Cabin* were so tightly linked to the social history of their times as Steinbeck's chronicle of the Joad family and their endurance. The Joads belong at once to history and myth. Exiled from their failed Oklahoma farm by the collusion between the drought and the bankers, and straggling westward in search of a new life, they are the representative figures of a dispossessed decade. At the same time, they are the last, unlikely pioneers, and their story echoes with the intermittent recollections of Jefferson, Emerson, and Whitman. The Joads travel across half a continent to find whatever might still remain of the American dream. Like John Dos Passos in *U.S.A.* and James Agee and Walker Evans in *Let Us Now Praise Famous Men*, Steinbeck attempted to enhance the authority of *The Grapes of Wrath* by employing a multiplicity of voices. To reinforce the novel's larger significance, he regularly interrupts the Joad family's adventures to insert a series of factual (and, frankly, sometimes semi-factual) "interchapters," as we usually call them. Used-car lots, tractors, banks, and the sad shacks of Hoovervilles are among Steinbeck's subjects in these sections. Some of these pages are abstract, but most are anecdotal. All are intended to broaden the novel's scope, generalize its themes, and confirm its documentary claims.

The novel opens with a description of the long drought:

> The sun flared down on the growing corn day after day until a line of brown spread along the edge of each [plant]. ... Then it was June and the sun shown more fiercely. The brown lines on the corn leaves widened. ... The air was thin and the sky more pale; and every day the earth paled.

> The hooves of the horses beat the ground. The dirt crust broke and the dust formed. Every moving thing lifted the dust into the air: A walking man lifted a thin layer as high as his waist, and a wagon lifted the dust as high as the fence tops.

Following this panoramic opening, the novel introduces its main characters. Tom Joad has just been released from prison, where he has done time for killing a man in a fight. It was, we are assured, justifiable homicide. Joined by an ex-preacher named Jim Casy, Tom returns home to find the farm vacant and his family gone. A half-crazed neighbor named Muley Graves tells Tom that the Joads, like almost every other family in the district, have been run off their land, victims of debt and drought. Muley is practically starving, himself, but he demonstrates his instinctive generosity by sharing a rabbit that he has trapped and cooked for dinner.

In Steinbeck's somewhat romantic view, poverty is associated with self-sacrifice. Late in the novel, Ma Joad will declare: "I'm learnin' one thing good. ... Learnin' it all a time, ever' day. If you're in trouble or hurt or need—go to poor people. They're the only ones that'll help—the only ones." Tom finds his family at Uncle John's nearby farm, packing up to leave for California. Despite his manifest sympathy, Steinbeck makes no effort to avoid stereotypes as he paints each portrait. Nevertheless, the Joads, conceived with monumental simplicity to illustrate the plight and the underlying integrity of America's victims, are memorable characters. Granma is toothless but feisty, Granpa is half-senile but still claims his patriarchal seniority. Pa guides with quiet resolution, while the earthy Ma quickly proves herself to be the family's heart and center. Along with Tom, who is the novel's major figure, the Joad children include the mentally impaired Noah, the pregnant teenager Rose of Sharon, and the younger children—Ruthie and Winfield. Casy and Rose of Sharon's restless and ultimately faithless husband, Connie Rivers, are also part of the company.

The novel is divided into two long sections. In the first, the Joads undertake their journey west. They are clutching yellow handbills that promise plentiful work in the California orchards. It seems that the big farmers have blanketed the Dust Bowl with boldfaced advertisements that read: "PEA PICKERS WANTED IN CALIFORNIA. GOOD WAGES ALL SEASON. 800 PICKERS WANTED.

As the farmers predict, the handbills attract tens of thousands, not mere hundreds. For most people, there will be no work. For the others, because of the over-supply of labor, wages will be held at criminally low levels. The Joad family's journey west is thick with cultural significance. Throughout much of American history, ordinary men and woman had followed the frontier in search of new spaces and new opportunities. In an earlier lecture, I discussed the shaping and even mythic power of this story, which provided the master narrative for much of American culture. *The Grapes of Wrath* is a text in that tradition. Steinbeck insists on the spiritual dimensions of the Joads' quest. In one of the early interchapters, the narrator makes a reference to *Pilgrim's Progress*, and the allusion is quite intentional. Like the hero of that earlier epic, and like the Israelites on the Exodus, the Joads believe that they are heading toward the Promised Land. When they cross the great southwestern desert, they almost literally reenact the Old Testament saga. Reality continuously intrudes. The journey west is a story of repeated disappointments. Piling their pitiful belongings in the back of a broken-down truck, the Joads head down Route 66, encountering one reversal after another. When they stop at a gas station, they are treated like thieves by the attendant, and Ruthie's dog is killed by a careless passing motorist. A few days later, Granpa dies of a stroke, and the family buries him in a shallow grave by the roadside. Tom recites a makeshift but heartfelt blessing over the old man's body. For Steinbeck, as for Mark Twain two generations earlier, the unlettered speech of the folk is more eloquent than the polished rhetoric of the elite.

The Joads get their first glimpse of what they will face in the West when they meet a ragged man, returning from California and crazed with grief. There is no work, he tells them. The handbills are a lie. His wife and two children starved to death while he could find no way to earn a dollar or a dime. Before they get to California, Noah simply walks away and Granma dies. The rest of the family find themselves in a "Hooverville," a squalid camp full of other hungry migrants. Here they learn about the power of the owners. Only starvation wages are paid, and anyone who complains is blacklisted, beaten, or even killed. The police and state troopers conspire with the companies. The law is in the pay of the owners.

The Joads meet a defeated fellow migrant who says of America: "She's a nice country. But she was stole a long time ago." There is no chance for the little people against the combined forces of money and power. Life improves for a while when the Joads get to Weedpatch, a government camp that provides sanitary facilities, protection from company thugs, and a portion of dignity, but they can only stay for a while. Then they have to move on and face again the prospects of hunger, violence, and defeat. The novel's final chapters recount yet another series of catastrophes. Rose of Sharon's husband disappears. Her baby is stillborn. Tom kills one of the deputies who is terrorizing the migrants, and has to hide. He joins a group of union organizers. He finds that Casy is one of the leaders, and he dedicates himself to achieving justice, whatever the cost. In a speech that intentionally paraphrases the Socialist leader Eugene V. Debs, Tom assures his mother that even though he has to go into hiding, he will always be near her. He says:

Maybe like Casy says, a fella ain't got a soul of his own, but on'y a piece of a big one—an' then. ... Then it don' matter. Then I'll be all aroun' in the dark. I'll be ever'where—wherever you look. Wherever they's a fight so hungry people can eat, I'll be there. Wherever they's a cop beatin' up a guy, I'll be there. ... I'll be there in the way guys yell when they're mad an'—I'll be [there] in the way kids laugh when they're hungry an' they know supper's ready.

As this speech demonstrates, a network of familiar American values lies not far below the novel's surface of melodrama and dissent. The reputed radicalism of the novel subsides at last into a celebration of the endurance of ordinary folk.

In one of the book's most famous passages, Ma Joad makes a speech about "the people." When Tom complains bitterly about the rich and powerful who have made their lives miserable, Ma replies:

You got to have patience. Why, Tom—us people will go on livin' when all them people is gone. Why, Tom, we're the people that live. They ain't gonna wipe us out. Why, we're the people—we go on. ... Rich fellas come up an' they die, an' their kids ain't no good, an' they die out. But, Tom, we keep-a-comin'. Don' you fret none, Tom. A different time's comin'.

It is the traditional democratic faith, almost religious in Steinbeck's formulation of it. Religion also suffuses the book's last scene. The Joads and a number of other migrants have taken refuge in a railroad boxcar. They are threatened with a flood of almost biblical proportions. A nameless old man is dying of starvation. Rose of Sharon saves his life by silently nourishing him with the breast milk meant for her dead baby. The novel ends with Rose of Sharon's wordless, mysterious smile. Once again, the image deliberately recalls the Madonna of Christian tradition.

The Grapes of Wrath quickly sold the 20,000 copies of its advance printing and continued to sell 10,000 copies a week for several months. Eventually, it was among the five bestselling novels of the 1930s. Steinbeck won the Pulitzer Prize. The novel was immediately adapted as a hugely successful and first-rate film. Not everyone applauded. The novel was denounced on the floor of the Senate and in the pulpits of the Midwest, reviled as a travesty by affronted Oklahomans and banned in dozens of libraries. Lyle Boren, an Oklahoma congressman, called the book "a lie, a black, infernal creation of a twisted, distorted mind." Californians also protested: Several libraries banned the book until the mid-forties. Needless to say, that sort of clamor—recall the similar case of *Huckleberry Finn*—only added to the book's caché among progressives, and it added as well to the sales figures.

While Steinbeck's literary status has remained problematic, *The Grapes of Wrath* has accumulated a reputation as reliable history. The radical writer, Anna Louise Strong, was among the first witnesses who testified to the novel's essential accuracy. Strong's book, *My Native Land*, is a record of her cross-country fact-finding travels in the latter years of the Depression. In the first section, she describes the Oklahomans who have trekked to California through the shorthand of invoking the film version of Steinbeck's book. She says: "You know these Oklahomans. You have seen them in *The Grapes of Wrath* in the movies. ... You remember Ma Joad, driving into the future." Strong goes on to itemize the same acts of injustice and inhumanity that Steinbeck dramatized: beatings inflicted by night-riding vigilantes in the pay of the Associated Farmers; children dying of malnutrition while food and milk rot in locked barns; and the complicity of local government.

There were also rebuttals to Steinbeck's depiction of migrant experience; most of them are now forgotten. A man named Marshall Hartranft produced one of the zanier efforts to debunk Steinbeck, a partisan screed called *Grapes of Gladness: California's Refreshing and Inspiring Answer to John Steinbeck's "Grapes of Wrath*. Somewhat more seriously, Ruth Comfort Mitchell published a novel called *Of Human Kindness* just a year after *Grapes* appeared. Mitchell's fictional counter-statement is told from the viewpoint of California farmers, who are presented as sympathetic men and women, in the narrator's words: "San Joaquin Valley pioneers, third generation in California; plain people, poor people, proud people; salt of the earth." In this novel, they treat the Dust Bowl migrants generously, but despise labor agitators who "moved among the workers like germs of virulent sicknesses."

Two of the most extended scenes in Mitchell's novel were clearly orchestrated as specific replies to Steinbeck. In the first, a character named Dexter says to Geoff Howard, one of the Farm Association leaders: "'I'm eager to get a copy of that famous hand-bill you sent to lure workers to the state.' '... so are we!' Howard answers. 'In fact we've had a reward out for months, but no takers up to date.'" And, in the book's final scene, a farm wife named Mary explains that a pregnant migrant woman could have found competent medical care. She says:

> You hav'n't understood. California does more for unfortunate people than any other state in the Union. ... [T]his girl needn't

have had her baby here on the ditch bank. There was a place for her in the hospital, one of the biggest and finest in the whole west.

Mary then gives the emaciated mother a large can of milk. The reconciliation between farmers and migrants is couched in the same sentimental image as Steinbeck's protest. Along with a nod to Shakespeare, the image also provides the novel with its title.

To put it crudely, Steinbeck won, and his critics lost. Today, seven decades after its publication, *The Grapes of Wrath* continues to attract readers and critical attention. Long after the disputes about its factual accuracy and the quality of its prose have subsided, Americans still turn to Steinbeck's big novel for its indelible rendition of human solidarity and the possibilities of hope.

Lecture Eighteen
Native Son

Scope: Richard Wright's *Native Son* was the first bestselling work of fiction by a black writer, selling over 200,000 copies within the first month of publication. Wright's troubled and troubling masterpiece permanently enlarged the possibilities for black literature in America: Bigger Thomas, *Native Son*'s protagonist, was neither a racial idealization nor a passive victim. Instead, Bigger inevitably acts out the violence that has stifled his humanity. The novel begins with Bigger accidentally killing a young white woman, which creates for him a new life, one that seduces with the increasing power he feels committing violent acts. Because of the challenge *Native Son* presents to consensual views of purpose and justice, the novel has evoked controversy among both black and white readers from the day of its publication nearly 70 years ago. The debates over Wright's novel testify to the enduring force of its narrative. The life and death of Bigger Thomas belie comforting assertions that might be offered about America's racial future. The novel remains one of the major texts in 20th-century American writing, and it continues to provoke controversy.

Outline

I. Richard Wright, the grandson of a slave, was born in 1908 on a plantation near Natchez, Mississippi.

    A. His father was a sharecropper and walked out on the family when Wright was a child.

        1. Wright grew up in poverty, spending several years with his grandparents as well as some time in an orphanage.

        2. He received little formal education.

    B. Wright moved to Chicago when he was 19 years old.

    C. In 1934, he joined the Communist Party, and he remained a member until 1942.

    D. After moving to New York in 1937, Wright published his first book, a collection of stories called *Uncle Tom's Children*.

1. Wright's stories, essays, poems, and novels distill his firsthand experience of the varieties of legally sanctioned American oppression.
2. Wright's literary growth in the 1930s coincided with the last years of the Harlem Renaissance.

II. Wright rejected the renaissance writers' subservience to white standards and patronage. He felt the job of the black writer was to identify himself with the masses and then use literature to "create values by which his race is to struggle, live and die."

   A. During the late '30s, Wright regularly measured black literature by the yardstick of revolutionary utility. Ironically, this was not the task he set out to achieve in *Native Son*.

   B. The violence Wright had seen and felt in his boyhood and later in Chicago and New York became the hallmark of much of his writing.

   C. His climactic accomplishment was *Native Son*, which upon publication permanently enlarged the possibilities for black literature in America.

III. *Native Son* is divided into three large sections, called with almost allegorical simplicity "Fear," "Flight," and "Fate." The first two sections take place in less than 72 hours, the third lasts for about a month.

   A. The first section, "Fear," recounts one day in Bigger's life. He shares a filthy one-room tenement apartment with his mother, sister, and brother.
      1. As they get dressed, a huge black rat crawls out of the wall, a grotesque symbol of the family's poverty and degraded existence.
      2. Wright's narrator gives the reader access to Bigger's rage and self-hatred—and predicts the violence to come as Bigger kills the rat.

   B. Bigger spends the day wasting time and getting into trouble; he hangs out with friends and plots a robbery.

   C. After applying for work as a driver for a rich white man, Mr. Dalton, Bigger's first job is to drive the Dalton daughter, Mary, to class.
      1. Mary orders him instead to drive her to meet her lover, a young communist.

2. After a night of drinking, Bigger carries the unconscious young woman to her room and puts her to bed.
3. The novel's turning point is when Mary's mother enters the room, and Bigger accidentally smothers Mary while trying to keep her quiet.

D. Though Mrs. Dalton is blind and cannot see him, Bigger knows that he will inevitably be charged with Mary's murder, and probably with rape. He burns Mary's body in the furnace.

IV. Part 2, "Flight," takes place across two days as Bigger tries to evade capture. In the morning after the murder, Bigger feels panic, which morphs into exaltation at the thought of what he had done.

A. During his flight, Bigger will commit another murder, this one brutal and intentional.
1. His girlfriend, Bessie, turns from him in despair when she learns of his crime.
2. He rapes her, and then beats her to death with a brick.

B. Once again, Bigger affirms the crime he has committed. He decides that "out of it all, over and above all that had happened, impalpable but real, there remained to him a queer sense of power … never had his will been so free as in this night and day of fear and murder and flight."

C. It was this moral stance, and not the brutality of its individual scenes, that gave *Native Son* the power of a physical blow.

V. In the novel's third section, "Fate," Bigger has been captured and imprisoned, and he is standing trial for the rape and murder of Mary Dalton; Bessie's death is never mentioned.

A. The trial in *Native Son* lacks any sense of urgency or drama; Bigger rightly knows that he has already been judged and convicted.
1. A communist lawyer named Boris Max defends Bigger, arguing that Bigger has been driven to murder by the squalor and bigotry that have defined his entire life.
2. Bigger himself rejects this interpretation, since it would erase the feeling of power and self-creation he derives from his actions and reduce him again to victim status.

B. In the novel's final scene, Bigger has embraced his fate, and he awaits execution with a "faint, wry, bitter smile."

VI. *Native Son* had its sources in Wright's own experience on Chicago's South Side, as well as the sociological insight of Louis Wirth. The novel also incorporates material from the sensational real-life trial of Robert Nixon.

    A. Wright acknowledges that Bigger was a composite of five different young black men he had known growing up in the South.

        1. What linked these men together was their shared defiance of Jim Crow's humiliating rules, and Wright uses their acts of defiance in the novel.

        2. However, Bigger collaborates with his circumstances of poverty and racism to increase the sum total of human misery.

    B. One of the earliest and most influential critics of *Native Son* was James Baldwin, whose view was that Bigger Thomas consists of nothing but his hate.

    C. Bigger is not the whole of America's racial truth, but a part of what had not been spoken before. Wright intended him to be a figure symbolic of America's future, a prophecy of "what we would encounter on a vast scale" in the days to come.

Suggested Reading:

Fabre, *The Unfinished Quest of Richard Wright.*

Walker, *Richard Wright, Daemonic Genius.*

Questions to Consider:

1. Race remains an integral part of America's identity and experience. What contribution does *Native Son* make today to the analysis of that issue, decades after its original publication? It is probably necessary to include the novel's presentation of violence in this analysis.

2. Although the reader is given a great deal of direct access to Bigger Thomas's consciousness, many readers find him mysterious and obscure. To what extent does Bigger exist as a fully realized character in the novel? Does his function in the book's thematic exposition interfere with his portrayal as a convincing human being?

Lecture Eighteen—Transcript
Native Son

Richard Wright's *Native Son* was the first novel by an African American to be named a main selection of the Book-of-the-Month Club. It was also the first bestselling work of fiction by a black writer, with sales of over 200,000 copies in the month following publication. The novel remains one of the major texts in 20th-century American writing, and, as we will see, it continues to provoke controversy.

The grandson of a slave, Wright grew up in poverty. He was born in 1908 on a plantation near Natchez, Mississippi. His father was a sharecropper who walked out on the family when Wright and his brother were young children. His mother moved from place to place across the South, trying to find and keep work. Wright lived for several years with his grandparents, and spent part of his childhood in an orphanage. He received little formal education; few American writers have endured as much simply to learn to read and write. Literacy was still considered dangerous for a black person in the South of Richard Wright's childhood. Wright moved to Chicago when he was 19, taking a long assortment of odd jobs, including several months caring for laboratory animals in a hospital research lab. He joined the left-wing John Reed Club, where he found a community of both white and black literary activists. In 1934, he joined the Communist Party, and he remained a member until 1942, shortly after the publication of *Native Son*. He announced his resignation from the party in a famous article called "The God That Failed.

After moving to New York in 1937, he published his first book, a collection of stories called *Uncle Tom's Children* that won a major prize from *Story* magazine. Wright's essays, stories, poems, and novels distill his first-hand experience of the varieties of legally sanctioned American oppression. He first came to attention as a poet, publishing, among some two-dozen poems, *I Have Seen Black Hands*, a call for the interracial revolution of exploited workers. His most famous poem, perhaps, was called "Between the World and Me," an appallingly successful re-creation of a lynching that Wright had personally witnessed: In that poem's anguished conclusion, Wright's voice merges with that of the lynch victim: "Panting, begging I clutched … the hot sides of death. Now I am dry bones and my face a stony skull.

This tone of outraged and baffled grievance would mark all of Wright's work. He had seen more of the cruelties of racial discrimination than almost any contemporary writer, black or white. While he was still a young man, he chose as his vocation the task of translating what he had seen and sometimes suffered into fictional terms. The 1930s, when Wright was growing into literary maturity, coincided with the last years of the Harlem Renaissance. The beginnings of the Renaissance have been traced to different events: the musical *Shuffle Along*, an African American play that opened on Broadway in 1921; or Jean Toomer's experimental novel *Cane*, published in 1923; or Alain Locke's landmark 1925 anthology, *The New Negro*. Whatever the particular catalyzing moment, the Harlem Renaissance was, quite self-consciously, a communal gathering of artistic forces, the first such movement in African American literature. Langston Hughes, Claude McKay, Zora Neale Hurston, Arna Bontemps, and James Weldon Johnson were among the poets and novelists who made major contributions. Though many of the Renaissance writers thought of themselves as co-workers, the group was never monolithic either in theme or technique. James Weldon Johnson's prophetic optimism in *Black Manhattan* is expressive of the movement, but so too is Claude McKay's call to racial judgment, "If We Must Die." If in fact we must die, McKay's poem declares, let us fight to the death, and never surrender. Conventional formality, for example the use of the sonnet form by McKay and Countee Cullen, was matched by the modernist experimentation of Jean Toomer and again by Langston Hughes's attempts to create rhythms in verse that would approximate the feel of jazz. Subjects ranged from racial protest, to romantic love, to African and Afro-American history.

In their essays and book reviews, the Renaissance writers posed a set of questions that would recur in black aesthetic debates throughout much of the 20th century. Was there, in fact or theory, a distinctively "Afro-American art"? Should black literary norms be the same as white? If not, what should be different and what should be held in common? What is the ideological function of literature?

Richard Wright arrived in New York as the Renaissance was winding down in the middle of the Depression. Motivated by his explicit political commitments, he stood outside the movement and in fact treated it with contempt. He was especially offended by what he saw as the subservience of many Renaissance writers to white standards and white patronage. In an important essay called "Blueprint for Negro Writing," Wright described the Renaissance writers—quite unfairly—as:

prim and decorous ambassadors who went a-begging to white America. ... They entered the Court of American Public Opinion dressed in the kneepants of servility, curtseying to show that the Negro was not inferior, that he was human, and that he led a life comparable to that of other people.

For the most part these artistic ambassadors were received as though they were French poodles who do clever tricks.

According to Wright, the job of the black writer was to identify himself with the masses and then use literature, in his words, to "create values by which his race is to struggle, live and die."

James Joyce's young hero, Stephen Dedalus, testified that he intended "to forge in the smithy of my soul the uncreated conscience of my race." Richard Wright, who felt an affinity between the colonized Irish and the oppressed African American, had the same intention. Wright adhered to a more or less dogmatic Marxism for only a few years, but during the late '30s he typically measured black literature by the yardstick of revolutionary utility. Ironically, as we will see, this was not the task he set out to achieve in *Native Son*, and Communist reviewers attacked the book for its deviation from the party line. Like several of his African American contemporaries, Wright underscored the central importance of folklore to black literature and black culture. In his "Blueprint," which I quoted earlier, he wrote that it was "in a folklore molded out of rigorous and inhuman conditions of life that the Negro achieved his most indigenous and complete expression." Wright's particular understanding of folklore, in other words, was shaped by his political convictions.

His book, *12 Million Black Voices*, published just a year after *Native Son*, is an angry documentary account of black life in Depression America. It is subtitled, *A Folk History of the Negro in the U.S.* The book is an inventory of the exploitation of blacks by whites, a chronicle in which all whites are reduced to one of two allegorical figures: Either they are the southern "Lords of the Land," or they are the northern "Bosses of Buildings."

As he enumerates the crimes of whites against blacks, Wright's prose accelerates toward a nearly physical confrontation. The one-room kitchenette apartment of northern ghettos, a sort of tenement housing that will feature so importantly in *Native Son*, is, says Wright: "our prison, our death sentence," imposed without a trial. He continues:

The kitchenette, with its filth and foul air, with its one toilet for thirty or more tenants, kills our black babies so fast that in many cities twice as many of them die as white babies. ...

The kitchenette, with its crowded rooms and incessant bedlam, provides an enticing place for crimes of all sort[s]—crimes against women and children or any stranger who happens to stray into its dark hallways. The noise of our living, boxed in stone and steel, is so loud that even a pistol shot is smothered. ... The kitchenette is the funnel through which our pulverized lives flow to ruin and death on the city pavements.

The violence Wright had seen and felt in his boyhood and later in Chicago and New York became the hallmark of much of his writing. In his memoir, *Black Boy*, he observed: "All my life had shaped me for the realism, the naturalism of the modern novel." His climactic accomplishment was *Native Son*, a troubled and troubling masterpiece that permanently enlarged the possibilities for black literature in America.

Bigger Thomas, the novel's protagonist, is descended neither from the racial idealizations nor the passive victims who populate most earlier American fiction. He is not class conscious nor indeed conscious of much of anything except the universal white injustice that suffocates his vague dreams of happiness. Virtually trapped into murdering his first victim, a white woman, he later murders again—a black woman this time, and in cold blood. Bigger relentlessly acts out the violence that has stifled his humanity.

Native Son is divided into three large sections, called with almost allegorical simplicity: "Fear," "Flight," and "Fate." The first two sections take place in less than 72 hours; the third lasts for about a month. The first section recounts one day in Bigger's life. He wakes up in the filthy one-room tenement apartment that he shares with his mother, sister, and brother. As they fumble to put on their clothes in the cluttered space, ashamed of dressing and undressing in front of each other, a huge black rat crawls out of the wall. The rat is Wright's grotesque symbol of the family's poverty and their degraded existence. All of them are trapped in a society that treats them as animals. So, too, are their neighbors, imprisoned in the squalor of a thousand identical tenement rooms. From the first page of the novel, Wright's narrator gives the reader access to Bigger's rage and self-hatred, and predicts the violence to come. Just after he kills the rat, we are told that

[Bigger] hated his family because he knew they were suffering and that he was powerless to help them. ... He knew that the moment he allowed what his life meant to enter fully into his consciousness, he would either kill himself or someone else. So he denied himself.

This is the primal fear from which the title of the first section comes.

Bigger spends much of the day, like most days, wasting time and getting into trouble. He hangs out with friends, with whom he plots a robbery that they don't commit. Then he goes to the movies, where Hollywood images of white affluence and romance fill him with anger and yearning. As Wright said in an essay about the novel, Bigger Thomas was simultaneously

> attracted and repelled by the American scene. He was [Wright explained] an American, because he was a native son; but he was also a Negro nationalist in a vague sense because he was not allowed to live as an American. Such was his way of life, and mine.

That last phrase is significant. Though Wright did star as his main character in a movie version of *Native Son*, he was not Bigger Thomas. Stirred to anger at injustice, Wright responded with his pen, not violence. Nonetheless, he insisted that he and Bigger shared a convulsive sense of dislocation. They were both citizens of a society that denied their rights to equality and even denied their identity.

Wright is here recapitulating the argument that W. E. B. Du Bois had made, almost four decades earlier, in *The Souls of Black Folk*. Every African American, wrote Du Bois, is torn into two parts by the burden of racism. In one of his most famous passages, Du Bois comments:

> It is a peculiar sensation, this double-consciousness, this sense of always looking at one's self through the eyes of others, of measuring one's soul by the tape of a world that looks on in amused contempt and pity.

> One ever feels his two-ness—an American, a Negro; two souls, two thoughts, two unreconciled strivings; two warring ideals in one dark body,

Bigger has none of the sophistication of Dr. Du Bois, but he exemplifies the same sense of alienation. Hoping for a job, he applies to work as a driver for a rich white man. His new employer, Mr. Dalton, also happens to own the squalid tenement in which Bigger lives. Bigger's first assignment is to drive the Dalton daughter, Mary, to classes at the university. Mary orders him instead to drive her to a seedy part of town, where she meets her lover, a young Communist named Jan Erlone. After a night of non-stop alcohol, Mary is too drunk to walk up the stairs of her house. Bigger carries the unconscious young woman to her room and puts her to bed. At that moment, the novel's turning point, Mary's mother enters the room looking for her. Bigger knows the inference that will be drawn if he is found in the room. He puts a pillow over Mary's mouth to keep her quiet and accidentally smothers her. Ironically, he has not been observed by Mrs. Dalton, who is blind. Nonetheless, he understands that if he is found out, he will be charged with murder and probably with rape. In the grisly final pages of the first section, Bigger takes Mary's body down to the basement, cuts off her head, and burns her body in the furnace. He walks home in the snow, a white blizzard that signals the inescapable world of whiteness in which he has always lived.

Part Two of the novel, "Flight," takes place across two days as Bigger tries to evade capture. Though he wakes in panic, his reaction to Mary's death is soon transformed into a strange species of exaltation. In the narrator's words:

> The thought of what he had done, the awful horror of it … formed for him for the first time in his fear-ridden life a barrier of protection between him and a world he feared. He had murdered and … created a new life for himself. It was something that was all his own, and it was the first time in his life [that] he had had anything that others could not take [away] from him. … His crime was an anchor weighing him safely in time. … His crime seemed natural; he felt that all of his life had been leading to something like this.

Bigger will maintain this shocking moral stance consistently through the novel. The second section will include another murder, this one altogether intentional. When he runs from one hiding place to another, trying to escape the police dragnet, he is accompanied by his girlfriend—a young black woman named Bessie. When he tells her what he has done, she turns from him in despair. He rapes her—then decides he will be safer if she is dead. He beats her head to bloody pulp with a brick and then throws her body down the air shaft of the abandoned building in which they have been hiding. Once again, Bigger affirms the crime he has committed. Although he is hungry, and broke, and threatened with imminent capture and certain death, he decides, as the narrator tells us, that:

> out of it all, over and above all that had happened, impalpable but real, there remained to him a queer sense of power. He had done

this. He had brought all this about. In all of his life these two murders were the most meaningful things that had ever happened to him. ... Never had he had the chance to live out the consequences of his actions; never had his will been so free as in this night and day of fear and murder and flight.

It was this moral attitude, and not the brutality of its individual scenes, that gave *Native Son* the power of a physical blow—and it still does. The novel's final section, "Fate," is at once the longest and the least successful portion of the book. Bigger has been captured and imprisoned, and he is standing trial for the rape and murder of Mary Dalton. Bessie's death is never mentioned. A Communist lawyer named Boris Max takes Bigger's case. Although courtroom scenes are often filled with high drama—we will look at such a scene when we discuss *To Kill a Mockingbird*—the trial in *Native Son* lacks any sense of urgency or suspense. For one thing, Bigger rightly knows that he has already been judged and convicted. Beyond that, the summation that Max delivers goes on for 30 repetitive pages, at which point the novel clunks to a halt. Max argues that Bigger has been driven to murder by the squalor and bigotry that have defined his entire life. In effect, Max concludes, Bigger is primarily guilty of the crime of being black. Bigger himself rejects this interpretation, since it would erase the feeling of power and self-creation that he has derived from his actions. It would reduce him again to the status of victim. In Bigger's view, those who want to kill him had never considered him as human. He was not included in their picture of Creation—and that, says the narrator, "was why he had killed. ... To live, he had created a new world for himself, and for that he was to die."

In this spirit, he embraces the guilty verdict and the sentence of death that follows. In the novel's final scene, Bigger is standing in his jail cell, holding the bars, waiting for his execution. In the last line, the narrator says that Bigger "smiled a faint, wry, bitter smile. He heard the ring of steel against steel as a far door clanged shut."

Native Son had some of its sources in Wright's own decade of experience on Chicago's South Side. It also included the sociological insights of Louis Wirth, a German immigrant and a social scientist at the University of Chicago. Wirth's publications included a 1938 essay called "Urbanism as a Way of Life." In that influential article, which Wright knew, Wirth declared that city life typically nurtured alienation. Densely packed tenements became a seedbed for what Wirth described as "the relative absence of intimate personal acquaintanceship [and the production] of human relations which are largely anonymous, superficial, and transitory." Translated from social scientific jargon into English, these views resonated with Wright's observations of Chicago's poorest neighborhoods.

Native Son also incorporates material from the sensational trial of Robert Nixon, an African American man who was tried, convicted, and executed for killing a white woman with a brick. The appalling racism that marked much of that trial's coverage in the white press is authentically documented in the novel. The press quotes in *Native Son* are taken verbatim from Chicago newspapers. One example will more than suffice:

> Though the Negro killer's body does not seem compactly built, he gives the impression of possessing abnormal physical strength. He is about five feet, nine inches tall and his skin is exceedingly black. His lower jaw protrudes obnoxiously, reminding one of a jungle beast.

Wright mentioned the Nixon case in an important essay called "How Bigger Was Born," his own account of the sources and background of *Native Son*. In part, according to Wright, Bigger was a composite of five different young black men he had known when he was growing up in the South. What linked them together was their shared defiance of Jim Crow's humiliating rules. One refused to move from the white section of a streetcar, another threatened a white bigot with a knife, and so on. Wright concedes that such gestures were doomed. White justice and the white lynch mob would soon eliminate black opposition. Nonetheless, there is a measure of nobility in saying no. However, these remembered outsiders do not adequately foreshadow Wright's fictional character. Bigger is not a victim who chooses to stand up in behalf of his dignity. He is a small-time gangster and bully who commits an accidental homicide to which he adds a deliberate and premeditated murder. Turning those acts into mythic deeds of self-invention does not subtract from the repugnance of his choices. Trapped from birth inside the prison of poverty and racial discrimination, he collaborates with his circumstances to increase the sum total of human misery. It is undeniably the case, as Bigger proposes at one point, that African Americans have always suffered unearned punishment simply for the color of their skin. Sadly, however, Bigger's actions have provided nothing more or less than a weird validation of white hostility. It has been proposed that Bigger's fate goes beyond race to encompass the helplessness of all humanity in a world of increasing violence and cruelty.

Wright himself suggests as much in his essay: "I made the discovery," he says, "that Bigger Thomas was not black all the time; he was white, too."

But that assertion simply enlarges the question that it begs: Can the murder of innocent bystanders confer dignity and meaning on the murderer? The victim of power, Bigger seeks salvation in the ungoverned use of power. It is not surprising that he finds himself attracted to forms of fascism. The narrator tells us that Bigger "liked to hear of how Japan was conquering China; of how Hitler was running the Jews to the ground; of how Mussolini was invading Spain." Note that Bigger even gets his fascist facts wrong: Mussolini had invaded the African country of Ethiopia, which lends an additional pathos to Bigger's adulation of totalitarian violence. Absolute power corrupts, according to a famous aphorism—but so, too, can powerlessness. Because of the challenge it presents to consensual views of choice and justice, *Native Son* has evoked controversy among both black and white readers from the day of its publication.

One of the novel's earliest and most influential critics was James Baldwin. In our discussion of *Uncle Tom's Cabin*, I referred to the 1949 essay, "Everybody's Protest Novel," in which Baldwin argued that Harriet Beecher Stowe had reduced her black characters to ciphers in a sentimental morality play. Baldwin attacked *Native Son* in that same essay and in approximately the same terms. To begin with, in Baldwin's view Bigger Thomas consists of nothing but his hate. He is ravaged by what Baldwin calls "a million indignities, the terrible, rat-infested house, the humiliation of home relief, the intense, aimless, ugly bickering, hating it; hatred smoulders through all these pages like sulphur fire." This, in turn, leads to Baldwin's famous juxtaposition of Richard Wright and Harriet Beecher Stowe. Below the surface of *Native Son*, argues Baldwin, lies what he calls "a continuation, a complement of [the] monstrous legend it was written to destroy. Bigger is Uncle Tom's descendant, flesh of his flesh." In other words, where humanity ought to reside, both characters are defined by the needs of propaganda. In consequence, Baldwin concludes, "Bigger's tragedy is not that he is cold or black or hungry, not even that he is American [and] black; but that he has accepted a theology that denies him life, that he admits the possibility of his being sub-human." In Baldwin's view, *Native Son* is protest literature, and all protest literature rejects the complex reality and contrariness of life.

As Baldwin often admitted, Wright had aided him early in his own career, and the two men had become rather close. Not surprisingly, the publication of the essay ended the friendship. When Baldwin re-printed "Everybody's Protest Novel" in a collection of essays, he called that volume *Notes of a Native Son*: an act of piety and parricide. The debates that Wright's novel has provoked testify to the enduring force of its narrative. The life and death of Bigger Thomas belie comforting assertions that might be offered about America's racial reality. In a lecture at Fisk University in the early 1940s, Wright said: "I had accidentally blundered into the secret, black, hidden core of race relations in the United States. That core is this: nobody is ever expected to speak honestly about the problem. Bigger is not the entirety of America's racial truth, but he was a part of it that had not been spoken before. He was also—at least in Wright's intensions—a figure symbolic of America's future, a prophecy of what "we would encounter on a vast scale," as Wright says, in the days to come.

At the same time, Wright also claimed that the genealogy of his dark vision could be traced back to earlier writers, white writers who had entertained a vision of the darkness that haunts the American spirit. In the final paragraph of his essay on Bigger Thomas, Wright suggests that:

> we have in the Negro the embodiment of a past tragic enough to appease the spiritual hunger of even a [Henry] James; and we have in the oppression of the Negro a shadow athwart our national life dense and heavy enough to satisfy even the gloomy broodings of a Hawthorne. And if Poe were alive, he would not have to invent horror; horror would invent him.

Lecture Nineteen
The Catcher in the Rye

Scope: It is the unmistakable voice of Holden Caulfield, snapping with a contempt for respectability, that has beguiled millions of young readers for decades. Holden is a 17-year-old boy burdened with a superior sensitivity to hypocrisy, eager to take on all the world's phonies single-handedly. An unlikely hero, Holden tells a story relatively free of adventure, complexity, excitement, or suspense. Nonetheless, *The Catcher in the Rye* was one of the bestselling novels of 1951 and has remained popular for over half a century. Salinger's principal achievement in *Catcher* was the creation of Holden's voice. Funny, earnest, crude, painfully honest, Holden speaks in a voice of uncanny authenticity as he is kicked out of his prep school and subsequently wanders Manhattan, all the while spewing contempt for liars, phonies, and just about everything else. Written during an age of conformity, expanding affluence, and sexual repression, J. D. Salinger's manifesto against the American status quo was actually part of an unorganized but decisive chorus of dissent. *Catcher in the Rye* both reflected and helped to initiate a countercultural movement with far-reaching consequences.

Outline

I. The poet Robert Lowell famously referred to "the tranquilized fifties," a metaphor which persists to this day. There is some merit to this assessment, as selective examples of politics, arts, and culture indicate. However, on closer inspection, the 1950s prove to have been a decade of considerable turmoil and dissent.

   A. The postwar civil rights movement began with the Supreme Court's 1954 decision that declared segregation in public schools unconstitutional.
      1. Rosa Parks refused to give up her bus seat to a white man in 1955, the same year that African Americans organized a successful boycott in Montgomery, Alabama.
      2. Ralph Ellison's *Invisible Man*, a rebuke to white complacency about race, was published in 1952.

B. Conformity was threatened by Elvis Presley's swiveling hips, and Alfred Kinsey published his first book, *Sexual Behavior in the Human Male*, in 1950.

C. Allen Ginsburg's *Howl* and Jack Kerouac's *On the Road*, both iconic statements of cultural dissent, appeared in the mid-1950s.

D. J. D. Salinger's manifesto against the American status quo, *Catcher in the Rye*, was a part of this increasing chorus of dissent.

II. Jerome D. Salinger was born and raised in Manhattan. Famously reclusive, there is very little information about his life, though he once said his boyhood "was very much the same as that of the boy in the book," Holden Caulfield.

A. He flunked out of schools prior to attending Valley Forge Military Academy, where he managed to graduate.

B. After dropping out of a couple of different colleges, Salinger became a soldier in World War II.

C. Unlike other veterans who were writers, Salinger did not often incorporate the war directly into his fiction. Salinger's attitude toward society's rules and regulations was shaped at least in part by his war experiences.

D. Salinger had published dozens of stories prior to *Catcher*, but it was this publication that transformed him overnight into one of the leading writers of his generation.

III. The story that Holden tells takes place over just three days, from a Saturday afternoon to a Monday morning. When it begins, Holden has just been kicked out of Pencey Prep for flunking all of his courses except English.

A. Holden called Pencey "a terrible school, no matter how you looked at it." The curriculum was boring, the teachers incompetent, and the typical student a phony.

B. A case study in alienation, Holden doesn't have either the energy or the insight to wage war against the machinery of societal demands, but he has an instinctive dread and mistrust of the system.

C. Holden's angry hostility is further provoked by a dissatisfying farewell to one teacher he had marginal respect for, as well as encounters with fellow students he holds in contempt.
1. One such incident involves Holden's roommate, Ward Stradlater, a good-looking athlete who is going out on a date with Jane Gallagher.
2. Jealous of his date with Jane, Holden forces a fight with Stradlater and loses to the stronger boy.
3. Impulsively, in the middle of the night, Holden leaves school and walks to the nearest train station in the snow.
4. On the train ride to Manhattan, Holden reveals himself to be exactly what he disdains in others: a liar and a phony. He makes up a story for a mother of a student he runs into, because he feels she doesn't deserve the truth.

IV. The rest of the novel takes place in Manhattan. He stays in a hotel, trying to find something to do, or some type of friendly companionship. He fails at both, due to his own lies and contemptuous attitudes.

A. The novel's most dramatic episode occurs when Holden is solicited by the elevator man, a pimp named Maurice.
1. Holden agrees to pay $5 for a prostitute, confessing to the reader that he is a virgin.
2. When Sunny arrives, Holden changes his mind and offers to her just to talk.

B. The only place in New York that gives Holden comfort is the Museum of Natural History. This is a place that is always familiar, always safe.
1. As many critics have pointed out, what Holden fears above all is growing up.
2. Childhood, with its dependence and lack of responsibility, is far more attractive than the compromises and disappointments of adulthood.

C. Holden goes on a date with Sally Hayes, despite her status in his mind as another phony. It is at Rockefeller Center that Holden makes one of the novel's best-known speeches, in which he itemizes the things he hates, which include just about everything.
1. He proposes that Sally leave New York with him and escape to a rural cabin in New England, where they would live happily ever after.

2. When Sally tells him that can't be done, he insults her and leaves.

V. Holden reserves his most fervent love and loyalty for his younger sister, 10-year-old Phoebe. She is smart, funny, and loyal to Holden; on Sunday night he sneaks into his parents' apartment to wake Phoebe up to talk.

   A. Holden calls her "old Phoebe," but she appeals to him precisely because she is so young. She makes no demands and offers Holden unhesitating affection.

   B. Only Phoebe is worthy to hear Holden's daydream, where he is standing in a field of rye grass, on the edge of a cliff, catching all the children who start to fall over. Though he can't manage his own life, he wants to rescue others, to protect other children from the various contaminations of the adult world.

   C. Holden only reaches a kind of peace after taking Phoebe to Central Park Zoo, where he watches her ride the carousel.

   D. The novel's final chapter makes clear that Holden has been institutionalized and has a psychoanalyst. Like many other novels and poems in the postwar years, *Catcher* makes use of insanity as a major theme.

Suggested Reading:

Hamilton, *In Search of J. D. Salinger.*

Salinger, *Dream Catcher.*

Questions to Consider:

1. *Catcher in the Rye* is frequently compared to *Huckleberry Finn*, usually as examples of coming-of-age novels. In addition, both novels have rather surprising endings that have generated much discussion. Do you find the comparison useful in understanding either or both novels? What distinctions and similarities would you propose?

2. Salinger introduces symbolic details and places throughout the novel, among them Holden's red hunting hat, Pencey Prep, Central Park, the carousel, and the cliff edge and rye of the title. Is *Catcher* to be read as a realistic novel or as a kind of fable, with a frequent dream-like quality?

Lecture Nineteen—Transcript
The Catcher in the Rye

It begins with one of the most famous sentences in American literature:

> If you really want to hear about it, the first thing you'll probably
> want to know is where I was born, and what my lousy childhood
> was like, and how my parents were occupied and all before they
> had me, and all that David Copperfield kind of crap, but I don't
> feel like going into it, if you want to know the truth.

That is the unmistakable voice of Holden Caulfield, bristling with contempt
for respectability, which has beguiled millions of readers for decades.
Holden is a 16-year-old boy burdened with a radar-like sensitivity to
hypocrisy, and eager to take on all the world's phonies single-handedly. A
child of privilege, he wants to protect other children from the various
contaminations of the adult world. Holden is an unlikely hero, and the story
he tells is relatively free of adventure, complexity, excitement, or suspense.
Nonetheless, *Catcher in the Rye* was a Book-of-the-Month Club selection
and one of the bestselling novels of 1951. It has remained popular for over
half a century.

To account for its success, we probably should turn first to the politics and
culture of the years following World War II. The 1950s have been codified
as an age of conformity, expanding affluence, sexual repression, and gray
flannel suits. The poet Robert Lowell famously referred to "the tranquilized
fifties," and his metaphor captured a widely shared opinion, which has
persisted to this day. As journalist David Halberstam put it, photographs of
the 1950s are usually black and white, while the decade that followed was
captured in living color. As usual, there is some merit in the received
opinion. Throughout most of the '50s, Dwight Eisenhower presided over
the country like a benevolent father, radiating the confidence and assurance
that befitted his stature as the nation's victorious commander in the war.
Stability was the order of the day. Business was in the ascendant.

Eisenhower nominated Charles Wilson, head of General Motors, as Defense
Secretary. In his confirmation hearings, Wilson famously shared his belief
that "what was good for our country was good for General Motors and vice
versa." Radicals were harassed by opportunistic politicians such as Joseph
McCarthy, the Wisconsin senator who promised to root out communists

from all their hiding places. Universities, sadly, lined up to demand loyalty oaths from their faculty, some of whom were fired for refusing to sign. Women, who had made substantial gains in the workplace during the war, went back to the kitchen, displaced by returning veterans and a resurgent gender discrimination.

Movies such as *The Greatest Show on Earth*, *Around the World in Eighty Days*, and *Gigi* won Academy Awards as best picture. Walt Disney released the animated features *Cinderella*, *Alice in Wonderland*, and *Peter Pan* in quick succession in the first years of the decade. The most popular songs included Mario Lanza's "Be My Love," Gene Autry's "Rudolph the Red-Nosed Reindeer," and Patti Page's "Doggie in the Window." In fact, however, the culture of the 1950s was considerably more complicated than my highly selective examples would imply.

On closer inspection, the 1950s prove to have been a decade of substantial turmoil and dissent. Recall that even the phrase "the man in the gray flannel suit," the title of Sloan Wilson's 1955 novel, was intended satirically. The following year, William H. Whyte delivered a similar warning against America's stifling corporate culture in his classic study, *The Organization Man*. Many of the themes that would define the Technicolor '60s traced their beginnings to the black-and-white '50s.

The postwar civil rights movement began with the Supreme Court's 1954 decision that segregation in public schools was unconstitutional. The movement gained momentum when Rosa Parks refused in 1955 to give up her bus seat to a white man, and African Americans organized a successful boycott of Montgomery, Alabama, businessmen.

Ralph Ellison's bestselling novel, *Invisible Man*, published in 1952, offered a rebuke to white complacency about race. If "Doggie in the Window" earned a gold record, the decade also saw the eruption of rock and roll—a term popularized by disk jockey Alan Freed in 1951. Elvis Presley made his first record in 1953, and in 1956 released "Heartbreak Hotel," the first of a hundred hits that would permanently transform American music and culture. Conformity was threatened by the sexual provocation of Presley's swiveling hips. Before Elvis, and even before the '50s opened, Alfred Kinsey had launched the attack on carnal denial. His first book, *Sexual Behavior in the Human Male*, appeared in 1948. *Around the World in Eighty Days* won an Oscar in the 1950s, but so, too, did tough-minded explorations of life's rougher edges, such as *On the Water Front* and *Marty*. Broadway filled seats with musicals and revivals, but in 1947 Tennessee

Williams's *A Streetcar Named Desire* had unleashed a storm of sexuality and violence across the stage. Allen Ginsberg's *Howl* and Jack Kerouac's *On the Road*, which remain iconic statements of cultural protest, both appeared in the mid-'50s.

In short, J. D. Salinger's manifesto against the American status quo was not at all anomalous. Rather, the novel was part of an unorganized but clamorous chorus of dissent. *Catcher in the Rye*, in short, both reflected and helped to initiate a counter-cultural movement with far-reaching consequences. Few of the historical or fictional characters associated with these changes imprinted themselves on the public mood more indelibly than Salinger's Holden Caulfield. Jerome David Salinger, to give him his full name, was born and raised in Manhattan. Famously reclusive, he has shared very little information about his life, though he did once say that his boyhood "was very much the same as that of the boy in the book," by whom he meant Holden Caulfield.

When he was about 13, Salinger's parents moved him from public school to the private McBurney School, from which he promptly flunked out. His father moved him again—this time to the Valley Forge Military Academy, where Salinger managed to graduate. He spent a semester at New York University, then dropped out and traveled in Austria and Poland as an employee of his father's meatimporting business. When he came back to the United States, he enrolled in Ursinus College, but left almost immediately. In his own words, and sounding indeed more than a little like Holden, Salinger said that he "tried college for half a semester, but quit like a quitter. There was already a defiantly non-conformist tone about those early years of J. D. Salinger, already a premonition of the poses that his most famous character would strike a few years later.

The Second World War transformed Salinger from a drifter into a soldier. He was part of the D-Day invasion force, landing on Normandy Beach five hours after the first troops. He also fought in the Battle of the Bulge, one of the bloodiest encounters of the European war, and he saw the horrifying reality of the concentration camps. Taken all together, Salinger probably had a more brutal personal experience of the war than most other soldiers. Unlike other veterans, including Norman Mailer and Joseph Heller, Salinger did not often incorporate the war directly into his fiction. But the case could be made that, like those other men, Salinger's attitude toward society's rules and regulations was shaped in part by what he experienced in the war.

In *Catcher*, Holden tells us that his older brother, D. B., was in the army for four years and fought in the D-Day landing. D. B. once said: "If he'd had to shoot anybody, he wouldn't've known which direction to shoot in. He said the Army was practically as full of bastards as the Nazis were." But even D. B. is a fan of Hemingway's *A Farewell to Arms*, which Holden thinks is just "a phony book. Salinger had written his first short stories before Pearl Harbor—including one that featured a character named Holden Caulfield—and he continued to write throughout the war. He had published two dozen stories before he was 30, but the appearance of *Catcher in the Rye* transformed him overnight from a promising young talent into one of the leading writers of his generation.

The story that Holden tells takes place over just three days, from a Saturday afternoon to a Monday morning. When it begins, a few days before Christmas, Holden has just been kicked out of a private school called Pencey Prep, because he has flunked every course except English. His teachers, like the teachers in the other schools from which he has been expelled, make the usual disappointed noises. He should apply himself; he should buckle down; he should make the effort. Holden regards the situation quite differently. Pencey, he says, was "a terrible school, no matter how you looked at it." In his view, the curriculum is boring, the teachers are generally incompetent, and the typical students are—you guessed it—phonies. To use a word that would soon be in wide currency in the early 1950s, Holden is a case study in alienation. He doesn't have either the energy or the insight to wage war against the machine, but he has an instinctive dread of the system. He is also, despite his individual eccentricity, enacting a familiar American gospel of anti-intellectualism. I first brought this topic up in connection with Cooper's *Last of the Mohicans*. Holden Caulfield doesn't have too much in common with Cooper's Hawkeye, but the two characters do share an ingrained preference for physical experience over abstract thought. This is one of the reasons Holden has so much trouble taking any school seriously—and particularly a school where, in his view, many of the teachers and just about all the students have so little interest in their academic tasks, in any case.

Despite his contempt for Pencey, Holden wants to find a dignified way to leave. Although he cannot construct a meaningful bond with the school, he would like to make his exit meaningful. As he says: "I don't care if it's a sad good-by or a bad good-by, but when I leave a place I like to know I'm leaving it. If you don't, you feel even worse." His efforts backfire. He pays a call on his history teacher, Mr. Spencer, the only faculty member for whom he has even an ounce of respect. However, the visit goes badly. Mr. Spencer is lying in bed, sickened by flu. Holden reports that "everything smelled like Vicks Nose Drops. It was pretty depressing." Instead of the affectionate farewell he is seeking, Holden is subjected to a speech about his defects and failures. The scene summarizes everything that Holden wants to escape, and he gets out as quickly as he can. Contrasting the literal stuffiness of the teacher with the free spirit of the pupil, Salinger labors without much subtlety to enlist the reader's sympathy on Holden's side.

When he returns to his room to finish his packing, Holden encounters a couple of his fellow students, who evoke his instant hostility. Robert Ackley is intellectually fatuous and physically repulsive: "I never once saw him brush his teeth. They always looked mossy and awful." Holden's roommate, Ward Stradlater, causes him even more distress. Unlike Ackley, Stradlater is "a secret slob. He always looked all right" when he finished shaving and combing his hair, but "he was a secret slob anyway, if you knew him the way I did." Stradlater, a good-looking athlete with a reputation for sexual conquests, is going out on a date with a girl named Jane Gallagher. Holden, who has known and respected Jane for years—she is one of the few people he actually admires—worries that Stradlater will take advantage of Jane.

In Holden's adolescent world, Jane represents a kind of feminine ideal. She is a figure of intelligence and physical appeal, but she is at the same time removed from the sordid sexual urges that threaten Holden's equilibrium. To make matters worse, Stradlater pressures Holden into writing an essay for him to hand in to his composition teacher. The assignment requires a description. Holden writes about his brother Allie's baseball mitt. Allie had written poems all over the mitt, to pass the time when he was in the field and nobody was batting. After telling us this, Holden adds: Allie's "dead now. He got leukemia and died when we were up in Maine, on July 18, 1946. The precision of that date is significant. Without reaching for explicit commentary, Holden makes it clear that Allie's mitt is one of his few cherished possessions, all that he has left of a brother whom he remembers as the most intelligent and the nicest member of his family.

The episode illustrates one of Salinger's chief strengths as a writer: his ability to locate powerful emotions in the commonplace images and objects that make up a boy's life. When Stradlater comes in from his night out, he complains that Holden's essay is not what the assignment intended. So Holden tears it up. In Holden's view, the episode captures the distance between his authenticity and the phoniness of everyone around him. Holden is also angry at the liberties he imagines Stradlater tried to take with Jane

Gallagher and forces a fight in which the stronger Stradlater beats him bloody. Impulsively, even though it is the middle of a cold night, Holden grabs his suitcase and leaves, walking to the nearest train station through the freezing temperatures and the snow.

On several occasions, Holden confesses that he is among the biggest liars in the world. He proves it on the train ride to New York. A middle-aged woman notices the school decal on his luggage and identifies herself as the mother of a Pencey student, Ernest Morrow. In Holden's view, "Her son was doubtless" the worst person "that ever went to Pencey, in the whole crumby history of the school," but he sings Ernest's praises, while inventing a false identity for himself. When Mrs. Morrow asks why Holden is going home before vacation begins, he confides that he has to have a brain tumor removed. "I'll be all right and everything. It's right near the outside. And it's a very tiny one. They can take it out in about two minutes." The point of the episode is that people like Mrs. Morrow don't deserve the truth. Although Holden decides that she is fairly likeable, she is irredeemably part of the adult world he despises.

The rest of the novel takes place in Manhattan. Holden registers at a shabby hotel and makes a couple of phone calls, trying to find someone who can provide some friendly companionship. When that fails, he spends a little time in the hotel dining room, where he is given a bad table and refused alcohol because of his age. Then he takes a cab to a place called Ernie's, where he is given another bad table and runs into a young woman who had dated his brother, D. B. She is with a sailor, and they invite him to sit at their table. In order to avoid sitting with them, he lies that he is just leaving, and then has to leave to cover the lie. As he says on the way out the door: "People are always ruining things for you."

The novel's most dramatic episode takes place when Holden goes back to his hotel. Solicited by the elevator man, a pimp named Maurice, Holden agrees to pay $5.00 for a prostitute. While he waits, he confesses that he is a virgin: "I really am. I've had quite a few opportunities to lose my virginity and all, but I've never got around to it yet." A woman named Sunny arrives, but Holden has changed his mind and offers to pay her just to talk. She walks out, calling him a "crumb-bum," and then returns with Maurice, who demands another $5.00. When Holden refuses, calling the beefy Maurice a moron, he is once again beaten up. As he lies on the floor, Holden complains that his sensitivity and neediness can find no echoing response in the hardboiled world around him.

The next morning, Sunday, Holden makes a date to go to a matinee with a girl named Sally Hayes, in spite of the fact that she is merely another of the phonies that make him miserable. He used to think she was intelligent, because she knew a lot about plays and literature and all, but he has revised his opinion. As he walks around Central Park to kill time before the 2:30 show, he thinks: "It didn't seem at all like Christmas was coming soon. It didn't seem like anything was coming."

However, when he hears a little boy singing "if a body catch a body coming through the rye," he says "it made me feel not so depressed anymore." The one place in New York that gives Holden comfort is the Museum of Natural History. This is where he had come a hundred times when he was a child, and the smell of the place makes him feel safe. It smelled, he says, "like it was raining outside, even if it wasn't, and you were in the only nice, dry, cosy place in the world. I loved that damned museum." As he walks toward it, across Central Park, he says that the best thing about the museum is that everything stays exactly where it was. "I knew that whole museum routine like a book," he says. Nothing changes. As many critics have pointed out, what Holden fears above all is growing up. Childhood, with its dependence and its lack of responsibility, is far more attractive to him than the compromises and disappointments of adulthood.

Holden dislikes the theater almost as much as he likes the museum. After all, actors are only pretending to be people they are not: just like all the phonies around him. Nevertheless, he confesses to a portion of admiration for the stars of the unnamed play, Alfred Lunt and Lynne Fontanne, though he is revolted when another member of the audience calls them "angels." After the play, he takes Sally ice-skating at Rockefeller Center. Neither of them can skate, so they sit down for a coffee, and Holden makes one of the novel's best-known set speeches. First he itemizes the things he hates, beginning with school:

> Boy, do I hate it. But it isn't just that. It's everything. I hate living in New York and all. Taxicabs, and Madison Avenue buses, with the drivers and all always yelling at you to get out at the rear door, and being introduced to phoney guys that call the Lunts angels, and going up and down in elevators when you just want to go outside.

Then he proposes that Sally come with him, leave New York and escape to some rural part of New England. They could live in a cabin, chop their own wood, live happily ever after. When Sally quite sensibly tells him that it can't be done, he insults her and leaves. Holden reserves his most fervent love and loyalty for his younger sister, 10-year-old Phoebe. On Sunday night, he sneaks into his parents' apartment and wakes Phoebe up to talk. She is smart, funny, and loyal. Holden calls her "old Phoebe," but she appeals to him precisely because she is so young. She makes no demands, and she offers Holden the sort of unhesitating affection that he can't find anywhere else. Only Phoebe is worthy to hear Holden's daydream, his fantasy of standing in a field of rye grass, on the edge of a cliff, catching all the children who start to fall over.

Though he is completely incapable of managing his own life, he wants to rescue others. Looking for somewhere to spend the night, Holden goes to the Sutton Place home of a former teacher, Mr. Antolini—but he wakes up in the middle of the night and finds Antolini caressing his hair. He makes a frightened exit, goes back to Grand Central Station, and sleeps for a few hours. Having decided that he is going to leave town, he wants to say goodbye to Phoebe. He walks to her school to leave her a note asking that she meet him at the museum. As he walks through the old school, which he had attended just a few years earlier, he is shocked by obscenities scribbled on the walls. He rubs out some of them, but quickly realizes that he won't be able to erase them all. When he gets to the museum, he finds more of the obscenities. They are emblems of the disease that corrupts society.

Holden takes Phoebe to the Central Park Zoo and persuades her to ride on the carousel. He promises her that he will go back home, that he won't run away. He sits on a bench, in the pouring rain, watching her circle around and reach for the brass ring. Only now does he achieve a kind of peace: "I felt so damn happy all of a sudden, the way old Phoebe kept going around and around. I was damn near bawling, I felt so damn happy, if you want to know the truth. I don't know why."

The novel's final chapter makes clear that Holden has been institutionalized and has been talking with a psychoanalyst. Like many other novels and poems in the postwar years, *Catcher* makes use of insanity or the threat of insanity as a major theme. Allen Ginsberg famously lamented that the best minds of his generation had been destroyed by madness. Robert Lowell published confessional poems about his electro-shock treatments. Philip Roth's Alexander Portnoy is famously in therapy with an analyst named Spielvogel, and Saul Bellow's Moses Herzog confides to the reader: "If I'm out of my mind, it's all right with me."

In a world in which normality had been redefined by the Holocaust and the atom bomb, the line between sane and insane seemed less clear. If these issues do not enter Salinger's novel explicitly, they do form part of its emotional and moral background. In his own analysis, Holden has apparently made some sort of recovery. He will be going to school in the fall, though he cannot promise that he will apply himself to the work, and he has misgivings about having told so many of his secrets. Recalling all these people and events, he is surprised to find that he misses many of the people he's known, even old Stradlater and Ackley, even the sleazy Maurice. "Don't ever tell anybody anything," he warns us. "If you do, you start missing everybody."

Understandably, many of *Catcher*'s first reviewers commented on the similarities between Salinger's novel and *Huckleberry Finn*. Both books are told in the first person by adolescent boys, both have plots that are little more than a sequence of incidents, both use language that was regarded in its time as indecent or indelicate, and both involve a critique of American society. The comparison has obvious limits. Holden's concerns seem to me, frankly, trivial compared with the questions of life and death, slavery and freedom, which lie at the center of Twain's novel. On the other hand, like Twain's achievement in *Huckleberry Finn*, Salinger's principal accomplishment in *Catcher* is the creation of Holden's voice. Funny, earnest, crude, painfully honest, Holden speaks in a voice of uncanny authenticity. His interjections—"one other thing I just thought of," or "I don't know exactly what I mean by that"—create a tone of spontaneity, the illusion of a young mind in the act of sharing whatever thoughts occur to him.

When he defends digressions in a conversation late in the novel, Holden is also defending this novel's method. The effect on readers has been magnetic. Early in the novel, when Holden gets back to his dorm room after visiting Mr. Spencer, he notices a book that he has taken out of the library. That leads to his thoughts about reading, in a passage that has become one of the most famous in the novel:

> I read a lot of classical books, like *The Return of the Native* and all, and I like them, and I read a lot of war books and mysteries and all, but they don't knock me out too much. What really knocks me out is a book that, when you're all done reading it, you wish the author that wrote it was a terrific friend of yours and you could call him up on the phone whenever you felt like it.

Thousands of Salinger's young readers have had precisely this reaction to *Catcher in the Rye*. At the same time, while the novel has had a long life, it has not exerted a substantial influence on the American fiction that followed. Among the major novels and bestsellers of the second half of the century, *Catcher in the Rye* does not appear in genealogies of influence and stylistic inheritance. Rather, the novel embodied almost perfectly a certain tone and set of gestures that helped to define a cultural moment. It continues to do that work.

Lecture Twenty
To Kill a Mockingbird

Scope: In 2006, the Museum, Libraries and Archives Council conducted a poll, asking simply, "Which book should every adult read before they die?" The book that respondents mentioned more than any other was Harper Lee's *To Kill a Mockingbird*. Published almost a half decade before, the novel won the Pulitzer Prize, was translated into more than 40 languages, and sold tens of millions of copies worldwide. *To Kill a Mockingbird* lies at the intersection of two important developments of the first half of the 20th century: the modern civil rights movement and the emergence of Southern literature. Harper Lee was one of the first white novelists to join those two streams of history together. She did so through the eyes of her narrator, Scout Finch, a feisty five-year-old girl, and her father, Atticus, the defense attorney of a black man accused of raping a young white girl in a small Southern town. Despite its candid portrayal of bigotry and violence, *To Kill a Mockingbird* concludes with an affirmation of human goodness.

Outline

I. Harper Lee was an airline reservations clerk living in New York City in the late 1950s when she began writing her only novel. She began with the working title *Atticus* but decided on *To Kill a Mockingbird*, perhaps to indicate her intentions for more than a character portrait.

   A. The book's sources of inspiration appear to be an unspecified trial of a black man for rape in Lee's hometown.

   B. Another probable source was the Scottsboro rape trial, which took place in March 1931.
      1. Despite incontrovertible evidence of the young black defendants' innocence, the young men were tried, convicted, and sentenced to die in less than three weeks.
      2. Harper Lee was nearly five years old when the first Scottsboro trial took place, about the same age as her narrator, Jean Louise Finch, who answers only to the nickname of Scout.

C. Harper Lee was one of the first white novelists to merge Southern literature with the modern civil rights movement.

    1. Literary culture was largely nonexistent in the South until after the turn of the 20th century.

    2. In the first half of the century, a formidable list of writers emerged from the South, including William Faulkner.

    3. The years of the Southern renaissance in literature coincided with the rise of the modern civil rights movement. This provides a framework for understanding *Mockingbird*, which was set in the early 1930s but written a quarter century later, when the debate over civil rights had been completely transformed.

II. The 1930s were dark years for African Americans, especially in the South: The most elementary justice in the courts eluded them, and lynching still remained a pervasive threat.

    A. In 1932, the U.S. Public Health Service embarked on the notorious Tuskegee syphilis experiment, where mostly poor black men were denied medical treatment they had been promised so doctors could record the disease's progress.

    B. During this decade, the Senate failed to pass an antilynching bill that was first proposed and passed by the House of Representatives in 1922.

    C. By the time Lee wrote *Mockingbird*, however, the situation had changed dramatically. While segregation and discrimination were widespread and pervasive, the civil rights movement had made undeniable strides.

        1. On May 17, 1954, the U.S. Supreme Court ruled unanimously in *Brown v. Board of Education of Topeka, Kansas* that segregation in public schools is unconstitutional.

        2. On December 1, 1955, Rosa Parks refused to give up her seat on a Montgomery, Alabama, bus.

        3. On February 1, 1960, four black students began a sit-in at a segregated Woolworth's lunch counter.

    D. This period of seismic change is that across which Harper Lee looks back at the nation's racial history in *To Kill a Mockingbird*.

III. The novel is divided into two parts. The first, shorter part introduces the small town of Maycomb, Alabama, as a sleepy, pleasant place to grow up for a young white girl with a beloved older brother, Jem, and affectionate father, Atticus.

    A. Scout's narration reveals her perceptions of Maycomb and the people who live in it.

        1. Maycomb is "an old town … a tired old town" that swelters and melts in the heat of Alabama summer.

        2. One of the near neighbors, Mrs. Dubose, was "plain hell," while the dilapidated Radley place, across the street, was whispered to harbor a ghost, which was reputed to be Arthur Radley, called "Boo."

    B. Scout Finch is one of the novel's principal achievements. Lee manages to recapture the world of a child who will move from sheltering innocence to a deeper perspective.

    C. Along with its easygoing sketches of small-town life, the first part of the novel contains premonitions of violence to come.

IV. The novel's main action commences in the final chapters of part 1 and occupies most of part 2. A black man, Tom Robinson, is accused of raping a white girl, Mayella Ewell. Atticus is assigned as defense attorney, though the town's white citizens have already decided that Robinson is guilty.

    A. Demonstrating great courage and integrity, Atticus determines to provide Robinson with a full and competent defense.

        1. Scout is confused by the town's anger at her father, and asks her father why he is defending the condemned. He responds that integrity is paramount, although he knows that the case is hopeless.

        2. Scout learns more about the reality that belies her comfortable world, and doing so she enacts a classical fictional role.

    B. The trial's outcome, as Atticus predicts, is a guilty verdict, despite the overwhelming evidence of Robinson's innocence.

        1. The novel's trial is justifiably celebrated as the high point of the novel. Atticus's summation to the jury makes up most of the book's 20th chapter.

2. Scout's point of view reinforces the shock of injustice, as only the children presume that Tom Robinson will be acquitted. Only later will Scout comprehend the fatality that has trapped Tom.

V. In the final chapters of the book, as the town returns to normal, one final cycle of violence erupts. Bob Ewell, the actual perpetrator of the rape, plans murderous revenge on Atticus for revealing him in the courtroom.

 A. On Halloween, he follows Jem and Scout home from a party and attacks them in the darkness.

 B. Boo Radley, the "ghost," saves the children's lives, while the villainous Ewell is stabbed to death.

 C. In the final scene, Scout declares "nothin's real scary except in books." After all, everyone thought Boo Radley was a ghost, and he turned out to be a hero.

Suggested Reading:

Johnson, *"To Kill a Mockingbird": Threatening Boundaries.*

Shields, *Mockingbird: A Portrait of Harper Lee.*

Questions to Consider:

1. In the novel's famous conclusion, Atticus Finch says, "most people are [nice], Scout, when you finally see them." Is this the novel's final judgment on the moral quality of its characters, and of men and women outside the novel as well? Do the events narrated in the book justify this conclusion, or is Atticus revealing an idealizing and perhaps naive attitude to moral questions?

2. Like most fictional places, the town of Maycomb plays an important role in the novel. It is presented as a place of potential violence and injustice that can also incorporate elements of a strong community. What are the human strengths and weaknesses of the town and its citizens?

Lecture Twenty—Transcript
To Kill a Mockingbird

In the last lecture, we looked at *Catcher in the Rye*, a novel with an adolescent central character, the teenaged Holden Caulfield. Children and their inexperienced points of view are also a central feature of today's text, *To Kill a Mockingbird*. Indeed, in their different ways, quite a few of the novels on our list—*Ragged Dick, Little Women, Huckleberry Finn*, as well as *Catcher in the Rye* and *To Kill a Mockingbird*—explore the world of moral choice from the vantage point of children and young adults. Writers know that this is a technique with profound implications for narrative. The consciousness of a child can provide a fresh entry into familiar questions. Children haven't yet exchanged their instinctive responses for the conventions and deceptions that govern adulthood. They tend to say what's on their minds.

Harper Lee's contribution to what we might call the "genre of ethical education" has earned a high place. In 2006, an organization called the Museums, Libraries and Archives Council conducted a poll, consisting of a single question: "Which book should every adult read before they die?" The book that respondents mentioned more often than any other was Harper Lee's *To Kill a Mockingbird*—strong testimonial. That was only the latest distinction that the novel has earned. *To Kill a Mockingbird*, which appeared nearly 50 years ago, was written by a woman who has not published another book and has lived for decades in near-seclusion in her Alabama home. The novel won the Pulitzer Prize, has been translated into more than 40 languages, and has sold tens of millions of copies worldwide.

Mockingbird appears frequently on high school reading lists. Teachers testify to the book's continued relevance and its portrayal of several major themes that, in their view, students should engage, including the search for justice, the threat of violence, racial conflict, and adolescent coming-of-age.

Harper Lee was living in New York City and working as an airlines reservation clerk when she began writing her novel in the late '50s. Truman Capote, a childhood friend who had already achieved considerable success, offered encouragement. Lee signed a contract with J. B. Lippincott and worked on the book for three years. She used the working title *Atticus*, the name of the main character, but decided on *To Kill a Mockingbird*, perhaps to indicate that the novel was intended as more than a character portrait. (I'll talk about that title later.)

The book's starting point seems to have been a combination of historical episodes. Lee herself has referred to an unspecified trial of a black man for rape in her hometown of Monroeville. Another probable source, which attracted such publicity that Lee would have heard a great deal about it, was the Scottsboro Case. In March 1931, nine young African American men, one of them 13-years-old, another 14, were arrested for the rape of two white women. The alleged crime was committed on a train traveling through Alabama, and the men were taken to a prison in Scottsboro. In less than three weeks, the young men were tried, convicted, and sentenced to die. For the next several years, the case of "The Scottsboro Boys," as they were called in news reports at that time, electrified the nation. The NAACP took the case and then withdrew. The Communist Party stepped in to provide defense counsel, which transformed a case that was already bristling with racial overtones into an explosive political event. The innocence of the defendants was incontrovertible. The evidence made it transparently clear that they were being victimized for the crime of their color.

Lee was nearly five years old when the first "Scottsboro Trial" took place, the same age as her narrator, Jean Louise Finch—an appealing, independent girl who answers only to the nickname "Scout." Without insisting that Scout be understood as a biographical surrogate, it seems reasonable to propose that the numerous parallels between the events in *Mockingbird* and the Scottsboro Trial had at least part of their source in Lee's emotional engagement and the national debate that surrounded it.

At a minimum, Scottsboro demonstrated the calamitous state of African American civil liberties in the South. *To Kill a Mockingbird* lies at the intersection of two important developments that emerged in the South in the first half of the 20th century: the flourishing of southern literature, and the maturing of the modern Civil Rights Movement. Harper Lee was one of the first white novelists to bring those two streams of history together.

With just a handful of exceptions, literary culture was virtually non-existent in the South until after the turn of the 20th century. A bad and flippant couplet was passed from hand to hand for decades: "Alas, poor South, her poets get fewer and fewer; She never was much given to literature." The novelist Ellen Glasgow, looking back on her childhood in late 19th-century Virginia, later said: "southerners did not publish, did not write, did not read." Glasgow's own work marked a turning point. What is sometimes called the "Southern Literary Renaissance" can be traced to her early novels. However, the Renaissance became a self-conscious movement after the First World War, with the gathering of the Nashville Fugitives n and around Vanderbilt University. These writers—all male, and white, and mostly young—played important roles in the reassessment of the South's past and prospects. They included important poets such as Donald Davidson, Allen Tate, and John Crowe Ransom. These men made it their job to seek out the strengths that, in their view, continued to reside in traditional values. They consistently attacked the North for its industrial culture, its alleged materialism, its hyperactivity, and its mongrel cities. They tended to talk less about southern disease and poverty.

In their poetry and fiction, southern authors created the most significant body of regional writing in the first half of the 20th century. Literature paid the debts of military defeat and sustained economic deprivation. The novelist Walker Percy, asking himself the question: "Why has the South produced so many good writers?" answered with a kind of gallows humor: "Because we got beat." Whatever the explanation, the list of writers that emerged in the South was formidable: Robert Penn Warren, Eudora Welty, Katharine Anne Porter, Flannery O'Connor, Tennessee Williams, Thomas Wolfe, James Agee, and above all, William Faulkner.

The years of the Southern Renaissance preceded and then corresponded to the rise of the modern Civil Rights Movement. That history is also important in approaching *To Kill a Mockingbird*. The novel is set in the first half of the 1930s but was written a quarter-century later, when the debate over African American rights had been completely transformed. The 1930s were dark years for African Americans, especially in the South. As the Scottsboro case demonstrated, black people could not expect even the most elementary justice. Lynching remained a pervasive threat. In 1932, the United States Public Health Service embarked on the notorious Tuskegee syphilis experiment. A cohort of mostly poor African American men were denied the medical treatment they had been promised in order that doctors could record the progress of their disease. This grisly enterprise, in which several hundred black men were used as laboratory animals, continued for 40 years. Recall that the 1930s were the years of the Great Depression, which multiplied the hardships that black people in the South suffered. African American sharecroppers and tenant farmers, already more impoverished than their impoverished white neighbors, saw their meager incomes drop further. In addition, the various relief provisions of the New Deal were distorted by racial discrimination. In many southern states,

African Americans were given only a fraction of the aid made available to whites—or, in many cases, were denied assistance altogether.

Throughout the 1930s, Congress refused even to enact an anti-lynching bill. First proposed and passed by the House of Representatives in 1922, the bill was continuously filibustered in the Senate throughout the '20s and '30s.

In a fairly typical speech opposing the bill, Allen Ellender of Louisiana declared on the floor of the Senate in 1938: "I believe in white supremacy, and as long as I am in the Senate I expect to fight for white supremacy." President Franklin Roosevelt, who needed the votes of Southern Democrats for his New Deal legislation, refused to support anti-lynching laws against men like Ellender and South Carolina Senator Ellison Smith, known as "Cotton Ed." This brief survey suggests the context in which the fictional events of *To Kill a Mockingbird* take place. By the time Lee wrote the book, the situation had changed quite dramatically. Southern Democrats, committed to segregation, still controlled the major committees of Congress. Discrimination in housing and employment still flourished across both the South and the North. African Americans still lagged behind whites in health and education. At the same time, however, the Civil Rights Movement had made undeniable strides. I mentioned some of these advances in the last lecture.

In the late 1940s, both the U.S. armed forces and major league baseball were integrated. On May 17, 1954, in *Brown v. The Board of Education of Topeka, Kansas*, the United States Supreme Court unanimously ruled that segregation in public schools is unconstitutional. On December 1, 1955, Rosa Parks refused to give up her seat on a Montgomery, Alabama, bus to a white man. On February 1, 1960, four black students from North Carolina Agricultural and Technical College began a sit-in at a segregated Woolworth's lunch counter.

To put it briefly: The years across which Harper Lee looks back at the nation's racial history in *To Kill a Mockingbird* had been a period of seismic change. Much remained to be accomplished—as it still does—but the assumptions and values that had authorized the injustices she describes had been challenged, and in at least some cases reversed. That chronology is important, because the book's narrator is an adult looking back from the 1950s at her childhood in the 1930s. Though the larger historical background is not explicitly introduced into the novel, it provided the foundation for the book's moral perspective. *To Kill a Mockingbird* examines the possibilities of change in an environment of racial stalemate.

In *Mockingbird*, Harper Lee consciously set out to make a contribution to racial progress. This was unusual for a white southern writer. While the South's black novelists and poets had worked hard for civil rights, the region's white writers were mostly indifferent—and, in some cases, hostile. In the late 1920s, Robert Penn Warren wrote an essay defending segregation. As late as 1956, the year that Harper Lee began working on *Mockingbird*, William Faulkner could say, in a magazine interview: "… if it came to fighting I'd fight for Mississippi against the United States even if it meant going out into the street and shooting Negroes. After all, I'm not going to shoot Mississippians." Harper Lee's quite different response to racial injustice has proven controversial, as we shall see, but the book was initially welcomed, at least in part, because of its demand for justice.

The novel is divided into two sections. The first, shorter part introduces the town and its many inhabitants. Maycomb, Alabama, is presented as a sleepy, generally pleasant place, at least for a white child living with a beloved brother and an affectionate father. It is "an old town … a tired old town," Scout says, slow moving, generally quiet. Even as a child, Scout knew that Maycomb was a backwater, and she evokes it without sentimentality. In the heat of the Alabama summer, in Scout's words:

> In rainy weather the streets turned to red slop, grass grew on the sidewalks, the courthouse sagged in the square. Somehow it was hotter then: a black dog suffered on a summer's day; bony mules hitched to Hoover carts flicked flies in the sweltering shade of the live oaks on the square.

> Men's stiff collars wilted by nine in the morning. Ladies bathed before noon, [and] after their three o'clock naps, and by nightfall were like soft teacakes with frostings of sweat and sweet talcum.

Scout portrays Maycomb, despite its discomforts, as a place where people know each other and do not lock their doors. She has no idea of the capacity for hate and violence that lie just below the tranquil surface.

Beginning with her recollection of the time her older brother, Jem, broke his elbow, Scout moves from one memory to another, sharing them like old photographs from a family album. Her father, Atticus Finch, is a lawyer with a tiny office in the courthouse. Scout's mother died when she was two, so her father has raised her and her brother alone, aided by Calpurnia, the Finch family's black cook. Calpurnia was "something else again," in Scout's account of her: near-sighted, tyrannical, almost always right. One of the near neighbors, Mrs. Dubose, was "plain hell," while the dilapidated

Radley Place, across the street, was reputed to harbor a ghost. The alleged phantom is Arthur Radley, called "Boo," a strange man who will appear at the end of the novel to save the lives of both Scout and Jem. Dill Harris—a precocious, tiny boy based loosely on Truman Capote—comes to spend summers in Maycomb and adds his eccentricity to the mix. Walter Cunningham, the malnourished son of a poor tenant farmer, provides an occasion for Calpurnia to teach Scout a lesson in courtesy. When Scout starts to make fun of the ragged Cunninghams, Calpurnia straightens her out: Poverty can coexist with dignity, and no man, woman or child should be treated with disrespect simply for being poor. Scout Finch is one of the novel's principal achievements.

Without condescending to a girl who is only five when the story begins, Harper Lee manages to recapture the world of a child who will move from sheltering innocence to a richer and sadder awareness in the course of the novel. Scout is independent and contrary: a "tomboy," in the phrase that is sometimes used to describe her. She is also funny, with a special knack for saying exactly what she thinks. Of her father (whom she always calls by his first name), she says: "Atticus was feeble: he was nearly fifty." Along with its easygoing sketches of small-town life, the first part of the novel contains premonitions of the violence that is to come. After recalling the time her older brother broke his elbow, in the book's opening line, Scout also includes episodes of racial insult and a fire that burns down the house of another neighbor, Miss Maudie, one of *Mockingbird*'s more admirable characters.

At Christmas, in the midst of the coldest winter in 60 years, Scout and Jem are given airguns as presents, along with the presents comes a warning from Atticus, "it's a sin to kill a mockingbird." Some birds can be hunted, but the mockingbird threatens no one and brings pleasure with its song. The famous exhortation embodies a moral caution about the rights of the innocent, a proposition that the book's plot will profoundly test. The novel's main action commences in the final chapters of part one and occupies most of part two. A black man, Tom Robinson, is accused of raping a white woman, Mayella Ewell. Atticus is assigned as defense attorney, although the town's white citizens have already decided that Robinson is guilty and should die. The defense, as in so many southern trials of black men for rape, is expected to be a formality. Instead, demonstrating extraordinary courage and integrity, Atticus determines to provide Robinson with a full and competent defense. He also faces down a lynch mob. For his affronts to the townspeople's racial assumptions, Atticus finds himself vilified and threatened with physical violence. By placing the narrative center in the imagination of a child, Harper Lee can spell out Atticus's motives with painstaking clarity. Scout is confused by the town's anger at her father and asks him why he is defending a man the town has condemned, a black man into the bargain. Atticus tells her that he has "a number of reasons. ... The main one is, if I didn't I couldn't hold up my head in town, I couldn't represent this county in the legislature, I couldn't even tell you or Jem not to do something again."

As he also explains to Scout, Atticus knows that the case is hopeless, regardless of the facts. He will lose, he says, "simply because we were licked a hundred years before we started." But that, he adds, "is no reason for us not to try to win." In the months leading up to the trial, the behavior of most of the white characters descends into ugly recrimination. They abandon even the pretense of decency and embrace an undisguised racial hate. Here again, Lee's use of a child's consciousness permits her to instruct her readers in the depths of southern discrimination. Scout learns a great deal about the reality that lies underneath her comfortable world, and in doing so she enacts a classic fictional role.

To Kill a Mockingbird is, among other things, a *Bildungsroman*, a tale of education and initiation. While most of the heroes of such narratives have been male—in American literature they include Huckleberry Finn and Hemmingway's Nick Adams—Scout's story is a memorable addition to the genre. The trial's outcome, as Atticus had predicted, is a guilty verdict. This despite the fact that no one in the courtroom could believe that Tom Robinson committed the crime of which he is accused. Among other things, Robinson has a shriveled left hand, while all the evidence points to a left-handed attack. The testimony, in fact, makes clear that if Mayella was raped, her own father, Bob Ewell, is the criminal. Ewell is a character of almost melodramatic villainy, a foil in his evil simplicity to both the highly principled Atticus Finch and the stoically enduring Tom Robinson. The courtroom is a favorite setting for novelists and playwrights. The scene is enclosed, as on a literal stage, with characters who play assigned parts. The stakes are typically high, often life and death. Ritual coexists with spontaneity. The scripted rhythm of the proceedings is often shattered by some sudden revelation, and the mechanism of the engagement—two attorneys using their verbal and emotional skills to persuade jurors of their point of view—justifies the inclusion of heightened and sometimes even eloquent language. Herman Melville's *Billy Budd*, Richard Wright's *Native Son*, Arthur Miller's *The Crucible*, and *Inherit the Wind* by Jerome Lawrence and Robert Edwin Lee are just a few examples.

The trial in *Mockingbird* has been correctly celebrated as the high point of the novel. Atticus develops an irrefutable line of argument to exonerate Tom Robinson. Mayella, we learn, has herself pursued Tom in a series of increasingly flirtatious encounters. In the climactic scene, as Tom reconstructs it, Mayella kissed him. As Tom tried to get away, Bob Ewell appeared, cursed at his daughter and threatened to kill her. Then, almost certainly, Ewell beat and raped his own daughter. Atticus's summation of his defense occupies a substantial portion of the book's 20th chapter and patiently reminds the jury that Robinson must be found guilty beyond a reasonable doubt, but the prosecution was riddled by doubt. Atticus declares that Mayella is trying to cope with her own guilt by having Tom Robinson killed: "She struck out at her victim," Atticus insists, "—of necessity she must put him away from her—he must be removed from her presence, from this world. She must destroy the evidence of her offense."

The pain and outrage that readers feel as they watch this travesty of justice is heightened once again by the novel's point of view. Scout, Jem, and Dill, who have been banned from the audience on the main floor of the courtroom by Atticus, hide in the balcony, among the African Americans. Scout's responses, for example that Mayella must be the "loneliest person in the world," seem at first peripheral to the great struggle over justice taking place on the courtroom floor. On the contrary, Scout inadvertently confers a dimension of humanity on the proceedings. Though she does not fully comprehend everything that is going on, her viewpoint rescues the scene from allegorical preachiness. It also reinforces the shock of injustice. Only the children presume that Tom Robinson will be acquitted. It seems so obvious to them. As everyone else expects, Tom is convicted and condemned to die in the electric chair. Only later will Scout comprehend the fatality that has trapped Tom. In her adult judgment: "Atticus had used every tool available to free men to save Tom Robinson, but in the secret courts of men's hearts Atticus had no case. Tom was a dead man the minute Mayella Ewell opened her mouth and screamed."

In these later stages of the novel, while Atticus is fully occupied with the trial, his older sister, Aunt Alexandra, moves in and more or less takes over the Finch household. She annoys Scout with her genteel behavior and demands. At the same time, she is obviously a strong and resolute woman. Alexandra exemplifies another of Harper Lee's interests: the contest between traditional southern femininity and the demands of conscience. For the most part, the women of Maycomb play the roles that regional history has assigned to them. They have little to say in the town's public spaces.

However, their silent assent ratifies the prejudice that poisons racial relations. Lee's portrayal of Maycomb's white women is anchored in southern reality. At about the same time as the events in *Mockingbird*, social scientist John Dollard was doing the research that led to his pioneering study of southern race relations, a book called *Caste and Class in a Southern Town*. Among other things, Dollard reports that "a Negro woman informant came forward with the unexpected idea that white women play a very aggressive role in the violent acts toward Negroes." That insight would not have been unexpected to Harper Lee.

Shortly after the trial, Aunt Alexandra hosts a tea party for the town's women. Scout surveys the group and instantly recoils: "Ladies in bunches always filled me with vague apprehension and a firm desire to be elsewhere." The party provides a setting in which the women can express their disapproval of Atticus's behavior. They embody the "dimity convictions" that Emily Dickinson famously ridiculed. They can be mortally offended by a raised voice and at the same time blind to the murderous hate that has condemned an innocent man to death. Atticus rushes in to this demure scene with the book's final tragic announcement. Rather than submit to execution, Tom Robinson has tried to break out of jail and has been killed in a fusillade of bullets. Atticus and Calpurnia leave to tell Tom's wife, Helen Robinson. The party returns to a kind of strained normality. Over the next weeks and months, the town also returns to normal.

Then, one final cycle of violence erupts. Bob Ewell, seething with resentment over the way in which Atticus has exposed him, plans a murderous revenge. On Halloween, he follows Jem and Scout home from a school party and attacks them. In the darkness, the terrified Scout can only feel and hear what is happening, including Jem's scream. The assault ends when another man intervenes. As she stumbles home, Scout sees a man carrying Jem, whose elbow has been broken. This is the event Scout had recalled in the novel's first line. When she gets home, Scout finds the sheriff, Heck Tate, and Boo Radley talking with Atticus. Boo has saved the children's lives, and in the course of the fight, Bob Ewell has been stabbed to death. Atticus, always alert to the demands of justice, suggests that there ought to be a police investigation. He thinks his son may have killed Ewell, and he is willing to act conscientiously on that possibility. Sheriff Tate, a less scrupulous, but perhaps more realistic man, sees no need to inflict that sort of exposure on anyone. The sheriff says: "There's a black boy dead for no reason, and the man responsible for it's dead. Let the dead bury the dead this time.

Despite its candid portrayal of bigotry and violence, *To Kill a Mockingbird* ends with an affirmation of human goodness. In the final scene, Scout asks Atticus to read her a ghost story before she goes to bed. When Atticus objects that she has "had enough scaring for a while," she tells him she wasn't scared. She has decided that "nothin's real scary except in books." After all, everyone thought that Boo Radley was a ghost, and he turned out to be a hero. "Atticus, he was real nice," Scout says, as she falls asleep. "Most people are, Scout," he answers, "when you finally see them."

Lecture Twenty-One
Catch-22

Scope: The title of Joseph Heller's novel, *Catch-22*, has entered the language as a "condition or consequence that precludes success, a dilemma where the victim cannot win" according to the *New Shorter Oxford English Dictionary*. This definition, however, doesn't quite capture the sheer scale of the frustration Heller had in mind while writing his novel that centers around the attempts of Captain Yossarian to escape a world governed by the logic of Catch-22. *Catch-22* doesn't have much of a plot in the conventional sense: Having marooned his soldiers on a fictional Mediterranean island, Heller simply illustrates their situation by piling one preposterous episode on top of another. Heller often insisted that *Catch-22* was not an antiwar novel, and it explicitly never objects to the fight against Hitler. The lunacy of war, however, is the book's central theme. With a combination of comedy and terror, the book effectively dissolves the concepts of patriotism and duty. War, as he reconstructs it, is both a terrible reality and a metaphor for a more systemic disease in the modern world as whole.

Outline

I. *Catch-22* is set mainly on the fictional Mediterranean island of Pianosa, in the summer and fall of 1944. From the Pianosa base, several squadrons of the Army Air Forces stage raids on German targets in Italy and France.

    A. The main character is Captain Yossarian, a not particularly heroic figure who is the reader's point of entry into a world that quickly reveals itself as essentially insane.

    B. It is a world governed by the logic of Catch-22, which is defined early in the novel in a famous conversation between Yossarian and Doc Daneeka, the unit's medical officer.

        1. The pressure of flying repeated bombing missions is pushing Yossarian's sanity to the breaking point. Desperate to be grounded by the doctor, Yossarian pleads craziness.

2. The doctor reveals the catch: Though insanity is a reason for grounding, the action of requesting such a dismissal is the inherent mark of sanity.
3. The men in Yossarian's unit must keep flying and dying because their commander, the megalomaniacal Colonel Cathcart, wants a promotion.

C. *Catch-22* is one of the funniest novels written by an American, and also one of the most despairing. Many of the novel's huge cast of characters die in the course of the book, most because of the stupidity, incompetence, or downright corruption of their commanding officers.

II. Kurt Vonnegut, author of his own war novel, *Slaughterhouse-Five* (1969), had also seen the action he wrote about. Like Vonnegut, Heller was more frightened than inspired by life in the military. Heller's fictional reconstruction resembles a long hallucination, a series of events that almost invariably lead to death.

A. Heller and Vonnegut stand in a venerable tradition of writing about war. The nation's long military history has elicited a fair-sized library of literary response. A few war novels contextualize *Catch-22* and its distinctive achievement.
1. Stephen Crane's *The Red Badge of Courage* (1895) was the first enduring war novel produced by an American writer. His disillusioned portrait of death established a tone that subsequent writers have adopted.
2. The preeminent war novelist of the early 20th century was Ernest Hemingway. Personal injury shocked him into a reappraisal of the meaning of power and the fate of the individual trapped inside the mass bureaucracies of the 20th century.

B. That focus on language, on the limits of true speech in a world of lies, would become a leading theme of American war fiction from Hemingway to Heller and beyond. The novelists rejected the routine political debasement of language in the service of power.

III. Like his predecessors, Joseph Heller also revolted against a military and political regime in which language simply means whatever the men in power say it means. *Catch-22* is filled with examples of this, all of them at once funny and frightening.

A. A sinister example of the disconnect between power and truth is dramatized in the interrogation of Private Clevinger on such charges as "Failure to 'sir' to superior officers when not interrupting them."

B. Many readers have noted a likeness between *Catch-22* and George Orwell's *1984*. As in Orwell's novel, the soldiers in *Catch-22* are captive to an authority they cannot defy and cannot even comprehend.

C. The novel doesn't have much of a conventional plot; rather, there are a series of lethal comic actions. Darkly comic episodes follow each other in a continuous, nonstop sequence.

    1. The structure of *Catch-22* is kaleidoscopic, not linear. Consequently, the novel's chronology is impossible to pin down conclusively.

    2. While the story has a beginning and end, events in between often take place in an indeterminate time, as if to emphasize the chaos and randomness of the situation.

IV. In the world of *Catch-22*, chaos coexists with fate, and Heller employs a high degree of repetition as one way of documenting the trap in which his characters live. What happens, happens—and then it happens again.

    A. The situation that all the characters in *Catch-22* experience repeatedly is death, usually inflicted for no perceptible reasons at all.

        1. Yossarian's paranoia is a perfectly rational reaction to his circumstances, and the repetition of images and events merely emphasizes the inevitable fatality of the island.

        2. The most vivid of the repeated images, and the one that propels Yossarian to the point of mutiny, is the death of Snowden, one of his crew.

        3. It is not clear exactly when this climactic event occurs. It haunts Yossarian repeatedly through the novel, but the magnitude of the trauma only becomes fully clear when the calamity is told in full near the end of the book.

    B. Yossarian deserts after Snowden's death, though getting off the island to travel to Sweden is nearly impossible. But he will try, and the novel suggests that this will finally be a truly heroic act.

C. Heller's novel is about both war and modern society; whether in battle or not, he argues, all of us are subject to surveillance, interrogation, and unexplained intrusions. As crazy as the events of *Catch-22* might seem, they accurately reflect the arbitrary and inescapable exercise of power that can and will operate by its own rules.

Suggested Reading:

Pinsker, *Understanding Joseph Heller.*

Ruderman, *Joseph Heller.*

Questions to Consider:

1. *Catch-22* is a relentlessly satirical novel. As in all satire, the critique depends on an implied standard of judgment, a norm against which the characters and their behavior can be measured. Where in the book are such norms to be found, either explicitly or by implication? Which characters, if any, come closest to representing an alternative to the novel's moral quagmire?

2. Heller claimed that *Catch-22* was aimed not at the army or warfare but at the structure of America's capitalist and bureaucratic society. Presumably Milo Minderbinder would play a significant part in such a reading of the novel. Do you find Heller's commentary persuasive, or does it seem more like a retroactive proposition, intended to enlarge the scope of the book's thematic territory?

Lecture Twenty-One—Transcript
Catch-22

The novel's title has entered the language. Every paradox or insoluble problem is described as a "Catch-22." In 1993, the phrase was included in the *New Shorter Oxford English Dictionary*, where "Catch-22" was defined as "a condition or consequence that precludes success, a dilemma where the victim cannot win." That's not bad, as far as it goes, but I don't think that definition quite captures the sheer scale of the frustration that Joseph Heller had in mind. Let me share a personal experience. Several years ago, I lost my passport in Wuhan, China. No problem, I was assured in a phone call with the American Embassy in Beijing. Just go to a police station and ask for a temporary travel permit. Use that to get to the nearest American consulate—425 miles away in Shanghai—where you can apply for a replacement passport—all routine, except that the sergeant in the Wuhan police station wouldn't sign the temporary permit. He explained, quite sensibly I think, that to do so would make him responsible if, in fact, I was not who I said I was. "No problem," said I, cheerfully. "I have all sorts of identification: driver's license, credit cards, checkbook, and university photo ID. The sergeant refused the gambit. "There is only one form of identification I will accept," he told me. Correct. My passport. The first phrase that went through my head was, of course, "Catch-22." Joseph Heller had coined the universal formula, applicable in every domain of modern life—from medical insurance to travel, from product warranties to IRS audits. All of our transactions risk a fearful encounter with Catch-22.

A number of years ago, the Pakistan Academy for Rural Development published a study called *Catch 22: the Politics of Poverty, the Poverty of Politics*. A 1993 book on the Catholic Church and contraception is called *Catch-22 and a Way Out*. Just a couple of years ago, a professor of psychiatry published a book called *Coping With Depression: From Catch-22 to Hope*.

The novel that ignited this linguistic revolution is set on the fictional Mediterranean island of Pianosa, in the summer and fall of 1944. From an air base on Pianosa, several squadrons of the Army Air Forces stage raids on German targets in Italy and France. The main character is a Captain Yossarian, about whose life before the war we learn very little. He is not particularly heroic, and he leans toward paranoia. But Yossarian is the reader's more or less rational point of entry into a world that quickly reveals itself as essentially insane. It is a world governed by the logic of Catch-22, which is defined early in the novel in a famous conversation between Yossarian and Doc Daneeka, the unit's medical officer. The pressure of flying repeated bombing missions is pushing Yossarian's sanity to the breaking point. Desperate to be grounded by the doctor, Yossarian pleads craziness. Referring to a buddy who is also losing his mind, Yossarian asks:

"Is Orr crazy?"

"He sure is," Doc Daneeka said.

"Can you ground him?"

"I sure can. But first he has to ask me. That's part of the rule."

"Then why doesn't he ask you to?"

"Because he's crazy," Doc Daneeka said. "He has to be crazy to keep flying combat missions. ... Sure, I can ground Orr. But first he has to ask me to."

"That's all he has to do to be grounded?"

"That's all."

"And then you can ground him?" Yossarian asked.

"No, then I can't ground him."

"You mean there's a catch?"

"Sure, there's a catch," Doc Daneeka replied. "Catch-22. Anyone who wants to get out of combat duty isn't really crazy."

...

Yossarian was moved very deeply by the absolute simplicity of this clause of Catch-22 and let out a respectful whistle.

"That's some catch, that Catch-22," he observed.

The men in Yossarian's unit, the 256th squadron, must keep flying and dying because their commander, the megalomaniacal Colonel Cathcart, wants a promotion. So he keeps raising the number of missions required for rotation out of the duty roster.

When Yossarian has flown 48 missions, he finds out that the Twenty-seventh Air Force Headquarters defines a complete tour as 40 missions.

Convinced that this should get him discharged, he goes back to Doc Daneeka, who tells him there is more to Catch-22: "Catch-22 … says you've always got to do what your commanding officer tells you to." Yossarian points out that "Twenty-seventh Air Force says I can go home with 40 missions." "But," Doc tells him: they don't say you have to go home. And regulations do say you have to obey every order. That's the catch. Even if the colonel were disobeying a Twenty-seventh Air Force order by making you fly more missions, you'd still have to fly them, or you'd be guilty of disobeying an order of his. And then the Twenty-seventh Air Force Headquarters would really jump on you.

Joseph Heller often insisted that *Catch-22* was not an anti-war novel. That is true, but only to the extent that it never explicitly objects to the fight against Hitler. Heller did have additional targets in mind, as I will suggest later, but the lunacy of war is the book's central theme. With its combination of non-stop laughs in the face of non-stop terror, the book effectively dissolves the concepts of patriotism and duty. *Catch-22* is one of the funniest novels written by an American, and also one of the most despairing. A great many of the novel's huge cast of characters die in the course of the book, and most die because of the stupidity, incompetence, or downright corruption of their commanding officers.

Kurt Vonnegut assured a friend that his own war novel, *Slaughterhouse-Five*, would have no role for John Wayne. Vonnegut had been captured by the Germans and spent the last months of the war as a prisoner in a meat factory in Dresden. There, more or less safely underground, he survived the Allied bombing that destroyed the city. He saw nothing heroic in the ashes and debris, and *Slaughterhouse-Five* is the disillusioned result. Vonnegut subtitled his novel *The Children's Crusade*, an ironic recollection of the medieval madness that sent little boys off to die in the pope's armies. Unable to quite believe what he had experienced, Vonnegut combines science fiction and grim realism to capture the mad reality of war.

Joseph Heller had also seen the action that he writes about. A young bombardier based in Corsica, he flew 60 B-25 missions in the last years of the war. Like Vonnegut, he was more frightened than inspired by life in the military. His fictional reconstruction resembles a long hallucination, a series of events that almost invariably leads to death. Heller and Vonnegut stand in a venerable tradition of writing about war. Americans, who like to think of themselves as peace loving, have in fact fought in a remarkably long series of wars. The nation was born in the War for Independence, which was followed by the Barbary War against pirates in Tripoli, the War of

1812, the Mexican War, the Civil War, the Indian Wars, the Spanish-American War, the Philippine Insurrection, the First World War, the Second World War, the Korean War, the war in Vietnam, the first and second wars in Iraq, and the war in Afghanistan. This list does not include numberless skirmishes and undeclared armed conflicts, among them repeated invasions and incursions into Latin America under the aegis of the Monroe Doctrine.

The nation's military history has elicited a fair-sized library of literary response. I want to comment on just a few of the novels that have taken war as their subject, in order to provide a context for *Catch-22* and its distinctive achievement. By general agreement, Stephen Crane's *The Red Badge of Courage* was the first enduring war novel produced by an American writer. Crane was born several years after the Civil War ended. His portrayals of battle and death were written out of intuition rather than experience. He found in the exceptional savagery of the Civil War the scenes of terror that galvanized his imagination. The novel's most famous episode summarizes Crane's reaction to the carnage of the war. Henry, the young Union soldier who is the book's hero, is seized by fear. He deserts from the battlefield into a nearby woods to seek shelter. He reaches a secluded place where the unbearable noise of the guns has receded and "the high, arching boughs [over him] made a chapel." Suddenly he falls back, "horror-stricken, at the sight" of what he takes to be "a thing":

> He was being looked at by a dead man who was seated with his back against a columnlike tree. The corpse was dressed in a uniform that [had] once been blue, but was now faded to a melancholy shade of green.

> The eyes, staring at the youth, had changed to the dull hue to be seen on the side of a dead fish. The mouth was open. Its red had changed to an appalling yellow. Over the gray skin of the face ran little ants. One was trundling some sort of bundle along the upper lip.

The green color of the dead soldier's uniform, and the ant with its enigmatic bundle, are unforgettable physical correlatives for terror. Crane's disillusioned portrait of death established a tone that subsequent writers have frequently adopted.

The preeminent war novelist of the early 20th century was undoubtedly Ernest Hemingway. Unlike Crane, whose work he knew and admired, Hemingway had taken part in battle. In 1918, he traveled to the Italian front in search of adventure and was wounded while driving an ambulance. Personal injury shocked him into a reappraisal of the meaning of power and the fate of individuals trapped inside the mass military bureaucracies of the 20th century. What he now saw was the skull beneath the skin of modern politics.

In a famous passage in Hemingway's war novel, *A Farewell to Arms*, Lieutenant Frederic Henry laments the subjection of language to militarist ambition that has murdered truth. According to Lieutenant Henry, words like "sacrifice" and "glorious" have become embarrassing: He decides that the battlefields are like "the stockyards at Chicago." Only proper names and unanalyzed physical experiences retain their dignity. Lieutenant Henry continues in a famous passage:

> Certain numbers were the same way and certain dates and these with the names of the places were all you could say and have them mean anything. Abstract words such as glory, honor, courage, or hallow were [obscene] words beside the concrete names of villages, the numbers of roads, the names of rivers, the numbers of regiments and the dates.

That focus on language, on the limits of true speech in a world of lies, would become a leading theme of American war fiction from Hemingway to Joseph Heller and beyond. Above all, novelists recoiled against the political abuse of words, the routine debasement of language in the service of power.

John Dos Passos's *Nineteen Nineteen* was the major war novel of the 1930s. Like Hemingway, Dos Passos had also seen bloody action as an ambulance driver in 1917 and 1918. In his novel, he revisits the carnage he witnessed. He captures the nastiness, the tedium, the intermittent horror, and above all the sheer stupidity that propelled men repeatedly into meaningless death.

The novel's final pages include an embittered set piece called "The Body of an American." In this episode, Dos Passos indicts the misguided and ultimately murderous patriotism that made World War I possible. Dos Passos re-creates the ceremony that took place in Arlington National Cemetery on November 11, 1921. There, President Warren G. Harding presided over the burial of the Unknown Soldier. Dos Passos's focus is on language: the distance between official lies and unspeakable truth. Presidential rhetoric and newspaper headlines are juxtaposed against the grisly anatomical realities of "John Doe's" mutilated body, which Dos Passos describes vividly:

> The blood ran into the ground, the brains oozed out of the cracked skull and were licked up by the trenchrats, the belly swelled and

raised a generation of bluebottle flies … and Mr. Harding prayed to God and the diplomats and the generals and the brasshats and the politicians and the handsomely dressed ladies out of the society column of the *Washington Post* stood up solemn and thought how beautiful sad Old Glory God's Country it was to have the bugler play taps and the three volleys made their ears ring.

Like his predecessors, Joseph Heller also revolted against a military and political regime in which language simply means whatever the men in power say it means. *Catch-22* is filled with examples, all of them at once funny and frightening. Here is the form letter Corporal Whitcomb ghostwrites for Colonel Cathcart, to inform and console the relatives of dead soldiers:

> Dear Mrs., Mr., Miss, or Mr. and Mrs. Daneeka: Words cannot express the deep personal grief I experienced when your husband, son, father, or brother was killed, wounded, or reported missing in action.

The idiocy of that letter is compounded in this case because Doc Daneeka has not in fact been killed. But the system has fouled up, and he has been officially declared dead, despite being alive. For the rest of the novel, he cannot get his commanding officers to acknowledge that he has not died. The distance between reality and official statements is unbridgeable.

A more sinister example of the disconnect between power and truth is dramatized in the interrogation of Private Clevinger on such charges as "Failure to say 'sir' to superior officers when not interrupting them." As the narrator comments: "The case against Clevinger was open and shut. The only thing missing was something to charge him with." Clevinger tries to defend himself by suggesting that he hasn't done anything wrong, and that therefore the colonel cannot find him guilty without perverting justice. On the contrary, as the narrator tells us: "Clevinger was guilty, of course, or he would not have been accused, and since the only way to prove it was to find him guilty, it was their patriotic duty to do so."

Many readers have noted a likeness between *Catch-22* and Orwell's *1984*. A scene like this one, in which guilt and innocence are determined solely by the needs—or even by the moods—of men in power, suggests that the likeness is correct. As in *1984*, the soldiers in Heller's novel are captive to an authority they cannot defy and cannot even comprehend. Whether the name of the godlike authority is Big Brother or Colonel Cathcart, the victims go to jail, suffer, and die. Explanations are irrelevant, or lies, or both. What happens, happens.

Hollywood's movies about the Second World War—often starring John Wayne—tended toward the patriotic and heroic. Novels, on the other hand, including Norman Mailer's classic *The Naked and the Dead*, James Jones's *From Here to Eternity*, as well as Vonnegut's *Slaughterhouse-Five* and Heller's *Catch-22*, typically lingered over the waste and destruction. In a memoir called *Wartime*, his own disenchanted book about the war, the infantry veteran and writer Paul Fussell asked:

> What was it about the Second World War that moved the troops to constant verbal subversion and contempt? What was it that made the Americans, especially, so fertile with insult and cynicism, …
>
> It was not just the danger and fear, the boredom and uncertainty and loneliness and deprivation. It was the conviction that optimistic publicity and euphemism had rendered their experience so falsely that it would never be readily communicable.

Heller shared that opinion. He wanted to abolish euphemism and tell the truth, even if it meant that he had to abandon the trappings of narrative logic. *Catch-22*, therefore, does not offer much of a plot in the conventional sense. Having marooned his soldiers on the island, and defined the bizarre circumstances that govern the place, Heller simply illustrates the situation by piling one preposterous episode on top of another. Medical orderlies Wes and Gus treat every patient in the same way, regardless of what's wrong: They slather purple paint on their gums and toes, and pump laxatives into them. Neither Gus nor Wes knows whether any of the men they medicate in this tragicomic way get better or worse. Nor do they care. Nor does anyone expect them to care. They are just doing their job. A few chapters later, a man named Major Major is promoted to major because of a clerical error that confounds his name with his rank. His fellow officers resent him because of his promotion and also because he looks like Henry Fonda. Harassed and depressed, he begins to sign his letters with the name "Washington Irving."

In another episode, Captain Black embarks on what he calls a "Glorious Loyalty Oath Crusade." Black compels his men to sign multiple loyalty oaths, in order to prove his own patriotism to superior officers, which might in turn earn him a medal or even a promotion. So the men sign loyalty oaths to check out their maps, their flak suits and their parachutes, to get a ride to the airfield, to receive their pay, to have their hair cut. As with everything else that is upside down on Pianosa, soldiers who are going off to die are presumed guilty of treason. The novel's most elaborate series of lethal comic actions concerns Milo Minderbinder. Milo, the squadron's mess hall officer, is one of the lowest-ranking men on the island, but he proves to be the most powerful. He has organized a vast syndicate, M & M Enterprises, which has monopolized much of the commerce in Europe. Buying and selling food, clothes, cotton, medicine, and whiskey, he transports his shipments from one country to another in army planes and trucks. When he needs to do so, he rearranges the war to support the business. He occasionally cooperates with the Germans when shipments are threatened with delay. The people of Palermo have elected Milo mayor in gratitude for the prosperity he has brought. These and a hundred other darkly comic episodes follow each other in a continuous, non-stop sequence. The structure of *Catch-22* is kaleidoscopic, not linear, and it can induce a kind of vertigo in the reader.

Because of its fluid organization, the novel's chronology is impossible to pin down conclusively. Lively and, in my view, ultimately pointless debates over what came before what take up a fair portion of the critical literature addressed to *Catch-22*. Such an argument misses the point. While the story has a beginning and an end, the events in between often take place in an indeterminate time, deliberately emphasizing the chaos and randomness of the situation. But in *Catch-22*, chaos coexists with fate, and Heller also employs a high degree of repetition as one way of documenting the trap in which his characters live. Men fly their missions. If they survive, they fly again—until they don't survive. What happens, happens, and then it happens again.

The so-called "soldier in white" is one example. He is introduced in the first chapter: a dying soldier completely enclosed in a full plaster body cast. Only a couple of tubes connect him to the world. One tube drips nutrients into the cast; the other collects waste that drips out. The soldier cannot move, speak, or eat. Is he already dead? Is the cast, in fact, empty? The soldier re-enters the novel twice again, and each time brings a stronger prophecy of death. Chaplain Tappman talks about "déjà vu," which he calls "a weird, occult sensation of having experienced the identical situation before in some prior time or existence." The situation that all the characters in *Catch-22* experience repeatedly is death, usually inflicted for no perceptible reason at all. In one of the narrator's early descriptions, he says that Yossarian harbored what he calls: "an unreasonable belief that everybody around him was crazy, a homicidal impulse to machinegun strangers, retrospective falsification, an unfounded suspicion that people hated him and were conspiring to kill him." However, it rather quickly becomes clear that Yossarian's fears are neither unreasonable nor unfounded. His paranoia is a perfectly sensible reaction to his circumstances. The repetition of images and events merely emphasizes the inevitable fatality of the island.

So Yossarian does everything he can to avoid flying. He tries to plead insanity. He fakes a liver disease. He re-draws the lines on bombing maps. He shows up naked to receive a medal he doesn't deserve from General Dreedle. As the narrator says: "He had decided to live forever or die in the attempt." The most vivid of the novel's repeated images, and the one that propels Yossarian to the point of mutiny, is the death of Snowden. Snowden is a member of Yossarian's crew. On one of their bombing raids, their B-25 comes under heavy anti-aircraft fire and Snowden is wounded. Yossarian sees a terrible injury in Snowden's thigh and does his best to provide medical assistance. Only gradually does Yossarian realize that Snowden's more serious injury is a gaping hole in his chest and stomach. When he opens a medical kit, the morphine he wants to give Snowden is gone. The narrator tells us:

> There was no morphine in the first-aid kit, no protection for Snowden against pain [except] the numbing shock of the gaping wound itself. The twelve syrettes of morphine had been stolen from their case and replaced by a cleanly lettered note that said: "What's good for M&M Enterprises is good for the country. Milo Minderbinder."

At that moment, Snowden's intestines pour out of his body, reducing the terrified Yossarian to impotent rage. It is not clear exactly when this climactic event occurs. It has haunted Yossarian repeatedly throughout the novel, but the magnitude of the trauma only becomes fully apparent when the calamity is told in full near the end of the book.

With this scene, the joking ends and the horror takes over. Staring at Snowden's entrails, and soaked in Snowden's blood, Yossarian moves away from all convictions except self-preservation: "Man was matter," he says, "that was Snowden's secret. Drop him out a window and he'll fall. Set fire to him and he'll burn. Bury him and he'll rot, like other kinds of garbage. The spirit gone, man is garbage." Rather than continuing to cooperate, Yossarian deserts. He determines to travel to neutral Sweden and sit out the rest of the war, and several of his buddies point out, getting from an island in the Mediterranean to Scandinavia in the midst of a European war is approximately impossible, but Yossarian will try. The novel suggests that this will at last be a truly heroic act. As for the brass hats he leaves behind, he says: "Let the bastards thrive, for all I care, since I can't do a thing to stop them but embarrass them by running away. I've got responsibilities of my own now."

Three years after *Catch-22* was published, Heller said that the novel was really about what he called "the contemporary regimented business society depicted against the background of universal sorrow and inevitable death that is [our] lot." In fact, Heller's novel is both about war and about modern society. The war, as he reconstructs it, is both a terrible reality and a symbol of a more systemic disease in the modern world as a whole. Whether in battle or not, Heller argues, all of us are subject to surveillance, interrogation, unexplained intrusions. We are continually folded, bent, and mutilated by the apparatus of corporate and state power. As crazy as the events of *Catch-22* might seem, they accurately reflect the arbitrary and inescapable exercise of power that can and will operate by its own rules.

Franz Kafka's *Metamorphosis* opens with a sentence far more offensive to common sense than anything in *Catch-22*: "When Gregor Samsa woke up one morning from unsettling dreams, he found himself changed … into a monstrous vermin." Samsa's bad dream, like Yossarian's nightmares, has come true. Grant that first premise, and everything follows. My point is not that Heller was directly influenced by Kafka, though, like all 20th-century writers on both sides of the Atlantic, he probably was. Rather, I want to emphasize what might be called the art of extremity in the 20th-century imagination. Heller's novel is located in a tradition of carefully orchestrated craziness.

Like many of his predecessors and contemporaries, Heller had seen how cheaply human life is valued in a world of mechanized destruction. He had seen the monstrous turn into the normal. *Catch-22* is the record of that frightening transformation.

Lecture Twenty-Two
The Woman Warrior

Scope: When I was preparing to teach *The Woman Warrior* for the first time, I wrote to Maxine Hong Kingston and asked her if she had any suggestions. She suggested the students pose this question, found in the first chapter: "Who am I? Do I have an essential self? What are the influences which have made me who I am?" Kingston's comments speak to the motives behind all memoirs: the attempt to discover the self and its meaning by translating the shapeless cacophony of private life into the symmetry of an orderly narrative. *The Woman Warrior* was Kingston's first book, and it was the first bestselling memoir by an Asian American. The book is subtitled *Memoirs of a Girlhood among Ghosts*, a phrase that summarizes one of Kingston's main themes, her struggle between past and present. The book weaves together old tales with contemporary experience, finding in each the metaphor that clarifies the other. In the process, *Woman Warrior* dissolves the line between fiction and nonfiction. The volume is a splendid experimental text that opened up new possibilities for a familiar form.

Outline

I. Autobiography has a history that long predates American writing and leads back to the classical world.

    A. Beginning with the *Confessions* of Augustine of Hippo, an early Christian bishop, the most durable autobiographies have provided a mirror of their times, or some insight into permanent human aspirations and fears.

    B. Americans have been engaged in autobiography since the earliest days of the English settlement in New England.

        1. In discussion of *The Bay Psalm Book*, I described the Puritan passion for introspection that led many 17th-century New England colonists to keep journals as they searched for some sign of God's plans.

        2. The habit of self-scrutiny was passed down to their American descendants, including many who did not share the same religious beliefs.

C. The most famous example of American autobiography is Benjamin Franklin's.

D. The popularity of modern biographies may represent the triumph of America's democratic instincts. Where earlier writers tended to be people of prominence, recent practitioners are more typically anonymous—men and women who become famous precisely because of their memoirs.

E. African American autobiography had its origins in 19th-century narratives dictated by escaped slaves.

F. Women, who had been underrepresented in the tradition of both biography and autobiography, began producing an abundant literature of memoir in the 20th century.

II. Maxine Hong Kingston was born in 1940 in Stockton, California. As the first bestselling memoir by an Asian American, *The Woman Warrior* further enlarged the literary conversation embodied in the genre.

   A. The book's subtitle is *Memoirs of a Girlhood among Ghosts*, a phrase that summarizes one of Kingston's main themes, the struggle between past and present that defined her imaginative life.

   B. The past and present are both represented: America, with its human opportunities but its indifference to spirit, is her future, while China, which makes room for magic but values girl-children at nothing, is her past.

III. The book is divided into five chapters of varying length, which function simultaneously as interrelated chapters and as independent stories.

   A. The first chapter, the shortest, is called "No Name Woman." Set in the China of Kingston's parents and grandparents, these pages serve as a kind of prologue, introducing several of the book's important themes and images.

      1. The memoir's first ghost is a dead aunt, whose adultery and pregnancy brought shame on the family. She was driven to suicide by an angry mob, and her name must never be spoken.

      2. *Woman Warrior* is, in the first place, designed to recover such vanished women, to give them back their identities and their place in history.

      3. By telling her story—despite her mother's warning—Kingston duplicates her aunt's violation of family rules and thus associates herself with the outcast woman.

B. The second chapter, "White Tigers," offers a counterpoint to chapter 1. In this section, Kingston tells the story of Fa Mu Lan, the legendary woman warrior of Chinese folklore, who demonstrates all the strength and independence that No Name Woman lacked.

  1. She also serves as the book's title character, a choice of significance.

  2. Although Kingston cannot be Fa Mu Lan—she says that she doesn't like fighting and armies—the Warrior Woman can be a surrogate for Kingston.

  3. Kingston's task is to replace silence and acquiescence with speech and autonomy.

C. The third chapter is called "Shaman," a word that signifies magic and sorcery, and communication between humans and the world of the spirit. The principal character is Kingston's mother, who tells her own story: a kind of memoir inside Kingston's memoir.

  1. Ying Lan (Brave Orchid) Hong's life is a tale of disorientation: She is an immigrant who has never felt at home in the new world to which she has come.

  2. At the heart of *The Woman Warrior* is a world of shifting and increasingly hybrid populations, leading to one question: Where do any of us truly belong?

D. This point is underscored in the fourth chapter, "At the Western Palace." The events take place in California and in the present. Brave Orchid's younger sister, Moon Orchid, has come to the United States to claim her rights as an abandoned wife.

  1. Thirty years earlier, Moon Orchid's husband left her and established a successful new American life with a second wife and family.

  2. Kingston interweaves the events of the here and now with a counterpart legend from the past. Brave Orchid recalls the ancient tale of the Emperor's four wives, where the Empress of the East must free her husband-Emperor from the Empress of the West.

  3. Moon Orchid's husband rejects her claims and turns her away; gradually she deteriorates into insanity and dies.

E. The final chapter of *Woman Warrior* is called "A Song for a Barbarian Reed Pipe." Kingston introduces another legendary Chinese woman, Ts'ai Yen, a poet born almost 2,000 years ago. She is another woman warrior.

1. Like Fa Mu Lan, Yen finds power not merely in swords and spears but also in language.
2. Ts'ai Yen's story illuminates Kingston's situation as a Chinese American girl growing up in a land that is at once hers and strange.
3. Kingston's early school years had been marked by a choking, shameful silence when she was required to speak English.

IV. In a sense, the book *Woman Warrior* is Kingston's final triumph over her childhood silence, and her revenge on both American and Chinese culture for silencing the voices of women.

A. Only a relatively small portion of the text provides conventional sorts of autobiographical information. By weaving legend with actual experiences, she blurs the line between fiction and memoir.

B. Kingston's stylistic choices reflect the fragmented reality she is trying to represent.

C. *The Woman Warrior* is a book about speaking and telling, about the variety of stories and sources that shape each life: a complex testimony to a complex reality.

Suggested Reading:

Cheung, *Articulate Silences*.

Questions to Consider:

1. *The Woman Warrior* offers a set of reflections on the experience of immigrants and displaced people. Such questions are especially pertinent in a nation made up, as America has been, of immigrants. How does this portrait of people removed from their original home compare with the stories of other immigrants, for instance your own, or those of your family, or those you have read about in other books?

2. Since the five sections function simultaneously as interrelated chapters and as independent stories, they can be approached from both points of view. Keeping in mind subject matter as well as literary techniques, what are the main points of connection among the sections? What are the differences? Along with ghosts and the woman warrior, what are some of the other major images that recur throughout the book? (For example, trace Kingston's preoccupation with voice, story, and storytelling.) Finally, what explains the order in which the five sections are arranged?

Lecture Twenty-Two—Transcript
The Woman Warrior

Some years ago, when I was preparing to teach *The Woman Warrior* for the first time, I wrote to Maxine Hong Kingston and asked her if she had any suggestions. She proposed that my students and I begin with the questions she herself had raised in the beginning of the book. She asked that we pay particular attention to this passage from the first chapter:

> Chinese-Americans, when you try to understand what things in you are Chinese, how do you separate what is peculiar to childhood, to poverty, insanities, one family, your mother who marked your growing with stories, from what is Chinese? What is Chinese tradition and what is the movies?

"In other words," Kingston added in her letter, "Who am I? Do I have an essential self? What are the influences [that] have made me who I am?" "Of course, I am addressing the general reader," she says, "not only Chinese-Americans. I'd like all readers to ponder these questions as they read the book, and come up with answers not only about me but about their own lives."

Kingston's comments, as we will see, provide a useful entry into her book. But they also speak to the motives behind all memoirs: the attempt to discover the self and its meaning by translating the shapeless cacophony of private life into the symmetry of an orderly narrative. For many autobiographers, the stakes are very high. Some have said that they only began to understand themselves through the act of turning their experience into words and writing it down. Critic Alfred Kazin, who published three volumes of memoir, went further. Kazin said that the books in which he reconstructed his life were "an effort to find salvation, to make one's own experience come out right."

Autobiography has a history that long pre-dates American writing and leads back to the classical world. Scholars have traced its genealogy at least to the *Confessions* of the early Christian bishop, Augustine of Hippo. This may be the first book in the West in which a person discloses the intimate details of his own life in order to illuminate the human condition. The intervening 16 centuries have witnessed a distinguished heritage of writing about the self— from Benvenuto Cellini's *Life*, to Montaigne's *Essays*, to Rousseau's selfportrait, which he also called *Confessions*. What has separated such classic autobiographical texts from mere anecdotes and naval-gazing is that generations and even centuries of readers have found some larger significance in these self-studies. Beginning with Augustine, the most durable autobiographies have provided a mirror of their times, along with some insight into perennial human aspirations and fears. They may be addressed to the common reader, but they have told the stories of uncommon individuals. Americans have been engaged in autobiography since the earliest days of English settlement. In our discussion of *The Bay Psalm Book*, I described the Puritan passion for introspection that led many 17th-century New England colonists to record the details of their lives as they searched for some sign of God's plan.

The diaries and journals they kept, almost none of them published in their lifetimes, inadvertently comprise the nation's first flowering of autobiography. These early believers saw their lives as a mingling of personal and collective experience. They took themselves seriously because their mission was serious. They worried about their own spiritual condition because the welfare of the entire community demanded that each individual conform to God's word and law. That habit of self-scrutiny was passed down to their American descendants, including many who did not share their same religious beliefs.

The most famous example is surely Benjamin Franklin. I have mentioned Franklin at least twice before, in discussing the novels of Horatio Alger and the success manuals of Dale Carnegie. Here I want to note Franklin's pioneering contribution as an autobiographer. His commitment to self-advancement was motivated by a genuine devotion to the common good. Though he was detached from any conventional religious motives, Franklin shared with his more pious predecessors the idea that his personal story encoded a larger communal significance. As a young man, he was deeply influenced by *Pilgrim's Progress*, and he saw his own life as a journey toward both worldly success and civic virtue. When he wrote the pages that would become the *Autobiography*, he addressed them to his son, William, suggesting that his experience could provide his son with a model for a well-lived, purposeful life.

The great American historian Henry Adams also conceived of his life as a model, but of a completely different sort. Writing just after the turn of the 20th century, he called his autobiography *The Education of Henry Adams*. Instead of Franklin's focus on success, the theme of Adams's self-portrait is failure. Overwhelmed by the technological forces that shaped the modern world, Adams struggled in vain to find any purpose at all in his life or in the sequence of historical events. He appealed to religion, nationalism, science, and art, but all of his efforts led to disappointment. Like Franklin, Adams thought of his autobiography, from its title on, specifically in terms of its instructional value. However, the *Education* is a reverse image of Franklin's story. It teaches a lesson in skepticism and futility. If Franklin embodied American opportunity, and the movement up from raggedy beginnings to prosperity and wisdom, Adams exemplified defeat. He began at the top of American society, the grandson and great-grandson of presidents, but he ended, at least intellectually, in a ditch.

Between them, Benjamin Franklin and Henry Adams defined the opposed American limits of autobiographical inquiry. But note that, despite the radical difference between them in tone and theme, both men carried on the early tradition that finds in individual experience an expression of collective values. Both of these men conceived of their autobiographical writings as messages that would find a broad range of readers. They may have begun as private meditations, but they were ultimately intended for a public audience. In the century since Adams published his *Education*, memoirs have multiplied, finally emerging over the past 20 years or so as one of the most popular genres in American writing.

In a *New York Times* article complaining about the proliferation of these life stories, William Grimes wrote: "We All Have a Life. Must We All Write About It?" He describes readers staggering under a "memoir mountain." What might explain this explosion of memoirs? One obvious possibility is that we all enjoy stories, and we also enjoy access into hidden places. Autobiography offers both. In addition, we have a special regard for "true stories," and we respond to memoir differently than we do to fiction. The critic and scholar Wendy Steiner has suggested that "fiction provides occasions for *vicarious identification*, whereas the [memoir] multiplies possibilities for *real empathy*." Of course, that is why readers feel especially betrayed when they learn that many memoirs have proven to be downright fabrications.

Think of the fictionalized *I, Rigoberta Menchú*, which boosted its author to a Nobel Prize for Peace; or James Frey's *A Million Little Pieces*, which bamboozled a legion of readers, including Oprah Winfrey; or Misha Defonseca's invented *Misha: A Mémoire of the Holocaust Years*; or the more recent autobiographical fraud, the fictitious *Love and Consequences*, by the equally fictitious "Margaret B. Jones." Despite these deceptions, most of us continue to assume that authors of memoirs are doing their best to tell the truth. That assumption, to be sure, is deeply embedded in our culture. Eyewitness testimony is much prized in courtrooms, though research has repeatedly proven how fallible most of us are despite even our best efforts to tell the truth.

Beyond our fascination with inside stories, preferably true, the popularity of modern autobiographies may represent the triumph of America's democratic instincts. Where early writers tended to be people (usually men) of prominence, recent practitioners are typically less familiar. They're often, in fact, men and women who become famous precisely for their memoirs. (Think here of Frank McCourt's *Angela's Ashes*.) Beyond that, as more and different groups have mobilized to affirm their place in the American experience, they provide an audience for books that represent their own specific histories and identities. African American autobiography has its origins in the 19th-century narratives written or dictated by escaped slaves. The most famous, which I've mentioned before, was the *Narrative of the Life of Frederick Douglass*, in which this major abolitionist told of his harrowing escape from the bondage of slavery.

Half a century later, Booker T. Washington's *Up From Slavery* told the story of Washington's rise from enslaved beginnings to leadership and influence. In the 19th and 20th centuries, Native American life stories began to appear. Since many of the Indian authors could not read or write, white listeners often transcribed their tales. *Black Elk Speaks* is perhaps the most famous example.

Women, who had been under-represented in the tradition of both biography and autobiography, began producing an abundant literature of memoir in the 20th century. These are works that both recorded and helped to stimulate the modern feminist movement. Jane Addams's *Twenty Years at Hull House*, Edith Wharton's *A Backward Glance*, Maya Angelou's *I Know Why the Caged Bird Sings*, and Maxine Hong Kingston's *The Woman Warrior* are just a sample of this rich collection of titles.

Maxine Hong was born in 1940 in Stockton, California. Both of her parents, Tom and Ying Lan Hong, had immigrated to the United States from China—her father in 1924, her mother 15 years later. During Maxine's childhood, the family operated a laundry in Stockton in which all of the Hong children worked, often for long hours.

Maxine received a B.A. from the University of California at Berkeley in 1962. After teaching English and mathematics for a few years, she moved to Hawaii in 1967 with her husband, Earll Kingston. They returned to California in 1985 and now live in Oakland.

The Woman Warrior was Kingston's first book, and it was the first bestselling memoir by an Asian American. As such, it further enlarged the literary conversation embodied in the genre. Those facts alone would stimulate our interest, but the volume is, in addition, a splendid experimental text, which opened up new possibilities for a familiar form. The book's subtitle is *Memoirs of a Girlhood among Ghosts*, a phrase that summarizes one of Kingston's main themes, the struggle between past and present that defined her imaginative life.

The ghosts are, to begin with, the Americans and their machines, among whom young Maxine Hong grew up: "Taxi Ghosts, Bus Ghosts, Police Ghosts, Fire Ghosts, Meter … Ghosts, Tree Trimming Ghosts, Five-and-Dime Ghosts." But the ghosts are also the customs and stories of China, a legacy of pain and beauty bequeathed to Kingston by her mother's "talk-story." America, with its human opportunities but its indifference to spirit, is her future, while China, which makes room for magic but values girl-children at nothing, is her past. The book is divided into five essays of varying length, which function simultaneously as inter-related chapters and as independent stories. Let me review them briefly, suggesting as I do some of the differences and connections among the various parts. The first chapter, the shortest, is called "No Name Woman." Set in the China of Kingston's parents and grandparents, these pages serve as a kind of prologue, introducing several of the book's important themes and images. Here we learn the story of an aunt, a sister of Kingston's mother, who in the mid-1920s drowned herself in the communal well of her family's rural Chinese village. The first line of the section will resonate through the entire volume. As her mother, Ying Lan Hong, or "Brave Orchid," begins to tell the story to young Maxine, she says: "You must not tell anyone … what I am about to tell you." Maxine's dead aunt is the memoir's first ghost: a woman whose adultery and pregnancy brought shame on the family. She was driven to suicide by an angry mob, and her name must never be spoken. *Woman Warrior* is, in the first place, designed to recover such vanished women, to give them back their identities and their place in history. What her family would conceal, Kingston feels obliged to reveal. *Woman Warrior* is, in part, a record of the contest between secrecy and truth telling. In addition, however, Kingston tests the limits of truth telling by offering two conflicting versions of her aunt's sexual conduct. Perhaps she was raped by one of the village men, or perhaps she was lonely and seeking love. The question is deliberately left unresolved. Kingston's purpose is not to find or invent factual precision, but to confer on the woman the complexity and ambiguity that all human beings incorporate. Certitude is always dangerous when we try to understand other people or even, perhaps, ourselves.

As she tries to reconstruct the hardships of her mother's small village, Kingston admits that she respects the traditions of her Chinese forbearers. She acknowledges that customs forbidding adultery make sense, especially in a poor community. At the same time, she knows that her unnamed aunt was punished because she was a woman. The man who was the father of the bastard child was never even sought. In a later part of the book, Kingston quotes a Chinese proverb: "When fishing for treasures in the flood, be careful not to pull in girls." Kingston argues that death was not the worst penalty her aunt suffered. She says: "The real punishment was ... the family's deliberately forgetting her." To be forgotten, in other words, is to cease to exist. Even as a ghost, the No Name Woman will wander alone, abandoned by other ghosts. By telling her story—despite her mother's warning—Kingston duplicates her aunt's violation of family rules, and thus associates herself with the outcast woman.

The second chapter, "White Tigers," offers a kind of counterpoint to chapter one. In this section, Kingston tells the story of Fa Mu Lan, the legendary woman warrior of Chinese folklore, who demonstrates all the strength and independence that No Name Woman lacked. She also serves as the book's title character, a choice that bears some comment. Kingston's version of the tale includes the battlefield heroism—the triumphs over male soldiers—that are typically part of Fa Mu Lan's story. However, the woman warrior of "White Tigers" is also intimately connected to words and language. After she has completed her 15 years of military training and is preparing for her first combat, her father tells her: "We are going to carve revenge on your back, ... We'll write out oaths and names." That is exactly what he does, cutting a long list of grievances into Fa Mu Lan's flesh with a razor-sharp blade. She says: "If an enemy should flay me, the light would shine through my skin like lace." The point of this grisly episode is not merely to demonstrate Fa Mu Lan's filial obedience or her courage. More important, her scarred body symbolizes the power of language. When she looks at her back in a mirror, she says that the bloody characters march in "files, like an army, like my army."

Although Kingston cannot be Fa Mu Lan—she says she doesn't like fighting and armies—the woman warrior can be a surrogate for Kingston. Words find their realization in action, and action finds its meaning in words. That is why, at the end of this chapter, Kingston can say: "The swordswoman and I are not so dissimilar." The characters cut into Fa Mu Lan's back are emblems of Kingston's task: to replace silence and acquiescence with speech and autonomy.

The third chapter is called "Shaman," a word that signifies magic and sorcery, and communication between humans and the world of the spirits. The principal character is Kingston's mother, who tells her own story: a kind of memoir inside Kingston's memoir. Above all, Ying Lan Hong's life is a tale of disorientation: She is an immigrant who has never felt at home in the new world to which she has come. As this section opens, Kingston recalls the few times her mother took out her Chinese medical diplomas. Brave Orchid was a fully qualified doctor with a busy practice. In the United States, she has become a worker in the family laundry. Everything about America confuses and frightens her: the strange language, the food and clothing, the customs and behavior. Kingston offers a long and detailed recollection of life in the medical school in which her mother trained, all of it convincingly factual. This straightforward story suddenly gives way to a remarkable episode in which Brave Orchid spends an entire night fighting off the attack of a ghost that tries to suffocate her. Western science and ancient folk tales merge in this scene, which marks the efforts of an emancipated Chinese woman to throw off the weight of the anti-feminist traditions of her homeland. Sitting in the sweltering laundry in California, she tells her daughter: "You have no idea how much I have fallen coming to America." She and her family have chosen exile and a new start, but the price has been heavy. America has brought anxiety, indignity, and loneliness.

As a gesture of defiance, Brave Orchid has kept her Chinese name, refusing to use an American name. She gets her revenge against ethnic insults by calling white people equally insulting names in Chinese. Her memories are saturated with images of her life in China: delivering babies, nursing the wounded during Japanese air raids, and doing important work. Brave Orchid will always feel China, where time moves more slowly, remains her home. For Kingston, on the contrary, China has never been home. Turning the history of Chinese misogyny into a kind of dark joke, she says:

> I did not want to go to China. In China my parents would sell my sisters and me. My father would marry two or three more wives, who would splatter cooking oil on our bare toes and lie that we were crying for naughtiness. They would give food to their own children and rocks to us. I did not want to go where the ghosts took shapes nothing like our own.

For Kingston, America is home, despite its vexations, and strangeness, and intermittent bigotry. Kingston aspires to exchange the claims of national loyalty for a cosmopolitan identity. She says to her mother: "We belong to the planet now, Mama. Does it make sense to you that if we're no longer attached to one piece of land, we belong to the planet? Wherever we happen to be standing, why, that spot belongs to us as much as any other spot." This passage lies near the heart of *Woman Warrior*. In a world of shifting and increasingly hybrid populations, where do any of us truly belong? The 20th century witnessed the largest displacement of people in human history. Estimates vary, but it is probable that more than 200 million men, women, and children left voluntarily or were driven from their homes and countries by a combination of hunger, persecution, and warfare. Brave Orchid, born and educated in one society, raising children and growing old in another, exemplifies this enormous transformation.

The point is underscored in the fourth chapter, "At the Western Palace." The events take place in California and in the present. Brave Orchid's younger sister, Moon Orchid, has come to the United States to claim her rights as an abandoned wife. Thirty years earlier, her husband had left her in China and established a new American life. He has become a successful doctor with a second wife and a new family. In fact, Moon Orchid is a timid, self-effacing woman in her mid-60s, who would never have undertaken this journey on her own initiative.

Brave Orchid has devised the scheme and takes great pleasure in anticipating her sister's unexpected and triumphant eruption into her husband's life. "You have to ask him why he didn't come home [to China]," Brave Orchid says, and she tells her sister to ask her husband: "Why he turned into a barbarian. Make him feel bad about leaving his mother and father. Scare him. Walk right into his house with your suitcases and boxes. Move right into the bedroom. Throw her stuff out of the drawers and put yours in. Say, 'I am the first wife, and she is our servant.' "

Once again, Kingston interweaves the events of the here-and-now with the counterpart legend from the past. In this case, however, the relationship is ironic. Brave Orchid recalls the ancient tale of the Emperor's four wives. Each wife lived in a palace at one of the four points of the compass. The Empress of the West wanted to reign as preeminent, while the Empress of the East was generous and kind. In Brave Orchid's version, her sister is the Empress of the East, who must free her husband-Emperor from the connivance of the Western Empress. It is a harebrained idea, doomed to fail.

Moon Orchid's husband rejects her claims and turns her away. Crushed by the encounter, Moon Orchid gradually deteriorates into insanity, lingers for a few months in an asylum, and then quietly dies. The chapter has a wonderfully bracing final line. Watching the mess their mother has made, all of Brave Orchid's children, Kingston says, "made up their minds to major in science or mathematics." In short, if this is what tradition means, better to leave it behind.

The final chapter of *Woman Warrior* is called "A Song for a Barbarian Reed Pipe." Kingston introduces another legendary Chinese woman, Ts'ai Yen, a poet born almost 2,000 years ago. Taken in a raid by an enemy chief when she was 20, Ts'ai Yen becomes her captor's concubine, bears his children, and fights alongside him in battle. Kingston tells us that "she cut down anyone in her path during the madness of close combat." She is another warrior woman.

Like Fa Mu Lan, Ts'ai Yen finds power not merely in swords and spears, but also in language. She sings in a high, clear voice about her lost homeland and her family. The barbarians cannot understand the words, but they sense the anger and sadness they communicate. Ts'ai Yen's story illuminates Kingston's situation as a Chinese- American girl growing up in a land that is at once hers and strange. Her early school years had been marked by silence when she was required to speak English, a choking silence that leads to shame.

Eventually, she and her sister and the other girls they knew "found some voice," she says, "however faltering. We invented an American-feminine speaking personality, …" In a sense, the book *Woman Warrior* is Kingston's final triumph over her childhood silence, and her revenge on both American and Chinese culture for silencing the voices of women. Only a relatively small portion of the text provides conventional sorts of autobiographical information. More a *Portrait of the Artist As a Young Woman* than a straightforward memoir, the book links old tales with contemporary experience, finding in each the metaphor that clarifies the other. In the process, *Woman Warrior* dissolves the line between fiction and nonfiction.

At one point in the final chapter, Kingston rebukes her mother's stories: "I don't want to listen to any more of your stories; they have no logic. They scramble me up. You lie with stories. You won't tell me a story and then say: 'This is a true story,' or 'This is just a story.' I can't tell the difference." Despite her complaints, it is the indeterminate nature of her mother's stories that have made them essential. Kingston's stylistic choices reflect the fragmented reality that she is trying to represent. Contemporary America is a place of acceleration, mixture, ethnic transformation, pluralism, and suspicion that alternates with tolerance. Change is the hallmark, not stability, and the virtual threatens to overtake the real.

In another passage in that last chapter, Kingston briefly tells a Chinese story that bears directly on her narrative intentions:

> Long ago in China, knot-makers tied string into buttons and frogs, and rope into bell pulls. There was one knot so complicated that it blinded the knot-maker. Finally an emperor outlawed this cruel knot, and the nobles could not order it anymore. If I had lived in China, I would have been an outlaw knot-maker.

The Woman Warrior is a book about speaking and telling, about the variety of sources and stories that shape every life. We are each a human amalgam in which heritage and history, family and friends and genetics, and high culture and pop culture are mixed in unpredictable combinations. Most of us don't fit very neatly into one-dimensional ethnic or religious or social categories, and Kingston's book is a complex testimony to that complex reality.

Lecture Twenty-Three
John Adams

Scope: By the end of 2007, David McCullough's *John Adams* had sold over 3 million copies, making it—by a considerable margin—the bestselling biography in America's literary history. But why John Adams? Working with this apparently unlikely material, McCullough achieved something quite rare in historical writing: He produced a superb political biography that also rehabilitated his subject. Largely because of this effort, John Adams has been restored, at least tentatively, to his place among the leading figures of the founding and early republic. In McCullough's reconstruction of him, John Adams emerges as a flawed but fundamentally decent man, built on human dimensions but capable of heroic deeds. It may be precisely his humanness that has struck a chord with readers, who welcome a man who seems to share their own ordinary stature but seized the chance to reach beyond the ordinary. McCullough combines that compelling human story with the authority of extensive research and a gift for description and narrative. *John Adams* received the Pulitzer Prize, and deservedly so.

Outline

I. The popularity of biography partly lies in the curiosity we all feel about the lives of other people, especially those who have played some role on the public stage. Beyond that, biographies speak to the universal human appetite for stories and storytelling.

    A. Like the memoir, biography has an ancient pedigree. The most famous such text from antiquity is perhaps Plutarch's *Lives*.

    B. Early biographies strongly emphasized the importance of virtuous actions and correct religious beliefs.

        1. This devotional focus strongly influenced the first American practitioners of the genre.

        2. The tendency of early Americans to portray themselves as biblical surrogates has had lasting implications for the way in which subsequent generations have viewed the nation's role in history.

    C. Americans have typically treated their founders and leaders with a similar quasi-religious reverence.

        1. George Washington was the subject of a celebrated biography written by Parson Weems, where Washington is presented as a semidivine figure.

        2. In 1938, Carl Van Doren wrote a Pulitzer Prize–winning biography of Benjamin Franklin. Since that time, over 300 studies of Franklin have appeared; more than 30 just since the year 2000.

        3. Hundreds of books, some of them multivolume tomes, have addressed Thomas Jefferson's life.

        4. Lincoln has been the subject of no fewer than 1,000 book-length studies.

II. A terse summary of John Adam's career could be condensed into an unflattering portrait.

    A. Absent from the new nation throughout much of the Revolutionary War, Adams spent several years in France, where he was overshadowed by Benjamin Franklin.

    B. Upon returning to the United States, Adams accepted election as vice president and endured eight humiliating years in that office.

    C. Though he considered himself Washington's obvious successor, Adams defeated Jefferson in the election of 1796 by a margin of just three electoral votes.

    D. In 1800, he was ignominiously defeated in his reelection effort. He retired to his Massachusetts farm where he lived out the remaining quarter century of his life.

III. McCullough said that he originally planned a joint biography of Adams and Jefferson but soon found himself more attracted to Adams. The reason lies near the center of the book's appeal and success.

    A. Adams's letters reveal a man quite different from the one-dimensional caricature of conventional wisdom. He proved to have been a man of uncommon insight and good judgment and capable of affection and humor.

    B. McCullough's profile of Adams humanizes him but also brings to light his remarkable traits and accomplishments.

        1. Adams seems in certain key respects a man ahead of his time: Unlike Washington and Jefferson, he never owned a slave, and he never hesitated to declare his repugnance for the practice.

    2. Unlike many of the other founders, Adams was not born to wealth and position. He was the son of a Massachusetts farmer and shoemaker; both father and son earned their money through hard work.

    3. Adams enrolled in Harvard College at 15 years old, chose the law over ministry, and realized his own substantial talents for writing and argument.

  C. McCullough emphasizes Adams's ambition as well. He wanted to shine, as he put it, and the tumultuous events of the 1760s gave him the chance.

    1. Adams was an early advocate of independence, taking a dangerous stand before most others.

    2. For a while, Adams managed to work effectively with Jefferson, who would later become his great rival.

    3. McCullough provides a long and detailed review of Adams's self-appointed mission to Holland after his failed year in France.

    4. In 1788, Adams was elected vice president, and he spent eight mostly unhappy years serving as understudy to George Washington.

IV. The single presidential term Adams served was fraught with conflict and crisis, as he was the only president in our history whose vice president was also his leading political opponent—Thomas Jefferson.

  A. The nation was dividing into political parties—Jefferson the head of the Republicans, and Adams reluctantly leading the Federalists.

  B. The overriding issue Adams faced was to determine America's response to the war between France and England.

  C. Attempting to maintain domestic control, Adams signed the Alien and Sedition Acts, four bills passed by the Federalist Congress that placed restrictions on noncitizens and limited dissent.

  D. The first and only campaign in which an incumbent president and vice president faced each other became, in McCullough's words, "a contest of personal vilification surpassing any presidential election in American history."

    1. As expected, Adams was beaten by Jefferson, whose tactics were demonstrably nastier than his opponent's.

    2.   This contrast provides one of the book's principal organizing devices: Adams's elevation inevitably implies Jefferson's reduction.

V. Adams was a tired, 65-year-old man when he returned to his home outside of Boston. He was then finally able to spend uninterrupted time with his wife, Abigail, one of the more remarkable people of her time.

    A. Abigail Adams was widely considered a woman of uncommon intelligence and independence. She held strong views on the crime of slavery and the rights of women.

    B. Due to John's public life, he and Abigail spent extended periods of time apart, during which they wrote letters to one another, providing McCullough with much of his source material.

    C. The friendship between John and Abigail Adams, and the mutual esteem with which they regarded each other, had no precedent in American history.

        1. It provides the emblem of integrity McCullough consistently attributes to his subject.

        2. In effect, this portrait of Adams works from the inside out, using his decency as evidence of his political significance.

    D. This human story is one reason for the unparalleled success of McCullough's book; the other is the sheer skill with which the story is told.

    E. On July 4, 1826, on the 50th anniversary of the Declaration of Independence, John Adams and Thomas Jefferson remarkably died within hours of one another.

Suggested Reading:

Ellis, *Passionate Sage.*

Smith, *John Adams.*

Questions to Consider:

1.   One of the key narrative devices McCullough employs throughout the book is a sustained series of contrasts between Adams and the other founders—especially Benjamin Franklin, and above all Thomas Jefferson. What purposes would such a device serve in this biography?

2. Though Adams's conception of equality did not reach to African Americans, he denounced slavery. Nor did he endorse voting rights or property rights for women, but his relationship with his wife Abigail reveals a profound respect for her views and courage. From the evidence of the many surviving letters between them, this husband and wife would seem to have maintained a relationship of affectionate reciprocity. They addressed each other as "My Dearest Friend," and John frequently acknowledged the value of Abigail's advice and criticism. Was the marriage genuinely unusual for its time, and if so does the source of the distinction lie with John or Abigail or both? Is it possible that the relationship seems more uncommon than it might have been simply because we have so few other examples of marriages from this period that have been equivalently documented?

Lecture Twenty-Three—Transcript
John Adams

By the end of 2007, David McCullough's *John Adams* had sold over 3 million copies. This made it—by a considerable margin—the bestselling biography in America's literary history. A question immediately suggests itself: John Adams? Wasn't he the nation's second president, a one-term incumbent more or less squashed between the much larger figures of George Washington and Thomas Jefferson? John Adams—the irritable, self-righteous lawyer about whom Benjamin Franklin famously said: "he is always an honest man, often a wise one, but sometimes and in some things [he is] absolutely out of his senses."

For two centuries, Adams had no biographical luck. The national pantheon was crowded with the men who had surrounded and apparently outperformed him. Washington led his ill-equipped, ragtag army of American soldiers to an unlikely victory over the greatest empire in the world, and then defined the presidency in his two terms. In the process, he became a human symbol of the American nation. Jefferson is permanently revered as the author of the Declaration of Independence, with its soaring rhetoric of freedom and equality. During the Revolution and against all odds, Benjamin Franklin went to France and pulled off the implausible feat of securing the aid of a monarchy to establish a republic.

James Madison achieved his immortality by guiding the Constitution to completion and approval. So, the question recurs: How did any biography achieve such popularity as McCullough's, and in particular a biography of John Adams? Let's begin with some background on the biographical genre. Part of the popularity of biography lies in the curiosity we all feel about the lives of other people, and especially people who have played some role on the public stage. What were these men and women really like? How did their inner and outer lives correspond? Like the memoir, which we looked at in the previous lecture, biography seems to promise us access into the secret places of other lives. Beyond that, biographies speak to the universal human appetite for stories and storytelling. People across every culture we know of share an unquenchable fascination with the narratives that make up myth and history, fiction and memory, and biography. There seem to be basic human pleasures, perhaps even hard-wired, in hearing the events of a life reconstructed and arranged in a meaningful pattern. Again like the memoir, biography has an ancient pedigree. Several of the most popular texts that have come down to us from antiquity have a biographical focus. The most famous, perhaps, is Plutarch's *Lives*, a series of sketches of illustrious Greeks and Romans presented in parallel. The arrangement is designed to underscore the shared virtues or defects of the paired subjects. Along with his pioneering contribution as a biographer, Plutarch also declared a motivation that has been widely copied for two millennia. In the opening of his *Life of Alexander*, Plutarch declared that he was less concerned with writing history than with exploring the influence of character on behavior. In other words, each of the two dozen or so subjects in Plutarch's essays is presented as a case study, a touchstone of moral example and instruction for readers. That interpretive impulse, as we will see, can be found in many subsequent biographies, including McCullough's *John Adams*.

For centuries after the fall of Rome, the most common specimen of biographical writing across Christian Europe was the saint's life. Often basing their tales on little or even no factual material, the authors of these pious volumes put a single-minded emphasis on the importance of virtuous action and correct religious belief. Each member of the Church should emulate the saints. The rewards were substantial: a sanctified life on earth, and the promise of eternal salvation. Christ himself provided the most ideal subject for this genre of writing. *The Imitation of Christ* by Thomas à Kempis, which urges readers to follow Christ's life as a model, has been continuously in print in dozens of languages for nearly 600 years. Not surprisingly, the devotional focus of those early biographies strongly influenced the first American practitioners of the genre. As we have seen, the 17th-century Puritans brought their religion and many of their literary ideas with them when they migrated to the New World.

In our discussion of *The Bay Psalm Book*, I mentioned the Puritan habit of connecting this world and the next in close association. In their reconstruction of the lives of their leaders, they often found biblical precedents for their heroic figures. The writing of the legendary preacher, Cotton Mather, whom I have mentioned before, provides a splendid example. He called his history of the New World colonies, *Magnalia Christi Americana*, which can be translated as "Christ's Great Deeds in America." Mather told the story of Massachusetts as the collective biographies of the Colony's great men. The founders and those who followed are honored for their piety and for their persistence in the face of obstacles. William Bradford of Plymouth, for instance, is identified as a latter-day Moses, the man who led his people out of the Egyptian slavery of their lives in Anglican England into the Promised Land of the New World. John Winthrop, long-time governor of Massachusetts, is the American Nehemiah, a reference to the governor of Judea, who rebuilt the walls of Jerusalem after their destruction by the Babylonians. Emerson would later say that: "Institutions are the lengthened shadows of great men." The Puritans, who effectively transformed history into biography, anticipated that idea. The Puritans frequently referred to themselves as a "chosen people." They professed a breathtaking confidence in the special role that had been assigned to them by God in his providential plan for humanity. Not coincidentally, such a special providence required special leaders.

This tendency of early Americans to portray themselves as biblical surrogates has had lasting implications for the way in which subsequent generations have viewed the nation's role in history. In an earlier lecture, I quoted Thomas Paine, predicting that all of posterity to the end of time would be affected by the American experiment in independence, and I've made reference to Abraham Lincoln's declaration that the United States represented the "last, best hope of earth." Louisa May Alcott's preacher father, Bronson Alcott, went so far as to suggest that God would plant his second Eden on American soil. Given all this, it is not surprising that Americans traditionally treated their founders and leaders with a quasi-religious reverence. George Washington's life provides the first and fullest example. Within weeks of his death, in a famous memorial portrait called *The Apotheosis of Washington*, the newly deceased president was pictured being literally carried up to heaven by angels and saints. Grieving women surrounded the pedestal. A Native American hangs his head in sorrow, and the American eagle looks on in apparent distress. History, religion, and national myth join together, and we will see multiple versions of that linkage in several of the examples I will be discussing.

Washington's face was the most ubiquitous in the early republic. Thousands of copies of paintings by Gilbert Stuart, Charles Willson Peale, and other artists circulated all across the new country. In addition, Washington was the focus of what we would today call merchandise: Crude portraits appeared on drinking mugs, dinner plates, tablecloths, cigar cases, and dolls. In a literal as well as metaphorical sense, Washington has become our nation's common currency. Gilbert Stuart's *Athenaeum Portrait* provided the image for the one-dollar bill, which has been reproduced billions of times in the past century.

Washington was also the subject of a celebrated biography that appeared within a year of his death. In 1800, Mason Locke Weems—known universally as Parson Weems—published a worshipful life of the late president, festooned with a wonderful title that summarizes everything you need to know about its intentions: *A History of the Life and Death, Virtues and Exploits of General George Washington, ... Containing a Great Many Curious and Valuable Anecdotes, Tending to Throw Much Light on the Private as Well as Public Life and Character of That Very Extraordinary Man, the Whole Happily Calculated to Furnish a Feast of True Washingtonian Entertainment and Improvement Both to Ourselves and Our Children.* That is just a portion of the title, but you get the idea. Weems's Washington is God's particular gift to America and the world, a semi-divine figure. Washington embodies all virtues—though he himself is too modest to admit it, since modesty is one of the virtues that he possesses. He builds American freedom from a blueprint that had been drafted more or less literally by the Lord. Weems's biography was itself a bestseller, appearing in many editions throughout the 19th century.

In the fifth edition, in 1806, Weems invented and introduced the most famous of all Washington stories, including its immortal punch line about who cut down the cherry tree. Washington says to his father: "I cannot tell a lie, Pa." With no more basis in fact than the marvelous tales in medieval saints' lives, the anecdote nevertheless has remained lodged in the American imagination for two centuries. No other character in the nation's history would be remembered with the unembarrassed adoration that Washington elicited, but many of the other founders would become the subjects of extended biographical treatment. Franklin was the most down-to-earth of the founders, the man in the leather apron who earned his money with his hands and his brain. Back in 1938, Carl Van Doren wrote a Pulitzer Prize-winning biography of Franklin and said in the "Preface" so many volumes have already been written on so many periods and phases of Franklin's career and there have been so many countless studies that Van Doren wondered whether there was room for one more. Well, by my reckoning, nearly 300 of the 400 studies of Franklin that you can find on library shelves have appeared since 1938: more than 30 just since the year 2000. The Franklin industry is alive and well.

Thomas Jefferson has also provided material for a long library shelf. Hundreds of books—some of them multi-volume tomes—have addressed Jefferson's life, including his political thought, architectural accomplishments, and private behavior. Writers have found an audience for books on Jefferson's travel essays, his opinions of French wines, his prose style, and his musical taste.

Among American leaders that followed the founders, only Lincoln has captivated the American imagination to a similar extent. Indeed, even in his lifetime, Lincoln was paired with Washington, the two of them occupying the roles of Father and Savior in the public imagination. Lincoln's assassination, just days after the Union victory in the Civil War, ensured his quasi-divine status. In the years since his death, Lincoln has been the subject of no fewer than 1,000 book-length studies, which brings us back to John Adams. A cruel summary of Adams's career could be condensed into a few sentences. He was absent from the new nation throughout much of the Revolutionary War. He spent several of those years representing Congress in France, where he was outmatched and overshadowed by Benjamin Franklin. When he returned to the United States, he accepted election as vice president and endured eight humiliating years in an office that brought neither responsibility nor respect. Though he considered himself Washington's obvious successor, Adams defeated Jefferson in the election of 1796 by a margin of just three electoral votes. He served one miserable presidential term and is remembered principally as the signer of the Alien and Sedition Acts, a pair of horrendous affronts to the civil liberties guaranteed in the Bill of Rights.

In 1800, he was ignominiously defeated in his re-election effort and retired to his Massachusetts farm, where he lived out the remaining quarter-century of his life. He did live to see his oldest son sworn in as president in 1825. John Quincy Adams snatched the presidency from Andrew Jackson in the most disputed election since his father's 28 years earlier. After a single term as unhappy as his father's had been, John Quincy was crushed in his rematch with Jackson in 1828. John didn't live to see his son's defeat; he had died two years earlier.

Working with this apparently unlikely material, David McCullough has achieved something quite rare in historical writing: He simultaneously produced a superb political biography, and he also rehabilitated his subject. The eminent historian Gordon Wood has called McCullough's book "by far the best biography of Adams ever written." Largely because of McCullough's efforts, John Adams has been restored, at least tentatively, to his place among the leading figures of the early republic. McCullough has said that he originally planned a joint biography of Adams and Jefferson, but that he soon found himself more attracted to Adams. The reason lies near the center of his book's appeal and success. Stated briefly, John Adams's letters, of which thousands survive, reveal a man quite different from the one-dimensional caricature of conventional wisdom. Those letters, never intended for publication, became McCullough's basic biographical building blocks. Upon the closer inspection that those letters make possible, Adams proves to have been a man of uncommon insight and good judgment. He was even, despite his reputation as a crank, capable of affection and humor.

In McCullough's reconstruction of him, John Adams emerges as a flawed but fundamentally decent man, built on a human scale but capable of heroic deeds. He would never adorn Mount Rushmore, as do Washington, Jefferson, Lincoln, and the first Roosevelt. However, precisely for that reason he has struck a chord with readers ready to welcome a man who appears to share their own ordinary stature but seized the chance to reach beyond the ordinary. Furthermore, Adams seems in certain key respects a man ahead of his time. Unlike Washington and Jefferson, he never owned a slave, and he found the very idea of slavery repugnant. He never hesitated to declare his contempt for slavery and slaveholders, even when he offended key allies. Also unlike most of the other founders—and in this he resembles Benjamin Franklin—Adams was not born to wealth and position. He was the son of a smallholding Massachusetts farmer and shoemaker. Both father and son earned their money through hard work.

More than his celebrated contemporaries, Adams seems to be the genuine American article: the man who really was "of the people. He enrolled in Harvard College at 15, chose the law over the ministry, and quickly began to realize his own substantial talents for writing and argument. McCullough emphasizes Adams's ambition. He wanted to shine, and the tumultuous events of the 1760s and 1770s gave him the chance.

In an episode to which McCullough devotes a good deal of space, Adams agreed to defend the British soldiers who had been arrested following the so-called Boston Massacre. In March of 1770, the soldiers fired into a crowd of men who were protesting unpopular British taxes. Five civilians were killed. Adams agreed to defend the soldiers, in spite of the universal clamor for vengeance that contaminated the trial and despite threats to his own safety. Surprising even himself, Adams convinced judge and jury that the British had fired in self-defense. Looking back later, Adams decided, with justifiable pride, that his effort in the case was, in his words:

> One of the most gallant, generous, manly and disinterested Actions of my whole Life, and one of the best Pieces of Service I ever rendered my Country. Judgment of Death against those Soldiers would have been as foul a Stain upon this Country as the

Executions of the Quakers or Witches [a hundred years earlier]. As the Evidence was, the Verdict of the Jury was exactly right.

The courage and skill that Adams demonstrated in this trial ultimately enhanced his reputation as a leader. He emerged as an early advocate of independence. Indeed, he often complained that he never received the credit he deserved for taking such a dangerous stand before most others. You may recall, from our discussion of *Common Sense*, Adams's irritation that Tom Paine received more applause than he did for urging the colonies to take the great step toward disunion with Great Britain. For a while, Adams managed to work effectively with Jefferson, who would become his great rival. With uncharacteristic generosity, Jefferson would later describe Adams as "the colossus of independence."

In the early years of the Revolutionary War, Adams worked himself to exhaustion. He served on more than two-dozen committees. He was also president of the Continental War Board, carrying the weight of supplying Washington's army with the weapons and provisions that the troops desperately needed and that Congress was always reluctant to provide. The frustrations of that job were matched by the next chapter of Adams's wartime experience. He was posted to Paris to join Franklin as a Congressional Representative to the French king. Adams did not know a word of French, and his plainspoken contempt for aristocratic foppery quickly alienated both the French and Franklin. He was summoned home after a year. As always, he sulked and complained about the way he was treated.

As always, however, he also made good use of the time he now had. He drafted the Massachusetts Constitution, which survives as the oldest written constitution in the world. Congress then sent Adams back to Europe, where he had no more success dealing with the French than before.

At this point, McCullough provides a long and detailed review of Adams's self-appointed mission to Holland. There he ultimately persuaded the Dutch government to recognize the new republic and—more importantly—secured a loan of several million indispensable dollars from Dutch bankers. The episode has been erased from most histories of the Revolution. McCullough has restored both the events and Adams to their proper place. Adams then spent another unhappy period in France, as part of the American team that negotiated the treaty ending the war. That was followed by an unhappy period in England, where Adams served as the first United States ambassador to the English king—then home in 1788, where he was elected vice president and embarked on eight mostly unhappy years serving as understudy to Washington.

He spent much of his time trying to mediate between Jefferson, now Secretary of State, and Treasury Secretary Alexander Hamilton, the two most powerful men in the cabinet. He was the first but not the last vice president to conclude that the job was essentially ceremonial. In a letter to his wife, he famously said: "My country in its wisdom contrived for me the most insignificant office that ever the invention of man contrived or his imagination conceived." Adams's single presidential term was fraught with conflicts and crisis. In the first place, Jefferson—who had the second-highest number of electoral votes, and whom Adams barely defeated for the job—was elected vice president. The Twelfth Amendment, adopted in response to this bizarre outcome, eliminated the problem for future administrations—too late for Adams, the only president in our history whose chief deputy was also his leading political opponent. The nation was dividing into political parties, Jefferson at the head of what was called the Republicans, Adams reluctantly leading the Federalists. During his eight years as vice president, Adams had demonstrated absolute loyalty to Washington. The record 31 votes he cast to break ties in the Senate were all in support of his president. Adams received nothing like that sort of loyalty from Jefferson—quite the contrary, Jefferson spent much of his vice-presidential term conspiring to replace his boss.

The overriding issue that Adams faced as president was to determine America's response to the war between France and England. The Republicans determined to support France, while the Federalists, who shared Adams's horror at the excesses of the French Revolution, insisted that America support Britain. An undeclared naval war with France provoked debates that frequently exploded in violence. Adams quite reasonably worried that his own life was at risk. Attempting to maintain domestic control, he signed the Alien and Sedition Acts, four bills passed by the Federalist Congress that placed restrictions on non-citizens and limited dissent for all. In particular, the fourth bill, officially called "An Act for the Punishment of Certain Crimes against the United States," made it a crime to publish what it called "false, scandalous, and malicious writing" against the government or its officials.

The Sedition Act became a defining issue in the presidential election of 1800. It also provided a foretaste of the efforts that later administrations would make to curtail the constitutional liberties of American citizens. The election of 1800, the first and only campaign in which an incumbent president and vice president faced each other, became, in McCullough's words: "a contest of personal vilification surpassing any presidential election in American history."

As he expected, Adams was beaten by Jefferson. Jefferson's tactics were demonstrably nastier than Adams's. McCullough lingers over the unsavory details as a way of contrasting the two men to Adams's advantage. Indeed, that contrast provides one of the book's principal organizing devices. The elevation of Adams inevitably comes at Jefferson's expense. Adams was a tired, 65-year-old man when he returned to his home outside Boston. Here he could finally spend uninterrupted months and years with his wife, Abigail, one of the more remarkable people of her time, a woman of uncommon intelligence and independence. Even Adams's detractors have always acknowledged that any man who could sustain the love and loyalty of such a partner couldn't be all bad.

In the course of John Adams's long public life, he and Abigail had been apart for extended periods of time, in some cases years. Given their evident affection for each other, the separations caused them both a good deal of anguish, but posterity has been the winner. Without those absences, we would not have the extraordinary letters they wrote to each other, letters that have provided McCullough with much of his source material. Abigail's letters combined reports on weather and crops, political opinion, news of local events, and wonderfully candid comments on friends and neighbors. Some of her views, for example on the crime of slavery, were even stronger than John's. Nor did John share her dedication to the rights of women. Like most women in that period, she accepted her traditional role, but she yearned to live in a society that would at least acknowledge the capacities of women. In an earlier lecture, I quoted Abigail's famous request to John that he and the other men in Philadelphia should "remember the ladies, and be more generous and favorable ... than your ancestors." Neither John nor any of the other founders listened, but history was on Abigail's side. Though he didn't follow her advice on women's rights, on almost every other subject he clearly respected Abigail's mind and her judgment. On many occasions, she served as his only confidant. The friendship between John and Abigail Adams, and the mutual esteem with which they regarded each other, had no precedent in American political history. It provides the emblem of the integrity McCullough consistently attributes to his subject. In effect, this portrait of Adams works from the inside out, using his personal decency as evidence for his political quality. McCullough's book, which began as a double biography of Adams and Jefferson, emerges as a double biography of John and Abigail Adams.

This human story is one reason for the unparalleled success of McCullough's book. Another is the sheer skill with which the story is told. McCullough combines the authority of extensive research with a rare gift for description and narrative. The cold winters of New England, the heat of Philadelphia in July, the perils of ocean voyaging, the terror of smallpox, and the tensions of revolutionary debate: Every scene comes to vital life. Only a handful of writers possess McCullough's talent for marshalling details into a thick texture of foreground and background. McCullough suggests that Adams had the makings of a fine novelist. The comment applies to Adams's biographer as well. *John Adams* deserved the Pulitzer Prize it received.

As several reviewers of the book observed, McCullough's portrait of John Adams bears a rather striking resemblance to his earlier Pulitzer Prize biography of Harry Truman. In both cases, a man of middling origins had achieved a measure of distinction. Both had followed men of legendary proportions into the presidency, and neither would have gotten there without the patronage of their predecessors. Their historical reputations had repeated that subordination: Adams was no Washington, Truman no Franklin D. Roosevelt. McCullough doesn't try to reverse those ultimate judgments: Washington and Franklin Roosevelt remain towering figures in America's political history. But he has recovered the qualities in both Adams and Truman that had been obscured by the neglect of earlier historians. Perhaps precisely because he is not a professional academic, McCullough brought a degree of liberating skepticism to the standard narrative.

Abigail Adams died in 1818, ending a marriage of 54 years. John Adams was genuinely devastated, and his own last years were shadowed by his loss. The timing of his own death, 8 years later, seemed almost miraculous to his fellow citizens. On July 4, 1826, on the 50th anniversary of the Declaration of Independence, he and Thomas Jefferson died within hours of each other.

Lecture Twenty-Four
Recent Bestsellers

Scope: In this course, we have been mapping the terrain of the American bestseller over more than three centuries. In the past 20 years or so, that landscape has been quite dramatically transformed. The bestsellers of today are quite different products than some of those discussed in earlier lectures; today there are "brand-name" writers, or franchise authors, whose success is nearly guaranteed on their name alone. Film adaptations have become commonplace for bestsellers, and the rise of the "megapublisher" is interrelated with the mega-authors we will discuss. One case study of such an author, John Grisham, will help in evaluating a key question: If we only had bestselling novels as evidence, what sorts of conclusions would we draw about American life in the late 20th and early 21st century? And where do these contemporary bestselling writers fit in the longer history of American bestsellers?

Outline

I. One of the most striking changes in the landscape of American bestsellers has been the emergence and dominance of a handful of franchise authors.

   A. Danielle Steel. Steel has published more than 75 novels, more than 30 of which have been included in top-10 lists since 1983.
   1. On several occasions, Steel has remarkably published 2 novels that simultaneously made the top 10 in the same year.
   2. In two consecutive years, 1997 and 1998, Steel placed 3 books on the annual list.

   B. Stephen King. Since the publication of *Carrie* in 1974, Stephen King has placed approximately 30 different titles on the annual bestseller lists, an average of about one every year.
   1. On six occasions, King published 2 novels that made the top-10 list in the same year.
   2. In addition, King's novels have several times been named as the number one seller in the annual survey.

C. John Grisham. From 1994 through 2000, Grisham's novels placed first on the annual bestseller lists. *Publishers Weekly* declared Grisham the bestselling American author of the 1990s, with sales in excess of 60 million copies for the decade.

D. Tom Clancy. Beginning with *The Hunt for Red October* in 1984, Clancy has published a long series of political thrillers and nonfiction books whose sales place him among the four or five bestselling writers in the past two decades.

E. Add a few more names, such as Michael Crichton, Patricia Cornwell, James Patterson, and Sidney Sheldon, and you have identified a fair percentage of the most popular novelists of the present and recent past.

II. Adding further cultural clout to the books these writers publish are the movie versions that regularly follow.

A. A half dozen of Tom Clancy's thrillers and eight of John Grisham's novels have been adapted for film.

B. Stephen King has seen more than two dozen of his novels turned into full-length movies, along with dozens of his stories that have been made into shorter films or television shows.

C. Film adaptation is not new; from the film industry's earliest days, popular novels have provided material for movies.

    1. Many of the novels we have discussed in this course have been adapted for film: *The House of Mirth, The Good Earth, Gone with the Wind, The Grapes of Wrath,* and *Catch-22,* to give a few prominent examples.

    2. The contemporary scene is different, though. Earlier books first made their way to readers, long before movie rights were considered. Today, every book by a star author is assumed to be Hollywood-bound, even before its publication.

D. The rise of what might be called the mega-author has been aided and reflected by the growth of the megapublisher.

    1. According to one source, just five publishers—Random House, HarperCollins, Hachette, Penguin USA, and Simon & Schuster—are responsible for about 80% of the nation's bestsellers.

    2. These companies possess the marketing know-how, the advertising budgets, and the global reach that now drive and define the book business.

E. Book clubs also play a role. One in particular has affected the publishing industry significantly: Oprah Winfrey's nationally televised book club.

    1. With 13 million viewers, "Oprah's Book Club" has been very successful, making each title she selects a bestseller.

    2. One scholar estimated that, "In the first three years of the Book Club, Oprah books sold an average of 1.4 million each."

III. Where do the mega-authors, such as Grisham, King, and Clancy, fit into the longer history of American bestsellers?

A. Many of our bestselling books provide large quantities of information, sometimes quite specialized. Across several genres, one pattern that connects a number of the most popular writers is a shared commitment to professionalized talk.

B. Beyond satisfying our appetite for information, popular writing suggests another cultural generalization: Many of the most widely sold novels are thrillers, mysteries, and horror stories.

    1. Perhaps these types of books disclose something about our contemporary anxieties.

    2. Political historian Richard Hosftadter pointed out many years ago that paranoia has been built into the American grain since Colonial times.

C. Today's bestsellers differ in subject matter than some of those discussed in earlier lectures. Writers have typically drifted away from direct engagement with major public issues (as seen in *Uncle Tom's Cabin*, *The Jungle*, or *The Grapes of Wrath*.)

    1. Books no longer occupy the same cultural space they once did.

    2. Today's reformers choose nonfiction as their literary medium or choose other media such as documentary film.

D. Above all, however, the current generation of popular writers shares with its predecessors an ability to provide enormous entertainment for large numbers of readers.

IV. John Grisham occupies an unprecedented position in contemporary literature and serves as a good case study for contemporary bestsellers.

A. Grisham's books are usually called legal thrillers; more than any other previous writer, Grisham has tapped into the American fascination with the legal system.

B. Grisham includes in his novels all sorts of hot-button political and social issues: assassination plots and CEO villainy, CIA chicanery and nuclear weapons, capital punishment.

C. Grisham's latest, *The Appeal* (2008), received a coveted front-page notice in the *New York Times Book Review*. It follows a similar formula as his many other bestselling titles: The action takes place in a small Southern town, and the antagonists are an honorable pair of small-town lawyers on one side and a rapacious corporation on the other.

   1. The villains in Grisham's novels are clearly intended as moral and political statements, nearly allegorical emblems of Grisham's contempt for the excesses of corporate greed and political corruption that in his view threaten the nation's fabric.

   2. The author's good guys, on the other hand, often combine humanizing flaws with their idealism.

D. The good-bad conflict is dramatized in an intricate, generally well-made plot. The resulting stories combine forward-moving urgency with skillful narrative timing.

Suggested Reading:

Pringle, *John Grisham*.

Rooney, *Reading with Oprah*.

Questions to Consider:

1. As we have seen, a number of bestsellers have survived, sometimes over many decades, while others have vanished from reading lists and bookstores. What are the shared qualities, if any, that more durable popular books have in common?

2. Every scholar of popular literature agrees that popularity is unpredictable. There will certainly continue to be bestsellers, but the past is no guide to the future. At one level this opinion is probably undeniable. At the same time, perhaps some forecasts can be offered, based on the broad survey we have just concluded. What predictions would you be willing to make about popular literature over the next decade or so?

Lecture Twenty-Four—Transcript
Recent Bestsellers

In these lectures, we have been mapping the terrain of the American bestseller over more than three centuries. We've discussed books from a wide variety of American times and places, and we've tested some ideas about the relationship between these books and the public that bought and read them in such large quantities. Along the way, we've noted some differences and some points of continuity. In the past 20 years or so, the bestseller landscape has been quite dramatically transformed. I mentioned some of the most striking changes briefly in our first session. Here I want to begin by filling in more detail. Using a bit of business jargon, I referred to several authors as the equivalent of brand names. Let me document that statement, starting with a few relevant and sometimes startling facts.

Item: Danielle Steel. According to her website, "America reads Danielle Steel. And so does the rest of the world." Given her publishing record, that claim seems just about correct. Consider that she has published more than 75 novels, at least 30 of which have been included in the top ten lists since 1983. Perhaps even more remarkably, Steel has on several occasions published two novels that made the top ten in one year. In two consecutive years—1997 and 1998—Danielle Steel placed three books on the annual list. Only Stephen King presents a challenge to Danielle Steel in that department.

Item: Stephen King. Since the publication of *Carrie* in 1974, Stephen King has placed approximately 30 different titles on the annual bestseller lists: an average of about one every year. On six occasions, King published two novels that made the top ten list in the same year. In addition, unlike Steel, King's novels have several times been named as the number one bestseller in the annual survey. But King does not have a lock on the top spot—that distinction belongs to John Grisham.

Item: John Grisham. From 1994 through 2000—an astonishing seven consecutive years—Grisham's novels placed first on the annual bestseller lists. After settling for both the second and third positions in 2001, Grisham returned to his accustomed number one spot in 2002 and again in 2005. (A novel called *The Da Vinci Code* intruded in 2003 and 2004.) *Publishers Weekly* did the numbers and declared Grisham the bestselling American author of the 1990s, with sales in excess of 60 million copies for the decade.

If Grisham has had a patent on number one, another brand name, Tom Clancy, has appeared several times right behind him, at number two.

Item: Tom Clancy. Beginning with *The Hunt for Red October* in 1984, Clancy has published a long series of political thrillers and nonfiction books whose sales place him among the four or five bestselling writers of the past two decades. Clancy also has the distinction of loaning (presumably leasing) his name to other writers who have published bestselling books in such series as *Tom Clancy's Op Center* and *Tom Clancy's Net Force*. Clancy makes the term "franchise writer" quite literally descriptive. To some extent, the bestseller lists of the past couple of decades have come to resemble a small village inhabited by the members of just a few prominent families who live in very large houses. Take the 1996 list as both fact and symbol: John Grisham at number one, Tom Clancy at number two, Stephen King at number three, King again at number five, under the name Richard Bachman, Danielle Steel at both number six and number seven. Add a few more names, such as Michael Crichton, Patricia Cornwell, James Patterson, and Sidney Sheldon, and you have identified a fair percentage of the most popular novelists of the present and recent past. To change metaphors: There are many stars in the bestseller night sky, but only a few constellations. By the way, I apologize if I have left out the name of your favorite popular writer.

Adding further cultural clout to the books that these writers publish are the movie versions that quite regularly follow. A half-dozen, at least, of Tom Clancy's thrillers and eight of John Grisham's 20 novels have been adapted for film. Stephen King has seen more than two dozen of his novels turned into full-length movies, along with dozens of stories that have been made into shorter films or television shows. Danielle Steel has enjoyed almost the same level of Hollywood interest. Film adaptation is not new. From the earliest days of the movies, popular novels have provided material for films. Some of the most enduring silent films, including Erich von Stroheim's *Greed*, based on a book by Frank Norris. Frank Lloyd's version of *Oliver Twist*, among a host of others, used novels as the raw material for film. Many of the novels we have discussed in this course have been adapted for film, often with excellent results: *The Virginian*, *The House of Mirth*, *The Good Earth*, *Gone with the Wind*, *The Grapes of Wrath*, and *Catch-22*, to give a few prominent examples.

The contemporary scene is altogether different. Those earlier books first made their way with readers before film producers dropped by offering money for movie rights. Cooper's *The Last of the Mohicans* waited over a century for its first adaptation, a 1936 film starring Randolph Scott. Today, almost every book by Grisham and his fellow superstars is assumed to be Hollywood-bound even before it is published.

The rise of what we might call the "mega-author" has been aided and reflected by the growth of the mega-publisher. Along with the huge success of a relatively small number of popular writers, the past several decades have also witnessed a conspicuous increase in the reach of fewer and fewer publishers.

According to one source, just five publishers are responsible for about 80 percent of the nation's bestsellers: Random House, HarperCollins, Hachette, Penguin USA, and Simon & Schuster. These are the companies that possess the marketing know-how, the advertising budgets, and the global reach that now drive and define the book business. Perhaps these phenomena are related. The number of books published continues to grow each year. Critic Michael Greenberg recently made the colorful observation that each new title "is a drop in a sea of books that keeps swelling forward, obliterating those that came before." Readers, in Greenberg's phrase, confront "the tyranny of plenty." No one can even glance at 100,000 titles in a year, let alone read more than a handful. The big publishers intervene and sort the abundance into manageable units and segments. Personal choices are amalgamated into statistical forecasts and outcomes. In some measure, what sells in the future is what has sold in the past. As I've mentioned before, the new, new thing will undoubtedly come along, but its arrival is completely unpredictable. In the meantime, the old, new thing will continue to sell lots of copies.

Book clubs, as I have mentioned, can also play a role here, and one in particular deserves additional comment. Several years ago, Toni Morrison claimed that Oprah Winfrey had sparked a "reading revolution." Morrison's tribute was justified. With 13 million viewers at its peak, "Oprah's Book Club" had the muscle to make a difference in book sales. One scholar has estimated that, "In the first three years of the Book Club, Oprah's books sold an average of 1.4 million each." Winfrey deserves a great deal of credit. At a time when the National Endowment for the Arts has warned that Americans are reading less, Oprah's Book Club has probably done more to kindle interest in books and reading than all the English professors in the United States put together. I served as the literary consultant to the Club when Winfrey featured *The Good Earth*, and I considered it a privilege. However, even the titles she selects—beginning with Jacquelyn Mitchard's *The Deep End of the Ocean* and including Sue Miller's *While I Was Gone*, and Joyce Carol Oates's *We Were the Mulvaneys*, and Jane Hamilton's *A Map of the World*—have recorded sales that lagged far behind the brand-name novelists.

Where do those writers, John Grisham, Stephen King, Tom Clancy, Danielle Steel, and the others who command the top of the recent lists, fit in the longer history of American bestsellers? In what ways do they illuminate contemporary cultural debates, as so many of the earlier bestsellers we have examined did? Another way to phrase this question might be: If we had only these bestselling novels as evidence, what sort of conclusions would we draw about American life in the late 20th and early 21st centuries? Well, if ours is the information society, then our bestselling books may be said to match our prevailing temperament. Many of our most popular books provide large quantities of information, sometimes quite specialized. Indeed, across their several genres, one pattern that connects a number of the most popular writers is a shared commitment to professionalized talk. Plots that are often implausible are provided with a veneer of verisimilitude through elaborate displays of arcane knowledge.

Michael Crichton's thrillers include eye-glazing quantities of technical material on DNA sequencing, and computer programming, and artificial intelligence, and any number of scientific domains—some of it correct, some of it invented: How many readers can tell the difference? Tom Clancy knows a great deal about the technology of nuclear-powered submarines, and he shares it all. Danielle Steel offers an exhaustive taxonomy of high-priced accessories and luxury resorts. John Grisham parades his mastery of legal definitions and procedures. Patricia Cornwell lovingly includes long descriptions of autopsies in her thrillers. In part, she wants to heighten the atmosphere of danger in her stories, but she also intends to convince her readers of the reality of such scenes.

Here is Cornwell's sleuth, Virginia's Chief Medical Examiner Dr. Kay Scarpetta, patiently explaining to her buddy, police captain Marino, how she goes about slicing up an apparent drowning victim:

> I've already made a skin pocket on the side of the chest, filled it with water and inserted a blade in the thorax to check for bubbles. I'm going to fill the pericardial sac with water and insert a needle into the heart, again to see if any bubbles form. And I'll check the brain for petechial hemorrhages, and look at the soft tissue of the mediastinum for extra-alveolar air.

Whew—surely Cornwell doesn't really assume that her readers, except for a handful of physicians, understand any of this. Most of us, and I certainly include myself, couldn't tell a pericardial sac from a parking meter. Instead, Cornwell is using the inaccessible vocabulary of postmortem anatomy to establish her character's authority and control. Dr. Scarpetta is one competent, tough lady. Do not cross her, or you may wind up as a lab specimen.

Beyond satisfying our appetite for information, or at least the illusion of information, recent popular culture, popular writing, may suggest another cultural hypothesis. Given that so many of the most widely read novels are thrillers, mysteries, and horror stories, perhaps these books disclose something of our contemporary anxieties. Many of us apparently fear that something or somebody is out to get us, and we are attracted to books that confirm our suspicions. This is not an altogether new American attitude. The political historian Richard Hofstadter pointed out many years ago that paranoia has been built into the American grain since our Colonial beginnings. From witches to Redcoats to Reds under our beds, we have always been afraid of something. Nonetheless, as the world gets more crowded and as the risks we face grow more dangerous, more various, and more exotic, it may be that we find ourselves breathing the air of an edgier, more suspicious climate. This is the atmosphere that we repeatedly find represented in our popular entertainment.

To be sure, horror stories and apocalyptic thrillers have been around for a long time, but they seem to take up more cultural space today. One more proposal about the difference between today's bestsellers and at least some of those we've discussed in earlier lectures, the link between recent popular literature and social protest seems less strong. Indeed, a survey of the main names might suggest that contemporary writers have abandoned large sectors of the public sphere. Where is the fictional equivalent of *Uncle Tom's Cabin*, with its cry of outrage against slavery, or *The Jungle*, which exposed the barbarism of the meatpacking industry? Where's the descendant of *The Grapes of Wrath*, which dramatized the sufferings of battered Dust Bowl refugees? If my speculation is correct, if writers have typically drifted away from direct engagement with major public issues, the explanation may lie in the changing nature of our society and its media. To put it simply, books no longer occupy the cultural space they once did. When Harriet Beecher Stowe wrote her novel attacking slavery, whatever national conversation American citizens had was confined to print: books, magazines, pamphlets, and newspapers. Magazines were more plentiful when Upton Sinclair exposed the brutality of Chicago slaughterhouses, but electronic media had not yet appeared. John Steinbeck's sympathetic account of his luckless farmers was competing with the radio and the movie house newsreels, but not with television and the Internet.

Today's reformers typically choose nonfiction as their literary form, or choose other media, such as the documentary film or the Internet. For better or worse, more than one critic has compared Michael Moore to Upton Sinclair and John Steinbeck.

In short, much has changed in today's version of the bestseller. At the same time, much remains the same. Above all, the current generation of popular writers shares with its predecessors an ability to provide enormous entertainment for large numbers of readers. This, I want to insist, is not a small accomplishment.

If one writer is going to serve as a brief case study, I think it has to be John Grisham, who occupies an extraordinary position in contemporary literary culture. As *The New York Times* critic, Janet Maslin, commented several years ago: "Whether Grisham's books are forceful or meandering, quick or pokey, [they] have a track record that proves them Pavlovian stimuli to loyal readers. He writes it; you buy it, even if it's blank." In a similarly half-joking vein, columnist Dave Barry suggested that the Federal Aviation Administration must have circulated a regulation requiring everyone boarding an airplane to hold a Grisham novel. I've already given the numbers that summarize Grisham's remarkable success in the book market. Here I want to look a bit more closely at his novels and try to answer the question: What is it that makes them so popular? To begin with, Grisham, whose books are usually called legal thrillers, is exploring an attractive genre. He is not the first writer to work in this territory. Several lawyers have featured in mystery stories and thrillers. Beginning in the early 1930s, to give one especially successful example, Erle Stanley Gardner published 80 stories featuring the attorney Perry Mason.

However, more than any previous popular writer, Grisham has tapped into the American fascination with the legal system. It is, of course, a love-hate relationship. Indeed, the prevalence of lawyer jokes might suggest a hate-hate relationship. In fact, on the contrary, a reverence for the law coexists with the bad jokes. The United States was the first country founded on a legal document, and the first to insist that ours was a "government of laws, not men." If we have often failed to honor that commitment, nevertheless we continue to aspire to the ideals of impartial justice and equality before the law. We are also, quite notoriously, the most litigious nation on the planet. We go to law at the drop of a tort over every kind of major and minor dispute. Legal controversies are also inherently dramatic. In an earlier lecture, I mentioned that novelists and playwrights—and I should add, television producers—love to create courtroom scenes. In addition, at one point or another in his books, Grisham includes all sorts of hot-button political and social issues: assassination plots, blackmail, nuclear weapons, CIA chicanery, offshore bank fraud, capital punishment, and CEO villainy on a grand scale. In other words, Grisham has chosen a set of topics that resonate widely with a contemporary audience.

Let's review just a few examples of Grisham at work. Full disclosure: I have chosen some of my own favorites. *The Firm* (1991) was Grisham's second novel, and the first to earn a place on the bestseller list. The book's hero, Mitchell McDeere, a bright young Harvard Law School graduate, takes a job at a tax firm in Memphis. As the murdered bodies of the other lawyers in the company pile up, Mitch discovers that his firm is, in fact, controlled by a criminal organization in Chicago, the Morolto family. When he starts cooperating with the FBI, an informer tips off the Moroltos, who order a hit on Mitch. The rest of the book narrates a series of hairbreadth escapes, as Mitch, his wife Abby, and his brother run from both the cops and the crooks. Frantic chases end quite satisfactorily—the Moroltos will go to jail, and Mitch and Abby will live happily for a good while on the millions they have stolen from the Mafia bank account.

The Pelican Brief (1992), which remains one of Grisham's most popular titles, combines environmentalism with mayhem and suspense. Two justices of the Supreme Court, who share a concern for environmental protection, are murdered. The villain in this case is an oil tycoon—Grisham has a well-established dislike for tycoons of all sorts—who feared that he would lose drilling rights to a huge tract of land because of an endangered pelican species. The hero in this tale is a woman, Darby Shaw, a law school student who sorts out the tangled web of deceit that leads all the way to the White House. Once again, high-level skullduggery provokes a hair-raising sequence of murders and escapes. In the end, with the help of a Washington reporter, the schemes are exposed.

The Partner (1998), Grisham's eighth novel, opens with an episode of torture but proves to be a rather lighthearted romp. The plot involves a first-rate scam cooked up by a Mississippi lawyer named Patrick S. Lanigan. When Patrick discovers that his partners have conspired to defraud the government of $90 million but have left him out, he stages his own death, steals all the money, and disappears, settling in a small village in the jungles of Brazil. Captured by a gang of thugs, he is rescued by the FBI and charged with a long list of crimes. He beats every rap and walks away with a seeming victory. In the book's final pages, however, in one of Grisham's more delightful surprises, Patrick's Brazilian girlfriend re-steals the stolen money and leaves him penniless in his little jungle village. One more example: *The Appeal* (2008), which received a coveted and quite favorable front-page notice in *The New York Times Book Review*. Once again, the action takes place in Mississippi, and once again the antagonists are an honorable pair of small-town lawyers on the one hand, and a rapacious corporation on the other. Wes and Mary Payton win a huge verdict against Krane Chemicals, which has been blithely contaminating local drinking water with cancer-causing waste. The $41 million victory, however, is only the start of the tale. Krane's boss, a man of unredeemable evil named Carl Trudeau, appeals the case and then sets about buying the next election of state judges.

Like many of Grisham's novels, the story told in *The Appeal* could have jumped off the front page of the morning newspaper. However, that instinct for timely and riveting subjects only begins to explain Grisham's success. By themselves, subjects don't move books. No subject, however topical or controversial or sexy, can ensure popularity. It is Grisham's technique that matters: the elements of his style. Grisham does not dazzle with his prose, but he puts his sentences together with assurance and clarity. If he sometimes resorts to clichés, so do we all. Most important, he achieves a consistently engaging tone, establishing a relationship of shared interest and concern with his readers. His paragraphs radiate authority and professionalism. Grisham also has an underappreciated talent for description. He quite convincingly evokes the many settings in his books, especially the towns and landscapes of his Mississippi home. His dialogue is rarely memorable, but it demonstrates a good ear for the rhythms and sequence of credible speech.

The characters in Grisham's novels are not typically complex. His bad guys, in particular, tend to be unambiguously bad. The villains are clearly intended as moral and political statements, nearly allegorical emblems of Grisham's contempt for the excesses of corporate greed and political corruption that, in his view, threaten the nation's fabric. Grisham's good guys, on the other hand, often combine humanizing flaws with their idealism. The struggle is always unequal, and the odds against justice are long. The recurring conflict is dramatized in intricate, generally well-made plots, and here we come closer to the core of Grisham's success. He has said that he spends a great deal of time preparing each novel, sketching detailed outlines for the events of every chapter and every page. The resulting stories combine forward-moving urgency with skillful narrative timing. These are page-turners in the most accomplished sense. The British writer, E. M. Forster, once wrote that the novelist's most basic job is to make the reader ask: "What happens next?" Few writers of fiction do that job as well as John Grisham. Grisham and the other bestselling writers I have mentioned are often accused of writing for the money. Grisham has denied that money is the motive behind his books. Stephen King has responded even more aggressively: "Now, there are lots of people who will tell you that anyone who writes genre fiction or any kind of fiction that tells a story is in it for the money and nothing else. It's a lie [said King]. ... I never in my life wrote a single word for money.

In my own view, the question is impertinent and irrelevant. What difference would it make if a writer included money among his or her considerations? The great 18th-century man of letters, Dr. Samuel Johnson, once famously remarked: "No man but a blockhead ever wrote, except for money." I detect more than a hint of envy in the vigor with which Grisham and other popular writers are sometimes belittled precisely because of their popularity. There is also a bit more zeal than there needs to be in the way some critics patrol the border between high culture and pop culture. While aesthetic distinctions will always be appropriate, the arguments about the literary quality of popular writing have become a bit tired. In 2003, Stephen King received the National Book Foundation's Medal for his Distinguished Contribution to American Letters. It was an important symbolic moment, in both directions. At the end of his acceptance speech, King said: "My message is simple enough. We can build bridges between the popular and the literary if we keep our minds and hearts open.

This brings us back to one of the questions we began with in the first lecture. How do we evaluate literature—or any other art for that matter—and what is the significance of our evaluations? From my own experience over many years, as a reader of all sorts of literature, I would propose that the issue could be re-phrased. We bring different expectations and needs to different texts (or pictures or musical compositions). Some yield rewards that require intensive study and perhaps even special information. The great books do remain indispensable—the plays of Shakespeare, the poetry of Milton and Keats, the novels of Dickens, to give just a few examples and just from the canon of literature in the English language. Literary work on this scale recalls us to our humanness, enacting our deepest moral and emotional experiences in languages that transcend our own paltry powers of expression. Popular literature performs another but also useful role. One body of work need not exclude the other.

As I have tried to suggest in our discussions of American bestsellers, these are texts that can tell us much about the nation's social history, and its recurring debates, and the astonishing cast of characters who have populated this nation from its earliest days. Popular literature offers at least a part of the answer to the perennial question of American identity. In short, American literature has sustained a wide variety of writing over many years, and all of it has much to teach us.

John Grisham is not William Faulkner, and Stephen King is not Henry James, but Grisham and King can offer insights into our culture—and their books are a great deal of fun into the bargain.

Timeline

1619 .... Africans brought as slaves to
                                                                         Jamestown (Virginia).

1620 .... Pilgrims sign Mayflower
                                                                         Compact and disembark
                                                                         at Plymouth (Massachusetts).

1630 .... John Winthrop and Puritans arrive
                                                                         aboard the *Arbella* and settle the
                                                                         Massachusetts Bay Colony.

1636 .... Harvard College founded (first college
                                                                         in the English-speaking colonies).

1640 .... *The Bay Psalm Book.*

1774 .... First Continental Congress meets
                                                                         in Philadelphia.

1775–1783 .... American Revolutionary War.

1776 .... Thomas Paine, *Common Sense*;
                                                                         Declaration of Independence
                                                                         (voted on July 2).

1790 .... First U.S. census shows population of
                                                                         3.9 million.

1793 .... Eli Whitney invents the cotton gin.

1804–1806 .... Lewis and Clark expedition.

1807 .... Robert Fulton builds
                                                                         Clermont steamboat.

1808 .... United States prohibits further
                                                                         importation of slaves.

1820 .... Missouri Compromise outlaws slavery
                                                                         north of latitude 36°30′ (Missouri
                                                                         admitted as a slave state, Maine
                                                                         admitted as a free state).

1825 .... Erie Canal links Hudson River and
Great Lakes.

1826 .... James Fenimore Cooper, *The Last
of the Mohicans.*

1831 .... Nat Turner's slave insurrection;
McCormick Reaper invented.

1833 .... American Antislavery Society
founded; Oberlin College founded
as first coeducational institution of
higher learning.

1837 .... John Deere develops plow for
prairie lands.

1838 .... Regular steam travel across the Atlantic
begins with arrival of the British *Sirius*
and *Great Western* (crossing time a
little more than 16 days).

1839 .... Invention of the daguerreotype;
abolitionists found the Liberty Party.

1841 .... Brook Farm community established.

1846–1848 .... Mexican War (United States acquires
territory between Rocky Mountains
and Pacific).

1848 .... Seneca Falls Convention; Free Soil
party formed; gold discovered at
Sutter's Mill, California.

1850 .... Compromise of 1850.

1851 .... Telegraph lines extended across
the Mississippi.

1852 .... Harriet Beecher Stowe, *Uncle
Tom's Cabin.*

1854 .... Kansas-Nebraska Act repeals the
Missouri Compromise.

1857 .... Dred Scott decision (Supreme Court denies African Americans standing in court).

1859 .... John Brown's raid on Harpers Ferry (Virginia); petroleum discovered in Pennsylvania.

1861 .... April 12, Fort Sumter attacked (beginning of war between Confederacy and Union).

1865 .... Slavery abolished by 13th Amendment; founding of Freedmen's Bureau.

1865–1877 .... Reconstruction.

1868 .... Horatio Alger Jr., *Ragged Dick.*

1869 .... First transcontinental railroad completed.

1870 .... Louisa May Alcott, *Little Women.*

1879 .... John D. Rockefeller's Standard Oil Trust founded.

1884 .... National Equal Rights Party nominates Belva Lockwood as first woman candidate for president; Mark Twain, *The Adventures of Huckleberry Finn.*

1886 .... Formation of the American Federation of Labor (AFL); Haymarket bombing in Chicago.

1888 .... George Eastman introduces Kodak camera.

1889 .... Jane Addams establishes Hull House in Chicago.

1890 .... Eleventh U.S. census declares frontier closed.

1896	Supreme Court, in *Plessy v. Ferguson*, declares "separate but equal" the law of the land; first moving pictures shown on a public screen.
1898	February 15, USS *Maine* blown up in Havana Harbor; Spanish-American War (Puerto Rico and Guam ceded to United States, Hawaii annexed, Philippines occupied).
1901	United States Steel Corporation founded.
1902	Owen Wister, *The Virginian*.
1903	Wright brothers make world's first successful heavier-than-air flight; Panama Canal Treaty signed (canal opened to commercial traffic in 1914); first baseball World Series.
1905	Edith Wharton, *The House of Mirth*.
1906	Upton Sinclair, *The Jungle*; Pure Food and Drug Act passed.
1907	Peak year of immigration (1,285,000 immigrants enter United States).
1909	National Association for the Advancement of Colored People (NAACP) established.
1911	Triangle Shirtwaist Factory fire in New York City (146 employees die).
1913	Federal income tax introduced.
1914	Eight-hour day and $5 daily wage introduced in Ford plants.
1915	Opening of D. W. Griffith's *The Birth of a Nation*.
1917	United States declares war on Germany.

1918 .... November 11, armistice declared in Europe.

1920 .... Sinclair Lewis, *Main Street*; federal voting rights for women secured by the 19th Amendment; 14th U.S. census indicates that urban population exceeds rural.

1925 .... Trial of John T. Scopes for teaching evolution in Tennessee.

1927 .... Nicola Sacco and Bartolomeo Vanzetti executed.

1929 .... October 29, stock market crashes; Great Depression begins.

1930 .... Dashiell Hammett, *The Maltese Falcon*.

1931 .... Pearl S. Buck, *The Good Earth*.

1935 .... Social Security Act passed.

1936 .... Margaret Mitchell, *Gone with the Wind*; Dale Carnegie, *How to Win Friends and Influence People*.

1938 .... Congress of Industrial Organizations (CIO) formed.

1939 .... John Steinbeck, *The Grapes of Wrath*.

1940 .... Richard Wright, *Native Son*.

1941 .... December 7, Japan bombs Pearl Harbor; United States enters World War II.

1945 .... Germany surrenders to Allies; United States drops atomic bombs on Hiroshima and Nagasaki; Japan surrenders; United Nations Conference in San Francisco and signing of UN Charter.

1950 .... United States begins police action in Korea (ends in 1953).

1951 .... J. D. Salinger, *The Catcher in the Rye.*

1954 .... Supreme Court, in *Brown v. Board of Education*, rules doctrine of separate but equal unconstitutional.

1960 .... Harper Lee, *To Kill a Mockingbird*; black students sit in to desegregate lunch counters in Greensboro, North Carolina.

1961 .... Joseph Heller, *Catch-22.*

1966 .... National Organization for Women founded.

1975 .... Maxine Hong Kingston, *The Woman Warrior.*

1984 .... Geraldine Ferraro becomes first woman nominated for the vice presidency by a major political party.

1991 .... First Iraq war.

2001 .... David McCullough, *John Adams*; September 11 attacks.

2003 .... Second Iraq war begins.

Biographical Notes

Alcott, Louisa May (1832–1888): Daughter of Amos Bronson Alcott, a teacher and self-styled philosopher, and Abigail May. Louisa grew up in a financially poor but stimulating environment: Her parents' friends included Ralph Waldo Emerson, Margaret Fuller, and Henry David Thoreau. Throughout her adult life, she accepted responsibility for helping to support her family. Along with her writing, which included children's stories and melodramatic fantasies, she worked at the badly paid jobs open to her: sewing, domestic service, and lady's companion. She was deeply opposed to slavery and served as a nurse during the Civil War. After publishing several adult novels, she received an offer to write a girls' book; she later said that she agreed because she needed the money. The result was *Little Women*, which was published in two parts, in 1868 and 1869. Exploiting the success of the book, Alcott followed with a series of novels on similar themes, including *Little Men* (1871) and *Jo's Boys* (1886). In the years after the war, Alcott campaigned energetically for the rights of women. She added her signature to a women's suffrage petition in 1875 and published essays in such magazines as the feminist *Woman's Journal*.

Alger, Horatio, Jr. (1832–1899): Born in Massachusetts; son of Horatio Alger, a Unitarian minister, and Olive Fenno. He graduated with honors from Harvard in 1852, after which he took a series of badly paying teaching jobs. He supplemented his income with miscellaneous essays and journalism that he published in a wide assortment of literary weeklies and monthlies. He attended the Harvard Divinity School, received ordination as a Unitarian minister, and continued to supplement his income with his writing. Beginning in 1864, Alger began to publish the juvenile books that would bring him both fame and wealth. Expelled from his Massachusetts congregation following charges of sexual impropriety with young boys, Alger moved to New York, where he became involved in charitable institutions that worked on behalf of impoverished children. In 1868, he published *Ragged Dick*, his most successful juvenile book and the first in a long series that made Alger's name synonymous with tales of upward mobility. Over the final decades of his life, he combined those publications with biographies of such figures as Abraham Lincoln and Daniel Webster, along with adult fiction.

Buck, Pearl S. (1892–1973): Daughter of a Presbyterian missionary named Absalom Sydenstricker and his wife Carie Stulting. She lived most of the first 40 years of her life in China, growing up bilingual and, as she said, "culturally bifocal." She and her first husband, John Lossing Buck, lived in an impoverished rural village for several years; that experience would provide Buck with material for many of her stories and novels. Her second novel, *The Good Earth* (1931), won the Pulitzer Prize. In 1937, *The Good Earth* was adapted as a movie and produced by MGM; like the book, the film enjoyed immense commercial and critical success and was nominated for several Academy Awards. In 1938, Buck became the third American, and the first American woman, to win the Nobel Prize in Literature. After moving back to the United States in the mid-1930s, Buck continued to write prodigiously—she would eventually publish 80 or so books—and she also took an active role in a number of political activities, working for the rights of women, minorities, and children.

Carnegie, Dale (1888–1955): Originally named Dale Breckenridge Carnegey; born in Maryville, Missouri, and grew up in near-poverty on a farm. His mother, a fervent Methodist, encouraged Carnegie's public speaking in the hope that he would become a minister. In his early adulthood, he moved from one job to another, including sales. After moving to New York, he began teaching public speaking at the YMCA. He enjoyed the courses and discovered his calling; he had soon organized a nationwide staff of teachers who promoted his methods across the country and beyond, to Canada and Europe. In 1936, Carnegie published his landmark book, *How to Win Friends and Influence People*, an instant bestseller that has enjoyed strong sales throughout the following decades. Carnegie's courses in speaking also continue to thrive. Located in over 75 countries, the program has enrolled over 10 million people.

Cooper, James Fenimore (1789–1851): Son of a wealthy landowner, William Cooper, the founder of Cooperstown, New York. He attended Yale University for two years but was expelled for misconduct. He spent several years working as a common sailor and officer on merchant and military ships. He married in 1811, eventually having seven children with his wife, Susan De Lancey. In 1820, Cooper published his first work of fiction, an imitation of an English novel of manners called *Precaution*. His first literary success came with *The Spy* (1821), set in New York during the Revolution, and brought him international celebrity. His next book, *The Pioneers* (1823), inaugurated the Leatherstocking Tales. He and his family traveled in Europe, where he was welcomed by the leading political and literary figures. In his later years, Cooper engaged in a long series of lawsuits against his New York neighbors over his property rights. He continued to write, both fiction and nonfiction; by the time he died, in his early 60s, Cooper had published over 50 volumes of work.

Hammett, Dashiell (1894–1961): Attended high school in Baltimore before taking a job at the Pinkerton Detective Agency. He worked for less than four years as a Pinkerton agent, or "operative," but would use the experience as raw material for his pathbreaking crime stories and novels. Hammett served briefly in the U.S. Army but contracted influenza in the epidemic of 1918–1919; for the rest of his life, he suffered from weakness and pain in his lungs. His first detective stories, featuring an anonymous detective called "the Continental Op," began to appear in the pulp magazine *Black Mask* in 1923. Over the next decade, he created two of modern fiction's most celebrated sleuths, Sam Spade and Nick Charles (the central character in the "Thin Man" series). After the mid-1930s, Hammett wrote little fiction, devoting much of his time and energy to political causes, including freedom of artistic expression.

Heller, Joseph (1923–1999): The son of Isaac Heller, a delivery truck driver, and his wife Lena; grew up in New York. He graduated from high school and then in 1941 took a job at the Norfolk (Virginia) Navy Yard. He enlisted in the Army Air Forces, trained as a navigator, and was sent to Corsica in 1944. He flew 60 bombing missions over Italy and France. Following his discharge, Heller completed college at New York University and took a Master's degree in English from Columbia. For several years, while he moved among a number of jobs, mostly in teaching and advertising, he kept writing and published a few stories in high-circulation magazines, including the *Atlantic Monthly* and *Esquire*. In 1961, using his own wartime experiences as the basis, Heller published his first and most popular novel, *Catch-22*. Despite mixed reviews, *Catch-22* proved immensely popular, and its title has entered the language as shorthand formula for frustration. Over the nearly four decades between his first novel and his death, Heller worked as a television and movie scriptwriter, published half a dozen additional novels, and wrote three plays.

Kingston, Maxine Hong (b. 1940): Born in Stockton, California, the daughter of Tom and Yin Lan Hong. She received a B.A. from the University of California at Berkeley in 1962. After teaching English and mathematics for a few years, she moved to Hawaii in 1967 with her husband, actor Earll Kingston. They returned to California in 1985 and now live in Oakland; they have one child, a son named Joseph. *The Woman Warrior: Memoirs of a Girlhood among Ghosts* (1975), Kingston's first book, won the National Book Critics Circle Award for nonfiction. It is among the best-known works in contemporary American literature and one of the most frequently taught in college courses. Her second book, *China*

Men, was published in 1980 and received the National Book Award for nonfiction. (Kingston has said that *Woman Warrior* and *China Men* are "supposed to be one book," a two-part memoir.) In 1987, Kingston published a collection of 12 prose selections, *Hawaii One Summer*. Her fourth book and only novel, *Tripmaster Monkey: His Fake Book*, appeared in 1989. Kingston received the National Humanities Medal in 1997. She is currently Senior Lecturer in English at Berkeley.

Lee, Harper (b. 1926): Born in Monroeville, Alabama, the daughter of Amasa Lee, a lawyer, politician, and journalist, and Frances Finch Lee. As a child, Lee was known for her rough play and her wide reading. Her neighbors included Truman Capote, with whom she developed a warm friendship; Lee would later assist Capote in gathering material for Capote's celebrated nonfiction novel *In Cold Blood*. Lee earned an undergraduate degree at Huntingdon College and studied law at the University of Alabama. She did additional study at Oxford University, then moved to New York where she worked as an airlines reservation clerk to support her writing. In 1960, she published her only novel, *To Kill a Mockingbird*, which was an immediate bestseller and has remained popular for decades. The novel won the Pulitzer Prize and was adapted as an enormously successful film starring Gregory Peck, who won an Academy Award for his portrayal of the book's main character, attorney Atticus Finch. In the nearly five decades since she published *Mockingbird*, Lee has lived quietly in Monroeville. She received the Presidential Medal of Freedom in 2007.

Lewis, Sinclair (1885–1951): Born in Sauk Centre, Minnesota; his father was a physician, his mother a schoolteacher. After graduating from Yale University in 1908, Lewis worked as a journalist and editor for several years. He published several novels before the bestselling *Main Street* (1920), which brought him both fame and wealth. Throughout the 1920s, he published a sequence of successful novels, each of which explored some aspect of contemporary American life. *Babbitt* (1922), the story of a boorish and greedy businessman, was followed by *Arrowsmith* (1925), an examination of the medical profession. *Elmer Gantry* (1927) provided a savage portrait of a hypocritical evangelical preacher. *Dodsworth* (1929), the final novel in this productive decade, offered a kinder version of a businessman. In 1930, Lewis became the first American to win the Nobel Prize in Literature; the choice was unpopular with many academics and critics. Lewis continued to write for the next two decades, but his popularity steadily declined.

McCullough, David (b. 1933): Born in Pittsburgh; attended Yale University, graduating with honors in English literature in 1955. Describing Yale in the 1950s, McCullough has said: "People like John O'Hara, John Hersey, Brendan Gill, and Thornton Wilder were around on the campus. There were days when I sat down at the communal lunch table beside Thornton Wilder. There was the daily themes course, which was taught by Robert Penn Warren." After graduating, he worked as a writer and researcher for *Time* and *Life* magazines, then at the U.S. Information Agency and *American Heritage*. Beginning with *The Johnstown Flood* (1968), McCullough has published eight volumes of history and biography, including *The Great Bridge* (1972), the story of the construction of the Brooklyn Bridge; *The Path Between the Seas* (1977), about the Panama Canal; *Mornings on Horseback* (1981), a biography of Theodore Roosevelt; *Truman* (1992); and *John Adams* (2001). Both *Truman* and *John Adams* received the Pulitzer Prize. McCullough frequently serves as a narrator on public television.

Mitchell, Margaret (1900–1949): Born and lived most of her life in Atlanta. She spent one year at Smith College but returned home after her mother died in the influenza epidemic of 1918–1919. While she resisted formal education, she was a tireless reader and began writing at quite an early age. Mitchell worked for several years as a journalist. Her first marriage was brief and ended in divorce; her second lasted until her death. She began writing *Gone with the Wind* during an illness in 1926. For 10 years, she wrote and revised, unwilling to part with the manuscript. The book created a sensation when it was published in 1936, and it became the bestselling novel of the first half of the 20th century. The 1939 movie version, starring Clark Gable and Vivien Leigh, was an international event. *Gone with the Wind* proved to be Mitchell's only book. She died at 48, the victim of a drunk driver.

Paine, Thomas (1737–1809): Originally Thomas Pain; born to a Quaker father (a corset maker) and an Anglican mother in Thetford, England. After spending seven years in a local grammar school, he was apprenticed in his father's shop. After a brief tour as a naval crewman, Paine moved to London, where he attended lectures on science. He married in 1759, but his wife and their first child both died in childbirth the following year. Paine took a series of jobs over the next decade, including teaching, all without success. He married again in 1771, suffered bankruptcy three years later, and moved to America, carrying a letter of introduction from Benjamin Franklin. He took up residence in Philadelphia, the leading city in the colonies. As the controversy with Britain escalated, Paine allied himself with some of the most radical colonists, among them John Adams, Benjamin Rush, and David Rittenhouse. In January 1776, Paine published *Common Sense*, a repudiation of British rule and a ringing call for independence. During the years of the Revolution, Paine published a series of pamphlets under the collective title *The American Crisis*. Following the Revolution, Paine moved to France, where he emerged for a brief time as a leading figure in the revolutionary movement. His most important publication in these years, *The Rights of Man*, exerted wide influence on radical political opinion on both sides of the Atlantic.

Salinger, J. D. (b. 1919): Son of a Jewish businessman and his Scotch-Irish wife. Jerome David Salinger (his full name) lived with his family in a comfortable apartment on New York's Park Avenue. He dropped out of several schools (or was expelled) and took a few college courses at New York University. Salinger served in the American infantry in the Second World War, seeing fierce action during the Normandy invasion and later engagements. From the late 1940s through the mid-1960s, his stories appeared mainly in the *New Yorker*. They were subsequently gathered into successful collections. Salinger's novel, *The Catcher in the Rye* (1951), was a Book-of-the-Month Club selection and an immediate bestseller; it has remained popular for over half a century. Salinger has not published any fiction since 1965, though he may have continued to write. He has lived in rigorous seclusion, avoiding most outside contact, for over four decades.

Sinclair, Upton (1878–1968): Son of a hard-working mother, who encouraged his ambitions, and an alcoholic father. Sinclair was a precocious reader and writer. To earn money for his college expenses, he published dozens of "dime" and "half-dime" novels for the mass market. In 1904, Sinclair investigated the conditions of the "wage slaves" in the Chicago meatpacking industry. The result was his novel, *The Jungle* (1906), a bestseller that also galvanized the federal government to improve the regulation of food. For the next 60 years of his life, Sinclair took part in a long series of radical and utopian enterprises. He founded Helicon Hall, an experiment in communal living. He supported the miners in their violent strike in Ludlow, Colorado. In 1934, he ran for governor of California on the self-created party he called EPIC: End Poverty in California. He received over 40 percent of the vote. Along with his fervent political activism, Sinclair continued to write in every genre; his bibliography lists over 2,200 published items.

Steinbeck, John (1902–1968): Born in Salinas, California; the only son of businessman John Steinbeck Sr. and former teacher Olive Hamilton. His family was not poor, but Steinbeck spent much of his time as a teenager and young adult doing field and factory work with migrant laborers. He attended Stanford University but left without a degree. Steinbeck produced most of his important writing in the 1930s, a sequence of books set in various California locales that culminated in *The Grapes of Wrath* (1939), his most significant and most popular novel. Both the novel, which won the Pulitzer Prize, and the highly successful movie that quickly followed, established indelible images of the Depression's effects on the nation's poor farmers. Although Steinbeck continued to publish continuously until his death, few of his later books earned much critical or commercial success. In 1962, he received the Nobel Prize in Literature.

Stowe, Harriet Beecher (1811–1896): Born in Connecticut; the daughter of Lyman Beecher, a celebrated evangelical preacher in the years before the Civil War, and Roxanna Foote. Harriet received a thorough education and showed an early talent for argument and writing. The family moved to Cincinnati in 1832 when Lyman accepted the presidency of Lane Seminary; several years later, Harriet married Calvin Stowe, who was on the Lane faculty. Along with many other Northerners, Stowe was outraged by the Fugitive Slave Law, passed in 1850, which extended the reach and effectiveness of the slave power. She began writing *Uncle Tom's Cabin* almost immediately. The novel was serialized in the abolitionist magazine the *National Era* and became the century's bestselling novel when it was published in book form in 1852. Stowe became an international celebrity and devoted much of her writing and her royalties to the antislavery cause throughout the 1850s. Following the Civil War, Stowe continued to publish actively, moving between political subjects and more domestic stories. She lent her influential support to several reform movements, including expanded political and legal rights for women.

Twain, Mark (1835–1910): Born Samuel Clemens in rural Missouri, the son of John Clemens, a lawyer, and Jane Lampton. After the family moved to Hannibal, John's undertakings failed, and the family declined into relative poverty. After only a couple of years of formal schooling, the young Twain began working, first as a printer's apprentice and then as a freelance typesetter. He found his calling when he trained as a river pilot and earned a good living until the Civil War stopped the river's commercial traffic. During the war, he went west with his brother Orion, who had been appointed secretary of the new Nevada Territory. The experience broadened his knowledge of the country, which provided him with material for his writing. He worked as a journalist on several western papers and began to publish the humorous essays that established his celebrity. He also began the lecture tours that would provide the bulk of his income for the rest of his life. Twain married Olivia Langdon in 1870; eventually they settled in Hartford, Connecticut. Twain's many books included travel essays, satire, and several novels. Of these, the most substantial has proven to be *The Adventures of Huckleberry Finn* (1884). By the late 19th century, Twain had become America's most famous writer; when he took a trip around the world, he was greeted as celebrity in every city he visited. His last years were shadowed by personal crisis, in particular the deaths of his wife and younger daughter.

Wharton, Edith (1862–1937): Born in New York City; daughter of George Frederic Jones and Lucretia Rhinelander, a prosperous and socially distinguished couple. Wharton later recalled her childhood as a time of privilege and unhappiness: She was well provided for materially but felt neglected by her parents. In particular, Wharton blamed her mother for opposing her literary aspirations and for pressing her to accept a conventionally eligible suitor, Edward "Teddy" Wharton, to whom she was married in 1885. The marriage seems to have been a failure from the beginning and would eventually lead to divorce. Several of Wharton's early publications, including *The Decoration of Houses* (1897) and *Italian Villas and Their Gardens* (1904), grew out of her experience as a traveler and observer in Europe. Nearly 40 when her first novel appeared, Wharton quickly established herself as a popular writer. *The House of Mirth* (1905) was a bestseller, and several of her other books also earned significant sales. She was active in supporting France and Belgium in the First World War and was decorated by both governments. She was always more comfortable in Europe than America; she lived most of her last four decades in France. Her first postwar novel, *The Age of Innocence* (1920), won the Pulitzer Prize.

Wister, Owen (1860–1938): Grew up in an affluent Philadelphia home. His father was a distinguished physician, Owen Jones Wister; his mother, Sarah Butler, was the daughter of Pierce Butler and famed British actress Fanny Kemble. Wister went to private schools in Europe and America, then attended Harvard College, from which he graduated with honors in 1882. He also earned a law degree from Harvard in 1888. Wister suffered from a variety of ailments and traveled to Wyoming for his health. The landscape and people captured his imagination and became the subjects of his most important fiction, including the bestselling *The Virginian* (1902). In the years following, Wister published on a wide variety of topics, including prohibition and immigration (he opposed both). His books include biographies of three presidents: George Washington; Ulysses Grant; and Theodore Roosevelt, with whom he had been friends since college.

Wright, Richard (1908–1960): Born on a Mississippi plantation; son of Nathaniel Wright, a sharecropper, and Ella Wilson, a teacher. Nathaniel abandoned the family when Richard was five years old. The rest of his childhood included periods under the care of grandparents and even several months in an orphanage. After a few weeks in high school, Wright dropped out, worked at a variety of odd jobs, and taught himself to read. He left the South for Chicago before his 20th birthday. There he worked at the post office and at a hospital, where he took care of laboratory animals. Wright gravitated toward left-wing politics, taking an active part in the John Reed Club, which was affiliated with the Communist Party. Wright moved to New York City in 1937. His first volume of short stories, *Uncle Tom's Children* (1938), earned a major prize from *Story* magazine. With the publication of *Native Son* (1940), the first bestselling novel and selection of the Book-of-the-Month Club by an African American, Wright became the most prominent black writer in the country. Wright resigned from the Communist Party in 1942; a few years later, he moved to France, where he lived for the remainder of his life.

Bibliography

Lecture One: Why Do Bestsellers Matter?

Cawelti, John. *Adventure, Mystery and Romance*. Chicago: University of Chicago Press, 1976.

Elson, Ruth Miller. *Myths and Mores in American Best Sellers, 1865–1965*. New York: Garland, 1985.

Gelder, Ken. *Popular Fiction: The Logics and Practice of a Literary Field*. London: Routledge, 2004.

Hackett, Alice Payne, and James Henry Burke. *Eighty Years of Best Sellers, 1895–1975*. New York: R. R. Bowker, 1977.

Hart, James D. *The Popular Book: A History of America's Literary Taste*. New York: Oxford University Press, 1950.

Hinckley, Karen, and Barbara Hinckley. *American Best Sellers: A Reader's Guide to Popular Fiction*. Bloomington: Indiana University Press, 1989.

Korda, Michael. *Making the List: A Cultural History of the American Bestseller, 1900–1999; As Seen Through the Annual Bestseller Lists of Publishers Weekly*. New York: Barnes & Noble, 2001.

Mott, Frank Luther. *Golden Multitudes: The Story of Best Sellers in the United States*. New York: Macmillan, 1947.

Sutherland, John. *Bestsellers: A Very Short Introduction*. New York: Oxford University Press, 2007.

Lecture Two: *The Bay Psalm Book*

The Bay Psalm book. 1640. A facsimile reprint of the first edition with an introduction by Wilberforce Eames. New York: New England Society, 1903.

Miller, Perry, ed. *The American Puritans: Their Prose and Poetry*. Garden City, NY: Anchor Books, 1956.

Ruppert, James. *Colonial and Nineteenth-Century [American Poetry]*. Boston: G. K. Hall, 1989.

Scheick, William J. *Design in Puritan American Literature*. Lexington: University Press of Kentucky, 1992.

Scheick, William J., and JoElla Doggett. *A Guide to Seventeenth-Century American Poetry*. Boston: G. K. Hall, 1977.

Lecture Three: *Common Sense*

Aldridge, Alfred Owen. *Man of Reason: The Life of Thomas Paine.* London: Cresset Press, 1960.

Bailyn, Bernard. *The Ideological Origins of the American Revolution.* Cambridge, MA: Belknap Press of Harvard University Press, 1967.

Fruchtman, Jack, Jr. *Thomas Paine: Apostle of Freedom.* New York: Four Walls Eight Windows, 1994.

Larking, Edward. *Thomas Paine and the Literature of Revolution.* New York: Cambridge University Press, 2005.

Liell, Scott. *46 Pages: Thomas Paine, Common Sense, and the Turning Point to American Independence.* Philadelphia: Running Press, 2003.

Keane, John. *Tom Paine: A Political Life.* Boston: Little, Brown, 1995.

Jensen, Merrill, ed. *Tracts of the American Revolution, 1763–1776.* Indianapolis, IN: Bobbs-Merrill, 1967.

Thompson, Ira M. *The Religious Beliefs of Thomas Paine.* New York: Vantage Press, 1965.

Williamson, Audrey. *Thomas Paine: His Life, Work, and Times.* New York: St. Martin's Press, 1973.

Lecture Four: *The Last of the Mohicans*

Dekker, George. *James Fenimore Cooper: The Novelist.* London: Routledge & Kegan Paul, 1967.

Franklin, Wayne. *The New World of James Fenimore Cooper.* Chicago: University of Chicago Press, 1982.

Grossman, James. *James Fenimore Cooper.* New York: William Sloane Associates, 1949.

Person, Leland S., ed. *A Historical Guide to James Fenimore Cooper.* New York: Oxford University Press, 2007.

Ringe, Donald A. *James Fenimore Cooper.* Boston: Twayne Publishers, 1988.

Verhoeven, W. M., ed. *James Fenimore Cooper: New Historical and Literary Contexts.* Atlanta, GA: Rodopi, 1993.

Lecture Five: *Uncle Tom's Cabin*

Ammons, Elizabeth, ed. *Critical Essays on Harriet Beecher Stowe*. Boston: G. K. Hall, 1980.

Caskey, Marie. *Chariot of Fire: Religion and the Beecher Family*. New Haven, CT: Yale University Press, 1978.

Crozier, Alice. *The Novels of Harriet Beecher Stowe*. New York: Oxford University Press, 1969.

Hedrick, Joan D. *Harriet Beecher Stowe: A Life*. New York: Oxford University Press, 1994.

Kirkham, E. Bruce. *The Building of Uncle Tom's Cabin*. Knoxville: University of Tennessee Press, 1977.

Tompkins, Jane P. *Sensational Designs: The Cultural Work of American Fiction, 1790–1860*. New York: Oxford University Press, 1985.

Wilson, Forrest. *Crusader in Crinoline: The Life of Harriet Beecher Stowe*. Philadelphia: J. B. Lippincott, 1941.

Lecture Six: *Ragged Dick*

Bennett, Bob. *Horatio Alger, Jr.: A Comprehensive Bibliography*. Mt. Pleasant, MI: Flying Eagle, 1980.

Scharnhorst, Gary. *Horatio Alger, Jr*. Boston: Twayne, 1980.

Scharnhorst, Gary, and Jack Bales. *Horatio Alger, Jr.: An Annotated Bibliography of Comment and Criticism*. Metuchen, NJ: Scarecrow Press, 1981.

Scharnhorst, Gary, with Jack Bales. *The Lost Life of Horatio Alger, Jr*. Bloomington: University of Indiana Press, 1985.

Lecture Seven: *Little Women*

Baym, Nina. *Woman's Fiction: A Guide to Novels By and About Women in America, 1820–1870*. Ithaca, NY: Cornell University Press, 1978.

Bedell, Madelon. *The Alcotts: A Family Biography*. New York: C. N. Potter, 1980.

Saxton, Martha. *Louisa May: A Modern Biography of Louisa May Alcott*. Boston: Houghton Mifflin, 1977.

Stern, Madeleine, ed. *Critical Essays on Louisa May Alcott*. Boston: G. K. Hall, 1984.

———. *Louisa May Alcott*. Norman: University of Oklahoma Press, 1950.

Lecture Eight: *The Adventures of Huckleberry Finn*

Bloom, Harold, ed. *Mark Twain's The Adventures of Huckleberry Finn.* New York: Bloom's Literary Criticism, 2007.

Budd, Louis J. *Our Mark Twain: The Making of His Public Personality.* Philadelphia: University of Pennsylvania Press, 1983.

———, ed. *New Essays on The Adventures of Huckleberry Finn.* New York: Cambridge University Press, 1985.

Chapman, Laurie, ed. *The Critical Response to Mark Twain's Huckleberry Finn.* New York: Greenwood Press, 1991.

Emerson, Everett. *The Authentic Mark Twain: A Literary Biography of Samuel L. Clemens.* Philadelphia: University of Pennsylvania Press, 1983.

Hutchinson, Stuart, ed. *Mark Twain: Tom Sawyer and Huckleberry Finn.* New York: Columbia University Press, 1999.

Johnson, Claudia Durst, ed. *Understanding The Adventures of Huckleberry Finn: A Student Casebook to Issues, Sources, and Historical Documents.* Westport, CT: Greenwood Press, 1996.

Kaplan, Justin. *Mr. Clemens and Mark Twain.* New York: Simon and Schuster, 1966.

LeMaster, J. R., and James D. Wilson, eds. *The Mark Twain Encyclopedia.* New York: Garland Publishers, 1993.

Lecture Nine: *The Virginian*

Cobbs, John L. *Owen Wister.* Boston: Twayne, 1984.

Etulain, Richard W. *Owen Wister.* Boise, ID: Boise State College [Press], 1973.

Payne, Darwin. *Owen Wister: Chronicler of the West, Gentleman of the East.* Dallas, TX: Southern Methodist University Press, 1985.

White, Edward G. *The Eastern Establishment and the Western Experience: The West of Frederic Remington, Theodore Roosevelt, and Owen Wister.* New Haven, CT: Yale University Press, 1968.

Lecture Ten: *The House of Mirth*

Benstock, Shari. *No Gifts from Chance: A Biography of Edith Wharton.* New York: Charles Scribner's Sons, 1994.

Dwight, Eleanor. *Edith Wharton: An Extraordinary Life.* New York: Abrams, 1994.

Joslin, Katherine. *Edith Wharton.* New York: St. Martin's Press, 1991.

Lawson, Richard H. *Edith Wharton*. New York: Frederick Ungar, 1977.

Lee, Hermione. *Edith Wharton*. New York: Alfred A. Knopf, 2007.

Lewis, R. W. B. *Edith Wharton: A Biography*. New York: Harper & Row, 1975.

Wolff, Cynthia Griffin. *A Feast of Words: The Triumph of Edith Wharton*. New York: Oxford University Press, 1977.

Wright, Sarah Bird. *Edith Wharton A to Z: The Essential Guide to the Life and Work*. New York: Facts on File, 1998.

Lecture Eleven: *The Jungle*

Arthur, Anthony. *Radical Innocent: Upton Sinclair*. New York: Random House, 2006.

Bloodworth, William A., Jr. *Upton Sinclair*. Boston: Twayne, 1977.

Dell, Floyd. *Upton Sinclair: A Study in Social Protest*. New York: George H. Doran, 1927.

Herms, Dieter, ed. *Upton Sinclair: Literature and Social Reform*. New York: P. Lang, 1990.

Mattson, Kevin. *Upton Sinclair and the Other American Century*. Hoboken, NJ: John Wiley & Sons, 2006.

Scott, Ivan. *Upton Sinclair, the Forgotten Socialist*. Lewiston, NY: Edwin Mellen Press, 1997.

Yoder, Jon A. *Upton Sinclair*. New York: Frederick Ungar, 1975.

Lecture Twelve: *Main Street*

Bucco, Martin. *Critical Essays on Sinclair Lewis*. Boston: G. K. Hall, 1986.

Dooley, D. J. *The Art of Sinclair Lewis*. Lincoln: University of Nebraska Press, 1967.

Fleming, Robert E., and Esther Fleming. *Sinclair Lewis: A Reference Guide*. Boston: G. K. Hall, 1980.

Grebstein, Sheldon N. *Sinclair Lewis*. Boston: Twayne, 1962.

Light, Martin. *The Quixotic Vision of Sinclair Lewis*. West Lafayette, IN: Purdue University Press, 1975.

Lingeman, Richard. *Sinclair Lewis: Rebel from Main Street*. New York: Random House, 2002.

Lundquist, James. *Sinclair Lewis*. New York: Frederick Ungar, 1973.

Schorer, Mark, ed. *Sinclair Lewis, a Collection of Critical Essays.* Englewood Cliffs, NJ: Prentice-Hall, 1962.

———. *Sinclair Lewis: An American Life.* New York: McGraw-Hill, 1961.

Lecture Thirteen: *The Maltese Falcon*

Dooley, Dennis. *Dashiell Hammett.* New York: Frederick Ungar, 1984.

Gregory, Sinda. *Private Investigations: The Novels of Dashiell Hammett.* Carbondale: Southern Illinois University Press, 1985.

Johnson, Diane. *Dashiell Hammett: A Life.* New York: Random House, 1983.

Layman, Richard. *Dashiell Hammett's The Maltese Falcon: A Documentary Volume.* Detroit, MI: Gale, 2003.

———. *Shadow Man: The Life of Dashiell Hammett.* New York: Harcourt Brace Jovanovich, 1981.

Nolan, William F. *Hammett: A Life at the Edge.* New York: Congdon & Weed, 1983.

Symons, Julian. *Dashiell Hammett.* New York: Harcourt Brace Jovanovich, 1985.

Wolfe, Peter. *Beams Falling: The Art of Dashiell Hammett.* Bowling Green, OH: Bowling Green State University Press, 1980.

Lecture Fourteen: *The Good Earth*

Conn, Peter. *Pearl S. Buck: A Cultural Biography.* New York: Cambridge University Press, 1996.

Doyle, Paul A. *Pearl S. Buck.* Boston: Twayne, 1980.

Harris, Theodore F. *Pearl S. Buck.* 2 vols. New York: John Day Company, 1969, 1971.

Spencer, Cornelia. *The Exile's Daughter: A Biography of Pearl S. Buck.* New York: Coward-McCann, 1944.

Stirling, Nora. *Pearl Buck: A Woman in Conflict.* Piscataway, NJ: New Century, 1983.

Lecture Fifteen: *Gone with the Wind*

Farr, Finis. *Margaret Mitchell of Atlanta.* New York: Morrow, 1965.

Jones, Anne Goodwyn. *Tomorrow Is Another Day: The Woman Writer in the South, 1859–1936.* Baton Rouge: Louisiana State University Press, 1981.

Pyron, Darden Asbury. *Southern Daughter: The Life of Margaret Mitchell.* New York: Oxford University Press, 1991.

Lecture Sixteen: *How to Win Friends and Influence People*

Cawelti, John G. *Apostles of the Self-Made Man.* Chicago: University of Chicago Press, 1965.

Huber, Richard M. *The American Idea of Success.* New York: McGraw-Hill, 1971.

Kemp, Giles, and Edward Claflin. *Dale Carnegie: The Man Who Influenced Millions.* New York: St. Martin's Press, 1989.

Meyer, Donald. *The Positive Thinkers: A Study of the American Quest for Health, Wealth, and Personal Power from Mary Baker Eddy to Norman Vincent Peale.* Garden City, NY: Doubleday, 1965.

Lecture Seventeen: *The Grapes of Wrath*

Benson, Jackson. *The True Adventures of John Steinbeck, Writer.* New York: Viking, 1984.

Bloom, Harold, ed. *John Steinbeck.* New York: Chelsea House, 1987.

French, Warren. *John Steinbeck.* Boston: Twayne, 1975.

Kiernan, Thomas. *The Intricate Music: A Biography of John Steinbeck.* Boston: Little, Brown, 1979.

Levant, Howard. *The Novels of John Steinbeck: A Critical Study.* Columbia: University of Missouri Press, 1974.

Li, Luchen, ed. *John Steinbeck: A Documentary Volume.* Detroit, MI: Thomson Gale, 2005.

Lisca, Peter. *The Wide World of John Steinbeck.* New Brunswick, NJ: Rutgers University Press, 1958.

McCarthy, Paul. *John Steinbeck.* New York: Frederick Ungar, 1980.

Owens, Louis. *The Grapes of Wrath: Trouble in the Promised Land.* Boston: Twayne, 1989.

———. *John Steinbeck's Re-vision of America.* Athens: University of Georgia Press, 1985.

Parini, Jay. *John Steinbeck, a Biography.* New York: Henry Holt, 1995.

Lecture Eighteen: *Native Son*

Abcarian, Richard. *Richard Wright's Native Son: A Critical Handbook.* Belmont, CA: Wadsworth, 1970.

Fabre, Michel. *The Unfinished Quest of Richard Wright.* Urbana: University of Illinois Press, 1993.

Gates, Henry Louis, Jr., and Kwame Anthony Appiah, eds. *Richard Wright: Critical Perspectives Past and Present*. New York: Amistad, 1993.

Gayle, Addison. *Richard Wright: Ordeal of a Native Son*. Garden City, NY: Doubleday, 1980.

Joyce, Joyce Ann. *Richard Wright's Art of Tragedy*. Iowa City: University of Iowa Press, 1986.

Kinnamon, Keneth, ed. *Critical Essays on Richard Wright's Native Son*. Boston: Twayne, 1997.

————. *The Emergence of Richard Wright: A Study in Literature and Society*. Urbana: University of Illinois Press, 1972.

Walker, Margaret. *Richard Wright, Daemonic Genius: A Portrait of the Man, a Critical Look at His Work*. New York: Warner Books, 1988.

Webb, Constance. *Richard Wright: A Biography*. New York: Putnam, 1968.

Lecture Nineteen: *The Catcher in the Rye*

Belcher, William F., and James E. Lee, eds. *J. D. Salinger and the Critics*. Belmont, CA: Wadsworth, 1962.

Bloom, Harold, ed. *J. D. Salinger: Modern Critical Views*. New York: Chelsea House, 1987.

French, Warren. *J. D. Salinger*. Boston: Twayne, 1976.

Grunwald, Henry A., ed. *Salinger: A Critical and Personal Portrait*. New York: Harper's, 1962.

Hamilton, Ian. *In Search of J. D. Salinger*. New York: Random House, 1988.

Lundquist, James. *J. D. Salinger*. New York: Frederick Ungar, 1979.

Marsden, Malcolm M., ed. *"If You Really Want to Know": A Catcher Casebook*. Chicago: Scott, Foresman, 1963.

Miller, James E., Jr. *J. D. Salinger*. Minneapolis: University of Minnesota Press, 1965.

Salinger, Margaret Ann. *Dream Catcher: A Memoir*. New York: Washington Square Press, 2000.

Lecture Twenty: *To Kill a Mockingbird*

Bloom, Harold, ed. *Harper Lee's "To Kill a Mockingbird."* New York: Chelsea House, 2007.

Johnson, Claudia Durst. *"To Kill a Mockingbird": Threatening Boundaries*. Boston: Twayne, 1994.

————. *Understanding "To Kill a Mockingbird."* Westport, CT: Greenwood Press, 1994.

Meyer, Michael J. *Literature and Law.* New York: Rodopi, 2004.

Petry, Alice Hall, ed. *On Harper Lee: Essays and Reflections.* Knoxville: University of Tennessee Press, 2007.

Shields, Charles J. *Mockingbird: A Portrait of Harper Lee.* New York: Henry Holt, 2006.

Lecture Twenty-One: *Catch-22*

Bloom, Harold, ed. *Joseph Heller's "Catch-22."* New York: Bloom's Literary Criticism, 2008.

Keegan, Brenda M. *Joseph Heller: A Reference Guide.* Boston: G. K. Hall, 1978.

Kiley, Frederick T., and Walter McDonald, eds. *A "Catch-22" Casebook.* New York: Crowell, 1973.

Merrill, Robert. *Joseph Heller.* Boston: Twayne, 1987.

Nagel, James, ed. *Critical Essays on Joseph Heller.* Boston: G. K. Hall, 1984.

Pinsker, Sanford. *Understanding Joseph Heller.* Columbia: University of South Carolina Press, 1991.

Potts, Stephen W. *From Here to Absurdity: The Moral Battlefields of Joseph Heller.* San Bernardino, CA: Borgo Press, 1995.

Ruderman, Judith. *Joseph Heller.* New York: Continuum, 1991.

Seed, David. *The Fiction of Joseph Heller: Against the Grain.* New York: St. Martin's Press, 1989.

Lecture Twenty-Two: *The Woman Warrior*

Cheung, King-Kok. *Articulate Silences: Hisaye Yamamoto, Maxine Hong Kingston, Joy Kogawa.* Ithaca, NY: Cornell University Press, 1993.

Janette, Michele. "The Angle We're Joined At: A Conversation with Maxine Hong Kingston." *Transition*, Spring 1997.

Lesniak, James, and Susan Trosky, eds. "Maxine Hong Kingston." In *Contemporary Authors.* Detroit, MI: Gale Research, 1993.

Pollack, Harriet, ed. *Having Our Way: Women Rewriting Tradition in Twentieth-Century America.* Lewisburg, PA: Bucknell University Press, 1995.

Rainwater, Catherine, and William J. Scheick, eds. *Contemporary American Women Writers: Narrative Strategies*. Lexington: University Press of Kentucky, 1985.

Smith, Sidonie, ed. *A Poetics of Women's Autobiography: Marginality and the Fictions of Self-Representation*. Bloomington: Indiana University Press, 1987.

TuSmith, Bonnie. *All My Relatives: Community and Individualism in Ethnic American Literatures*. Ann Arbor: University of Michigan Press, 1993.

Yalom, Marilyn, ed. *Women Writers of the West Coast: Speaking of Their Lives and Careers*. Santa Barbara, CA: Capra Press, 1983.

Lecture Twenty-Three: *John Adams*

Brown, Ralph A. *The Presidency of John Adams*. Lawrence: University Press of Kansas, 1975.

Ellis, Joseph J. *Passionate Sage: The Character and Legacy of John Adams*. New York: W. W. Norton, 1993.

Ferling, John. *John Adams: A Life*. Knoxville: University of Tennessee Press, 1992.

Gelles, Edith. *Portia: The World of Abigail Adams*. Bloomington: Indiana University Press, 1992.

Howe, John R. *The Changing Political Thought of John Adams*. Princeton, NJ: Princeton University Press, 1966.

Kurtz, Stephen G. *The Presidency of John Adams: The Collapse of Federalism, 1795–1800*. Philadelphia: University of Pennsylvania Press, 1957.

Shaw, Peter. *The Character of John Adams*. New York: W. W. Norton, 1976.

Smith, Page. *John Adams*. 2 vols. Garden City, NY: Doubleday, 1962–1963.

Withey, Lynne. *Dearest Friend: A Life of Abigail Adams*. New York: Free Press, 1981.

Lecture Twenty-Four: Recent Bestsellers

Pringle, Mary Beth. *John Grisham: A Critical Companion*. Westport, CT: Greenwood Press, 1997.

Rooney, Kathleen. *Reading with Oprah: The Book Club That Changed America*. Fayetteville: University of Arkansas Press, 2008.

Notes

Notes

Notes